SO-ARV-503

Cases in Global Marketing Strategies

Fifth Edition—2002 Update

DISCARDED

Cases in Global Marketing Strategies

Fifth Edition—2002 Update

Jean-Pierre Jeannet
F. W. Olin Distinguished Professor of Global Business
Babson College, Wellesley, Massachusetts

Professor of Global Marketing and Strategy
International Institute for Management Development (IMD)
Lausanne, Switzerland

H. David Hennessey
Associate Professor of Marketing and International Business
Babson College, Wellesley, Massachusetts

Associate, Ashridge Management College
Berkhamsted, United Kingdom

Houghton Mifflin Company   **Boston**   **New York**

Cases in global marketing
strategies : 2002 update
658.84 J438a
30531001309481

OHIO CHRISTIAN UNIVERSITY

Associate Sponsoring Editor: *Joanne Dauksewicz*
Senior Project Editor: *Maria Morelli*
Editorial Assistant: *Tanius Stamper*
Senior Production Design Coordinator: *Jennifer Meyer Dare*
Senior Manufacturing Coordinator: *Marie Barnes*

Copyright © 2002 by Houghton Mifflin Company. All rights reserved.

No part of this book may be reproduced or transmitted in any form or by any means, electronic or mechanical, including photocopying and recording, or by any information storage or retrieval system without the prior written permission of Houghton Mifflin Company, unless such copying is expressly permitted by federal copyright law. Address inquiries to College Permissions, Houghton Mifflin Company, 222 Berkeley Street, Boston, Mass. 02116-3764.

Printed in the U.S.A.
ISBN: 0-618-15947-9

1234567879-HPC-05 04 03 02 01

Contents

Preface

This 2002 casebook update has been designed to accompany *Global Marketing Strategies,* Fifth Edition. By combining the cases in a separate book, we expect to provide regular annual updates rather than be limited to the revision cycles of the main text.

In choosing the collection of cases provided here, we have aimed to provide ample opportunity for both students and instructors to apply the concepts and principles appropriate to global marketing in a changing world and across a variety of industry and geographic settings.

The case collection has undergone substantial additions from the previous version (© 2001). Four new cases have been added while all the cases from our previous version have been retained. The new cases reflect our drive toward more global marketing issues, and an attempt to include more service industry cases.

Here is a brief description of the four new cases for this casebook update:

- Tonernow.com deals with an existing bricks and mortar business that wants to change into clicks and mortar while taking advantage of e-business opportunities. This case covers both B2C and B2B opportunities in the office supply market. This is also a small, entrepreneurial firm raising the issue of critical mass for global marketing.

- Deloitte Touche Tohmatsu, a leading financial services firm with global operations, deals with the potential integration of the firm's Eastern European practice and its use as a business model for the established practices in Western Europe.

- Euro RSCG deals with the global branding and account management practices of one of the largest advertising agencies with global operations. Students are challenged to find a working model on global account management that goes beyond what is practiced in this industry today.

- Swatch Project is a classic case that was part of earlier versions of our text. It deals with the establishment of global distribution channels in the initial cycles of the Swatch launch with special emphasis on the U.S. market.

Cases that have been retained from the previous edition include the following:

- "Alcon Laboratories" deals with a U.S.-based company that is the world leader in the ophthalmic industry and discusses global resource allocation across multiple geographies, product lines, and other competing priorities.

- The Ericsson case ("Make Yourself Heard: Ericsson's Global Brand Campaign") opens the discussion of global branding for the company's mobile phones in an intensively competitive industry.

- "Delissa in Japan" deals with a European food company in the process of entering the Japanese market.

- "Siemens Automotive Systems: Brazil Strategy" deals with a subsidiary of the large German international firm and its electronic automotive parts supply business.

- "Interactive Computer Systems Corp." deals with the issues of pricing, parallel imports, and gray markets.

- "ICI Paints (A): Strategy for Globalization" and "ICI Paints (B): Considering a Global Product Organization" focus on global strategy and global organizations.
- Gillette International's TRAC II" highlights competitive strategies within the global marketplace.
- A group of four cases, "Note on the World Over-the-Counter Drug Industry," "Note on Competitors in the Over-the-Counter Drug Industry," " Note on OTC Brands," and "Ciba Self-Medication," describe the situation in the over-the-counter drug industry prior to the merger of Ciba with Sandoz to form Novartis Consumer Health.

Acknowledgments:

The content of the cases would not have been possible without the generous participation of a number of companies and executives: Herman Scopes and John Thompson (ICI paints); Jose Helio Contador Filho and Walter Kunerth (Siemens Brazil); Roland Jeannet (Novartis Consumer Health and OTC Series), and Ed Schollmaier (Alcon Laboratories), Henry Kasindorf and Richard Katz (Tonernow.com), Bob Schmetterer (Euro RSCG), Libero Milone and Tom Presby (Deloitte Touche Tohmatsu Europe), and Ernst Thomke (Swatch). These executives, and others who prefer to remain anonymous, gave generously of their time so that other current and future managers could learn from their experiences. We would like to thank our colleagues Kamran Kashani (Ericsson), Dominique Turpin (Delissa Japan) and Bob Collins (co-author on Deloitte Touche Tohmatsu Europe) from IMD for their willingness to have their cases reprinted in our new casebook version. We would also like to thank Persita Egeli, head of Case Administration at IMD, who provided us crucial support in guiding our cases through the approval, release, and copyright process.

To turn the collected material and data into readable form, we could always count on a number of students, graduate assistants, and research associates. We wish to thank Babson College students Peter Mark, Christine Menz, Shauna Pettit, and Sameer Kaji, who wrote parts of the cases used in this text. We are grateful to Barbara Priovolos, Susan Nye, Robert Howard, Sam Perkins, and Martha Lanning, who in their roles as research associates wrote several of the cases at IMD and Babson College.

J.P.J.

H.D.H.

Case 1

Siemens Automotive Systems: Brazil Strategy

In the spring of 1992, Jose Helio Contador Filho, General Manager of Siemens Automotive Ltda., the Brazilian subsidiary of Siemens Automobile Group, prepared himself for the upcoming strategy meetings in Germany with Walter Kunerth, who had worldwide responsibility for the Automotive Systems Group at Siemens. Contador realized that he would not only have to present a medium-term strategy for Brazil, but he also needed to consider Siemens' global aspirations and strategy for the Automotive Systems Group. "What role should and can the Brazilian operation play when the parent company is essentially pursuing a global strategy? What can we, operating in a developing country, contribute to the global strategy of our division?" Those were the questions Contador needed to resolve before he could present a more detailed plan and expect to receive any additional funds for investment.

Corporate Background

Siemens AG was one of Europe's largest industrial companies, with annual sales of DM 73 billion in 1991 ($50 billion), more than 400,000 employees worldwide, and a comprehensive range of products. Internationally, Siemens was one of the world's major electrical engineering and electronics firms.

Siemens had recently been reorganized along fifteen major product groups. Each group was respon-

sible for worldwide operations in development, manufacturing, sales activities, and earnings performance. Two newly formed embryonic divisions and two separately organized operating subsidiaries completed the roster of operating groups. They were supported by corporate divisions and departments as well as some centralized services. Furthermore, there was a range of regional organizations around the world which were coordinated by two central departments. (Refer to Exhibit 1.)

Siemens' largest operating groups were: information systems with some DM 12.1 billion in sales, power generation and transmission (DM 10.3 billion), public communications networks (DM 11.3 billion), industrial building systems (DM 8.8 billion), and medical engineering (DM 7.4 billion). Other groups concentrated on automation, electrical and electronic components, and data and information systems. (Refer to Exhibit 2.)

Almost half of Siemens' sales were in Germany (46 percent), while the rest of Europe accounted for another 30 percent of sales. North America accounted for about 10 percent. As for worldwide sales, Asia had 7 percent; Latin America, 3 percent; and the rest of the world, 3 percent. Siemens was present in more than 130 countries and had some 159,000 employees outside Germany. The company operated about 200 plants abroad. (Refer to Exhibit 3.)

THE MARKET FOR ELECTRONIC AUTOMOTIVE COMPONENTS

The Worldwide Automobile Market

The market for automobiles had experienced major expansion during the second part of the 1980s. In the early 1990s, the markets in several regions were depressed and showed declining sales. However, market experts had forecast substantial growth throughout

This case was prepared by Professors Jean-Pierre Jeannet and Kurt Schär as a basis for class discussion rather than to illustrate either effective or ineffective handling of a business situation. Copyright © 1993 by the International Management Development Institute (IMD), Lausanne, Switzerland. Not to be used or reproduced without permission directly from IMD.

Exhibit 1 ● Siemens AG Corporate Structure

Managing Board Corporate Executive Committee				
Groups			**Corporate Divisions**	**Central Departments**
Power Generation (KWU)	Power Transmission and Distribution	Drives and Standard Products	Corporate Finance	Corporate Relations
Automation	Private Communication Systems	**Automotive Systems**	Corporate Research and Development	Berlin Executive Offices
Transportation Systems	Industrial and Building Systems	Public Communication Networks	Corporate Human Resources	International Regions
		Defense Electronics		
		Medical Engineering	Corporate Production and Logistics	**Centralized Services**
		Semiconductors	Corporate Planning and Development	Domestic Regional Administration
Special Divisions	Electro-mechanical Components	Audio and Video Systems		Berlin
Passive Components and Electron Tubes				Munich
Legally Independent Units	Siemens Nixdorf Informations-systeme AG			Personnel
Osram GmbH				

Regional Organization
Regional offices, international Siemens companies, sales companies, representative offices, agencies

Exhibit 2 ● Siemens AG Sales by Business Segments

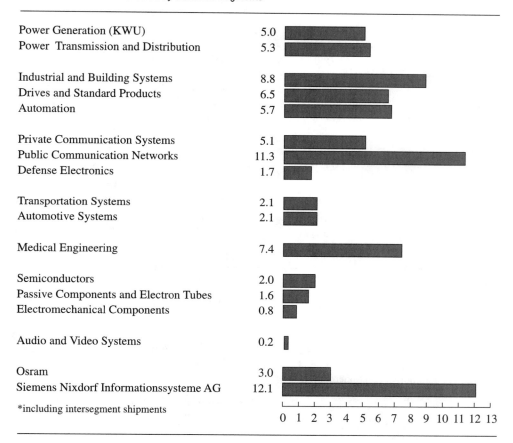

Power Generation (KWU)	5.0
Power Transmission and Distribution	5.3
Industrial and Building Systems	8.8
Drives and Standard Products	6.5
Automation	5.7
Private Communication Systems	5.1
Public Communication Networks	11.3
Defense Electronics	1.7
Transportation Systems	2.1
Automotive Systems	2.1
Medical Engineering	7.4
Semiconductors	2.0
Passive Components and Electron Tubes	1.6
Electromechanical Components	0.8
Audio and Video Systems	0.2
Osram	3.0
Siemens Nixdorf Informationssysteme AG	12.1

*including intersegment shipments

0 1 2 3 4 5 6 7 8 9 10 11 12 13

the decade for cars and trucks. The number of vehicles produced exerted a substantial influence on the automotive components business, as did the fortune of the leading companies. There were twenty-eight vehicle producers worldwide. The changes affecting their business had a strong and direct effect on the independent components and parts manufacturers. (Refer to Exhibit 4.)

The Worldwide Market for Automotive Components

Purchased components typically represented 50 percent of the cost of a car. As a result, efficient compo-

nent purchasing was an important aspect of the cost structure of car companies, which were always under pressure to improve efficiency. Ford Motors' worldwide purchasing bill amounted to $53 billion in 1990.

Automobile manufacturers were essentially makers of the car body shell. In most instances, they manufactured car engines as well as the transmission. The rest of the components and parts were purchased for installation either from outside suppliers or company-owned component operations.

The size of the worldwide automotive component market was vast. For the United States alone, which was the largest single market, the amount was

Exhibit 3 ● Siemens AG Geographic Sales Distribution (in DM mn)

	Sales		Capital Investments	
	1991	*1990*	*1991*	*1990*
Germany	51,245.0	44,504.0	3,332.0	3,882.0
Attributable to exports	(17,982.0)	(16,152.0)		
Europe excluding Germany	23,338.0	19,532.0	1,284.0	2,241.0
Included therein:				
European Community	(14,761.0)	(12,090.0)	(800.0)	(1,808.0)
North America	8,517.0	7,543.0	576.0	704.0
Latin America	1,563.0	1,771.0	138.0	113.0
Asia	2,715.0	2,088.0	219.0	85.0
Other Regions	1,100.0	1,011.0	46.0	41.0
Minus intersegment shipments	(15,469.6)	(13,264.1)		
	73,008.4	**63,184.9**	**5,595.0**	**7,066.0**

$96 billion in 1989 (refer to Exhibit 5). Germany's market, ranked third behind Japan, amounted to $32 billion. Included under automotive components were not only the electronic systems for cars but also tires, glass, bearings, plastic parts, and many other components purchased for direct installment.

The size and growth of the market depended largely on trends that affected the volume of the automotive OEM market and the annual vehicle output. The replacement market, important for those components that were subject to wear and tear—such as tires, was under constant pressure since quality was constantly improving and the typical life expectancy was therefore rising.

Major trends in the components market came from new technologies and the pressure on automotive manufacturers to continue to improve the efficiency and environmental impact of their cars. Vehicles were expected to have higher fuel efficiency which, in turn, required having lighter components to reduce the car's overall weight. Higher emission standards required improved engines and alternative fuel systems. Safety standards around the world were also

becoming stricter. All these factors called for the use of more electronics in automobiles.

The Worldwide Market for Electronic Automotive Systems

For the lay person, automotive electronics might be described as a "black box" inside a car. For this "black box" to work properly, some key components had to be present. The most important ones were sensors (input devices) and actuators (output devices such as electric motors that acted on information transmitted by sensors). Without their proper functioning, the automotive electronics systems would not be able to perform the required function. As a result, these areas were also where R&D concentration was the highest.

The market for automotive electronic systems was in a phase of rapid growth. Currently, an average automobile contained about $1,000 worth of electronic systems and components. By the year 2000, this amount was expected to reach $2,000 for a typical car. Despite the slow growth in total car output, the

Exhibit 4 ● World Car Production and Sales Statistics and Forecast, 1991–1995

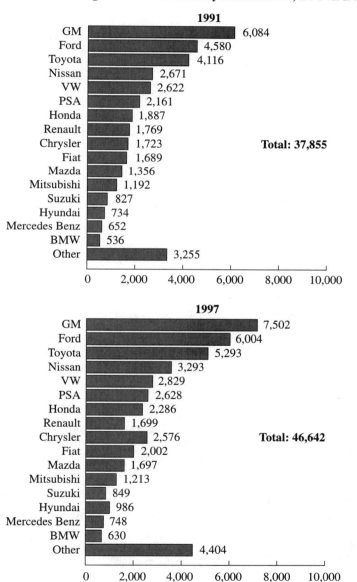

Total Car and Light Truck Production by Manufacturer, 1991 vs. 1997

1991

Manufacturer	Production
GM	6,084
Ford	4,580
Toyota	4,116
Nissan	2,671
VW	2,622
PSA	2,161
Honda	1,887
Renault	1,769
Chrysler	1,723
Fiat	1,689
Mazda	1,356
Mitsubishi	1,192
Suzuki	827
Hyundai	734
Mercedes Benz	652
BMW	536
Other	3,255

Total: 37,855

1997

Manufacturer	Production
GM	7,502
Ford	6,004
Toyota	5,293
Nissan	3,293
VW	2,829
PSA	2,628
Honda	2,286
Renault	1,699
Chrysler	2,576
Fiat	2,002
Mazda	1,697
Mitsubishi	1,213
Suzuki	849
Hyundai	986
Mercedes Benz	748
BMW	630
Other	4,404

Total: 46,642

Note: Thes numbers include US, Canada, Mexico, Japan, Korea, and Western Europe only.

Note: These numbers include United States, Canada, Mexico, Japan, Korea, and western Europe only.

Exhibit 4 ● World Car Production and Sales Statistics and Forecast, 1991–1995 (*continued*)

	World Car Sales Forecast (000s)[a]				
	1991	*1992*	*1993*	*1994*	*1995*
WORLD TOTAL	*34,202*	*34,649*	*36,746*	*38,143*	*39,643*
Germany	4,158	3,687	3,471	3,552	3,648
Italy	2,340	2,324	2,256	2,287	2,345
France	2,031	2,167	2,283	2,369	2,416
United Kingdom	1,592	1,697	1,894	2,008	2,153
Spain	887	997	1,095	1,197	1,296
EU TOTAL	*12,580*	*12,440*	*12,582*	*13,034*	*13,512*
WEST EUROPE TOTAL	*13,526*	*13,391*	*13,584*	*14,100*	*14,629*
Eastern Bloc	1,630	1,713	1,987	2,033	2,326
United States	8,373	8,695	9,805	10,032	10,175
Canada	871	916	987	1,040	1,100
Brazil	583	569	608	679	747
Mexico	392	421	439	447	462
Japan	4,868	4,674	4,814	4,970	5,108
South Korea	745	836	919	993	1,067

a. 1991 actual; 1992–1995 forecast.

Source: DRI World Automotive Forecast Report.

increase in the electronics for each new model was expected to cause the segment to grow 10–15 percent annually over the next decade. Eventually, electronics would account for as much as 15–20 percent of the product costs of a typical car.

Major applications for automotive electronics were engine control systems, controls for automatic transmission, controls of drive trains or chassis in the form of braking systems or suspension, safety systems such as airbag controls, control electronics for instrumentation and driver information (speed, distance, location), and a whole range of entertainment electronics (e.g., radios, CD players). In the area of engine control, the trend was toward a single computer controlling both ignition and fuel injection.

Control of automatic transmission systems was experiencing considerable growth as the use of automatic transmissions in Japan was rapidly reaching the U.S. level, and Europe was expected to follow this trend. In the area of chassis or drive train, the focus was on electronically controlled anti-lock brake systems (ABS) and suspension systems designed to adapt to different road surfaces.

Automotive Electronics Suppliers

Siemens faced three groups of competitors in the automotive electronics field. First, there were the large international merchant suppliers who were independent car manufacturers, among them Bosch of Ger-

Exhibit 4 ● World Car Production and Sales Statistics and Forecast 1991–1995 (*continued*)

World Car Production Forecast (000s)[a]

	1991	1992	1993	1994	1995
WORLD TOTAL	34,266	34,958	37,053	38,339	39,868
Germany	4,659	4,652	4,541	4,574	4,612
France	3,187	3,118	3,404	3,476	3,529
Spain	1,773	1,730	1,806	1,858	1,954
Italy	1,634	1,627	1,580	1,695	1,758
United Kingdom	1,236	1,390	1,691	1,778	1,838
EU TOTAL	12,826	12,866	13,464	13,867	14,297
WEST EUROPE TOTAL	13,103	13,179	13,815	14,265	14,725
Eastern Bloc	1,895	1,859	2,028	2,236	2,531
United States	5,733	6,238	6,702	6,798	7,066
Canada	1,066	1,071	1,322	1,406	1,454
Brazil	705	703	754	848	942
Mexico	673	708	757	793	841
Japan	9,753	9,618	9,682	10,005	10,210
South Korea	1,128	1,268	1,429	1,551	1,636

a. 1991 actual; 1992–1995, forecast.

Source: DRI World Automotive Forecast Report.

many and Valeo of France. Secondly, there were the in-house—or captive—suppliers of large automobile manufacturers, such as GM and Ford, and Nippondenso (Japan) to some extent. Finally, there were a large number of smaller and regional players in certain niches, both in terms of products and geographical location. (Refer to Exhibits 6, 7, and 8.)

Among the captive players was GM, which had volume in electronic parts and components of about DM 6–8 billion (three to four times Siemens' sales). Ford had a volume of about DM 4 billion. Both companies realized that their own captive sources were increasingly uncompetitive and were under heavy pressure to reduce costs. GM, due to its size, was even

further backward integrated, making its own semiconductors and chips.

The ***Robert Bosch Group,*** with sales of $22.4 billion in 1991, was the world leader in automotive electronics. Bosch had some 50 percent of its corporate sales in automotive components, with ABS systems, lighting, engine control systems, chassis electronics, injection systems for diesel engines, starters, and generators as the major product lines. The company employed some 180,000 people, with one third of those working abroad.

In automotive electronics, Bosch was the most important merchant supplier and Siemens' biggest competitor. Bosch, estimated to have a volume of DM

Exhibit 5 ● U.S. Automotive Components Industry, 1987–1989

Component Sector[a]	1987	1988	1989
Value of product shipments ($bn)	87.8	91.4	96.0
Employment (000)	631	639	649
Shipments per worker ($000)	139	143	148
Value of imports ($bn)	26.8	31.0	33.2
Import penetration	26.7	29.5	29.8
Value of exports ($bn)	14.4	17.8	17.8
Exports as % of shipments	16.4	19.0	18.5
Trade deficit ($bn)	12.4	13.5	15.5

a. Excludes services provided by establishments in the automotive parts and accessories industry and tires and batteries.

Source: The Economist Intelligence Unit.

Exhibit 6 ● Major U.S. Automotive Component Suppliers, 1989

Companies with Annual Sales of More Than $1 bn.

Rank	Corporation	Sales ($bn)
1	GM Automotive Components Group	$29.0
2	Ford Automotive Components Operations	13.5[a]
3	Goodyear Tire and Rubber	10.9
4	Dana	4.9
5	Allied Signal Automotive	3.8
6	GM Hughes	3.5
7	Cummins Engine Company	3.5
8	TRW Automotive	3.4
9	Acustar	3.4
10	ITT Automotive	2.9
11	Rockwell Automotive	2.4
12	Eaton	2.1
13	United Technologies Automotive	1.9
14	Magna International	1.9
15	Tenneco Automotive	1.8
16	Masco Industries	1.7
17	Echlin	1.5
18	Arvin	1.2
19	Kelsey-Hayes	1.2
20	Lear Seating	1.1
21	Federal Mogul	1.1
22	Borg-Warner Automotive	1.0
23	Gates Rubber Company	1.0

a. Estimate.

Source: The Economist Intelligence Unit.

4 billion in electronics, was competing directly with Siemens' entire electronics line. In ABS, Bosch was a leader; 28 car manufacturers offered Bosch ABS systems in more than 100 models. Fuel injection systems had experienced substantial growth. Bosch also operated a large company in Brazil.

Valeo, based in France, was one of the world's leading automotive suppliers, with $4 billion in sales and some 30,000 employees. More than half of its sales were abroad. Valeo was a publicly owned company with almost 40 percent of its voting stock controlled by Carlo de Benedetti's Cerus Group. Although larger than Siemens as a component supplier, in the automotive electronics field Valeo's sales were about DM 1 billion, or half those of Siemens. Valeo was not competing in engine management systems or airbag systems, but it competed with Siemens on all other product lines.

One of Valeo's important product lines was air conditioning systems, which accounted for $600 million in sales. The company also produced around 5 million heating units, 500,000 air conditioning systems, and 100,000 electronic air control systems. Valeo was represented in Brazil through several operating companies.

Nippondenso was a Japanese firm with sales of $11.8 billion in 1991—a 2 percent decrease from the previous year. The company had gained its independence from Toyota in 1949, which remained its largest shareholder with about 23 percent of shares.

Exhibit 7 ● Major European Automotive Systems Suppliers, 1990

			Companies with Annual Sales of More Than $2 bn		
Rank	Company	Sales ($mn)	Principal Country of Manufacture	Parent	Country of Parent
1	Bosch	10,757	Germany	Robert Bosch	Germany
2	Michelin	10,311	France	Michelin	France
3	Philips	4,793	Netherlands	NV Philips	Netherlands
4	Continental	4,649	Germany	Continental	Germany
5	Valeo	3,936	France	Valeo	France
6	Magneti Marelli	3,370	Italy	Fiat	Italy
7	ZF	3,112	Germany	Zahnradfabrik Friedrichshafen	Germany
8	BASF	3,092	Germany	BASF	Germany
9	GKN	2,750	United Kingdom	GKN	United Kingdom
10	Pirelli	2,620	Italy	Pirelli	Italy
11	Lucas	2,448	United Kingdom	Lucas Industries	United Kingdom
12	ACG-GM	2,400	France	General Motors Corp.	United States
13	Goodyear	2,190	Belgium	Goodyear Tire Co.	United States

			Companies with Annual Sales of $1 bn–$1.999 bn		
14	Teves	1,807	Germany	ITT Inc.	United States
15	BTR	1,804	United Kingdom	BTR	United Kingdom
16	Allied-Signal	1,770	France	Allied-Signal	United States
17	TRW	1,770	United Kingdom	TRW Inc.	United States
18	Tenneco Automotive	1,731	Belgium	Tenneco Corp.	United States
19	Saint-Gobain	1,616	France	Compagnie de Saint-Gobain	France
20	T & N	1,496	United Kingdom	T & N	United Kingdom
21	Pilkington	1,262	United Kingdom	Pilkington	United Kingdom
22	Mahle	1,248	Germany	Mahle	Germany
23	SKF	1,226	Sweden	SKF	Sweden
24	VDO	1,222	Germany	VDO Adof Schindling	Germany
25	BBA	1,215	United Kingdom	BBA	United Kingdom
26	Siemens	1,163	Germany	Siemens	Germany
27	Hella	1,139	Germany	Hella	Germany
28	Du Pont	1,075	Germany	Du Pont de Nemours & Co.	United States
29	Freudenberg	1,029	Germany	Carl Freudenberg	Germany
30	Epéda-Bertrand Faure	1,008	France	Epéda-Bertrand Faure	France

Source: The Economist Intelligence Unit.

Exhibit 8 ● Major Japanese Automotive Component Suppliers, 1989

Companies with Annual Sales of More Than $1 bn

Company	Sales ($mn)
Nippondenso	$9,056
Bridgestone	8,799
Sumitomo Rubber	3,015
Sumitomo Metal	2,951
Alsin Seike	2,898
Sumitomo Electric	1,970
Yazaki	1,848
Diesel Kiki	1,757
Yokohama Rubber	1,664
Mitsubishi Electric	1,515
Koyo Seiko	1,507
Hitachi	1,500
Toyo Tire & Rubber	1,362
Calsonic	1,283
NTN	1,275
Toyoda Gosel	1,258
NEC Corporation	1,159
Koiti Manufacturing	1,099
Atsugi Unisia	1,032
Asaki Glass	1,014
Nippon Seiki	1,006
TOTAL	*$48,968*
Number of Companies	21
Segment Average	2,332

Source: The Economist Intelligence Unit.

Another 10 percent was owned by Bosch, whose shareholding came about as a result of capitalizing licensing agreements. About 50 percent of the company's sales were transacted with Toyota. Nippondenso's major product lines were car heaters and air conditioners (35 percent), electrical and electronic automotive controls (30 percent), fuel management sys-tems (15 percent), with the rest consisting of a variety of other automotive component products. Its automotive electronics product line was comparable to that of Bosch in depth, and the company's sales were estimated at about DM 4 billion.

Heaters and air conditioners were Nippondenso's biggest line, with 5.45 million air conditioners shipped, a 1.3 percent decrease over the previous year. In its Control Product units, standard products such as starters, alternators, and small motors declined about 2 percent. Growth was recorded in other lines—ABS, airbag related devices, and relays for expensive cars. In fuel management systems, sales showed negative trends for electronic fuel injection, but they increased for electronically controlled distribution pumps.

Nippondenso had $2.5 billion in overseas sales. Internationalization was pushed ahead and the company embarked on a drive to increase the amount of local manufacturing overseas. The company operated thirty-six facilities, in fifteen different countries, including six in the United States and—among other plants—one in Brazil.

OEM Purchasing Practices

Traditional purchasing practices, where an adversarial relationship existed between the OEM and the component supplier, were giving way to long-term partnerships. In Europe and the United States, a car manufacturer typically used two to five suppliers for a component of a given car model. By splitting the supply contracts, the OEM felt that there was less risk of a supplier dictating the price level. Contracts were issued annually to local suppliers, with the lowest price bidder receiving the largest portion—about 30 percent—of the annual volume, and others receiving smaller portions, ranging from 20 percent to 10 percent each.

With respect to automotive electronics, a significant amount of the cost base was research and product development, since each new model range required its own type of components. After choosing several suppliers, with each one including R&D in its cost base and the resulting price, European and U.S. car manufacturers realized that the savings through price control did not make up for the additional costs of paying redundantly for several manufacturers' development. By comparison, Japanese firms tended to use only one supplier. They were thus able to save the multiple costs of development. As component costs were the largest cost factor in car manufacturing, competitive pressures forced changes to take place, but they had only come about in the last two to three years.

Since purchased components accounted for about half of the unit cost of a car, cost reductions in components was an important element in the purchasing strategy of most car manufacturers. The latest trend was to give a supply contract to just one or two suppliers for the entire life cycle of a car model, which typically lasted five years. Prices for each of those five years were negotiated from the beginning, with substantial price reductions agreed to from the outset. There was a strong trend to purchase from wherever the cheapest source could be found (global sourcing), as opposed to buying exclusively from local suppliers. With contracts being much larger than formerly, companies from around the world would compete for them. Logistics also became more important as JIT [just-in-time distribution] reached new levels of capability. Some new car plants were known to be located near airports (such as the one planned by BMW in the United States) so that regular shipments could be made by air from anywhere to the place of assembly.

Companies were engaging in a process of "deverticalization," whereby they would make less internally and rely more on component manufacturers. Increasingly, the preference was to rely not only on fewer suppliers but to delegate more responsibility—such as for inventory, R&D, tooling, logistics—to each supplier. The lead suppliers would handle entire systems rather than only components, thus car companies could purchase more preassembled modules from fewer sources. These lead suppliers were expected to be financially strong enough to assume the added responsibility. Quality would become an ever more important element in the purchasing system. In Japan, suppliers had only 50 rejects per one million parts, whereas the relevant standard in the United Kingdom was still at 1,000 rejects per one million parts.

Several firms had already reduced the number of suppliers. Ford had cut its supplier base worldwide in half since 1980 and was expected to cut another third by 1995. Ford Europe had had 900 suppliers in 1988, but intended to have only 600 by 1995. Renault, with 1,000 suppliers in 1991, anticipated reducing the number to 600–700. In addition, Renault, through its alliance with Volvo, was developing a joint purchasing strategy, which would eventually increase the commonality of suppliers from the current level of 15 percent of purchased components to 80 percent. Two suppliers—Siemens and Bosch—would be particularly affected, as Bosch had 80 percent of the Volvo account and Siemens the other 20 percent, while the percentages were reversed for Renault. Peugeot moved from 1,700 suppliers in 1984 to 740 in 1991. At the same time, both French companies pushed purchased components up to two-thirds of total component costs, a steep increase from previous years. In comparison, Nissan used only 160 suppliers. By concentrating on fewer suppliers and larger average volumes, cost reductions that could be passed on to the car companies were expected to occur.

GM served as another example of changed purchasing strategies. In early 1992, the company appointed an executive to the key strategy board of both GM North America and GM Europe who would have worldwide responsibility for purchasing. GM announced a 10–20 percent price cut to be made incrementally over three years from its suppliers. A 6 percent savings in the first year represented a savings of $4 billion in 1991. As part of this new program, GM was expected to pursue global sourcing for all its operations. Lean production strategies with lower inventories were to be rigorously pursued. The number of types of car platforms (basic underbodies) was to be reduced, thus permitting greater use of common components. And finally, the practice of making up-front payments to component suppliers for new tooling was to be abolished. In return, companies could compete to sell components to GM on a worldwide basis on long-term contracts with some stretching over the life cycle of a car model.

Partnerships with suppliers were increasingly being sought. At Ford, where the development time for new car models was to be cut by 25 percent, the company was looking for suppliers who could make a commitment early on in the development cycle. In this way, the company would be better able to design, integrate, and manufacture the new model, and to provide a "full-time and full-service" function all the way to the market. Japanese car companies had moved toward taking direct interest—even sometimes making investments—in the operations of their suppliers. They then expected to share in the resulting profit and cost savings derived from the partnership.

Dependence on their customers could affect the fate of component suppliers. When Fiat saw its market share slip from 55 percent to 45 percent in its important Italian market over the past two years, its component suppliers faced substantial volume reductions and, consequently, most of them suffered losses.

Verticalization, or the amount of backward integration pursued by car companies, was also under debate. Practices differed by country. In the United States, both GM and Ford maintained large component manufacturing operations. GM Automotive Components Group had annual sales of $29 billion. Its Delco subsidiary was the largest supplier of ignition systems worldwide, whereas its Harrison Radiators subsidiary was the leader in radiators. Ford operated the Ford Automotive Components Operations with sales of $13.5 billion. In Europe, Fiat owned 66.5 percent of Magneti Marelli, Italy's largest automotive supplier.

German car manufacturers tended to purchase from independent companies. As far as automotive electronics was concerned, in-house or captive volume accounted for two-thirds of total purchasing. Merchant suppliers, which included Siemens, could therefore only compete for a fraction of the market. However, as companies changed their policies on merchant versus captive suppliers, the available market volume for merchant suppliers would become larger.

Economics of the Business

Electronic components could not be made in-house unless the car manufacturer had sufficient volume. Few companies were in such a situation; at GM, Ford, and Toyota, these activities tended to take place in separately established subsidiaries.

The economics of automotive components manufacturing were driven by cost requirements on one side and research costs on the other. R&D costs tended to be around 10 percent of sales. To achieve low-cost status and thus offer competitive prices to car manufacturers, component suppliers were relocating to low-cost production areas. JIT requirements were still in force, but car manufacturers came to reappraise the process. Typically, they preferred a nearby supplier that shipped components by truck on a regular basis.

On the other hand, minimum size and manufacturing efficiencies were only guaranteed with a plant producing about DM 200 million in output on a given product line. To reach this level, component suppliers were producing in a low-cost area, then shipping by air on a regular basis to just a few plants or even only one plant per product line. It was expected that a supplier would reserve airlift capacity from faraway plants several years in advance for a given customer, and maintain minimal buffer stocks nearby.

Delivery reliability, however, was still believed to be the number one criteria, as the cost of having an assembly line idle was extremely high. Car manufacturers required that a component supplier absorb any costs caused by a delay that was the supplier's fault.

SIEMENS AUTOMOTIVE SYSTEMS (AT)[1]

Historic Development and Growth

The Automotive Systems Group, organized as one of Siemens' industry groups, was one of the company's new businesses. Started in 1981 with about 150 employees and just DM 20 million in sales, the business had grown to a volume of DM 2.1 billion by 1991 (up 17 percent from the previous year). Capital spending for 1991 amounted to DM 236 million, down 27 percent from the previous year. Research and development spending had reached DM 250 million, or 12 percent of sales, and total employment had passed 14,000 for the entire Automotive Systems Group.

Siemens' business in automotive systems passed through several phases in its growth. (Refer to Exhibit 9.) Initially, Siemens had built the business from internal growth, consistently adding new product lines. In the mid-1980s, related businesses from other Siemens activities were combined into Automotive Systems. In 1988, Siemens acquired the automotive components business of Bendix Electronics from Allied-Signal, a large U.S.-based company. This acquisition had many strategic advantages for Siemens. Traditionally, Siemens Automotive Systems had had its strength in automo-

---

1. AT (Automobil Technologie) is Siemens' international abbreviation for this business. The company recommended using the term "Automotive Systems Group" in English.

Exhibit 9 ● Siemens Automotive Systems Division: Historic Development, 1980–1991

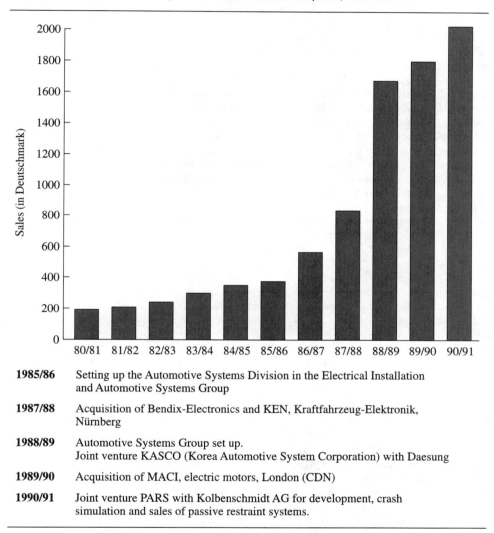

1985/86	Setting up the Automotive Systems Division in the Electrical Installation and Automotive Systems Group
1987/88	Acquisition of Bendix-Electronics and KEN, Kraftfahrzeug-Elektronik, Nürnberg
1988/89	Automotive Systems Group set up. Joint venture KASCO (Korea Automotive System Corporation) with Daesung
1989/90	Acquisition of MACI, electric motors, London (CDN)
1990/91	Joint venture PARS with Kolbenschmidt AG for development, crash simulation and sales of passive restraint systems.

bile electronics, combined with a strong presence in the European—primarily German—market. Bendix, on the other hand, had well-established product lines in the more conventional technologies and electromechanical components.

Most important, however, was Bendix's established customer relationships with leading U.S. companies and its long-standing position in the U.S.

market. Bendix also had built up an international market presence in Latin America, Asia, and Europe. As well, the company brought its line of engine management systems into the merger. Bendix, located in Troy, Michigan, was 20 miles from important technical development centers of the "Big Three" U.S. automobile companies. In Europe, the merger brought in Renix, a JV [joint venture] between Renault and Bendix, with a plant in Toulouse and access to France, the world's fourth-largest automobile manufacturing market.

The merger and the resulting increased volume catapulted Siemens Automotive Systems into second place worldwide—behind Bosch—among the merchant suppliers of automobile electronics. It was Siemens' strategy to solidify its position as the number two merchant supplier worldwide and to maintain a first-tier supplier role, i.e., a supplier that dealt directly with automobile manufacturers rather than supplying other component companies. Its line of products covered the entire spectrum of automotive electronics, with the exception of driver information systems (speed and distance indicators, and instrumentation). Siemens was in the running to acquire VDO, a German company whose main emphasis was instrumentation. But, in the end, that company was acquired by Mannesmann, a large German engineering firm.

Siemens' AT Organization

Siemens supplied various product lines and was grouped into five divisions: Vehicle Electronic Systems, Plastic Systems and Air Management, Electrical Motors and Electrical Motor Systems, Vehicle Electrical Distribution Systems, and Engine Management Systems. Each of these components divisions had worldwide responsibility for product development, manufacturing, and distribution. (Refer to Exhibits 10 and 11.)

Engine management systems was one of Siemens' most important product categories. A fully operable system used a combination of twenty-one individual components and controlled the car's drivability and exhaust emissions. Its principal clients were Chrysler, Renault, Peugeot, VW, and BMW. Siemens was also rapidly becoming a major supplier of electronic control modules and sensors for anti-lock braking systems (ABS). In some ABS systems, as many as half of the components were from Siemens. As yet, the company did not supply complete systems, but it sold to companies which, in turn, delivered complete systems to car makers. (Refer to Exhibit 11.)

Air management systems supplied entire cooling and air systems, heating, ventilation, and air conditioning systems. Siemens manufactured the plastic parts that held the systems in place and sourced the key components—such as compressors, fans, control electronics, and electric motors—both from other di-

visions and outside suppliers. With a volume of DM 200 million, the division sourced from plants in Rodach (Germany), Turkey, Canada, and the United Kingdom.

Electrical distribution systems, which conveyed power and signals in the car, had become increasingly important (typically $200–$300 worth of components per car). This area accounted for sales of DM 250 million for Siemens and employed 3,000 people in plants in Germany and Portugal. Modular networks and multiplex systems were the latest systems under development.

Siemens was an active supplier of *electric motors.* Some luxury cars required as many as 70 motors for various activities. Its Wuerzburg plant in Germany, one of the most modern plants for small electric motors in Europe, alone had sales of DM 280 million. A new plant for this range was planned for the North American market. In 1991, Siemens acquired the electronics group of Magna International in Canada (sales of U.S. $150 million).

In 1992, as much as 8 percent of the total electronics required for an automobile was made up of various *sensors.* They tended to create as much as 20–25 percent of warranty costs due to corrosion and wrong signals sent. Automotive electronics could not be effective without sensors as they supplied all inputs. Present sensor technology still lagged behind the requirements. Sensors were expected to represent as much as a $4 billion market by 1995. Siemens had a total of 1,000 employees in the sensor area, spread over two plants in Canada and France, and total sales of DM 120 million. Within the next three years, sales were expected to reach some DM 300 million. Key products were RPM sensors, sensors to measure air mass according to the hot film principle, and knock, oil, and pressure sensors for gasoline suction systems. In anticipation of future car engines with mixed fuels (gasoline and methanol), Siemens was developing a sensor that could measure the alcohol content of the gasoline. Furthermore, Siemens was developing crash sensors for airbag systems to be supplied from its Canadian plant and already had half of the GM business in the US. Airbags alone were expected to grow into a $7 billion segment by the mid-1990s. Siemens was supplying eleven of the world's twenty-eight OEMs with components for airbag systems.

The *Fuel System Components Division* included such elements as actuators, fuel injectors, and

Exhibit 10 ● Siemens Automotive Systems Product Line

RESTRAINT SYSTEMS

- Airbag systems
- Airbag diagnostic and control units
- Electromechanical and electronic crash sensors

POWER TRAIN AND CHASSIS CONTROLS

- Electronic transmission control system
- Automatic four-wheel drive
- Automatic limited-slip differential
- ABS electronics
- All-wheel steering
- Damping control systems
- Ride-height control systems
- Wheel speed sensors
- Hydraulic pressure sensors
- Hydraulic valves
- Application systems

INFORMATION SYSTEMS

- Trip computers
- Check control
- Navigation systems
- Traffic management systems
- Outside-temperature sensors
- Wheel speed sensors
- Ultrasound level sensors

VEHICLE ELECTRICAL DISTRIBUTION SYSTEMS

- Vehicle wires
- Components
- Main and secondary wiring harnesses
- Modular vehicle electrical systems
- Brake wear indicators

CONVENIENCE SYSTEMS

- Infrared locking systems
- Seat memory
- Anti-theft warning systems

AIR-CONDITIONING SYSTEMS

- Heaters and air-conditioners
- Electronic and mechanical controls
- Air-quality systems
- Air jets
- Plastic parts and components

INDUCTION SYSTEMS

- Air cleaners
- Resonators
- Secondary air pumps
- Integrated air/fuel systems
- Plastic parts and components

ENGINE MANAGEMENT

- Integrated engine management
- OBD 2
- Ignition control units
- Ignition trigger boxes
- Fuel-injection control
- Single-point fuel injection
- Multi/single-point fuel injectors
- Fuel rails
- Throttle potentiometers
- Methanol-sensors
- Coolant temperature sensors
- Inlet manifold temperature sensors
- Knock sensors
- Camshaft angle sensors
- TDC sensors
- MAP sensors
- Mass air-flow sensors
- Lambda sensors
- Catalysts
- Tank venting systems
- Canister purge solenoids
- Exhaust-gas recirculation valves
- Mini pressure regulators
- Three-way solenoid valves
- Vacuum regulator valves
- Air-bypass valves
- Coolant bypass valves
- E-gas
- Application systems

ELECTRIC MOTORS, ELECTRICAL MOTOR SYSTEMS

Motors for

- Power window
- Seat adjustment
- Sun roof
- Steering
- Transmission
- Clutch
- Flap adjustment

Pump drives for

- ABS Steering
- Central hydraulic units

Fans for

- Heating and air conditioning
- Engine cooling
- Electrical maindrive

RELAY DEVICES for

- Flasher unit
- Wash/wipe interval
- Rear window wiper
- Courtesy light delay
- Compressor protection
- Fuel pumps
- Glow time
- Overvoltage protection
- Seat heating
- Diesel filter heating
- Headlamp cleaning
- Motoraggregate control

Exhibit 11 ● Siemens Automotive Systems Division: Worldwide Organization Chart

Automotive Systems
Prof. Dr. Kunerth/Mache

Vehicle Electronic Systems Sensor Systems		*Air Management and Plastic Systems*		*Electric Motors, Electrical MotorSystems*		*Vehicle Electrical Distribution Systems*		*Actuators and Fuel Systems Components*		*Central Staff*	
Regensburg	(D)	Rodach	(D)	Würzburg	(D)	Brake	(D)	Newport		Regensburg	(D)
Toulouse	(F)	Chatham	(CDN)	London	(CDN)	Elsendorf	(D)	News	(USA)	Auburn	
Boussens	(F)	Windsor	(CDN)	Burlington	(CDN)	Zwickau	(D)	Pisa	(I)	Hills	(USA)
Foix	(F)	Tilbury	(CDN)			Berlin	(D)				
Nürnberg	(D)	Kartal	(TR)			Seixal	(P)				
Lohmar	(D)	Corby	(GB)			Cerkezköy	(TR)				
Alzenau	(D)										
Wien	(A)										
Kyungki-Do	(ROK)										

Regional Sales—Germany, France, United Kingdom, Spain, Sweden, Italy, United States, Brazil, Japan, South Korea, Czechoslovakia, Mexico.

solenoid valves for adaptive suspension. These components were expected to work within very small tolerances—withstanding tremendous heat, cold, and vibration—during the lifetime of an automobile, and thus required high-precision engineering and manufacturing. The fuel components division had sales of DM 120 million and employed 760 persons in Newport News, Virginia. At its Virginia plant, Siemens produced 30,000 fuel injectors daily and had achieved a 60 percent share of all factory orders placed during the last twenty-four months.

Siemens AT's Manufacturing and Technology Strategy

Siemens operated factories throughout the world, with the major concentration in Europe and North America. Plants were located in Germany, France, Italy, Spain, Portugal, Austria, the United States, Canada, Turkey, the Czech Republic and Korea. Typically, each factory produced a specific range of components, which were then sold to different product divisions and delivered to customers worldwide. (Refer to Exhibit 12.)

Since new sales growth depended heavily on obtaining contracts from new automobile models, a substantial amount of the budget was committed to R&D. For 1991, R&D costs amounted to DM 250 million and equalled 10–20 percent of sales, depending on the product line. Most of the R&D was spent on product ranges not yet in production and represented the company's commitment to further growth. R&D was managed by the five product divisions, which maintained major technical centers in different parts of the world. R&D for "the car of the future" was being performed by some 100 engineers in centers in Toulouse (France), Regensburg (Germany), and in the United States. In January 1991, the company opened a new sales and technical center near Detroit (Auburn Hills), Michigan, for a total cost of DM 40 million. An application development center was under construction in Korea with a JV partner.

In Regensburg, Germany, engineers were working in close cooperation with many customers around the world. Future projects included adaptive suspensions, electronic steering, engine control systems, airbag control modules, and ABS electronics.

Exhibit 12 ● Siemens Automotive Systems Division: A Global Presence

HEADQUARTERS				
	• Auburn Hills	• Regensburg		

R&D, MANUFACTURING, SALES				
• Alzenau	• Chatham	• Lohmar	• Rodach	• Windsor
• Berlin	• Corby	• London (CND)	• Salto	• Würzburg
• Boussens	• Elsendorf	• Newport News	• Seixal	• Zwickau
• Brake	• Foix	• Nürnberg	• Tilbury	
• Burlington	• Kartal	• Pisa	• Toulouse	
• Cerkezköy	• Kyungki-Do	• Regensburg	• Wien	

REGIONAL SALES CENTRES				
• Auburn Hills	• Köln	• München	• Salto	• Turin
• Barcelona	• Kyungki-Do	• Nanterre	• Sölvesborg	• Wolfsburg
• Bayreuth	• London (GB)	• Prag	• Stuttgart	
• Ingolstadt	• Mexico	• Rüsselsheim	• Tokyo	

Siemens AT's Marketing Strategy

Siemens had three goals when it created the Automotive Systems Division. First, the division was to operate internationally. Second, the company was to be located close to its customers. Third, it was to offer a full range of electronic products. To date, Siemens maintained operations in Europe, North America, and the Far East, with production, marketing, and development centers in each of those regions.

Kunerth described the company's strategy: "Siemens is focused on the customer and not on the region. We plan to conduct at least three-quarters of our business with the top ten automobile manufacturers because they account for 70 percent of all vehicles made. If we supply Ford Motor, we wouldn't just focus on Ford's business in the United States, Europe, or Asia; we would strive for a large percentage of its worldwide business." To date, some twenty-five of the world's twenty-eight major auto manufacturers were Siemens customers, including all "Top 10" companies. Siemens maintained sales centers close to major customer plants—such as Stuttgart, Wolfsburg, Gothenberg, Barcelona, and Detroit.

The automotive business required that merchant suppliers tailor their products to the particular demands of each automotive manufacturer. As a result, there were no real "global" products in the strictest sense. Instead, products tended to be geared to certain car models, although there were substantial similarities for given systems across OEM requirements. But, even for Ford, requirements differed between Ford North America and Ford Europe.

Siemens AT's Sales Strategy

Marketing was essentially in the hands of the five product divisions, each with worldwide responsibility. Individual sales teams handled Siemens' 25 customers worldwide. For each one, Siemens deployed a sales team close to the major decision makers for purchasing and engineering. These key account teams reported directly to Kunerth. For example, an account manager for Ford was responsible for supplying Ford with the most effective components, wherever they were made. If a certain component could be sourced at a lower cost from Korea rather than the United States, the Ford account manager was expected to follow through—provided the customer agreed with the sourcing location. (Refer to Exhibit 6.)

Siemens' strategy in the United States reflected the particular purchasing patterns of U.S. car companies. American automobile manufacturers owned large parts assembly facilities which purchased individual components from outside sources and assembled them into complete systems or modules to be installed in the car at the company's assembly plant. As a result, Siemens sold components to GM's and Ford's automotive components groups.

In Europe, car companies had traditionally bought components from independent outside suppliers. There was a move toward sourcing entire systems or modules. As a result, Siemens was offering full systems or, where necessary, sold components to independent companies which, in turn, supplied European car firms with complete systems. Siemens' business in Asia was concentrated in Korea where it operated with the help of a JV partner. A technical assistance center was under construction in Korea, and the local plant could deliver both electronic and electromechanical components. Siemens cooperated closely with Japanese automobile firms on new developments.

SIEMENS AUTOMOTIVE SYSTEMS IN BRAZIL

Siemens acquired its automotive operations in Brazil with the Bendix merger in 1988. The operation had been founded by Bendix and had operated in Brazil since 1957. Sales amounted to DM 40 million ($22.3 million), but had fluctuated considerably over the past three years (DM 52, 36, and 42 million, respectively). Total employment was about 860. With regard to sales, 75 percent were to automotive OEMs and 25 percent to the after-markets; export sales of both categories amounted to about 5 percent.

For the first two years after the Bendix merger, Siemens' automotive operations in Brazil remained under the original Bendix management and reported to the Siemens-Bendix management in Detroit. However, operating losses brought in a new management team recruited from other Siemens operations in Brazil. It was when this change took place that Contador assumed the role of general manager in January 1991.

Product Lines in Brazil

Siemens marketed some 600 product items grouped into seven product families:

Fuses	U.S.$1.3 million
Relays/connectors	4.9 million
Filters/carbon canisters	3.5 million
Relay panels	2.1 million
Switches and sensors	4.3 million
Cigarette lighters	2.1 million
Fuel level sensors/indicators	4.0 million

Although the product categories partly overlapped with the Siemens AT items elsewhere, the general technology level was considerably below what the company offered in other countries. For cigarette lighters and gasoline tank sensors, the technology was about the same worldwide. In connectors, however, Brazil was at the bottom level compared to other countries. Similarly, in Brazil, Siemens was not yet providing any very small-scale types of fuses; only normal sizes were available. In fact, the company did not consider Siemens' AT products for Brazil saleable outside that country, as they were made for local demand only. In several instances, cars in Brazil were an older generation of models that had been discontinued in Europe.

Siemens competed in product categories that were relatively small. Relays, fuel sensors, and sensors were segments with a total market of about $30 million each. The other four categories ranged from a low of $2 million to a high of $8 million for canisters.

The OEM Segment

Siemens' business with the major automobile and truck manufacturers (OEMs) in Brazil accounted for 75 percent of its operations. Included in its customer lists were: Autolatina (a Ford and VW joint venture for

Latin America, with $9.5 million); General Motors ($4.7 million); Fiat ($0.5 million); Mercedes-Benz ($1 million); Scania ($0.3 million). The company had been qualified as a supplier for specific products and was typically invited to offer a tender for any new projects related to its present line. In cigarette lighters, the company was the only domestic supplier and enjoyed a market share of 90 percent. In connectors (relays) it was third behind Kostal of Germany and HL. In indicators, Siemens had one-third of the market and was competing with Indebras, a local supplier, and VDO of Germany.

Due to its size in Brazil, Autolatina accounted for some 50% of Siemens' AT sales. Autolatina, the common group of both Ford and VW in Brazil, purchased together. Filters for gasoline tanks were sold only to Autolatina. However, for each of these two partner firms, the model range was different and had to be adapted and/or customized accordingly.

The After-market Segment

The after-market, accounting for about 25 percent of sales (or $5.4 million), was served through 25 large wholesale distributors who sold through smaller dealers. These distributors had exclusive contracts and territories by product lines, and did not carry competitive products. Siemens' position was hampered by insufficient quality and nondependable delivery times. Problems had occurred in sensor products and also with relays. Although Siemens was able to achieve a price premium of 40–50 percent over OEM prices and higher margins than with its OEM business, Siemens' market position in the after-market had been characterized by losing market share and increasing operating losses. Siemens' after-market business consisted of: relays, 25 percent; switches, 18 percent; and fuel sensors, 45 percent.

The size of the after-market was determined by Brazil's total car fleet of about 14 million cars and trucks. The average life of a car was 13.5 years, and the typical distance driven was some 270,000 km over this time. This resulted in an after-market of two to four times the OEM market for segments such as relays, fuel sensors, and fuel pumps. Siemens achieved price premiums of 40–50 percent over OEM prices, a factor which encouraged even some OEMs to enter the after-market through their own outlets and sell

parts for two to three times the original cost. Another reason for the higher prices in the after-market was the lack of any direct price competition.

Manufacturing Operations

The Siemens Automotive plant in Brazil (150,000 sq. ft.) accounted for the bulk of its employment. The factory, located west of Sao Paulo in Salto, contained many older machines. The tools in general were poorly maintained. The plant included a stamping facility and injection molding operations.

Marketing Operations

Marketing was performed by about ten professionals out of an office in San Bernardo, the same city where Autolatina and GM were located. The local sales office also had some development professionals who were separate from the small R&D staff in the main plant.

Financial Situation

"When I took over at the end of January this year, I found an incredible financial situation. Monthly interest costs for accumulated deficits for the past years had reached the size of our monthly sales levels," explained Contador. The company had to continue to borrow just to keep itself afloat. This was primarily caused by the very steep inflation—about 30 percent per month—and the high real interest rates charged by financial institutions. A complicated transaction to recapitalize the company led to a first stabilization.

Under the economic circumstances that prevailed in Brazil, it was very difficult for Contador to have complete information on his costs. With inflation rates of more than 20 percent per month, figures derived from historical cost control records were meaningless by the time they reached his desk. Following the stabilization of his business, the cost categories were:

	Percent of sales
Purchased materials and components	29%
Wages and salaries	38%
Capital and financing costs	13%
Other costs (overhead, etc.)	18%

Actions Taken During the First Half of 1991

Given this cash crisis, Contador made a number of key decisions. The product range was reduced by about 40 percent. A rigid cost control program was introduced that achieved savings in many company functions. The organization was restructured and streamlined—from seven to five layers, which resulted in better communications throughout the company. By September 1991, employment levels had been reduced by 20 percent—to about 700 people.

Contador also restructured the entire manufacturing area. To increase flexibility, communications, and to obtain better employee morale, manufacturing was organized around three major cells. These cells were again subdivided into sub- and mini-cells. Each cell was made responsible for its own production program and priorities, and took care of its own ordering system. The required space was duly allocated, and the reorganization was completed by September 1991. The only functions retained centrally for all cells were purchasing, accounting and control, and inventory. This was a change from the previous system where, although inventory was maintained throughout the production lines, the lines were often down for lack of component parts. With the new system, all buffer stocks at the plant level were eliminated.

Quality had been another issue that had been targeted. With the assistance of a quality expert from the head office in Regensburg, Germany, Contador introduced a total quality program—using JIT—which was aimed at suppliers and customers. Every production cell included one quality expert who was integrated into the team. Sampling was used to maintain quality control centrally.

In terms of costs, Contador felt that he was better off than most of his local competitors. Local labor costs were about $200 per month, and clerical costs averaged $400 per month.

THE BRAZILIAN MARKET

The Brazilian Automobile Industry

The Brazilian automobile industry has undergone substantial changes during the previous decade (refer to Exhibit 13). In 1980, at its peak, the industry had produced 1.16 million vehicles and ranked eighth in the world. Output in 1990 amounted to 914,000 vehicles, making Brazil the eleventh highest producer. In between, output fell 33 percent in 1981, then—as a result of the first Cruzado Plan—it slowly recovered, to reach slightly above the million unit level by 1986. The 1990 slump came as a result of the New Brazil Plan instituted after the Collor regime took over.

These abrupt changes in economic policy and economic conditions greatly affected the financial performance of the larger players. GM incurred a loss on sales of $2.5 billion in 1990. Fiat, the third-largest group in Brazil, had a loss of $200 million in 1990, but managed to break even in 1991.

The Brazilian automotive industry accounted for about 10 percent of Brazil's GNP. It directly employed about 125,000 people. Industry sources estimated that some 4.1 million jobs in Brazil were generated, directly or indirectly, by the industry.

The Brazilian industry produced both for the local market and for export. (Refer to Exhibit 14 for domestic sales levels.) Substantial variations due to

Exhibit 13 ● The Brazilian Vehicles Industry: Total Unit Output by Category, 1986–1990

Year	Passenger Cars	Light Commercial Vehicles	Buses	Trucks	Total
1986	815,152	145,418	11,218	84,544	1,056,332
1987	683,380	148,847	13,639	74,205	920,071
1988	782,411	196,108	18,427	71,810	1,068,756
1989	730,992	205,008	14,553	62,699	1,013,252
1990	663,084	184,754	15,026	51,807	914,671

Exhibit 14 ● Brazilian Domestic Unit Sales for Motor Vehicles, 1986–1990

Year	Passenger Cars	Light Commercial Vehicles	Buses	Trucks	Total
1986	672,384	114,002	84,488	71,854	866,728
1987	410,260	103,372	10,068	56,385	580,085
1988	556,582	123,092	12,968	54,912	747,716
1989	566,582	137,380	9,485	48,178	761,625
1990	532,927	128,336	10,091	41,344	712,698

changes in the country's economic policies were largely responsible for the fluctuating output. The record sales level of 1979 (1,014,925) had never again been reached. Because of a severe local recession in 1981, domestic sales had declined by 40 percent. Due to severe inflation, high interest rates and the difficulty of obtaining financing, consumers banded together in purchasing cooperatives. Having accounted for as much as 40 percent of passenger car sales, the funds of the consortios were blocked as part of the New Brazil Plan, to be made available only in eighteen installments. This could inject a substantial amount of new financing into the market.

Government policies tended to affect domestic sales. To date, imports were virtually impossible, as domestic industry had been protected since the 1950s by very high tariffs. Import tariffs averaged 60 percent for assembled vehicles. Completely Knowed Down (CKD) imports had only been recently permitted, with duties levied at 55 percent. Brazil, despite its domestic output, had some of the world's highest car prices. By comparison, a Ford Escort with a 1.6-liter engine retailed for $16,000 in Brazil. The corresponding price was $7,400 in the United States, $14,500 in France, and $16,500 in Argentina. Before taxes were added, that same Escort would cost only $9,400 in Brazil.

The government announced that import duties on assembled vehicles were to be lowered in steps—to 35 percent in 1994 and 30 percent for CKDs. As part of a broad trade liberalization policy instituted by the Collor government, imported cars were entering Brazil for the first time in seventeen years. Brazilian car companies finally had the freedom to import machinery, raw materials, and components from abroad. The average import tax on vehicles sold was also to be reduced from 60 percent in 1991 to 20 percent in 1995.

Domestically, the Brazilian government levied high sales taxes on vehicles, amounting to 43 percent for cars. Only very small cars with engines of less than 1000 cc were favored with lower taxes. Until July 1990, car prices had been controlled by the government, which ensured that price increases tended to equal the increase of the consumer price index (CPI). Only a few months later, prices were again placed under government control and price increases had fallen behind the CPI. This also affected the prices paid to component makers, which brought about partial shortages. As a result, more than 10,000 "crippled" cars with partially missing components were assembled and awaiting final components before they could be sold. This hurt the industry, as more cars could have been sold if supplies had been available.

Competition in the Brazilian market differed by vehicle category. In passenger cars, the market was dominated by Autolatina, a joint venture between Volkswagen and Ford, accounting for about 50 percent of sales. GM accounted for 20 percent of volume, but had recently lost its number two position to Fiat which had 25 percent of sales—helped by its small 1000 cc Fiat Uno model.

In the light commercial vehicle segment, Autolatina (Ford and VW) had a commanding lead (44 percent), followed by Fiat (30 percent) and GM (20 percent). Toyota imported 5,000 vehicles annually in CKD form. In the heavy truck segment, Mercedes-Benz, Saab Scania, and Volvo dominated the 30-ton-plus segment. In the small truck market, Autolatina was the leader. Mercedes-Benz, Autolatina, and GM were the key players in the middle market range.

The car manufacturers had announced substantial investment programs: more than $4 billion over the next four to five years, amounting to double that of the previous five years. Given the fleet range of currently 13 million vehicles operating in Brazil, annual sales of some 1.3 million would be normal, assuming a ten-year replacement cycle. This level would represent a doubling of present domestic sales. With the right economic conditions, it was felt that this estimate for domestic sales was possible. The addition of exports to this figure would lead to a substantial increase from the present levels.

THE BRAZILIAN MARKET FOR AUTOMOTIVE COMPONENTS

In 1991, the automotive components industry in Brazil reported a drop in sales—to $9 billion from $12.2 billion in 1990 and $15.5 in 1989, the best year the industry had ever experienced. About 55 percent of these sales were made to Brazilian OEMs, 30 percent to the replacement and after-sales market, and about 15 percent for export. Employment dropped from 282,200 to 260,000 during the same period. The average unused capacity reached about 25 percent. There were 960 different supplier companies active in Brazil at the time.

The after-market was huge—amounting to 40 percent of the OEM market. This situation was largely caused by the long life span of vehicles in Brazil. Of importance to parts manufacturers was the absence of price controls for parts and the resulting higher profitability to manufacturers.

The market for automotive parts was driven by the three largest car companies, GM, Autolatina (Ford and VW), and Fiat. These three makers offered some twenty models, the majority of which had been introduced during the late 1970s and early 1980s from German and U.S. plants. The average annual volume per model was about 35,000 units. Use of automotive electronics was only about $100 per car in Brazil. Some experts thought that this level might reach as much as $500 per car within three years or so.

Total exports, both in the form of direct and indirect parts (i.e., installed in 175,000 exported cars that were assembled in Brazil), brought in $2.1 billion and were thus a significant factor. Indeed, Brazilian automotive components represented almost 12 percent of all manufactured products exported. This growth was a substantial and steady climb from 1984 when the exports (both direct and indirect) had amounted to $1.2 billion.

Typically, the U.S. market had absorbed 50–60 percent of Brazil's components exports, followed by the United Kingdom, Germany, Mexico, and Italy. Mexico was rapidly becoming the second most important market, with almost 10 percent in 1990. Among components and parts, engines accounted for 23 percent and car radios for 15 percent of sales in 1990.

Direct exporting of components was dominated by the United States and Germany—with about 25 percent each—then Japan—with about 14 percent—followed by the United Kingdom, France, and Italy. The leading product was gear boxes (20 percent); there was also a range of other components, but none of them accounted for more than 50 percent of export sales.

Due to the differences in product lines and technology, Siemens' competitors were not the same in Brazil as elsewhere. Most of them were local firms, such as Indebras, Outros, Instron, and Polimatic. Only VDO (fuel sensors) was a major international competitor.

The Economic Climate in Brazil

Brazil, with 150 million inhabitants and a GNP per capita of $2,200, was one of the ten largest economies in the world. The country had been plagued by very high inflation for years (450 percent in 1991) and was still considered a developing country. Due to difficult economic, political, and social circumstances, Brazil had not yet been able to live up to its long-term economic potential.

During much of the 1974–1982 period, inflation tended to stay below the 100 percent per annum level. The trade balance usually was slightly negative, particularly as the country became involved in heavy borrowing abroad for infrastructure projects. In 1983, the government started to change its economic policies and pursue a strategy of export growth, because Brazil—like many other Latin American countries—could not service its foreign debt of $120 billion. At the height of the crisis in the mid-1980s, debt service consumed some 90 percent of its total exports. Inflation, however, continued to grow, reaching 235 percent by 1986. Devaluation of the local currency at a pace faster than inflation created a substantial balance of trade surplus, i.e., $12 billion in 1985. In 1986, however, with the arrival of a new civilian government for the first time in over twenty years, the government changed the local currency from cruzeiros to the cruzaro, exchanging 1,000 old cruzeiros for each new cruzaro. By enhancing the currency, inflation sank to only 65 percent in 1986. However, inflation soon picked up again, reaching extremely high levels even for Brazil—1,500 percent in 1990.

A new government, headed by President Collor, came into power in 1990. Termed the New Brazil Plan, the new government pursued an aggressive policy of deregulation and of opening the Brazilian markets to the dictates of the world trade. Introduced just one day after his inauguration on March 15, 1990, the New Brazil Plan froze all bank and savings accounts for eighteen months, exchanged the cruzaro for cruzeiros, and froze wages and prices. Some $110 billion was removed from circulation, a very large amount considering the size of the economy.

The New Brazil Plan (also called the Collor Plan) threw Brazil into a deep recession. Although inflation came down, the plan failed to halt it completely. Prices, initially frozen, were deregulated in July 1990, which meant that Brazilian car companies could—for the first time since 1968—set their own prices. Arguing that price increases in the past had not compensated them for all inflationary increases, car companies raised prices by some 400 percent by the end of 1990. This situation produced a strong reaction from the Collor government, which then reintroduced price controls for cars in early 1991.

Controlled prices caused problems for parts suppliers and resulted in parts shortages in 1991.

The newly adopted policy of trade liberalization, applied to many industry sectors, had tremendous implications for the car industry. Vehicle imports were allowed, tariffs were to be reduced, external sourcing of components would be allowed, machinery for production could be imported without taxes, and some key industrial areas that had formerly been reserved for local nationals were suddenly available to all comers.

These changes immediately attracted newcomers. Lada, the Russian car company, entered the market through importing and reached a respectable volume of some 30,000 units over eighteen months. Land Rover was interested in setting up a plant for CKD assemblies in Brazil—where a market for four-wheel-drive vehicles had been completely absent. Peugeot, Citroen, and BMW, not represented before, were considering import dealerships. Foreign cars were aided by the high prices caused by inefficiencies in the Brazilian car market.

The Collor Plan did not reach its main goal—to eliminate inflation from the economy. Down to 25–30 percent monthly, with real interest rates at 2 percent per day, the industry was still in a recession.

Summary

In May 1992, Contador was expected to make a proposal to the management of Siemens Automotive Systems in Germany on the future possibilities for doing business in Brazil. It was up to Contador and his small team to come up with a realistic presentation. He knew that all the details would not have to be worked out at this point. Nevertheless, management would want to know what its options were and what directions the company could take.

Case 2

Note on the World Over-the-Counter (OTC) Drug Industry

In early December of 1994, Roland M. Jeannet, recently appointed to head Ciba's global Self Medication (OTC) business, convened a three-day strategy meeting near Geneva Airport.

By next spring we need to develop a complete road map of how we want to compete in this industry. Before we do this, however, we need to answer some fundamental questions about our industry. The questions foremost on my mind include how any company, to be successful, will have to compete in this industry, now and in the future. Will past industry practices be applicable as we move into the 21st century? Is this a global industry, run on a global scale, that will lend itself to global marketing approaches, or is this a regional or even local industry that will have to be directed accordingly? Unless we can come to some understanding of the rules of this industry, we cannot make real progress towards a strategy that will secure an important place for Ciba in Self-Medication.[1]

OTC INDUSTRY OVERVIEW

Over-the-counter (OTC) pharmaceutical products were consumer health care products approved but nonprescription bound. In 1995, the global market was estimated at US$51 billion. The pharmaceutical industry

and, specifically, the OTC sector, was characterized by fragmentation. The entire industry was changing rapidly. There were changes in ownership of the players, growing consumer awareness, and new government regulations. Realizing that marketing OTC products to consumers required a different skill set than the one needed for ethical pharmaceuticals aimed at health care professionals, many international pharmaceutical companies were developing separate self-medication divisions or forming relationships with experienced OTC companies to market OTC products and switches based upon prescription products.

In broad terms, user segments were categorized as Self-Medicators, Doctor Seekers, Home Remedy Users, Non-treaters, and Don't Knows (refer to Exhibit 1). However, users often changed from one category to another depending on the type and severity of the ailment.

Not only was it difficult to lump consumers into consistent market segments, but their demographics and attitudes were changing (refer to Exhibit 2). Top OTC markets, such as Europe, Japan, and the United States, had to adapt to aging populations. Consumers and government alike tended to turn to self-medication to fight rising health care costs. Consumers in most markets were also moving toward more alternative, natural remedies.

OTC INDUSTRY SIZE AND STRUCTURE

It was estimated that the world market for OTCs would reach U.S.$53 billion in 1996 and sustain a compound annual growth rate (CAGR) of over 7 percent through the year 2004. The United States was estimated to have the majority of the 1996 sales in the world OTC market at 31 percent, with Europe following closely behind at 29 percent.[2] Japan's share of the revenues was estimated at 17 percent (refer to Exhibit 3).

This case was written by Kristi Menz and Shauna Pettit, MBA candidates at the F. W. Olin Graduate School of Business at Babson College, under the direction of Professor Jean-Pierre Jeannet. Copyright © 1996 by IMD—International Institute for Management Development, Lausanne, Switzerland. Not to be used or reproduced without written permission directly from IMD.

1. Ciba prefers to use the term *self-medication* instead of *over-the-counter* (OTC).

2. Excluding sales of most eastern European countries.

Exhibit 1 ● Analysis of Consumer Segments by Source of Treatment: % of Adult Populations Suffering Minor Ailments

	Self-medicators	Doctor Seekers	Home Remedy Users	Non-treaters	DK
FRANCE	26%	48%	4%	19%	3%
GERMANY	25	55	4	14	2
SPAIN	26	54	5	11	4
UNITED KINGDOM	30	22	3	45	0

Self-medicators—Those who usually or always buy OTCs instead of visiting a doctor.
Doctor seekers—Those who usually or always go to the doctor for advice and a prescription.
Home remedy users—Those who often use something they have at home rather than seeking a prescription or buying an OTC. This category has some overlap with doctor seekers and self-medicators.
Non-treaters—Those who usually or always do not treat an ailment.
DK—Those who don't know.

Historically, the United States had experienced the highest growth of any country or region. By the year 2004, growth rates of Asian countries were expected to surpass all other regions (refer to Exhibit 4).

The top ten OTC companies accounted for almost 35 percent of worldwide industry sales in 1995 (Exhibit 5). Mergers and acquisitions were common in the industry. With that trend expected to continue, market analysts predicted the top ten companies would command more than 50 percent of global OTC revenues by the year 2005 (see Exhibits 6 and 7).

RELATIONSHIP TO PHARMACEUTICAL INDUSTRY

An important relationship existed between OTCs and the pharmaceutical industry as a whole, since OTCs accounted for 17 percent of total 1995 pharmaceutical industry sales. Of sixty-six new OTC brands introduced over a seventeen-year period by fourteen leading United States marketers, 30 percent were switches.[3] In the United States, the ten top-selling switched products since 1975 accounted for sales of U.S.$1047 million in 1994 compared to only U.S.$316 million for the ten top-selling new OTC brands introduced during the same period. Increasingly, pharmaceutical companies

3. Switches were pharmaceutical products approved for OTC status.

found OTC switches an important means of justifying the heavy R&D costs associated with developing new prescription drugs. As an executive at Ciba Self Medication stated, "We think that with investment in consumer advertising and some changes to a drug (i.e., taste, delivery system, etc.) we can extend the life cycle of a prescription drug significantly" (Exhibit 8).

There were two ways to develop new OTC products. The first, and most common, was to reformulate a prescription-bound product for use as an OTC. This usually meant lowering the dosage and/or strength and perhaps changing the drug delivery system. In the industry, this was referred to as a switch. The other way was to scan the world market for ingredients that had already been tested and approved. Often by introducing a new combination of ingredients, companies had been able to make innovations in the OTC market without developing new substances from scratch. For example, Procter & Gamble was awaiting final patent approval of a new cold remedy which combined ibuprofen and an antihistamine, both commonly available ingredients used in other products, but never before used together.

If a company did not have its own products moving through its research and development pipeline, there were several other ways of adding a new product: licensing, acquisitions, joint ventures, and comarketing.

Exhibit 2 ● Changing Consumer Demographics

% of Population by Age 1994						
Age	France	Germany	Italy	United Kingdom	United States	Japan
0–14	9.9%	17.1%	15.7%	19.6%	21.9%	17.1%
15–64	65.4	68.2	69.0	64.8	65.5	69.5
65–79	10.8	10.8	12.0	11.8	9.7	10.9
80+	3.9	3.8	3.4	3.6	2.9	2.5

Estimated % of Population by Age 1998						
Age	France	Germany	Italy	United Kingdom	United States	Japan
0–14	19.5%	17.1%	15.1%	20.0%	21.8%	16.5%
15–64	65.1	67.8	67.3	64.6	65.7	68.2
65–79	11.6	11.7	13.1	11.6	9.4	12.4
80+	3.8	3.4	3.4	3.8	3.0	2.9

Growth in Self-medicators			
	% Adult Pop. 1993	% Adult Pop. 2000	% Growth
USA	38%	45%	18%
FRANCE	26	33	30
GERMANY	25	45	80
SPAIN	26	32	23
UK	30	45	50

Annual OTC Consumption per Capita (US$ ex-manu. sales)		
	1990	1995
US	27	55
GERMANY	20	85
FRANCE	16	80
UK	13	23
ITALY	8	23
JAPAN	36	67

Source: Scrip Reports & OTC Review 1996.

Exhibit 3 ● World Self-medication Market by Volume, 1996 (estimated)

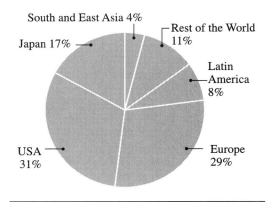

World OTC Market

- South and East Asia 4%
- Japan 17%
- Rest of the World 11%
- Latin America 8%
- Europe 29%
- USA 31%

Source: James Dudley International Ltd. trade estimates 1996; from *Self-Medication in Europe,* vol. 1, *The European Market,* p. 1-1.

Exhibit 4 ● Historic and Forecast Growth Rates in the World OTC Market

| | *Average Growth* | |
	1989–1993	*1993–2004*
Europe	4.3%	5.8%
USA	6.0	5.9
Japan	3.4	5.2
Others[a]	4.7	6.7

a. Historic estimate based on average IMS Asia growth rate.
Source: OTC Insight (IMS), Kline, 1994; from Zyma.

American Home Products and Warner-Lambert each chose different strategies for developing their product portfolio. American Home Products often used licensing and acquisition. To develop the brand Advil, AHP licensed the U.S. distribution rights for the active ingredient, ibuprofen, from Boots, a British company. To enter the vitamin, mineral, and supplement (VMS) market, on the other hand, AHP acquired American Cyanamid.

Warner-Lambert was well known for entering into joint venture agreements. It had two major joint venture agreements with pharmaceutical companies Glaxo and Wellcome. Since the merger of Glaxo and Wellcome in 1995, Warner-Lambert had pledged to repurchase its share of the OTC Warner Wellcome Consumer Healthcare joint venture.

Another frequently used strategy was comarketing agreements with other companies. In this case, a company would sell its brand to another OTC company to be marketed under a different brand name in the same geographic market. This strategy was used when it was not in the strategic interest of a company to employ a larger sales force in a secondary market.

OTC INDUSTRY PARTICIPANTS

The lines between participants in the OTC industry were fuzzy at best. The level of vertical integration varied greatly among the players. In general, however, they could be classified as chemical intermediate suppliers, OTC manufacturers distributors, and retailers (refer to Exhibit 9). In addition, consumers, doctors, governments, and managed care organizations had an important impact on the industry.

Chemical Intermediate Suppliers

Fine chemical companies produced the active ingredients which were the building blocks of OTCs. They started with base chemicals of natural origins or made from petrochemicals. These base chemicals were then combined to form the intermediates or active ingredients. OTC companies could either source the active ingredients from the fine chemicals industry or produce them internally.

OTC Manufacturers

OTC manufacturers provided the critical link from active ingredient to the pharmacy shelf. Most of the major international competitors were divisions of larger companies.

OTC manufacturers were generally responsible for developing, registering, manufacturing, packaging, and marketing OTC products. This varied greatly according to the level of integration of the company and the specifics of the product involved. Manufacturers began their part of the process by either switching a product from prescription status or by reformulating commonly available active ingredients. They performed efficacy and safety tests in an effort to get the

Exhibit 5 ● OTC Company Rank, 1995

	World			Europe		
Rank	Company	Home Country	Share of Market	Company	Home Country	Share of Market
1	J&J	US	6.9%	Rhone	France	4.1%
2	AHP	US	4.8	Bayer	Germany	3.2
3	Bayer	Germany	3.9	SmithKline	UK	3.0
4	P&G	US	3.8	Roche	Switz.	2.7
5	SmithKline	UK	3.2	AHP	US	2.5
6	W-L	US	3.0	Boehringer	Germany	2.4
7	Rhone	France	2.6	Ciba	Switz.	2.2
8	BMS	US	2.5	Pierre Fabre	France	2.0
9	Ciba	Switz.	2.3	Servier	France	2.0
10	Roche	Switz.	1.6	Sanofi	France	1.9
Top 10 Share of Market			34.6%			26.0%

	United States			Japan		
Rank	Company	Home Country	Share of Market	Company	Home Country	Share of Market
1	J&J	US	14.3%	Taisho	Japan	19.2%
2	AHP	US	9.1	Takeda	Japan	8.1
3	P&G	US	7.2	Sato	Japan	7.5
4	W-L	US	5.8	SS Pharma	Japan	7.0
5	Bayer	Germany	5.3	Kowa	Japan	5.1
6	SmithKline	UK	3.9	Chugai	Japan	4.1
7	BMS	US	3.7	Sankyo	Japan	3.4
8	Abbott	US	3.7	Eisai	Japan	3.1
9	Schering	US	2.8	Zevia	Japan	2.9
10	Ciba	Switz.	2.7	Zenyaku	Japan	2.8
Top 10 Share of Market			58.5%			63.2%

Source: OTC Review 1996.

product registered for sale as an OTC. Once the product received regulatory approval, full-scale manufacturing started. Manufacturers packaged the products themselves and then either distributed them to a wholesaler or directly to a retailer. Their final responsibility was to market the product to health care professionals, retailers, and consumers.

Distributors

Distributors were responsible for the transportation of OTC products from the manufacturer to the retailer, or in some cases, directly to the consumer. Manufacturers had the choice of either distributing the products themselves, distributing their products

Exhibit 6 ● Share of World OTC Market (%) Held by Top Ten Players

	World	*USA*	*Europe*	*Japan*
1991 SOM[a] by top 10 Players	30%	47.7%	27.3%	55.1%[b]
1995 SOM by top 10 Players	34.6	58.4	25.7[c]	63.2
2005 SOM by top 10 Players	50+		54.0	

a. SOM=Share of market
b. 1990 for Japan.
c. If self-medication sales only are included, the percentage goes up to 28.7.
Source: Scrip Reports: *Rx to OTC Report* (p. 6), *OTC Review 1995, OTC Bulletin,* January 25, 1996.

Exhibit 7 ● Merger and Acquisition in the OTC Industry, 1993–1995

Business	*Buyer*	*Seller*	*Price (millions)*	*Sales (millions)*	*Pretax profit (millions)*	*Price/profit ratio*	*Price/sales ratio*
JV to market OTC products	Warner-Lambert	Wellcome	n/a	—	—	—	—
License agreement for WW to market Glaxo's switches	Glaxo	Warner Wellcome	n/a	—	—	—	—
Sterling Health	SmithKline Beecham	Eastman Kodak	U.S.$2,900	U.S.$1,006	—	—	2.9
Sterling Health North American business	Bayer AG	SmithKline Beecham	U.S.$1,000	U.S.$346	—	—	2.9
American Cyanamid	American Home Products	Takeover	U.S.$9,600	U.S.$4,277	—	—	2.2
North American OTC business	Ciba	Rhône-Poulenc Rorer	U.S.$407[a]	U.S.$154	—	—	2.6
43.57% stake in Lipha of France (took holding over 96%)	E Merk	Coopération Pharmaceutique Française	Undisclosed	FF 2,820	FF 306	—	—
Wellcome	Glaxo	Takeover	£9,000	£2,280	£738	12.2	3.9
Planta-Subtil of Germany	Boeringer Ingelheim	Takeover	Undisclosed	DM 22	—	—	—
Soekami Lefrancq of France	Roche	Roussel Uclaf	Undisclosed	FF 200	—	—	—
Marion Merrell Dow	Hoechst	Dow/Takeover	U.S.$7,150	U.S.$3,060	U.S.$438[b]	16.3	2.3

Exhibit 7 ● Merger and Acquisition in the OTC Industry, 1993–1995 (*Continued*)

Business	Buyer	Seller	Price (millions)	Sales (millions)	Pretax profit (millions)	Price/profit ratio	Price/sales ratio
Gastrocote brand[c]	Seton Healthcare	Boeringer Mannheim	£10.0	£2.6	£1.8 gross	—	3.8
Pharmacia & Upjohn	Merger	Merger	—	U.S.$6,800	—	—	—
Milupa of Germany	Nutricia	Atlanta Group	DM 820	DM1,000	DM 25	36.9	0.9
Fisons	Rhône-Poulenc Rorer	Takeover	£1,830	£500[d]	£100[d]	—	3.7[d]
Ferrosan of Denmark (70% stake)	Management buyout	Novo Nordisk	DKK 400	DKK 600 app.	—	—	—
Woodward's brand	Seton Healthcare	London International	£4.8	£2.2	£1.0 gross	—	2.2
Biogal of Hungary (78% stake)	Teva of Israel	—	U.S.$26	U.S. $102	U.S.$5.4 net	—	0.3
Setlers Brand	Stafford-Miller	SmithKline Beecham	Undisclosed	—	—	—	—
Pharmavit of Hungary	Bristol-Myers Squibb	Takeover	U.S.$110	U.S. $39.6	U.S.$6.05	18.2	2.8
Diocalm and Ralgex brands	Seton Healthcare	SmithKline Beecham	£7.85	£2.16	£1.4 gross	—	3.3
Abtei Pharma of Germany	SmithKline Beecham	Private owner	DM 203	DM 110	—	—	1.8
Warner Wellcome (acquisition)	Warner-Lambert	Glaxo Wellcome	U.S.$1,050	U.S.$360	—	—	2.9

a. Estimated net value of transaction over seven years, Ciba has U.S.$143 million option to purchase intellectual property rights after seven years.

b. Net income 1994.

c. Worldwide rights excluding Austria, Slovakia, and Portugal in Europe. Most U.K. sales on prescription.

d. Fisons' pharmaceutical operation had sales of £254 million in the six months to June 20, 1995. Operating profit was £47.6 million.

Source: OTC Bulletin, January 25, 1996, p. 18.

through wholesalers, or using an agency distribution system.

Wholesalers bought in volume from the manufacturer and then resold the inventory to retailers. Often, carriers acted as middlemen between manufacturers and wholesalers to physically transport the product from one to another. However, ownership of the inventory went directly from the manufacturer to the wholesaler.

Agency distribution differed from wholesaling only in the ownership of the products. With an agency, the manufacturer retained ownership of the products until they were distributed to retailers. The agency was responsible for distributing the products and re-

Exhibit 8 ● Product Life Cycle Extension Through a Prescription-to-OTC Switch

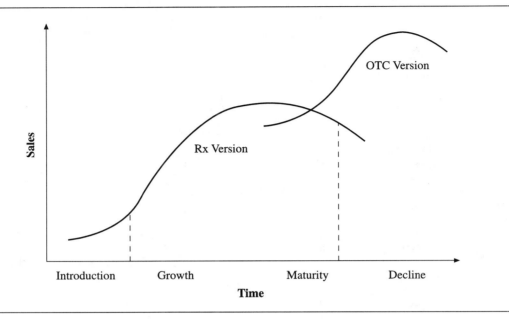

Exhibit 9 ● The Generalized Distribution Channel for OTC Products (Manufacturers, Wholesalers, Retailers, Consumers)

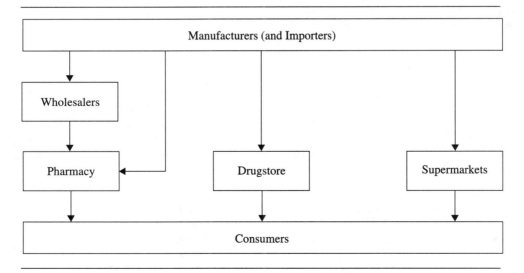

Source: Datamonitor; from *European Pharmaceuticals,* "Switching to OTC Status," p. 26.

Exhibit 10 ● Possible Distribution Channels for OTC Products

Country	Pharmacy	Chain Pharmacy	Drugstore	Chain Drugstores	Grocery
France	X				
Germany	X		X[a]	X[a]	X[a]
Italy	X	n/a			
United Kingdom	X	X	X[a]	X[a]	X[a]
United States	X	X	X	X	X
Japan	X	X	X	X	

n/a = data not available

a. Limited to OTC products that have been available for a long time and are frequently purchased by consumers (e.g., confectionery cough drops and chewable antacids).

ceived a management fee for its services. The manufacturer still had the ultimate control over the price of its products to retailers. Glaxo used this system extensively and with much success. Because of this, other pharmaceutical and OTC manufacturers were considering a switch to agency distributors.

Retailers

The most common retail outlet varied from one geographic region to the next. In part, government regulation was to blame, but consumer lifestyles and retail preferences were also important determinants. Pharmacies were the most common distribution outlet in Europe, Japan, and to a lesser extent in the United States. Other retailers included food stores, drugstores,[4] mass merchandisers, and mail order companies (refer to Exhibit 10).

Europe In 1993, OTC sales through pharmacies accounted for 85 percent of the total market in Europe, which made them the most important OTC distribution channel for all countries except the Netherlands (refer to Exhibit 11). In the future, sales in pharmacies were expected to fall as governments deregulated the

4. Drugstores differed from pharmacies in that the former did not require a pharmacist to be on staff. In addition, pharmacies could dispense prescription-only medicines, whereas drugstores could not.

retail sector. Several EU countries were beginning to discuss legislation which would allow distribution of OTCs in outlets other than pharmacies. In the United Kingdom and Germany, for instance, some categories of OTCs were frequently sold in drugstores and supermarkets.

United States Thirty-eight percent of all OTC sales in the United States came from pharmacies. Combination stores made up an additional 25 percent of sales (refer to Exhibit 12). The growth of mass merchandisers and in-store pharmacies in the United States caused a continuing decline of sales through independent pharmacies. More and more "mom and pop" stores closed down. Distributing OTC products through the mail represented a very small portion of the industry but was a growing trend in the United States, especially to care facilities that required products in bulk. This trend was most evident in the sale of vitamins and nutritional supplements. It was attractive for consumers and governments who wanted to cut health care costs since it was often cheaper than other distribution and retailing methods. In 1990, more than half of the pharmaceutically-oriented mail order companies carried OTCs.

Japan Japan had five categories of pharmaceutical retailers. At each level, there were more and more restrictions on the activities retailers could perform.

Exhibit 11 ● European Consumer Purchases of OTC Medicines in Pharmacy Compared to Nonpharmacy Outlets, 1993

	% Purchases by Value		
Country	*Pharmacy Purchases*	*Nonpharmacy Purchases*	*Commentary*
France	100%	<1%	Restricted to limited vitamin products only
Germany	87	13	Excludes analgesics, antacids, and cough, cold, and flu medicines
Hungary	65	35	Herbal medicines largely sold through herbalists
Netherlands	36	64	Druggists licensed to sell OTC brands in limited pack sizes
United Kingdom	69	31	General sale list for nonpharmacy outlets

Source: James Dudley International Ltd. Trade.

Pharmacies were at the top level and were allowed to both sell and dispense drugs. Drugstores usually fell into the first-class retailer category, which was one step below pharmacies. First-class retailers could not dispense drugs and were only allowed to sell them. Traditionally, most OTCs were sold through pharmacies. However, drugstores were becoming a popular channel for OTC sales in Japan, as the government continued its effort to separate the prescribing and dispensing activities traditionally taking place at the doctor level.

Consumers

Rising health care costs, delisting of reimbursable drugs, and increasing health-conscienceness caused a growing number of consumers to turn to OTCs. Unlike the prescription pharmaceutical industry, consumers had the ultimate choice over brands and products.

This was less the case in Europe, where 36 percent of the overall OTC sales came from doctors "prescribing" non–prescription-bound products (commonly known as semi-ethicals). In many European countries, semi-ethicals were used by the government as a stepping stone to a product becoming a completely nonreimbursable OTC.[5] Consumers often sought

5. In many European countries, governments reimbursed consumers for prescription drugs through government-controlled health insurance.

prescriptions for OTCs, knowing that medicines purchased on prescription were government-reimbursable. This practice was especially prevalent in Germany and France with 41.8 percent and 46.1 percent of their respective OTC sales in 1994 generated through these semi-ethical products. Both British and German law allowed advertising of reimbursable OTCs directly to consumers, which continued to drive sales of semi-ethical products. In France, consumers shied away from self-medicating and preferred to get prescriptions from doctors. Other European markets had similar characteristics.

Doctors

Other than prescribing semi-ethicals in Europe, doctors did not impact the OTC industry in the same manner as for Rx products. OTC manufacturers sometimes found it difficult to persuade doctors to recommend OTCs. This was partly because they lacked sufficient information about OTCs and their efficacy and partly because doing so effectively cut them out of the payment loop. Doctors in the United Kingdom were the exception, and they had a reputation for being in favor of OTC medicines.

Doctor recommendations were not critical, but they did significantly impact a product's sales in some cases. A good example was the marketing of Advil and Nuprin in their launch year (1984). Advil spent

Exhibit 12 ● U.S. OTC Distribution by Outlet, 1993

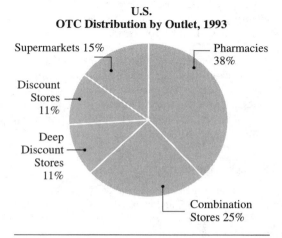

**U.S.
OTC Distribution by Outlet, 1993**

Supermarkets 15%

Pharmacies 38%

Discount Stores 11%

Deep Discount Stores 11%

Combination Stores 25%

Source: Contributors/James Dudley International Ltd/Calc JDI.

U.S.$1 million on advertising to professionals with a dedicated sales team, while Nuprin completely neglected advertising to this segment. After one year, Advil achieved sales of U.S.$79 million, compared to only U.S.$15 million for Nuprin. This and other examples proved to manufacturers that, at the very least, they needed passive support from doctors. If a consumer asked for a recommendation on a particular product, the worst possible situation from the manufacturer's standpoint was for a doctor to dissuade the consumer from buying that product.

Government and Managed Care Organizations

Governments, insurance companies, managed care organizations (e.g., HMOs and PPOs), and pharmacy benefit managers (PBMs) played an important role in the OTC industry. By delisting drugs from reimbursement, or adding OTCs to their formularies, or purchasing OTC products for distribution to consumers, these institutions had a direct impact on the industry. Rising health care costs forced a growing number of consumers and governments to look for help from OTCs. The United States set the trend in

this area, mostly due to its privatized health care system.

Experts estimated that some 18 percent of U.S. managed care organizations offered reimbursement for some OTC products. Furthermore, future sales and marketing strategies were affected, as OTC manufacturers began lobbying HMOs to add OTCs to their lists of reimbursable drugs. Products with the highest chance of being added to HMO or PBM formularies were those that could possibly reduce future costs to the organization through prevention or substitution. SmithKline Beecham (SB), for example, lobbied HMOs to reimburse its OTC smoking cessation aid, Nicorette. SB's main selling point was that the relatively inexpensive Nicorette would reduce future, expensive-to-treat degenerative diseases. Similar advantages were touted for home diagnostic products, which could curtail costs due to doctor visits and unnecessary surgery.

In the United States, the drive to lower costs came from consumers. In other countries, governments shouldered most of the burden for health care; thus, HMOs were not as prevalent. Rather than privatize their health care systems through HMOs, governments preferred to contain costs in other ways (e.g., with price controls for OTCs or pressure on doctors to prescribe fewer reimbursable drugs). Still, the state health care systems operating in many European countries were similar to managed care organizations, since they, too, bought in volume and had considerable leverage with a full range of health care suppliers. As U.S. managed care organizations looked to expand, it was possible for them to become advisors to foreign organizations.

Regulators

Regulators played an integral role in the OTC industry. They governed which products could be switched from Rx to OTC status, determined manufacturing guidelines to be followed, had an impact on where products could be sold, and how the marketing could be done. This was especially true for the European and Japanese markets. Each country had its own set of rules regarding OTC products. However, as the member countries of the European Union worked toward harmonization, adapting to the local countries' regulations was expected to become easier.

OTC COMPANY OPERATIONS

Research & Development

R&D for OTCs differed from prescription-bound products. With OTCs, the active ingredients had already been developed, causing most research to center on new delivery systems, flavors, and product stability. Typically, products only incurred 2–5 percent of their final retail cost at this stage (refer to Exhibit 13). In the case of switched products, OTC firms benefited from the basic clinical and safety work done by the pharma division of its parent company or the licensor. Increasing price pressure in the industry further caused many companies to focus their attention on new formulations of existing compounds as opposed to searching for new ones.

The Registration Process

OTC manufacturers were responsible for conducting clinical trials before being granted regulatory approval to market. In the case of a switch, this was less extensive than for the original Rx approval. Many of the required trials were completed by the pharma company which had initially developed the drug. The main element of this process was to prove effectiveness at the OTC dose and a side effect profile safe enough for consumers to use without doctor supervision. In cases where the product in question utilized a new drug delivery system, the company had to prove to regulators that it did not dramatically alter the effects of the drug compared to its original prescription form.

Production Processes

Production centered around active ingredients. The trend was for OTC and pharma firms to divest themselves of this task, however, preferring instead to spend their investment dollars on R&D and marketing. Some of the larger companies had their own chemical divisions, which perhaps also did synthesis

Exhibit 13 ● Cost Structure of the OTC Industry, by Percentage of Total Cost

The cost structure of the industry varied depending on the country, the size of the players, and the level of integration. The general trends can be observed with the following breakdown:

MANUFACTURERS			*60–70%*
Cost of Goods Sold		17–23%	
Raw Materials	*2–4%*		
Packaging	*5–9*		
Direct Labour	*2–4*		
Equipment	*1–2*		
Quality Control	*1–2*		
Manufacturing Overhead	*5–8*		
Transportation		2–5	
Research & Development		2–5	
General & Administrative		2–5	
Marketing & Sales		17–23	
Profit		7–12	
WHOLESALERS			*7–12*
RETAILERS			*15–25*
CONSUMERS			*100%*

for smaller OTC companies to gain economies of scale. Rhone-Poulenc Rorer, for instance, had a fine chemicals division generating between U.S.$400–U.S.$500 million per year on overall company sales of about U.S.$4.2 billion (10–12 percent).

Dosage manufacturing began after the production of the active ingredients. There were several guidelines which had been adopted first by the United States and then by Europe to regulate the manufacturing process. Good Manufacturing Practices (GMPs) were followed by all international companies, since most of the major markets required it for products that were sold in their countries.

Packaging Operations

Unlike prescription pharmaceuticals, OTCs packaging was an extremely important part of the manufacturing process. Packaging had to be eye-catching and appealing to consumers. Safety, as in the case of child-resistant packaging, was also a major concern. Thus, packaging accounted for almost twice as much of the cost of a product as the active ingredients themselves. Manufacturers generally packaged the product themselves, mostly in small packages ready for resale to consumers. Specific guidelines governing the required information for the inside and outside packages were stipulated by each country. All countries required that labeling be printed in the native language of the country where the product was marketed (which was another reason that packaging absorbed a large part of product cost). The EU, in working toward harmonization, hoped to specify one set of packaging guidelines for all member countries.

As with packaging, labeling was regulated by individual countries. Labeling requirements were relatively stringent in most countries; however, it was up to manufacturers to decide how much warning information to include on the package in excess of the requirements. In the case of Europe, EC Directive 92/27/EEC identified sixteen standard OTC labeling requirements for all member countries. The United States did not have a similar labeling procedure, although it hoped to adopt stricter regulation in the future.

Distribution of OTCs

There were several distribution alternatives available to manufacturers. These alternatives included wholesaling, direct and self-distribution, parallel importing, and direct-to-consumer. The preferred method of distribution varied widely, depending on the geographic region. In the United States and Japan, the distributors tended to be the manufacturers themselves, perhaps hiring a carrier to physically transport the goods. As with the chemical synthesis process, manufacturers tended to stick to their core competencies rather than concentrating on distribution.

In Europe, a bulk of the distributing was done through independent wholesalers. The distributors added little value; however, in the case of wholesalers, they had a fair amount of leverage. The wholesaling trend toward large-scale operations and quantity discounts meant eroded profit margins for manufacturers. A growing trend in wholesaling was to develop business on an international level. This allowed wholesalers to buy in greater volume and at lower prices. In Europe, wholesalers tried to gain the needed critical mass by integrating in all directions: vertically, horizontally, forward, and backward (refer to Exhibit 14). For example, Gehe, Germany's leading pharmaceutical wholesaler, began producing branded generic and nonprescription-bound products. These products, while accounting for less than 10 percent of 1994 sales, contributed to over 25 percent of the profits.

Exhibit 14 ● Vertical Integration of OTC Wholesalers

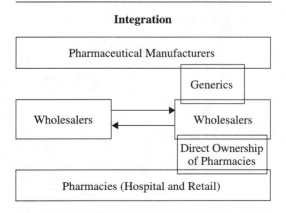

Source: Datamonitor; from *European Pharmaceutical,* "Switching to OTS Status," p. 29.

Direct distribution and self-distribution cut the middlemen out of the process. OTCs went directly from the manufacturer to the retailer. Direct distribution differed from self-distribution with respect to transportation. The manufacturer transported OTCs under direct distribution, and the retailer performed the task under self-distribution. Fewer OTCs in Europe were distributed through these channels, since retailers preferred delivery several times in one day due to a lack of storage space. Shelf space was divided among an increasing number of products, and it was difficult to stock in significant quantities.

In the United States direct distribution played a more significant role, since the trend in the United States was away from the independent pharmacies. The larger outlets that distributed OTCs in the United States did not need the frequent deliveries required by smaller pharmacies. Japanese manufacturers also pre-ferred direct distribution to doing business with wholesalers. This was especially true of the major manufacturers such as Taisho, SS Pharmaceutical, and Sato (refer to Exhibit 15). The Japanese trend was furthered by government initiatives toward separation of prescribing and dispensing activities. As the main prescriber role shifted from doctor to pharmacist, it became much more economical to distribute in this fashion. Direct-to-consumer distribution was unique to the Japanese market and was only allowed for herbals and first-aid kit replenishing supplies.

Parallel importing, which involved the buying of OTCs in one country and selling them in another, was a factor in Europe. Distributors took advantage of regulated prices to buy products much cheaper in one country than they could be sold in another. Generally, distributors required a price differential of 20–25 percent between the same product in different countries

Exhibit 15 ● Taisho Pharmaceutical Company Direct Marketing System for OTC Drugs

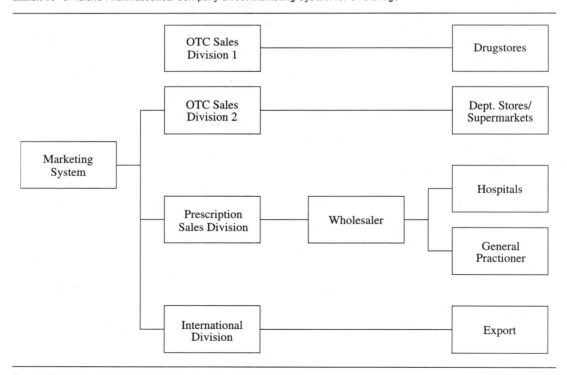

Source: MarketLine Annual Report.

for parallel importing to be lucrative. Parallel importing affected the prescription portion of the pharma industry much more than the OTC sector due to higher margins on the former.

Sales and Marketing Activities

The main role of a manufacturer in the marketing process was to create and maintain brand awareness. The OTC industry was increasingly competitive, so marketing and education were vital at all levels: consumers, retailers, distributors, and the medical community. Manufacturers used a combination of push and pull strategies, which included brand awareness advertising, keeping retailers shelves stocked with products, and detailing medical professionals.

Approximately one-fifth of the final cost of an OTC product (at consumer level) was spent on marketing and sales at the manufacturer level. Various activities contributed, the most common being customer service, brand management, sales, advertising, and promotion. Exhibit 16 shows a typical allocation of an OTC manufacturer's marketing budget.

There were essentially three types of product introductions that took place in the OTC industry, each with different launch costs. The most expensive launch was the introduction of a new brand (refer to Exhibit 17). The advertising-to-sales (A/S) ratio in the first year was almost always over 100 percent. The cheapest product introduction was to extend an existing brand. This required much less effort and money, since consumers were already familiar with other OTC products of the same brand name. Switching a prescription product to OTC status using the same name fell in between the two extremes.

Exhibit 16 ● Typical Marketing Budget for an OTC Manufacturer

Marketing Activity	Proportion of Budget
Customer service	6–9%
Brand management	10–14
Sales force	15–20
Advertising & promotion	65–75
Advertising	*30–40*
Consumer promotion	*7–10*
Trade promotion	*15–20*
Medical promotion	*10–13*
Total marketing & sales	100%

Consumer marketing programs relied primarily on television advertising and points-of-purchase displays. Supporting ads were sometimes placed in print media and billboards. Consumer education was an important part of the advertising campaign. For the consumer to understand the scientific message, a different level of advertising and education was needed. Pamphlets produced by manufacturers played an important part in the education process. They were given to retailers who then distributed them to the consumer. The pamphlets could specifically advertise the brand or could simply provide information on health care subjects. Furthermore, information contained on the packaging was an important educating tool, since most self-medicators did not have contact with informed health professionals.

Exhibit 17 ● New Product Launch Costs

	New OTC Product Launch Using New Brand Name	New OTC Product Launch Using Rx Brand Name	OTC Line Extension Using Existing Brand Name
Advertising $/year (millions)	U.S.$40–45	U.S.$25	U.S.$20
AS ratio after 3 or 4 years	40–50%	40%	30–40%
Breakeven point	5–7 years	3–5 years	3–4 years

Consumer education was even more important in Asian countries, such as Japan, where there was less differentiation between prescription and OTC medicines. Also, Asian consumers were very company and brand loyal, which made it difficult for new entrants.

Another source of information for consumers came from pharmacists and doctor recommendations. As such, a strong relationship with these groups was invaluable. It was the manufacturer and/or the distributor who educated the retailer on the use of the OTC product. Companies such as SmithKline Beecham, Glaxo, and others even started including training packages complete with reference manuals and videos in their professional and trade promotional campaigns for new OTCs.

OTC companies also marketed their products to the various managed care organizations. They positioned their products as preventive tools and/or an alternative to the higher-cost prescription drugs. However, since there was a fine line between being cost-conscious and providing quality care, there was a limit to how far this relationship could go. Managed care organizations needed to ensure to their subscribers that they were receiving as good, if not better, benefits than from competing providers.

GEOGRAPHIC SEGMENTS & TRENDS

There were four basic geographic regions that were important markets for the OTC industry: Europe, North America, the Pacific Rim, and the developing regions (the Far East and Latin America). These markets were grouped together because they had a similar infrastructure, and in some cases, harmonization efforts were underway via free trade pacts and other trade alliances. Exhibit 18 describes each region and its OTC sales.

The European Market and Trends

The European market was comprised of the fifteen European Union (EU) members, the associated countries of the European Free Trade Area (EFTA), eastern Europe, and the Community of Independent States (CIS).[6] This market accounted for 32 percent of in-

6. The Community of Independent States replaced the Soviet Union in 1990 and comprises Russia, Ukraine, and other former Soviet republics.

Exhibit 18A ● OTC Sales by Region, 1995

Country	OTC Sales (U.S.$bn)	% of World Total
Europe (including eastern Europe and CIS)	16.45	32%
North America	15.10	29
Pacific Rim	8.78	17
Latin America	4.14	8
Far East and China	4.55	9
Others	2.43	5
Total World	51.45	100%

dustry sales. Germany, France, and the United Kingdom were the dominant markets in this region (refer to Exhibit 18). Most European countries had a semiethical category for OTC products, and therefore, it was not uncommon for a consumer to receive partial reimbursement for a purchase.[7]

As a region, Europe was developing into a unified market, similar to the United States in size and scope. However, there were many aspects that made it more difficult to compete in this market. For one thing, there were as many different languages as countries. In the United States, there was one primary language. Furthermore, in all countries, governments played a strong role in the health care system, be it through compulsory health insurance programs, such as in France, or through administration of health funds, as in the case of Germany. In contrast, the majority of U.S. residents had private insurance policies which were administered by corporations. There was increasing pressure by governments to reduce health care expenditures, and since most medical plans included the reimbursement of pharmaceutical products, health authorities were more eager than before to see some pharmaceuticals switched to OTC status and/or taken off the reimbursement list.

European consumers had strong relationships with pharmacists and often relied on them as a source of information. This was especially true in countries where consumer advertising was either strictly controlled or altogether banned (refer to Exhibit 19).

7. Exceptions were the Netherlands and Finland.

Exhibit 18B ● OTC Sales Breakdowns by Region, 1995

**Europe
Share of Total Sales of Non Rx-Bound Products
by Country, 1995**

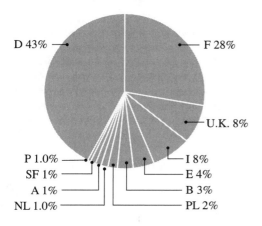

Total Sales in U.S.$ 16.45 billion
Ex-Manufacturer Sales in U.S.$

Source: OTC Review 1996, pp. 2-19, 3-1, 5-1.

**North America
Self-Medication Sales by Country, 1995**

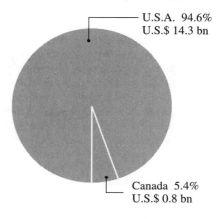

Total Sales in U.S.$ 15.1 billion
Ex-Manufacturer Sales in U.S.$

Consumer differences were subtle but nevertheless existed. Of all the European countries, the British were the least likely to treat ailments, but when they did, they were most likely to use OTCs. Germans were noted for their interest in using OTCs as preventative treatments. The French consumed the highest level of pharmaceuticals in the EU; however, they were culturally attached to reimbursable products. In general, reimbursement was less for OTCs and the French preferred the advice of doctors rather than reliance on self-diagnosis.

Government regulations differed from country to country as well. Price controls on ethical and semi-ethical pharmaceuticals existed in some countries, such as France, but not as much in others, such as the United Kingdom. Likewise advertising restrictions varied from one country to another, making some populations easier to reach than others.

Eastern Europe was rapidly developing as governments restructured their health care and reimburse-

**Pacific Rim
Self-Medication Sales by Country, 1995**

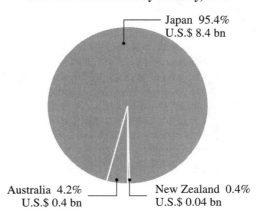

Total Sales in U.S.$ 8.8 billion
Ex-Manufacturer Sales in U.S.$

**Latin America
Self-Medication Sales by Country, 1995**

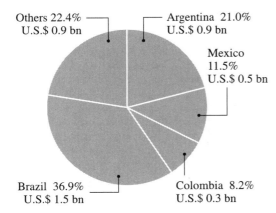

Others 22.4%
U.S.$ 0.9 bn

Argentina 21.0%
U.S.$ 0.9 bn

Mexico
11.5%
U.S.$ 0.5 bn

Brazil 36.9%
U.S.$ 1.5 bn

Colombia 8.2%
U.S.$ 0.3 bn

Total Sales in U.S.$ 4.1 billion
Ex-Manufacturer Sales in U.S.$

**Far East and China
Self-Medication Sales by Country, 1995**

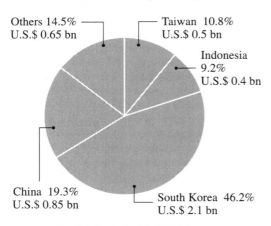

Others 14.5%
U.S.$ 0.65 bn

Taiwan 10.8%
U.S.$ 0.5 bn

Indonesia
9.2%
U.S.$ 0.4 bn

China 19.3%
U.S.$ 0.85 bn

South Korea 46.2%
U.S.$ 2.1 bn

Total Sales in U.S.$ 4.5 billion
Ex-Manufacturer Sales in U.S.$

ment policies came more in line with those of the European Union. As a result, countries such as Hungary and the Czech Republic were aggressively developing the necessary marketing infrastructure for OTC products. Significant opportunities for expansion of OTC sales were predicted (refer to Exhibit 20).

Harmonization efforts were underway, and governments realized that open borders and cable television limited their ability to maintain the same kind of control. Furthermore, the propensity for consumers to self-medicate was increasing at a very fast pace. By the year 2000, Germany, France and the United Kingdom expected to have 45 percent of the population self-medicating, the same proportion as the United States.

The North American Segment and Trends

North America included Canada and the United States. The United States dominated the region with 95 percent of the sales (refer to Exhibit 18). The North America OTC market was well developed in comparison with the other regions of the world.

North America was an attractive market for OTCs not only because of its large, relatively homogeneous population, but due to its relatively loose advertising regulations. Both OTCs and prescription pharmaceuticals could be promoted directly to the public. However, these liberalized laws meant that regulatory bodies, such as the FTC, and other OTC competitors kept a close eye on advertising claims. Unsupported claims of safety and efficacy in Rx-to-OTC switches resulted in numerous lawsuits.

U.S. consumers were considered to be the most advanced in the world in terms of propensity to self-medicate. In 1993, 38 percent of the adult population were self-medicators. This was expected to grow to 45 percent by the year 2000. This was in part due to their history of privatized medicine, and the fact that American consumers were accustomed to taking both financial and personal responsibility for their health care.

Prescription products played an important role in the U.S. OTC industry. The driving forces behind new product introductions were the recent switches from prescription to OTC status. One reason was the threat of patent expiry on pharmaceutical products. Once a nonprescription product's patent expired, generic pro-

Exhibit 19 ● Advertising Regulation Differences Between Major Countries

Market	OTC Versions of Rx Brands Permitted	Advertising Reimbursed Brands Permitted	Advertising Limited to OTC Status Only	Media Permitted
France	Yes	No	Yes	All
Germany	Yes	Yes	No	All
Netherlands	Yes	Yes	No	All
UK	Yes	Yes	No	All
Italy	No	No	Yes	All
USA	Yes	Yes	No	All
Japan	Yes	n/a	n/a	All

n/a = not available

Source: James Dudley Self-Medication in Europe Volume 1, pages 1-39.

Exhibit 20 ● Eastern Europe OTC Growth

Region Totals	
1995 Sales in $US mn	*% Growth in 1994/1995*
$737	34.7

Sample Country Breakdowns		
Industry Activity[a]	*Number of OTCs 1995*	*Recent Developments*
HUNGARY — 100+ Switches in 1994/5	348	Non-Prescription Pharmaceutical Manufacturers and Wholesalers Association created
CZECH REPUBLIC — 638 Switches 1994/5	1660	Gov't encouraging OTC switching and liberating prices

a. In 1994, Italy had approximately 190 switches, Germany had 5 switches, and France had 3 switches.

ducts inevitably appeared on the market, stealing profits from the original manufacturer. Also, a growing number of managed care organizations began adding OTCs to their formularies of approved medications. This gave added incentive to pharmaceutical companies to switch their products to OTC status. Finally, as mentioned above, the United States was the most lib-

eral country with respect to the advertising of pharmaceutical products directly to consumers. Thus, Americans tended to be much more aware of a switch product's prescription and medical heritage.

Influential organizations in the United States, aside from the FDA, included the American Medical Association, and various specialty organizations such as the American Heart Foundation and the Arthritis Foundation. The FDA was the only organization which played a role in getting products approved. The other organizations were involved in independent research and their buy-in was very important to gaining the trust of the public. OTC companies had begun to pursue relationships with these organizations to help market their products. For example, Johnson & Johnson and the Arthritis Foundation partnered to introduce an anti-inflammatory product which carried the organization's name instead of a Johnson & Johnson brand name.

Canada, unlike the United States, was under a socialized health care system. Still, consumers in that market were much the same as their southern neighbors, since the socialized system did not cover pharmaceuticals. Only those people with private health insurance policies or those qualifying for social assistance received partial or full reimbursement for prescription and nonprescription products (much like Medicare, SSI, and Medicaid in the United States). To further development of the Canadian pharmaceutical market, regulators began to standardize pharma categories across provinces. A new registration system for OTCs was developed, which legislators hoped would result in faster registration times and a more efficient switching procedure. Additionally, more governmental resources were allocated for processing switch applications.

The Pacific Rim Segment and Trends

The Pacific Rim, comprising Japan, New Zealand, and Australia (refer to Exhibit 18), were separated from the other Far East countries primarily because they shared a similar level of sophistication regarding their consumers and their health care systems. All three were advanced economies with significant consumer purchasing power. Though all three countries were under socialized health care systems, private insurance plans were encouraged by the governments and were on the rise.

Japan was the dominant player in this area, accounting for approximately 17 percent of world OTC sales. Public health care was provided to all citizens through one of two ways: Employee Health Insurance (EHI) and National Health Insurance (NHI). Approximately two-thirds were provided for by EHI. Pre-scription drugs were reimbursed, under both policies. EHI members contributed 10 percent of prescription drugs' cost whereas NHI members and EHI dependents contributed 30 percent.

Historically, it was difficult for western OTC companies to achieve critical mass in the Japanese market. First there were significant philosophical differences between Eastern and Western medical heritage. Eastern medicine was based on herbal remedies and acupuncture. The Japanese viewed OTCs as products for prevention rather than for treatment. Evidence of this was found in both the overwhelming popularity of tonics and vitamins and mineral supplements in Japan (the tonics segment was virtually nonexistent anywhere else with the exception of Germany) and the low usage of pain relief products compared to other countries (refer to Exhibit 21).

Second, there was a reluctance by the Japanese companies to expand internationally. This was illustrated by the fact that the industry structure in Japan had been unaffected by the wave of mergers and acquisitions taking place in North America and Europe. None of the Japanese companies consolidated to gain critical mass nor did they appear interested in buying any of the big OTC divisions that were up for sale (e.g., Sterling in 1994) in the United States or Europe.

Finally, retail prices for OTC products were unusually high in Japan (up to six times the ex-factory price). Thus, consumers still tended to seek medical advice for a majority of ailments. The high cost of OTCs was mostly due to Japan's resale price maintenance (RPM) scheme, which the government planned to dismantle by 1999. The disappearance of the RPM system was expected to lead to increased price cutting and discounting of OTC products. Margins for retailers ranged from 15–20 percent for tonics to 35–60 percent for other OTCs.

New Zealand experienced the highest growth rates in the region, but accounted for only .4 percent of sales in 1995. It was considered to be one of the most progressive OTC markets in the world. Switching was common, and regulators had an open attitude on advertising aimed at consumers.

Emerging Regions

Emerging regions included countries in Latin America, the Far East, and China (refer to Exhibit 18). Although

Exhibit 21 ● Market Segment Sales Breakdown for Non–Prescription-based Products, by Region and Major Country, 1995

Europe
Leading Markets for Non–Prescription-bound Products, 1995

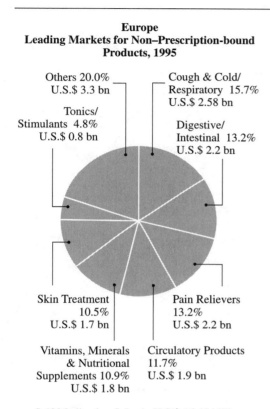

Others 20.0%
U.S.$ 3.3 bn

Cough & Cold/
Respiratory 15.7%
U.S.$ 2.58 bn

Tonics/
Stimulants 4.8%
U.S.$ 0.8 bn

Digestive/
Intestinal 13.2%
U.S.$ 2.2 bn

Skin Treatment
10.5%
U.S.$ 1.7 bn

Pain Relievers
13.2%
U.S.$ 2.2 bn

Vitamins, Minerals
& Nutritional
Supplements 10.9%
U.S.$ 1.8 bn

Circulatory Products
11.7%
U.S.$ 1.9 bn

Self-Medication Sales in U.S.$ 16.45 billion
Ex-Manufacturer Sales in U.S.$

France
Leading Markets for Non–Prescription-bound Products, 1995

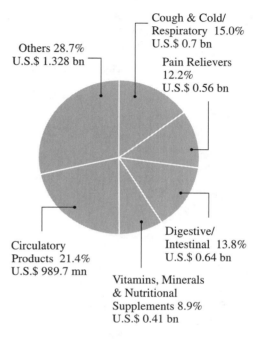

Others 28.7%
U.S.$ 1.328 bn

Cough & Cold/
Respiratory 15.0%
U.S.$ 0.7 bn

Pain Relievers
12.2%
U.S.$ 0.56 bn

Circulatory
Products 21.4%
U.S.$ 989.7 mn

Digestive/
Intestinal 13.8%
U.S.$ 0.64 bn

Vitamins, Minerals
& Nutritional
Supplements 8.9%
U.S.$ 0.41 bn

Self-Medication Sales in U.S.$ 4.62 billion
Ex-Manufacturer Sales in U.S.$

there were many cultural and geographic differences between emerging markets, there were also many similarities in the way they were viewed in the context of the OTC industry. For instance, their economies were still developing and, in some cases, governments were going through major restructuring. This impacted the OTC industry because historically there was less of a distinction between prescription-bound and non–prescription-bound products.

Most emerging markets showed a high incidence of illegal distribution of prescription-bound products. This suggested that part of the population was self-medicating. Because there was no infrastructure to encourage the introduction of new OTC drugs, distributors were doing so illegally.

Rapidly developing economies such as those in Southeast Asia, China, and Latin America were developing a more formalized health care system which included a more official place for OTC products. As this progressed, opportunities for OTC companies would increase.

MARKET SEGMENTS AND TRENDS

The OTC market was divided into eighteen different market segments followed by various therapeutic segments. The leading market segments varied somewhat

**Germany
Leading Markets for Non–Prescription-bound
Products, 1995**

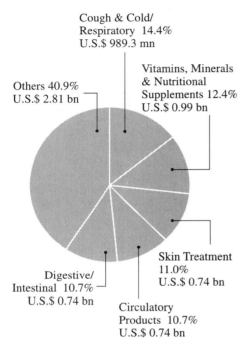

Cough & Cold/
Respiratory 14.4%
U.S.$ 989.3 mn

Vitamins, Minerals
& Nutritional
Supplements 12.4%
U.S.$ 0.99 bn

Others 40.9%
U.S.$ 2.81 bn

Digestive/
Intestinal 10.7%
U.S.$ 0.74 bn

Skin Treatment
11.0%
U.S.$ 0.74 bn

Circulatory
Products 10.7%
U.S.$ 0.74 bn

Self-Medication Sales in U.S.$ 6.88 billion
Ex-Manufacturer Sales in U.S.$

**Italy
Leading Markets for Non–Prescription-bound
Products, 1995**

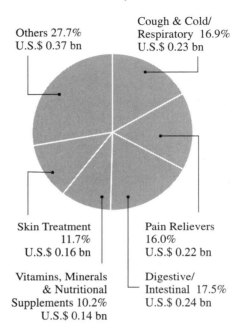

Others 27.7%
U.S.$ 0.37 bn

Cough & Cold/
Respiratory 16.9%
U.S.$ 0.23 bn

Skin Treatment
11.7%
U.S.$ 0.16 bn

Pain Relievers
16.0%
U.S.$ 0.22 bn

Vitamins, Minerals
& Nutritional
Supplements 10.2%
U.S.$ 0.14 bn

Digestive/
Intestinal 17.5%
U.S.$ 0.24 bn

Self-Medication Sales in U.S.$ 1.36 billion
Ex-Manufacturer Sales in U.S.$

by geographic region, but in general, the majority of the volume was concentrated on six main categories: cough, cold, and other respiratory; pain relief; digestive and other intestinal remedies; vitamins, minerals, and nutritional supplements; tonics and other stimulants; and skin treatments (refer to Exhibits 21 and 22).

The highest growth segments were diagnostic tests, habit treatment, and herbal and homeopathic remedies. Growth in these segments represented the changing attitudes of consumers in favor of more preventative medicating and healthier lifestyles. This move toward overall wellness was also evident within existing top segments. For example, products were introduced to *prevent* heartburn, cold sores, and other

ailments rather than just to treat them once they happened. Growth in market segments also occurred because borders were becoming more open. The world was, in effect, becoming a smaller place. Thus, consumers contracted new strains of viruses from other cultures and were more likely to pass them on to others. OTC manufacturers addressed this issue by introducing a wider variety of antiviral and antifungal products.

Major OTC Categories

Pain Relief Sales for the pain relief segment were U.S.$7.3 billion in 1994, making it the largest in the industry. Growth was predicted to reach U.S.$9 billion in 1999. Pain relief was one of the first market

**UK
Leading Markets for Non–Prescription-bound
Products, 1995**

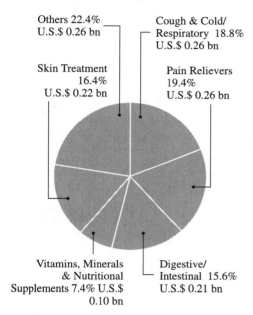

Others 22.4%
U.S.$ 0.26 bn

Cough & Cold/
Respiratory 18.8%
U.S.$ 0.26 bn

Skin Treatment
16.4%
U.S.$ 0.22 bn

Pain Relievers
19.4%
U.S.$ 0.26 bn

Vitamins, Minerals
& Nutritional
Supplements 7.4% U.S.$
0.10 bn

Digestive/
Intestinal 15.6%
U.S.$ 0.21 bn

Self-Medication Sales in U.S.$ 1.35 billion
Ex-Manufacturer Sales in U.S.$

segments to be developed by pharmaceutical companies. Even so, the segment was very dynamic. The sheer size and sales opportunity enticed new entrants and made the segment very competitive. Most segment growth came both from switches of new non-steroidal anti-inflammatory drugs (NSAIDs) and the proliferation of niche products aimed at taking some category business away from entrenched leaders, such as Tylenol and Bayer.

The major therapeutic categories are illustrated in Exhibit 22. Note that the general pain relief category accounted for close to 70 percent of the entire segment. Higher than average growth was expected from the second largest segment, muscular pain relief, between the years 1995 and 2000. In general, environmental factors that contributed to the use of pain relief included lifestyle, stress, the pressure to "keep

going," and an aging population. Users of pain relief products covered most of the population segments. For example, in Europe, 75 percent of the population used analgesics in any one year.

The global market leader was Johnson & Johnson with its Tylenol brand, although Tylenol was not a global brand. It had gained its rank due to its success in the large U.S. market. The leading brands in Europe and Asia were different from those in the United States. For example, Bayer Aspirin was the only analgesic with a European-wide presence. In Japan, Bufferin was the number one pain relief product.

Products in the pain relief category were differentiated based on their efficacy in treating specific types of pain. The oldest and most common form of pain relief product was analgesics, which treated pain caused by headaches, cold/flu, and fever. In the 1980s and 1990s, significant activity was observed when a new treatment was introduced to the OTC market in the form of nonsteroidal anti-inflammation drugs (NSAIDs). Much of the success of this OTC treatment was attributed to its prior success and efficacy reputation in the prescription market. Another form of differentiation was based on the delivery system, as in the case of topical pain remedies which usually contained analgesics or NSAIDs. This was useful to some consumers because it tended to have a lower incidence of side effects.

Finally, a growing trend in the pain relief segment was the use of these products for prevention rather than for treatment of a specific ailment. For example, in the United States and the United Kingdom medical professionals began recommending a daily dose of aspirin to prevent cardiovascular problems. This trend had a positive impact on sales of lower-dose aspirin products.

Cough, Cold and Other Respiratory Remedies
Sales for this category reached U.S.$7.1 billion in 1994 and were expected to grow between 7.7 percent and 10.2 percent from 1995 to 2000. Key therapeutic categories included cough remedies, cold remedies, sore throat, hay fever, and asthma. Growth in this segment came from new switches from the prescription-only segment. The worldwide market leader for this category was Procter & Gamble with the Vicks brand franchise. Product offerings were differentiated based

**USA
Leading Markets for Non–Prescription-bound
Products, 1995**

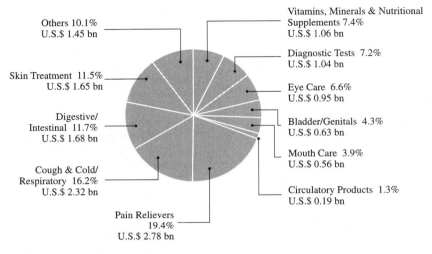

Others 10.1%
U.S.$ 1.45 bn

Skin Treatment 11.5%
U.S.$ 1.65 bn

Digestive/
Intestinal 11.7%
U.S.$ 1.68 bn

Cough & Cold/
Respiratory 16.2%
U.S.$ 2.32 bn

Pain Relievers
19.4%
U.S.$ 2.78 bn

Vitamins, Minerals & Nutritional
Supplements 7.4%
U.S.$ 1.06 bn

Diagnostic Tests 7.2%
U.S.$ 1.04 bn

Eye Care 6.6%
U.S.$ 0.95 bn

Bladder/Genitals 4.3%
U.S.$ 0.63 bn

Mouth Care 3.9%
U.S.$ 0.56 bn

Circulatory Products 1.3%
U.S.$ 0.19 bn

Self-Medication Sales in U.S.$ 14.30 billion
Ex-Manufacturer Sales in U.S.$

**Japan
Leading Markets for Non–Prescription-bound
Products, 1995**

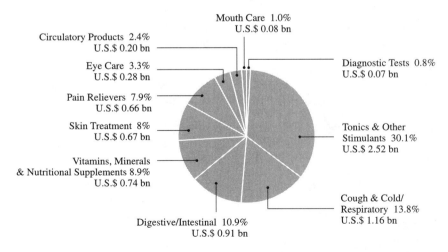

Mouth Care 1.0%
U.S.$ 0.08 bn

Circulatory Products 2.4%
U.S.$ 0.20 bn

Eye Care 3.3%
U.S.$ 0.28 bn

Pain Relievers 7.9%
U.S.$ 0.66 bn

Skin Treatment 8%
U.S.$ 0.67 bn

Vitamins, Minerals
& Nutritional Supplements 8.9%
U.S.$ 0.74 bn

Diagnostic Tests 0.8%
U.S.$ 0.07 bn

Tonics & Other
Stimulants 30.1%
U.S.$ 2.52 bn

Cough & Cold/
Respiratory 13.8%
U.S.$ 1.16 bn

Digestive/Intestinal 10.9%
U.S.$ 0.91 bn

Self-Medication Sales in U.S.$ 8.37 billion
Ex-Manufacturer Sales in U.S.$

Exhibit 22 ● 1995 OTC Industry Product Classification and Sales Figures

Category	Major Therapeutic Segments	Share of Segment Sales[a]	% Growth 1995–1998	Top U.S. Brands
World OTC	*Total Sales: U.S.$51.45 Billion*			
Pain relief	*Percent of Total Sales: 17%*		4.6%	
	General pain relievers	69.5%	4.2	Tylenol, Advil, Aleve
	Muscular pain	26.4	6.1	Ibuprofen (PL), Ben-Gay
	Migraine remedies	.25	5.8	Migraclear
	Mouth pain relief	1.97	3.9	Anbesol, Orajel
Cough, cold, and respiratory	*Percent of Total Sales: 17%*			
	Cough remedies	29.0	5.9	Halls, Robitussin DM
	Cold remedies	44.0	8.1	NyQuil, Alka Seltzer Plus C
	Sore throat	12.9	8.5	Chloraseptic, Sucrets
	Hayfever	11.5	9.4	Benadryl OTC, Tavist-D
	Asthma	2.6	9.2	Bronkaid, Primatene Mist
Digestive preparations	*Percent of Total Sales: 12%*		3.4	
	Stomach remedies	53.0	4.1	Pepcid AC, Pepto Bismol
	Laxatives	28.1	2.7	Metamucil, Milk of Magnesia
	Antidiarrheals	14.1	2.0	Imodium-AD, Pedialyte
	Liver remedies	4.2	2.1	Lipoflavonoid, Decholin
	Worm treatment	0.6	2.0	Combantrin, Pin-X
Skin treatments	*Percent of Total Sales: 12%*		7.6	
	Skin protection	28.3	8.7	Coppertone
	Skin irritation relief	18.2	8.8	Campho Phenique
	Antiseptics	11.2	8.2	Alcohol (PL), Campho Phenique
	Antifungals	11.0	9.2	Lotrimin AF, Desenex
	Spot and blemish care	8.2	4.5	Clearasil, Oxy
	Antidandruff	5.7	7.7	Head & Shoulders
	Antiparasites	3.1	2.2	Lice Treatment Kit
	Cold sore remedies	1.3	31.3	Zovirax, Blistex
	Antibaldness	0.7	17.3	Rogaine
Vitamins, minerals, and nutritional supplements	*Percent of Total Sales: 10%*		8.1	Centrum, One-A-Day, Ensure
Diagnostic tests	*Percent of Total Sales: 5%*		15.5	One Touch, E.P.T
Tonics and stimulants	*Percent of Total Sales: 4%*		6.5	Vivarin, No Doz, Ginseng
Eye care	*Percent of Total Sales: 4*		4	Renu, Opti-Free, Aosept
Oral care	*Percent of Total Sales: 4%*		1.2	Listerine, Polident, Fixodent
Circulatory remedies	*Percent of Total Sales: 4%*		5.5	Preparation H, Tucks
Ear care	*Percent of Total Sales: .5%*		7.3	Murine Ear Drops
Bladder and genitals	*Percent of Total Sales: 2.5%*		-1.6	Monistat-7, Trojans
Habit control	*Percent of Total Sales: .3%*		21	Nicorette, Nicotinell
Other	*Percent of Total Sales: 7.7%*			

a. 1995 sales for ten countries: Belgium, France, Germany, Italy, the Netherlands, Spain, United Kingdom, Canada, United States, and Japan.

on whether or not they were a single- or multiple-symptom–relieving product, or a time-release product. Further differentiation came from alternative delivery systems such as capsules, liquids, nasal sprays, and topical treatments.

Most of the sales in this category were generated by the population aged twenty-five to forty-four. This segment of the population had the greatest concentration of workers who, for convenience sake, opted to use OTC products rather than visit a doctor. It was important to note that these preferences differed from region to region. For example, in the United Kingdom, 50 percent of allergy and hay fever sufferers purchased OTCs as a first line of treatment. In Italy, most of the sufferers preferred to treat hay fever with doctor prescribed formulas.

There were several external factors that affected sales of this category. Mild winters or unusually high pollen counts in spring could significantly impact sales for that year. In addition, consumer misdiagnoses and confusion between cold, flu, hay fever, and sinus ailments distorted segment sales to some degree in the United States and the United Kingdom. There was evidence that this segment was somewhat price sensitive, especially in Japan, where there seemed to be significant correlation between raising the price of a product and the sales volume decrease. Finally, the recent availability of allergy and flu vaccinations in some markets also impacted sales.

Digestive and Other Intestinal Remedies   This category had sales of U.S.$5.8 billion in 1994 and was expected to reach U.S.$6.75 billion in 1999. The United States commanded the largest share of the market with 39 percent, followed by Japan (32 percent). The number one subcategory was stomach remedies which accounted for approximately 53 percent of all category sales. Users purchased digestive remedies to treat a range of ailments including: colic, constipation, diarrhea, flatulence, heartburn, and indigestion.

Prescription-to-OTC switches in the United States, Europe, and Japan had the most impact on this segment. The first switch of this kind was loperamide, a derivative of opium, which was known as a very effective treatment for diarrhea. Until this ingredient was made available for OTCs, consumers had not been able to effectively treat the symptoms. Addition-

ally, the switch of H_2 antagonists, such as Tagamet 100, Pepcid AC, and Zantac 75, known for the treatment for ulcers, received considerable attention. Having received approval to be marketed as a heartburn prevention, H_2 was introduced to the OTC market and brought indigestion remedies to a new level. As a result, several companies had to expand the market segments to maintain their competitive position. This meant either extending the existing product line or developing new attributes for existing products.

Vitamins, Minerals, and Nutritional Supplements
This market segment experienced sales in 1995 of U.S.$5 billion and was expected to reach U.S.$6.4 billion in 1999. This category was broadly defined and encompassed many different therapeutic categories. Unlike the other segments, vitamins, minerals, and nutritional supplements (VMS) was highly fragmented. For example, in Germany, the top ten brands accounted for no more than 22 percent of self-medication sales. Furthermore, user trends regarding the most sought-after substances and delivery systems varied from country to country. For example, fish oil supplements was one of the most popular categories in the United Kingdom, vitamin E in Germany, and bottled nutritive drinks in Japan.

Despite these differences, there were a few common characteristics of the category. First, there was a reliance on science to lend credibility to this market segment. Since dietary supplements could not be patented, there was no incentive for pharmaceutical companies to conduct independent studies. As a result, much of the research for this segment was done by government agencies. Second, to a certain extent, these items were considered commodities. In some markets, such as the United States and the United Kingdom, private labels dominated and branded products had to rely on heavy consumer advertising. Some companies tried to differentiate themselves from the competition by offering products that were highly targeted to specific groups, or to package them in easy-to-use containers (like vitamin packs or calendar packs). Finally, in part due to the characteristics listed above, this industry was predisposed to fads, which made predicting growth and sales opportunities very difficult. Nevertheless, the sheer size of the market and the increasing interest in preventive measures meant that this segment had the potential to be very profitable for those players who entered at the right time.

The trend for VMS in the future was in the creation of new forms of dietary supplements called medico-foods, functional foods, or nutraceuticals.[8] With this new market segment. the line between food and OTCs became less distinct.

Tonics and Other Stimulants Sales for tonics and other stimulants were $2.46 billion in 1993.[9] The market was expected to grow to U.S.$3.3 billion by 1998, with most sales generated in Japan (80 percent) and Germany (14 percent). Similar to the VMS segment, this segment was broadly defined and meant different things in different markets. For example, in Japan, tonics were the largest OTC segment. One of the most common applications there was to consume tonics containing caffeine to combat fatigue. In fact, caffeine was the second most commonly used molecule in this segment. On the other hand, in Germany, tonics accounted for a fairly small portion of the country's OTC sales, and consumers there used tonics more as "health" drinks. Caffeine did not even make the country's top twenty list of most commonly used ingredients.

The most notable trend in Japan was a line of "mini-drinks" that were similar to the bottled nutritive drinks of the VMS segment. These products were positioned as both energy boosters and nutritional supplements. Mini-drinks were targeted primarily at the young and fashionable. Industry analysts believed this market had matured by the late 1990s, and while still a strong presence in the Japanese OTCs, it was not going to be an area of growth and opportunity for other areas. The strongest players in this segment were national companies like Chugai Seiyaku and Kowa Shinyaku in Japan and Klosterfrau in Germany.

Skin Treatment Worldwide OTC sales for this segment were $5.4 billion in 1995 and were anticipated to grow to $6.8 billion in 1999 (compound annual

growth rate [CAGR] of 7.6 percent). Historically, OTC skin treatments were defined as products that offered a medicinal benefit such as treating excessively dry skin, dandruff, or protecting skin from sun damage. However, a trend was emerging where more and more pharmaceutical applications were aimed at creating cosmetic improvements rather than treating an ailment. The industry buzz word for products such as these was "cosmeceuticals."

The dominant therapeutic segment was general skin protectors, followed by skin irritation treatments, such as lotions and lip balms. The highest growth was anticipated from two new segments which were created from prescription-only switches: cold sore prevention and antibaldness. For cold sore prevention, acyclovir, marketed under the brand name of Zovirax, was anticipated to attract new users based on its capability to stop cold sores from developing. The antibaldness category was created by the switch of minoxidil and tested the barriers of whether or not an image-enhancing product should be considered an OTC.

Growth Areas The diagnostics, habit treatment, and herbals/homeopathic segments were emerging categories in the OTC industry. With increasing emphasis placed on prevention and wellness, they offered the most interesting growth opportunities.

Diagnostics The OTC diagnostics segment was defined as products that enabled consumers to obtain information about their health by performing a test, similar to those done in clinics, but at home and without the supervision of health care professionals. Sales in this segment were $872 million in 1993.[10] While relatively small, this market was considered to be in the growth stage with potential as technology improved and retail prices declined. Examples of self-diagnostic kits were pregnancy tests, ovulation kits, blood glucose tests for diabetics, and cholesterol tests. Expected to move through the pipeline were home HIV test kits and some types of cancer screening tests.

As consumers everywhere were forced to take more and more responsibility for their health care, in-

---

8. Medico-foods, functional foods, and nutraceuticals refer to the cross-classification of traditional food products that had proven therapeutic benefits and were therefore used as therapeutic or preventative remedies.

9. Figures for ten countries only: Belgium, France, Germany, Italy, the Netherlands, Spain, the United Kingdom, Canada, the United States, and Japan.

10. Figures for ten countries only: Belgium, France, Germany, Italy, the Netherlands, Spain, the United Kingdom, Canada, United States, and Japan. *OTCforesight*, Vol. 1, London: SelfMedication International, 1995, pp. 11–177.

dustry analysts believed diagnostics would become more popular. In the United Kingdom, the government started charging for pregnancy tests, creating the market for at home pregnancy tests. However, the ultimate success of self-diagnostic kits depended on affordability, ease of use, accuracy, and consumer awareness.

Habit Treatment   A newly created segment, habit treatment amounted to $64 million in 1993 and was expected to grow to $166 million in 1998. This segment was brought to life by the prescription switch of nicotine replacement therapies. The driving force behind this category's increasing popularity was the growing interest from governments, managed care organizations, and employers who had a financial stake in the future health of their constituents. Furthermore, in the United States, antismoking campaigns succeeded in the prohibition of smoking at work and many public places. The antismoking movement developed at a much slower pace elsewhere in the world.

Herbal Remedies and Homeopathic Treatments   Natural remedies did not have OTC classification. They were often considered alternatives to the chemically-based products produced by OTC companies. Herbals and homeopathics were not required to be registered. As such, it was difficult to value the market. Industry analysts suggested, however, that the total worldwide market for these products was around U.S.$2 billion in 1994. However, because these products were distributed in so many different outlets and defined in so many different ways, an accurate estimate was difficult to obtain. More than 75 percent of the herbal and homeopathic market was in China, Japan, and other Far Eastern countries. The U.S. share of the market was estimated at about 1 percent.

The main attraction of natural remedies was the medicinal benefit (with fewer side effects) received by consumers. Also, as rising health care costs in many countries caused consumers to take more personal responsibility for their health, the relatively inexpensive natural remedies looked more attractive. Even though, traditionally, OTC producers did not offer products that fit the natural remedies definition, many began to seriously consider this emerging market. Initially, OTC producers seemed to test the market by offering herbal and homeopathic line ex-

tensions of their current products. For example, Bayer marketed a One-A-Day Extra garlic line extension.

TECHNOLOGY TRENDS

The driving forces behind technology were changes in consumer demographics, dissatisfaction with taste, form of dosage, the desire for fast-acting therapies, and changing consumer attitudes. A technology breakthrough potentially gave a company a significant competitive advantage. One of the most important decisions was how a product was going to interact with the human body. This was referred to as the delivery system, or "galenics," of a drug.

A drug could be introduced to the body a number of ways, and once there, it chose from a variety of transportation systems to reach its final destination. The most common dosage forms of OTCs were tablets, capsules, and liquids.

Advancements were made whereby the different modes of the drug delivery system offered consumers a more desirable form of treatment. Companies who wanted to maximize their growth potential in a mature market needed to look for ways to differentiate themselves from the competition. Technological breakthroughs played an important role.

Gelatin capsules and effervescent tablets were two examples of new delivery systems that changed the competitive landscape by offering consumers new benefits in terms of taste, improved efficacy, and convenience. More recent developments included transdermal patches for delivering a substance through the skin, time-release capsules which decreased the frequency of dosages, and topical creams which made the need to swallow pills (difficult for some people, especially the elderly) unnecessary.

REGULATORY ISSUES

The regulatory process for getting OTCs approved differed in every country and, in the case of some developing countries, was nonexistent. However, most countries had government-chosen regulatory bodies composed of health care professionals and academics. The role of these organizations was to classify OTCs according to their characteristics and potential impact on the welfare of the public. The following list describes the questions most commonly asked when evaluating whether or not a product was safe for OTC use.

- Was the medicine likely to present a danger, either directly or indirectly, if utilized without medical supervision?

- How likely was it that the medicine was going to be used incorrectly and, as a result, was it likely to present a direct or indirect danger to human health?

- Had the medicine been fully proven to be safe and effective with the target population?

- Was the substance addictive?

All pharmaceuticals and most OTCs had to be registered. The registration application needed to prove two things: the proposed product was safe and effective. However, each country had its own definition of safety and efficacy, requiring specific dossiers to be prepared for each country.[11]

The time required to pass the application procedure depended on the quality of the document, the potential impact on the public health, the efficiency of the health authority, and whether or not the product was a new drug or a copy of an existing product. The average time spent in the OTC registration process was two to three years, but there was an economic incentive for some countries, especially in Europe, to improve on this process. For example, in 1995, the United Kingdom streamlined its procedure so that it could process OTC registrations in less than a year.

The differences in regulatory practices made it difficult for companies to initiate global product launches. Inevitably, some products were OTC-registered in one country and still prescription-bound in another (refer to Exhibits 23 and 24). However, with the breakdown of trade barriers, European, American, and Japanese regulatory authorities initiated the International Conference on Harmonization. This organization was to establish a consensus for all pharmaceutical regulatory practices, including OTCs.

The U.S. Experience

The regulation and registration process was controlled by the Food and Drug Administration (FDA). In the 1970s, the FDA realized the value of enabling consumers to purchase medical products on their own. There was a flood of applications for switches. To streamline the process, the FDA established the monograph system. A monograph was a public standard spelled out by the FDA, which aimed at standardizing labeling, indications, and dosages for very common products generally recognized as effective and safe. Once a monograph for a substance was established, products using a monograph could quickly pass through the approval process.

Products introduced to the market were classified as either a new OTC or a monograph. If a product was considered a new OTC, the company had to get labeling approved from the FDA and then undergo postmarketing surveillance. It generally took longer for a new drug application (NDA) to pass through the

11. "Dossier" referred to an application which was prepared and included all the necessary documentation and proof the company thought necessary to submit for regulatory approval.

Exhibit 23 ● Comparison of OTC Regulation Between Regions

Regulated Activity	United States	Europe	Japan
New OTC drug approval	1–3 years	1–3 years	4 years
Advertising and promotion restrictions	No	Yes	Yes
Monography system	Yes	No	Yes
Postmarketing surveillance of new substance	3 years	2 years	6–10 years
Banned dosage forms	No	No	Yes[a]
Resale price maintenance	No	Yes[b]	Yes

a. Includes chewable tablets, effervescent powders, and chewing gum.

b. Only in Germany, Italy, Spain, Switzerland, and the United Kingdom.

Exhibit 24 ● Regulatory Differences by Country for R-to-OTC Candidates

			Country	
Substance	*Product Segment*	*Sample Brand Name*	*Austria*	*Belgium*
Loperamide	Antidiarrheals	Imodium	Rx	OTC
Hydrocortisone	Anti-itch treatment	Hydrocortisone cream	Rx	OTC
Clotrimazole	Antifungal	Gyne-Lotrimin	OTC	OTC
Miconazole	Antifungal	Monistat 7	Rx	OTC
Nicotine	Smoke cessation	Nicorette	OTC	OTC
Acyclovir	Cold sore/herpes treatment	Zovirax	OTC	OTC
Ketoprofen	Analgesic	Oruvail gel	Rx	OTC
Cimetidine	H_2 antagonist	Tagament	Rx	(OTC)
Loratidine	Antihistamine	Clarityn	Rx	OTC
Ranitidine	H_2 antagonist	Zantac	Rx	(OTC)
Famotidine	H_2 antagonist	Pepcid AC	Rx	Rx

a. Previously OTC, but switched back to Rx status.

b. As of 1993.

registration process than for an application based on a monograph (refer to Exhibit 25).

OTC companies often chose to submit an NDA because this path offered many benefits. A private license was granted to the new drug holder or sponsor. In addition, it was possible to secure exclusivity for up to three years, which, if granted, offered companies high profit potential.

In general, it was more difficult to get prescription products switched in the United States than in some European countries, such as the United Kingdom. This was due to the fact that once a product has been granted OTC status, there were no other safety nets in place (in terms of advertising and distribution restrictions) to protect the consumers.

The European Experience

Historically, companies had to register each new product in each country. This meant up to fifteen different registration applications and fees to market a product throughout western Europe.

In order to harmonize the process for registering

and regulating OTC products, the EU developed directives[12] relating to the registration, classification, labeling, and advertising of OTC medicines. Effective January 1, 1995, companies that wished to register a nonprescription medicine in more than one EU country had three options:

- **National Procedure:** Prepare separate applications for each country (until 1998 only).

- **Decentralized System:** Apply for registration in one country and, if approved, application was circulated to other member states. There was a specified process for resolving disputes, and final decision was legally binding for all member states.

- **Centralized System:** The applicant submitted one dossier to the European Medicines Evaluation Agency (EMEA). The EMEA coordinated the process, but evaluation of the dossier was done by the Committee for Proprietary

12. A directive was legally binding legislation passed by the European Union. Member states needed to put the directive into effect through national laws by a specified date.

Exhibit 24 ● Regulatory Differences by Country for R-to-OTC Candidates (*Continued*)

			Country				
France	*Germany*	*Italy*	*Netherlands*	*Spain*	*UK*	*Japan*	*US*
OTC	OTC	Rx[a]	OTC	Rx	OTC	OTC	OTC
OTC	Rx	OTC	Rx	OTC	OTC	OTC	OTC
OTC	OTC	OTC	OTC	OTC	OTC	OTC	OTC
OTC	OTC	OTC	OTC	Rx	OTC	OTC	OTC
(OTC)	OTC	OTC	OTC	OTC	OTC	(OTC)	OTC
OTC	OTC	Rx	OTC	Rx	OTC	Rx	(OTC)
Rx	Rx	Rx[a]	(OTC)	Rx	OTC	Rx[b]	OTC
(OTC)	Rx	OTC	Rx	Rx	OTC	(OTC)	OTC
Rx	OTC	Rx	Rx	Rx	OTC	Rx[b]	(OTC)
Rx	(OTC)	OTC	(OTC)	Rx	OTC	(OTC)	OTC
Rx	Rx	OTC	(OTC)	Rx	OTC	(OTC)	OTC

a. Previously OTC, but switched back to Rx status.

b. As of 1993.

Medicinal Products (CPMP). If approved, a single marketing authorization was granted, and it was valid for all member countries.

Reimbursement status was also subject to regulatory control. OTC producers determined whether it was in their strategic interest for the product to be reimbursed. If the product was approved for reimbursement, the product was subject to price controls and advertising restrictions. Products for easily self-diagnosed ailments, such as the common cold, rarely applied for reimbursement status.

A major difference from the U.S. process was that European regulatory restrictions went a step further and controlled the distribution and advertising activities of the products as well. Some countries were more stringent than others, with the United Kingdom and the Netherlands on the liberal end and France and Italy on the conservative side (refer to Exhibit 19). With harmonization efforts under way, these differences were expected to become less distinct.

Most OTCs had to be distributed in pharmacies owned by a licensed pharmacist. The only products that could be sold in the mass market were those that were considered general health and beauty aids such as cough drops, skin care, and general antiseptics.

The Japanese Experience

Japan imposed the tightest regulations of all the developed regions. The registration process was similar to other countries, except that in most cases the health authority did not accept western clinical trials. If a company wanted to register a product in Japan but the substance was not a registered prescription product, it had to first register the product as a prescription substance. The cost for a new product registration was approximately $5 million dollars and required about six years of surveillance as a prescription substance before it could be available OTC.

There were no advertising restrictions applied to different product classifications. However, OTC companies were not allowed to make references to medical endorsements or previous ethical use in public advertisements. Finally, some dosage forms were not allowed if they resembled a food product too closely.

Exhibit 25 ● OTC Registration/New Product Development Process

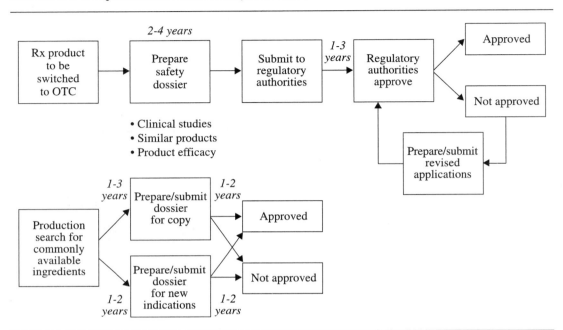

Previously banned delivery forms were chewable tablets, effervescent powders, and chewing gum.

CONCLUSION

As the strategy meeting drew to a close, Roland M. Jeannet spoke to the group:

In the past, most traditional OTC companies operated based on their individual core competencies and tried to apply these strengths to the regions and markets to which they were best suited. A pharma approach was applied to the OTC market and OTCs were often a by-product of the pharma business. As such, OTCs were not usually differentiated from their other businesses. For us at Ciba, we need to think about the evolving self-medication industry and reflect on whether these traditional practices still apply, and if not, what specific changes any firm needs to adopt if it wants to remain or become a world-class player in this industry.

Case 3

Note on Competitors in the OTC Drug Industry

INDUSTRY OVERVIEW

Over-the-counter (OTC) pharmaceutical products were consumer health care products that were approved and nonprescription bound. In 1995, this was a U.S.$51 billion industry and was growing at more than 7 percent per year. OTC products covered a broad array of consumer health products ranging from vitamins and minerals to self-diagnostic kits (refer to Exhibits 1 and 2.)

The industry was rapidly growing and changing as both ends of the spectrum expanded. On one end, the lines between consumer products such as beauty aids and food products were becoming fuzzier. On the other end, a growing number of prescription-bound products were being switched to over-the-counter products. This was in response to consumers looking for alternatives to the oftentimes higher-priced prescription drugs, governments trying to reduce health care expenditures, and pharmaceutical companies trying to expand the product life cycle of key products.

What started as a fragmented industry became a rapidly changing one with mergers and acquisitions (M&A) the order of the day. Many OTC companies used M&A to grow a product portfolio, gain econ-

●

This case was written by Kristi Menz and Shauna Pettit, MBA candidates at the F. W. Olin Graduate School of Business at Babson College, under the direction of Professor Jean-Pierre Jeannet. This case is to be used in conjunction with Cases 2 and 4. Copyright © 1996 by IMD—International Institute for Management Development, Lausanne, Switzerland. Not to be used or reproduced without written permission directly from IMD.

omies of scale, and boost their traditionally lower profit margins.[1]

COMPETITOR OVERVIEW

Strategies among OTC companies varied, but competitors could generally be grouped into one of the following categories: Global OTC, Global Pharma, Regional OTC, National OTC, Niche Player, and Pharmaceutical Only (see Exhibit 3).

Global OTC companies were those that generated the majority of their pharmaceutical sales from nonprescription products. Typically, these companies competed in a majority of the top market segments and geographic regions. Global OTCs generally offered products that were closer to being consumer products than to prescription pharmaceuticals.

The opposite of a Global OTC company was a Global Pharma company, whose products were oftentimes more technically-oriented and innovative. Prescription-bound pharmaceutical sales exceeded OTC sales for these companies. As with Global OTC companies, Global Pharma companies offered OTC products in a broad range of market segments and geographic regions.

The core strengths for a Regional OTC company lay in one particular geography, such as Europe or North America. A regional player usually chose to attack each geography on a country by country basis and did not generally market brands on a regional basis. This was less true for companies in North Amer-

---

1. An OTC company earned lower profits on average than a pharmaceutical company, since the former usually had a lower retail selling price for its products and spent money on consumer advertising (although in the United States, even prescription-bound drugs could be advertised to consumers.)

Exhibit 1 ● OTC Industry Market Segment Share and Growth

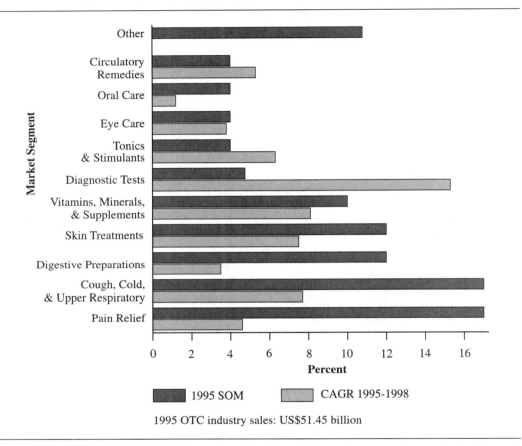

1995 OTC industry sales: US$51.45 billion

Source: OTC Review 1996, OTC Foresight 1995.

ica, since consumers in the United States and Canada shared many common attitudes.

National OTC companies realized the majority of their annual turnover in one country. The Japanese market, for example, spawned many companies that did not cross national borders with their products. In some cases, the intricacies of the individual country made it hard to apply the same principles elsewhere. This could be caused by peculiar government practices or consumer attitudes.

In contrast to companies with core competencies in a particular geography, Niche Players specialized in a specific nongeographical segment of the OTC industry. Some niche companies focused on a particular market segment such as eye care in the case of Bausch and Lomb or vitamins in the case of Pharmavite. Other niche companies, like Perrigo, followed a "me too" strategy and concentrated their efforts on private label versions of popular nonprescription products.

The final competitor category contained companies that chose not to directly compete in the OTC industry, but were important players due to their

Exhibit 2 ● 1995 Split of OTC Sales by Geography

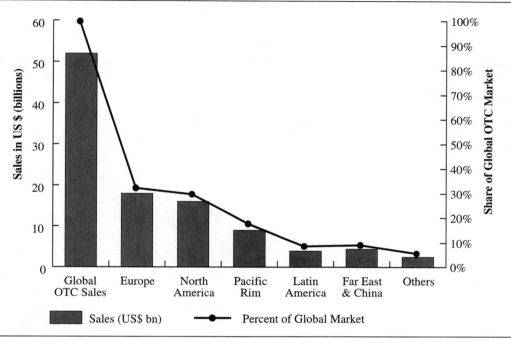

Source: OTC Review 1996

pipelines of potential Rx-to-OTC switches. Prescription Only companies generally signed licensing agreements and formed joint ventures to market Rx-to-OTC switches. Glaxo and Marion Merrell Dow both used this strategy and were significant suppliers of products to the OTC industry.

Exhibits 4 through 10 show the major players in these categories and their competive advantages in different makets, as discussed below.

COMPETITORS

Procter & Gamble

In 1995, the United States-based Procter & Gamble (P&G) reached sales of U.S.$33,434 million (Exhibit 11). Nonprescription sales accounted for just under 6 percent of that total, making it the fourth-largest OTC company in the world. Unlike some of its OTC competitors, P&G had no significant presence in the prescription pharmaceutical industry. P&G divided its operations into six categories: Laundry & Cleaning, Paper, Beauty Care, Food & Beverage, Health Care, and Corporate (refer to Exhibit 12). Most of its corporate sales came from North America and Europe, although it had a growing presence in Asia and Latin America (Exhibit 13). P&G employed 99,200 people worldwide.

The company entered the health care market in 1982, when it acquired Norwich Eaton and its OTC products, the most notable of which were Pepto-Bismol and Chloraseptic. Following this trend, Vicks and Clearasil were added to P&G's portfolio in 1985 through the purchase of Richardson-Vicks. Metamu-

Exhibit 3 ● Strategic Groupings of OTC Competitors

Global OTC	Global Pharma	Regional OTC	National OTC	Niche Player	Rx Only
Procter & Gamble	SmithKline Beecham	Rhône-Poulenc Rorer	Taisho	Pharmavite/ Otsuka	Glaxo Wellcome
Warner-Lambert	Bayer	Schering-Plough	Angelini	Perrigo	Merck
	American Home Products	Boots PLC	Takeda	Ross/Abbott Laboratories	Eli Lilly
	Roche	Boehringer Ingelheim	SS Pharmaceutical	Bausch and Lomb	Tanebe
	Johnson & Johnson		Sato Pharmaceutical	Seton	
	Bristol-Myers Squibb		Gehe	Thompson Medical	
	Sandoz		Kowa	Rexall	
	Ciba-Geigy		Klosterfrau	Allergan	
			Sanofi	Vitamex	
			Pierre Fabre	Boiron	
			Servier	Standard Homeopathic	
			Synthelabo	Boericke and Tafel	

cil, Blendax (a German oral hygiene product), and Noxzema were acquired in a similar fashion by the end of the 1980s.

P&G competed in all major market segments except vitamins, minerals, and supplements. Most of P&G's OTC sales came in the cough and cold and skin treatment segments through the Vicks, NyQuil, and Clearasil brands. It also had strong brands in the gastrointestinal segment in the United States with Metamucil and Pepto-Bismol (see Exhibit 14). In its domestic market, P&G entered the pain relief segment with Aleve in 1994 through a joint venture agreement with Syntex. It also announced an agreement with Cygnus Therapeutic to launch an OTC version of its smoking cessation skin patch. Neither of these joint venture agreements carried into any other geographies, however.

Part of P&G's success came from its ability to extend global brands such as Vicks and Clearasil into new products. For example, Vicks was a company name whose first product was a vaporub. When P&G purchased the company and its products, Vicks remained as an umbrella brand name. P&G expanded the Vicks line through new delivery systems such as liquid gel caps and other product segments such as cough drops. Clearasil had a similar success story. What started as only an acne treatment evolved into a full line of facial cleaning products.

P&G's product portfolio aimed at treating ailments that required little doctor intervention, such as cold and cough, acne treatment, and mild indigestion. Thus, P&G was able to focus its attention on what it did best: winning over retailers and consumers. P&G also concentrated on a value pricing strategy with many of its products. It relied on fast-moving consumer goods with low prices and high volumes for much of its turnover.

Geographically, P&G was dependent on its home

Exhibit 4 ● Competitive Positioning Map

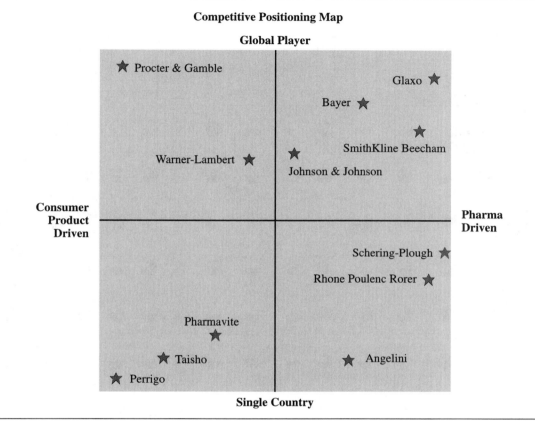

Competitive Positioning Map

Global Player

Procter & Gamble

Glaxo

Bayer

SmithKline Beecham

Warner-Lambert

Johnson & Johnson

Consumer Product Driven

Pharma Driven

Schering-Plough

Rhone Poulenc Rorer

Pharmavite

Taisho

Angelini

Perrigo

Single Country

market in the United States for 64 percent of self-medication sales (refer to Exhibit 14).[2] While Japan did not account for a great percentage of annual turnover, P&G was the largest overseas manufacturer there, with 1993 sales of U.S.$70 million. In the European market, self-medication sales were concentrated in Germany, France, and Italy. P&G's strategy for entering new markets was to first introduce fast-moving consumer goods that were not regulated, such

2. The total sales figure that this percentage was based upon does not include semi-ethicals in Europe.

as cleaning products and paper goods, and follow with OTCs.

Warner-Lambert

Warner-Lambert (W-L) was another strong U.S.-based competitor, with a 3 percent share of the world OTC market. W-L's 36,000 employees generated sales in 1995 of U.S.$7,040 million. Sales and earnings growth were positive from 1993–1995, but somewhat less stable in prior years (refer to Exhibit 15). The Consumer Health Care division accounted for nearly

Exhibit 5 ● Relative Competitive Position of OTC Competitors

Legend (top to bottom): ● Very Strong ◕ Strong ◑ Good ◔ Moderate ○ Weak

Company	Relationship with Retailers	Relationship with Healthcare Professionals	Willingness to Form Partnerships	Presence in Growth Segments/ Geographies	Presence in Key Market Segments	Rx-to OTC Switch Experience	Protection from Generics/ Private Labels	Consumer Brand Awareness	Innovation	Financial Position	Relationship with Pharma Industry	Rx-to-OTC Pipeline	Global Presence
Procter & Gamble	●	○	◑	◑	◔	◔	◑	●	◔	◑	◔	◔	●
Warner-Lambert	●	◑	●	◑	◑	◔	◑	◔	◑	◕	◕	◕	◑
Bayer	◑	◕	◑	◕	◕	◑	◑	◑	◑	◔	◑	○	◔
Johnson & Johnson	◑	●	◕	●	●	◑	◑	●	●	◔	◕	◕	◑
SmithKline Beecham	◑	●	◕	●	●	◔	◑	◑	◔	◕	●	●	◔
Rhone Poulenc Rorer	◔	●	◔	◕	◔	◑	●	◑	◔	◑	◑	○	◔
Schering-Plough	◑	●	◑	◑	◔	◑	◔	◑	●	◑	◔	◑	◔
Angelini	◔	N/A	◑	◔	○	◔	●	◔	○	○	◑	◔	○
Taisho	N/A	N/A	◑	◔	◔	◑	●	●	◔	◑	◑	◔	○
Perrigo	●	○	◔	●	●	○	N/A	○	○	◑	○	◔	○
Pharmavite	●	○	◔	◔	○	N/A	○	○	○	N/A	N/A	○	◔
Glaxo	N/A	●	●	◑	◔	N/A	◔	◔	◕	●	N/A	◕	●

Exhibit 6 ● Geographic and Market Segment Strength of OTC Competitors: *Overview*

	France	Germany	Italy	United Kingdom	United States	Japan	Latin America	Far East
PAIN RELIEF		J&J			P&G			
					J&J			
	Rhône			Rhône				
					SB		SB	SB
	Bayer	Bayer	Bayer	Bayer	Bayer	Bayer	Bayer	
						Taisho		
			Angelini					
					Perrigo			
COUGH/COLD	P&G	P&G	P&G	P&G	P&G			
	J&J	J&J		J&J	J&J			
	S-P		S-P	S-P	S-P			S-P
	W-L	W-L	W-L	W-L	W-L			W-L
	Rhône	Rhône	Rhône					
		SB	SB	SB	SB	SB		SB
		Bayer	Bayer		Bayer			
						Taisho		
					Perrigo			
DIGESTIVE	P&G				P&G	P&G		
	J&J	J&J		J&J	J&J			
					S-P			
	W-L	W-L			W-L			W-L
	Rhône	Rhône	Rhône	Rhône				
	SB			SB	SB			
		Bayer	Bayer	Bayer	Bayer		Bayer	
						Taisho		
			Angelini					
					Perrigo			
SKIN TREATMENT	P&G	P&G	P&G	P&G	P&G			
				J&J	J&J			
			S-P	S-P	S-P			
		W-L	W-L	W-L	W-L			W-L
				Rhône				
			SB	SB	SB			
					Bayer	Bayer		
						Taisho		
					Perrigo			
VITAMINS					J&J			
	Rhône	Rhône						
		SB		SB	SB			
			Bayer		Bayer			
						Taisho		
					Perrigo			
					Pharma	Pharma		

Exhibit 6 ● Geographic and Market Segment Strength of OTC Competitors: *Overview (Continued)*

	France	Germany	Italy	United Kingdom	United States	Japan	Latin America	Far East
DIAGNOSTICS					J&J W-L Bayer			
						Taisho		
TONICS	Rhône	Rhône						
						Taisho		
					Perrigo			
CIRCULATORY			W-L		W-L			
	Rhône	S-P						
				SB				
						Perrigo		
GENERAL PRESENCE						P&G		
			J&J					
						W-L	W-L	
	SB							
								Taisho
			Angelini					

half of the company's sales (refer to Exhibit 16) and the percentage was growing. W-L split itself geographically into the United States; Europe, Middle East and Africa; and Americas and Far East. Sales were relatively even between the segments, but the United States accounted for slightly more than the other regions at 43 percent (refer to Exhibit 16).

Even though W-L did have a pharmaceutical division, most of its products came through joint venture agreements with other companies.[3] In general, its prescription products focused on more chronic ailments such as angina and epilepsy, not on products that were conducive to OTC sales.

W-L's most notable joint venture agreement was with Glaxo Wellcome. Through this arrangement, W-L received the OTC marketing rights to two important

3. The most notable exception to this strategy was the Halls brand franchise, one of W-L's most successful brands.

products: Zovirax and Zantac 75. In the prescription world, Zovirax was a genital herpes treatment that also proved to be effective for the prevention and treatment of cold sores. In the United Kingdom and Germany, Zovirax was switched to OTC as a cold sore treatment. Glaxo Wellcome delayed the U.S. launch in an effort to get it approved as an OTC treatment for genital herpes. However, there was some doubt as to whether or not it was going to get FDA approval.

Zantac 75 was an H_2 antagonist, an often prescribed anti-ulcer medicine. The switch of H_2 antagonists received a lot of attention. By adding Zantac to its product mix, W-L was increasing its interest in the gastrointestinal market. Heavy competition existed from two products: SmithKline's Tagamet and Johnson & Johnson's Pepcid AC, both hitting the market before Zantac 75.

Cough and cold was W-L's dominant market

Exhibit 7 ● Geographic and Market Segment Strength of OTC Competitors: *Individual*

	France	Germany	Italy	United Kingdom	United States	Japan	Latin America	Far East
PROCTER & GAMBLE								
Pain relief					X			
Cough/cold	X	X	X	X	X			
Digestive	X				X	X		
Skin treatment	X	X	X	X	X			
Vitamins								
Diagnostics								
Tonics								
Circulatory								
General presence						X		
WARNER-LAMBERT								
Pain relief								
Cough/cold	X	X	X	X	X			X
Digestive	X	X			X			X
Skin treatment		X	X	X	X			X
Vitamins								
Diagnostics					X			
Tonics								
Circulatory			X		X			
General presence						X	X	
BAYER								
Pain relief	X	X	X	X	X	X	X	
Cough/cold		X	X		X			
Digestive		X	X	X	X		X	
Skin treatment					X	X		
Vitamins			X		X			
Diagnostics					X			
Tonics								
Circulatory								
General presence								
JOHNSON & JOHNSON								
Pain relief		X			X			
Cough/cold	X	X		X	X			
Digestive	X	X		X	X			
Skin treatment				X	X			
Vitamins					X			
Diagnostics					X			
Tonics								
Circulatory								
General presence			X					

Exhibit 7 ● Geographic and Market Segment Strength of OTC Competitors: *Individual (Continued)*

	France	Germany	Italy	United Kingdom	United States	Japan	Latin America	Far East
SMITHKLINE BEECHAM								
Pain relief					X		X	X
Cough/cold		X	X	X	X	X		X
Digestive	X			X	X			
Skin treatment			X	X	X			
Vitamins		X		X	X			
Diagnostics								
Tonics								
Circulatory				X				
General presence	X							
RHÔNE-POULENC RORER								
Pain relief	X			X				
Cough/cold	X	X	X					
Digestive	X	X	X	X				
Skin treatment				X				
Vitamins	X	X						
Diagnostics								
Tonics	X	X						
Circulatory	X							
General presence								
SCHERING-PLOUGH								
Pain relief								
Cough/cold	X		X	X	X			X
Digestive					X			
Skin treatment			X	X	X			
Vitamins								
Diagnostics								
Tonics								
Circulatory	X							
General presence								
ANGELINI								
Pain relief			X					
Cough/cold								
Digestive			X					
Skin treatment								
Vitamins								

Exhibit 7 ● Geographic and Market Segment Strength of OTC Competitors: *Individual* (*Continued*)

	France	Germany	Italy	United Kingdom	United States	Japan	Latin America	Far East
ANGELINI								
Diagnostics								
Tonics								
Circulatory								
General presence			X					
TAISHO								
Pain relief						X		
Cough/cold						X		
Digestive						X		
Skin treatment						X		
Vitamins						X		
Diagnostics						X		
Tonics						X		
Circulatory								
General presence								X
PERRIGO								
Pain relief					X			
Cough/cold					X			
Digestive					X			
Skin treatment					X			
Vitamins					X			
Diagnostics								
Tonics					X			
Circulatory					X			
General presence								
PHARMAVITE								
Pain relief								
Cough/cold								
Digestive								
Skin treatment								
Vitamins					X	X		
Diagnostics								
Tonics								
Circulatory								
General presence								

Exhibit 8 ● OTC Competitor Overview

	Procter & Gamble	Warner-Lambert	Bayer	Johnson & Johnson	SmithKline Beecham[d]
Home country	USA	USA	Germany	USA	UK
Type of company	Global OTC	Global OTC	Global Pharma	Global Pharma	Global Pharma
1995 corporate sales ($mn)	$33,434	$7,040	$31,110	$18,842	$11,077
Corporate profit margin	7.9%	10.5%	5.4%	12.8%	14.7%
Corporate ROE	25.0%	32.9%	13.1%	26.6%	58.3%
1995 # of employees	99,200	36,000	142,900	82,300	52,400
OTC divisional sales ($mn)[a]	$3,025	$3,293	$7,746	$5,831	$3,171
Div. operating profit	$360	$858	$1,273	$298	$526
Div. net assets[b]	$2,882	$1,759	$5,236	$4,334	$2,209
Div. RONA	12.5%	48.8%	24.3%	6.9%	23.8%
1995 est. global OTC sales ($mn)	$1,955	$1,540	$2,007	$3,550	$1,646
1995 U.S. OTC sales ($mn)	$702	$760	$662	$1,555	$602
1995 % TME of sales[c]	26.4%	17.2%	22.2%	38.2%	19.8%
World rank	4	6	3	1	5
World SOM	3.8%	3.0%	3.9%	6.9%	3.2%
USA rank	3	4	5	1	6
USA SOM	7.2%	5.8%	5.3%	14.3%	3.9%
Europe rank	—	—	2	—	3
Europe SOM	—	—	3.2%	—	3.0%
Japan rank	—	—	—	—	—
Japan SOM	—	—	—	—	—

n/a=not available.
a. Sales of the corporate division handling OTC sales.
b. Identifiable assets less capital expenditures and depreciation & amortization.
c. U.S. nonprescription drug advertising expenditures as a percentage of U.S. OTC sales.
d. 1994 figures instead of 1995.

segment, due to the success of the Halls brand of products (refer to Exhibit 17). Oral care and skin treatments were also important segments for the company. Lacking in the company's product portfolio was a pain relief product.

Within the self-medication sector, W-L derived 76 percent of its 1994 sales in the United States. Sales in Europe were far behind at 18 percent, and the rest of the world accounted for only 6 percent.[4] Thus, W-L was heavily dependent on its domestic market for its revenues and profits. Its major markets in Europe were the United Kingdom, Germany, and France, which accounted for 84 percent of sales in that region.

4. Does not include sales of semi-ethical products in Europe.

Rhône-Poulenc Rorer	Schering-Plough	Angelini[d]	Taisho	Perrigo	Pharmavite[d]	Glaxo
France	USA	Italy	Japan	USA	Japan	USA
Regional	Regional	National	National	Niche	Niche	Pharma Only
$5,142	$5,104	$173	Est $2,400	$717	Est $140	$11,247
6.9%	17.4%	0.3%	13.1%	6.2%	n/a	9.4%
15.1%	54.6%	0.8%	9.6%	13.0%	n/a	13.6%
28,000	20,100	750	4,816	4,410	650	52,419
$1,557	$633	$67	$1,605	$517	$140	$—
N/A	$154	n/a	n/a	n/a	n/a	$—
N/A	$373	n/a	n/a	n/a	n/a	$—
—	41.2%	—	—	—	—	—
$1,338	$545	$67	$1,605	$517	$140	$—
$—	$436	$—	$—	$517	$140	$—
—	12.2%	—	—	—	n/a	—
7	—	—	—	—	—	—
2.6%	—	—	—	—	—	—
—	9	—	—	—	—	—
—	2.8%	—	—	—	—	—
1	—	—	—	—	—	—
4.1%	—	—	—	—	—	—
—	—	—	1	—	—	—
—	—	—	19.2%	—	—	—

Bayer

The German corporation, Bayer, was a significant player in both the United States and Europe, holding the number five and number two positions in those respective markets. Bayer's 1995 corporate sales of about U.S.$31,110 million and OTC sales of U.S.$2,000 million ranked them as the third-largest OTC company worldwide. Bayer was the largest chemical conglomerate in the world, which explains the fact that almost half of the company's annual turnover came from chemical products (refer to Ex-

hibit 18). This made the company somewhat vulnerable to the cycles of the chemical industry, as can be seen by the variability in sales and profits (refer to Exhibit 19). In contrast, the Health Care division accounted for 51 percent of Bayer's profits while generating only 25 percent of sales. Not surprisingly, the bulk of Bayer's sales came from Europe, its home continent (refer to Exhibit 18).

In general, Bayer's product portfolio was old and lacked innovation. The company's strongest market segment was analgesics, with its Aspirin brand. As recently as 1994, Bayer recovered the use of its own

Exhibit 9 ● Common Size 1994 Income Statements: Parent Corporations

	Procter & Gamble	Warner-Lambert	Bayer	Johnson & Johnson	Smithkline Beecham
1994 Sales	100.0%	100.0%	100.0%	100.0%	100.0%
COGS	57.3%	33.6%	56.6%	33.7%	37.7%
Gross margin	42.7%	66.4%	43.4%	66.3%	62.3%
SG&A	30.9%	43.5%	26.4%	40.4%	41.1%
R&D		7.1%		8.1%	9.8%
Other			9.4%		
EBIT	11.8%	15.8%	7.6%	17.8%	11.4%
Interest	1.6%		-0.2%	0.5%	0.8%
Other	-0.8%	1.4%	0.2%	0.3%	-0.1%
EBT	11.0%	14.4%	7.6%	17.0%	10.7%
Taxes	3.7%	3.4%	3.0%	4.3%	8.8%
Profit margin	7.3%	11.0%	4.6%	12.7%	1.9%
DUPONT MODEL					
Financial Leverage	2.9	3.0	1.6	2.2	2.9
Asset Turnover	1.2	1.2	1.6	1.0	1.9
Profit Margin	7.3%	11.0%	4.6%	12.7%	1.9%
ROA	8.7%	12.5%	7.2%	12.8%	3.5%
ROE	25.0%	38.2%	11.5%	28.2%	10.4%

a. Used Otsuka numbers for Pharmavite since Pharmavite's were not available.

name and trademark in North America by purchasing it from Sterling Health. During World War II, the U.S. government confiscated Bayer's U.S. assets, causing Bayer to operate under the name of Miles in the United States.

The Alka Seltzer family performed well in both the cough and cold and digestive categories. Other strong Bayer brands included Mycelex 7, Phillips' Milk of Magnesia,[5] Campho-Phenique, and Flintstones vitamins. In addition, Bayer had significant presence in the emerging diagnostic market with its blood glucose self-test kits.

Within the Consumer Care division, Bayer's annual sales were split more evenly between geogra-

5. Originally a Sterling Health product.

phies. Europe still retained the lead with 36 percent, followed by North America with 33 percent, Latin America with 19 percent, and Asia Pacific with 12 percent. Most European business was generated in Germany, Spain, and Italy. Bayer showed its commitment to growing business in other parts of the world by building a manufacturing facility in Japan. In addition, its strong presence in Europe gave Bayer a strong foothold in the emerging eastern European markets.

Johnson & Johnson

Johnson & Johnson's (J&J) top rank in its home country, the United States, also made it the largest OTC company in the world. J&J had 1995 sales of U.S.$18,842 million, of which U.S.$3,550 million

Rhône-Poulenc Rorer	Schering-Plough	Angelini	Taisho	Perrigo	Otsuka[a] (Pharmavite)	Glaxo
100.0%	100.0%	100.0%	100.0%	100.0%	100.0%	100.0%
34.7%	20.0%	62.3%	28.0%	71.0%	56.5%	
65.3%	80.0%	37.7%	72.0%	29.0%	43.5%	100.0%
35.8%	38.7%	36.5%	14.2%	14.6%	35.5%	34.9%
13.5%	13.4%		8.9%	0.9%		15.2%
2.7%	0.8%		25.3%			17.8%
13.3%	27.1%	1.2%	23.6%	13.5%	8.0%	32.1%
1.0%		0.6%	-2.5%	0.5%	0.3%	-0.4%
0.9%					0.1%	
11.4%	27.1%	0.6%	26.1%	13.0%	7.6%	32.5%
3.2%	6.6%	0.3%	13.0%	4.8%	4.1%	9.5%
8.2%	20.5%	0.3%	13.1%	8.2%	3.6%	23.0%
2.2	2.8	2.0	1.3	1.6	1.9	1.5
1.0	1.1	1.2	0.6	1.4	1.5	1.1
8.2%	20.5%	0.3%	13.1%	8.2%	3.6%	23.0%
7.9%	21.3%	0.4%	7.4%	6.1%	5.2%	24.6%
17.4%	58.6%	0.8%	10.1%	18.5%	9.9%	36.9%

came from OTC products. Sales and profits enjoyed especially strong growth from 1994 to 1995 (refer to Exhibit 20). J&J's three divisions, Consumer, Pharmaceutical, and Professional, accounted for roughly one-third each of the corporation's sales. As with many other global competitors, J&J relied on the United States for critical mass, generating almost 50 percent of its sales in that market (refer to Exhibit 21).

With the exception of a joint venture agreement with Merck, J&J's primary means of growing its OTC portfolio was through innovative developments from its 150+ autonomous operating units. These units were decentralized such that it was easy to get rid of those that were unprofitable. J&J's main OTC operating units were McNeil Consumer Products in the United States and Janssen-Cilag in Europe.

Tylenol was the highest revenue generator in J&J's OTC portfolio. This was due to its great success in the United States, where Tylenol sales accounted for almost 36 percent of company turnover. The Tylenol brand franchise was particularly successful in leveraging its brand name in the pain relief segment to other segments such as cough and cold and pediatrics.

Besides the analgesics segment, J&J had significant presence in all key segments and played a strong role in growing new segments. For example, it competed in gastrointestinals, diagnostics, cough and cold, skin treatments, habit control, and wound care (refer to Exhibit 22). Mylanta brought in half of gastro-intestinal sales, with Imodium accounting for another third. Pepcid AC, an H_2 antagonist, was the rising star in the GI segment.

Exhibit 10 ● Main Product Offerings of OTC Companies

Company	Top Brands	Indication	Future Switches	Indication
P&G	Aleve	Pain relief	smoking cessation patch	Habit control
	Clearasil	Acne treatment		
	Lactulose	Laxative		
	Metamucil	Fiber laxative		
	NyQuil	Cough/cold		
	Pepto-Bismol	Stomach remedy		
	Vicks	Cough/cold		
W-L	Anusol	Hemorrhoid treatment	Zovirax (in the US)	Genital herpes treatment
	Benadryl	Allergy relief & cold/flu		
	Caladryl	Anti-itch treatment		
	e.p.t.	Pregnancy test		
	Halls	Cough/cold		
	Listerine	Mouthwash		
	Neosporin	Topical antibiotic		
	Rolaids	Antacid		
	Sudafed	Cold/flu & sinus relief		
	Zantac	Antacid		
Bayer	Alka-Seltzer	Cough/cold, antacid	bone resorption and formation	Diagnostic kits
	Aspirin	Pain relief		
	Bactine	Antiseptic		
	Bayer Select	Pain relief		
	Campho-Phenique	Antiseptic		
	Flintstones	Multivitamin		
	Midol	Pain relief		
	Milk of Magnesia	Laxative		
	Mycelex	Vaginal yeast infection		
	One-A-Day	Multivitamin		
	Stri-Dex	Acne treatment		
J&J	Children's Motrin	Pain relief	Confide	HIV Test Kit
	Fact Plus	Pregnancy test	Hismanal	Allergy relief
	Imodium	Antidiarrheal	Nizoral	Dandruff shampoo
	Micatin	Athlete's foot	Renova	Protocamage
	Monistat 7	Vaginal yeast infection	Retin-A	Acne treatment
	Mylanta	Antacid	Spectazole	Athlete's foot
	Nicotrol	Habit control		
	One Touch	Glucometer test		
	Pepcid AC	Antacid		
	Tylenol	Pain relief, cough/cold		

Exhibit 10 ● Main Product Offerings of OTC Companies (*Continued*)

Company	Top Brands	Indication	Future Switches	Indication
SmithKline	Citrucel	Fiber laxative	Bactroban	Topical antibiotic
	Contac	Cough/cold	Nicoderm	Habit control
	Ecotrin	Pain relief	Relafen	Pain relief
	Gaviscon	Antacid	Seldane	Allergy relief
	Geritol	Dietary supplement		
	Nicorette	Habit control		
	Oxy	Acne treatment		
	Panadol	Pain relief		
	Sucrets	Cough/cold		
	Tagamet	Antacid		
	Tums	Antacid		
Rhône	Anthisan	Insect bites and stings		
	Brol-eze	Eye drops		
	Bronchicum	Cough/cold		
	Doliprane	Pain relief		
	Maalox (Europe)	Antacid		
	Oruvail	Topical pain relief		
	Resiston One	Allergy remedy		
Schering	Afrin	Cough/cold	Carafate	Antiulcerent
	Chlor-Trimeton	Cough/cold	Claritin	Allergy relief
	Correctol	Laxative	Proventil	Asthma treatment
	Drixoral	Cough/cold		
	Gyne-Lotrimin	Vaginal yeast infection		
	Lotrimin	Athlete's foot		
	Polaramin	Allergy relief		
	Tinactin	Athlete's foot		
Angelini	Moment	Pain relief		
	Tachipinna	Pain relief		
	Tantum Verde	Sore throat relief		
Taisho	Dermarin	Athlete's foot	Minoxidil	Hair loss
	Kanpo Ichoyaku	Stomach remedy	Zantac	Antacid
	Lipovitan	Bottled nutritive drinks		
	Pabron	Cough/cold		
	Preser	Antihemorrhoidal		
Perrigo	N/A			
Pharmavite	Nature Made	Vitamin		
	Nature's Resource	Herbal remedy		
Glaxo			Beconase	Allergy treatment
			Flonase	Allergy treatment
			Zovirax (in the US)	Genital herpes treatment

Exhibit 11 ● Procter & Gamble Sales and Earnings Growth

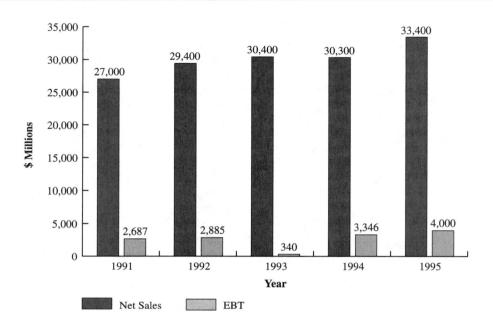

Source: Company reports.

Closely aligning itself with the medical community, J&J tried to create a feeling of reassurance with its self-medicating customers. For example, the slogan for Tylenol had always been "Hospitals use it," and with Mylanta, the slogan was ". . . my doctor said 'Mylanta.'" In addition, J&J had an entire sales force in the United States that was dedicated to health care professionals.

SmithKline Beecham

SmithKline Beecham (SB), head-quartered in the United Kingdom, generated 1995 sales of U.S. $11,077 million. SB was ranked number five worldwide for its OTC sales, number four in Europe, and number six in the United States. Before tax earnings showed solid growth in 1995, rebounding from lower-than-usual profits in 1994 (refer to Exhibit 23). The company was

organized into three divisions: Pharmaceuticals, Consumer Health, and Clinical Laboratories. Pharmaceuticals was the highest revenue-generating division, accounting for almost 60 percent of 1995 sales. Consumer Health, which contained mostly OTC products, accounted for 29 percent of total sales (refer to Exhibit 24). While SB as a corporation derived almost half of its sales from the United States, OTCs were more evenly divided among geographic regions (Refer to Exhibit 25).

SB, in its effort to be a truly global company, participated in numerous marker segments. It had a strong presence in gastrointestinals with its Tums and Gaviscon[6] products. Tums had a 45 percent share of the United States antacid market. In skin care, SB's

---

6. Gaviscon was marketed by SmithKline in the US only. Reckitt & Coleman sold it in Europe.

Exhibit 12 ● Procter & Gamble 1995 Sales Breakdowns by Geography and Activity

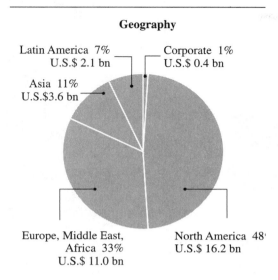

Geography

Latin America 7%
U.S.$ 2.1 bn

Corporate 1%
U.S.$ 0.4 bn

Asia 11%
U.S.$3.6 bn

Europe, Middle East,
Africa 33%
U.S.$ 11.0 bn

North America 48ᵃ
U.S.$ 16.2 bn

Total Sales in U.S.$ 33.43 billion

a. Includes OTC sales.

Source: Company reports.

Oxy ranked only behind Clearasil in the United States. Contac, for coughs and colds, had a truly global reach and was particularly strong in Japan and China. Geritol was the company's main product in the dietary supplements category. SB entered the analgesic market with its purchase of Sterling Healthcare, who brought along the Panadol brand.

SB was among the first to market with two newsworthy products: Tagamet, an H_2 antagonist, and Nicorette, a smoking cessation aid.[7] Both technologies were expected to grow their market segments, but SB faced stiff competition from other OTC competitors.

SB grew its OTC portfolio through acquisition of other companies, joint ventures with pharmaceutical companies such as Marion Merrell Dow, and Rx-to-

7. Nicorette was first to market for SB in the U.S. market only. It was licensed from Pharmacia & Upjohn, who marketed the product outside the U.S.

Activity

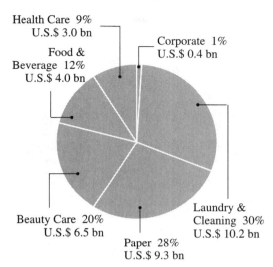

Health Care 9%
U.S.$ 3.0 bn

Food &
Beverage 12%
U.S.$ 4.0 bn

Corporate 1%
U.S.$ 0.4 bn

Beauty Care 20%
U.S.$ 6.5 bn

Paper 28%
U.S.$ 9.3 bn

Laundry &
Cleaning 30%
U.S.$ 10.2 bn

Total Sales in U.S.$ 33.44 billion

Exhibit 13 ● Split of Procter & Gamble's Self-Medication Sales, 1992–1993

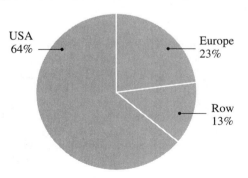

**Procter & Gamble
Split of Global Self-Medication Sales, 1992-1993**

USA
64%

Europe
23%

Row
13%

Source: James Dudley International Ltd. Trade Estimates 1996; © *James Dudley Management.*

Exhibit 14 ● Procter & Gamble's Top 5 OTC Brands (U.S. Sales)

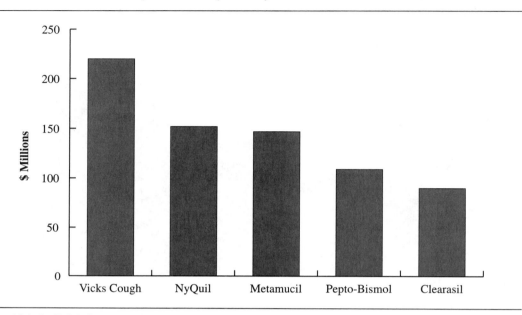

Source: Nicholas Hall & Company estimates.

OTC switches from its own pharmaceutical division. SB closely aligned itself with managed care organizations in the United States for both its pharmaceutical and OTC divisions. SB's goal was to position its products, particularly Nicorette, as wellness and prevention tools for managed care organizations.

Rhône-Poulenc Rorer

Rhône-Poulenc Rorer (RPR) was the leading OTC company in Europe, commanding a 4.1 percent share of the market in 1995. The French company employed 22,100 people who generated U.S.$5,142 million in sales. Around 26 percent of those sales were self-medication, making RPR the seventh-ranked OTC company in the world. Similar to Bayer, RPR was dependent upon the cyclical chemical industry for much of its sales, which caused its sales and earnings to fluctuate from one year to the next (refer to Exhibit 26). RPR's health sector accounted for around 37 percent of sales and consisted of human pharmaceuticals,

veterinary pharmaceuticals, and animal nutrition. Thirty-five percent of the company's overall sales came from France and another 23 percent from the rest of Europe (refer to Exhibit 27).

RPR had many joint venture agreements within its pharmaceutical operations; however, the OTC portfolio was built up mostly by acquisition. Furthermore, even though the type of research and products coming through its pharmaceutical division was revolutionary, RPR's Rx-to-OTC pipeline was empty.

RPR's key market segments were cough and cold, pain relief, and gastrointestinals. It also had strengths in vitamins and tonics (refer to Exhibit 28). The Maalox line was a particularly strong global brand for the company, except in the United States. RPR no longer controlled Maalox in that market since it sold its North American OTC business to Ciba at the end of 1994. Within France, Germany, and the other European countries, RPR approached each country individually. As a result, the leading brands in each country differed dramatically, with the exception of

Exhibit 15 ● Warner-Lambert Sales and Earnings Growth

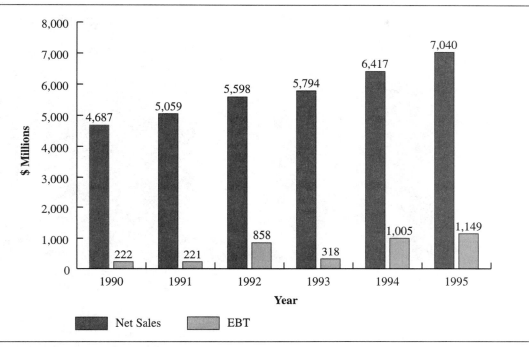

Source: Company reports.

Maalox. For example, one of RPR's most successful products was its analgesic, Doliprane. However, this product was only a top seller in France. Likewise, the innovative Oruvail, a gel-based topical analgesic, was launched only in the United Kingdom.

In the self-medication sector, RPR was even more reliant on France for its sales. Sixty percent of its European self-medication sales came from that market and another 25 percent from Germany. The North American OTC business contributed 35 percent of annual turnover before it was divested. That segment was mostly dependent upon Maalox, whose sales were consistently falling over time. In an attempt to become less reliant on France and Germany, RPR acquired the United Kingdom pharmaceutical company, Fisons, in 1995. Fisons brought with it mostly prescription-bound products, especially in the

asthma category, but also a couple of OTC hay fever remedies.

Schering-Plough

Schering-Plough (S-P) generated about 10 percent of its overall corporate sales of U.S.$5,104 million with OTC products.[8] This was enough to rank them number nine in the United States, but S-P did not make the top ten in any other market. The OTC division's share of the overall corporate sales fell from 7 percent in 1993 down to 5 percent in 1995. S-P had one of the highest earnings before taxes of the companies stud-

8. The OTC division only accounted for 5 percent of sales. However, some OTC products were accounted for in the foot care and sun care divisions.

Exhibit 16 ● Warner-Lambert Sales Breakdowns by Geography and Activity, 1995

Geography

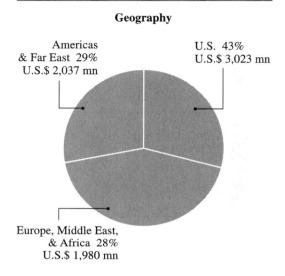

Americas & Far East 29%
U.S.$ 2,037 mn

U.S. 43%
U.S.$ 3,023 mn

Europe, Middle East, & Africa 28%
U.S.$ 1,980 mn

Total Sales in U.S.$ 7,040 million

*Includes OTC sales, shaving products, and pet care products.
Source: Company reports.

Activity

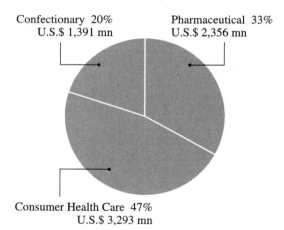

Confectionary 20%
U.S.$ 1,391 mn

Pharmaceutical 33%
U.S.$ 2,356 mn

Consumer Health Care 47%
U.S.$ 3,293 mn

Total Sales in U.S.$ 7,040 million

Exhibit 17 ● Warner-Lambert OTC Sales by Category and Brand, 1994*

Warner Lambert OTC Sales by Category, 1994* (RSP)

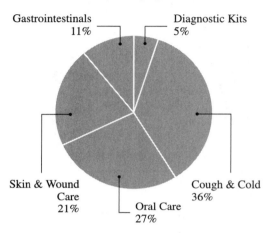

Gastrointestinals 11%

Diagnostic Kits 5%

Skin & Wound Care 21%

Oral Care 27%

Cough & Cold 36%

* Including Warner Wellcome brands

Source: UPDATE U.S.A. based on trade estimates.

Warner Lambert Cough & Cold Sales by Brand, 1994* (RSP)

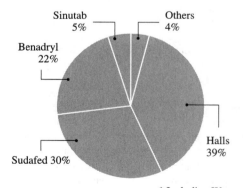

Sinutab 5%

Others 4%

Benadryl 22%

Sudafed 30%

Halls 39%

* Including Warner Wellcome brands

Warner Lambert
Skin & Wound Care Sales by Brand, 1994* (RSP)

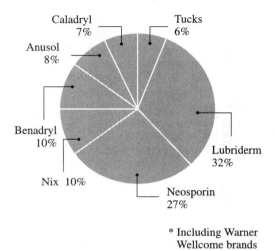

* Including Warner
Wellcome brands

Exhibit 18 ● Bayer Group Sale Breakdowns by
Geography and Activity, 1995

Activity

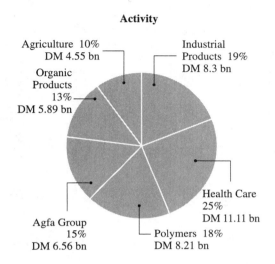

Total Sales in DM 44.6 billion

*Includes OTCs, diagnostics, pharmaceuticals.

Source: Company reports; *Nonprescription Drugs USA 1995.*

Geography

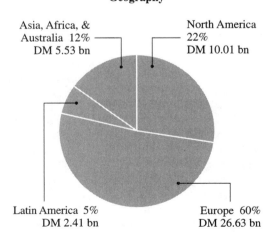

Total Sales in DM 44.6 billion

ied (refer to Exhibit 29). S-P generated 55 percent of its sales in the United States, followed by 25 percent in Europe, the Middle East, and Africa (refer to Exhibit 30).

In the OTC industry, S-P concentrated in a few selected product markets: skin treatments, cough and cold, and gastrointestinals. Most of the products in its OTC portfolio were the result of switches. Of eight successful switches in the United States between 1951 and 1991 (refer to Exhibit 31) seven went on to become top-selling brands. Skin treatments were its top category in the United States. S-P held the top two spots in antifungals with Lotrimin and Tinactin. Afrin, Drixoral, and Chlor-Trimeton were S-P's top products in cough and cold. Correctol rounded out the top products in the gastrointestinals market in the United States. Europe was a much smaller OTC market for S-P, generating only 5 percent of sales, com-

Exhibit 19 ● Bayer Group Sales & Earnings Growth

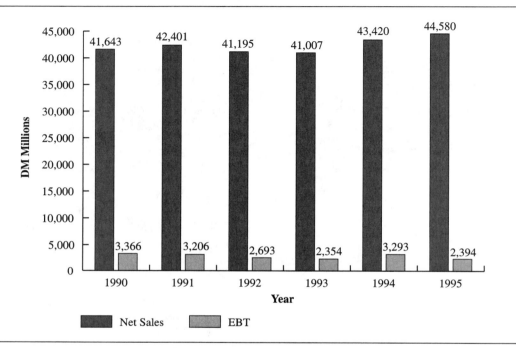

Source: company reports.

pared to the United States' 80 percent. Allergy and hay fever remedies were the strongest products for S-P in that region (refer to Exhibit 31).

S-P held the patent for Clarityn, the number one prescription for allergies. The company had already switched this product to OTC status in the United Kingdom and was gearing up for a U.S. switch with a consumer advertising campaign.

Two of S-P's consumer divisions, foot care and sun care, had OTC products in its mix. S-P was able to create several OTC products by leveraging the brand name of its two biggest franchises: Dr. Scholl's and Coppertone.

Angelini

Angelini, an Italian pharmaceutical company, generated 1994 sales of about U.S.$174 million. Over one-

third of the company's sales came from OTCs, making Angelini the third-largest OTC company in its domestic market. This was also enough to rank them first among the local players in Europe in 1994. Angelini was mostly an Italian company, although two wholly owned subsidiaries, one in Spain and one in Venezuela, generated U.S.$16–18 million and U.S.$14–16 million of pharmaceutical sales in their respective countries. The four divisions of the company included, Dispecial (ethicals), Area "C" (OTC, hospital, and veterinary). Pharma International (export), and Materie Prime (fine chemicals). Angelini had negative sales and earnings growth from 1991–1993, but began to rebound in 1994 (refer to Exhibit 32).

Pain relief was Angelini's biggest market segment (refer to Exhibit 33). Two analgesic products, Moment and Tachipirina, accounted for a majority of sales in this category. In fact. Tachipirina was a top-

Exhibit 20 ● Johnson & Johnson Sales and Earnings Growth

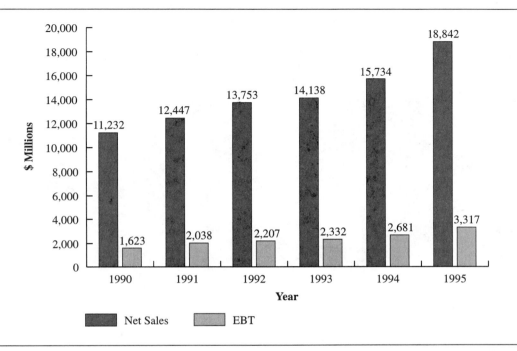

Source: Company reports.

selling product in the Italian OTC industry. It shared the second-place position with Halls (by W-L) in 1994. Moment ranked fourth in 1994. The throat preparation, Tantum Verde, generated the majority of sales in Angelini's second-biggest category, oral care. Angelini also competed in the gynecological segment with another Tantum product, Tantum Rosa P.

In Italy, the pharmaceutical market was changing rapidly. For example, pressures from the government to reduce health care expenditures and changing consumer attitudes enabled OTC companies to expand. Angelini was a well-known Italian company and had a strong foundation in its home country.

An example of how Angelini was able to leverage its nationally known name happened with the launch of Moment. There was a battle in the analgesics market between Moment and the British company Boots' Nurofen. Being the home country paid

off for Angelini as it was able to ward off the market penetration of Nurofen to take the number two spot in the Analgesics market behind Bayer's Aspirin.

Taisho

Japan's number one OTC company, Taisho, generated 1995 sales of approximately U.S.$2,400 million. Exhibit 34 shows Taisho's steady sales growth from 1990–1994. Roughly two-thirds of its sales were generated from OTC products (refer to Exhibit 35). The remaining sales came primarily from other pharmaceuticals (25 percent) and consumer products (5 percent). The main market segments for Taisho were cough and cold, gastrointestinals, pain relief, diagnostics, skin treatments, and tonics. Taisho had a strong OTC Drug Research Division and planned to diversify into other OTC product segments in the future. While Japan was

Exhibit 21 ● Johnson & Johnson Sales Breakdowns by Geography and Activity, 1995

Exhibit 22 ● Johnson & Johnson U.S. OTC Sales by Category and Brand, 1994–1995

Geography

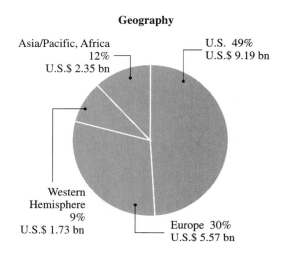

Asia/Pacific, Africa
12%
U.S.$ 2.35 bn

U.S. 49%
U.S.$ 9.19 bn

Western Hemisphere
9%
U.S.$ 1.73 bn

Europe 30%
U.S.$ 5.57 bn

Total Sales in U.S.$ 18.84 billion

Activity

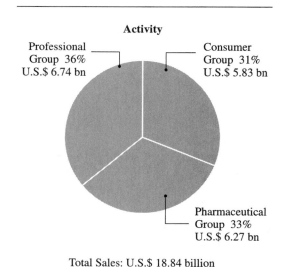

Professional Group 36%
U.S.$ 6.74 bn

Consumer Group 31%
U.S.$ 5.83 bn

Pharmaceutical Group 33%
U.S.$ 6.27 bn

Total Sales: U.S.$ 18.84 billion

*Includes OTCs and personal care products.
Source: Company reports.

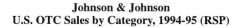
**Johnson & Johnson
U.S. OTC Sales by Category, 1994-95 (RSP)**

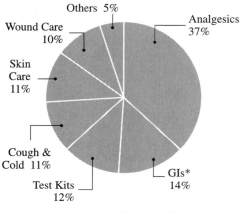

Others 5%

Wound Care
10%

Skin Care
11%

Cough & Cold 11%

Test Kits
12%

Analgesics
37%

GIs*
14%

* Includes first few months of Pepcid AC sales

Source: UPDATE U*S*A based on Towne-Oller data from 1994–1995.

**Johnson & Johnson
GI Portfolio Shares, 1995 (RSP)**

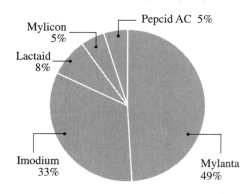

Mylicon
5%

Lactaid
8%

Pepcid AC 5%

Imodium
33%

Mylanta
49%

Source: Based on Towne-Aller food and drugstore tracking service, 12 months to 7/95.

Exhibit 23 ● SmithKline Beecham Sales and Earnings Growth

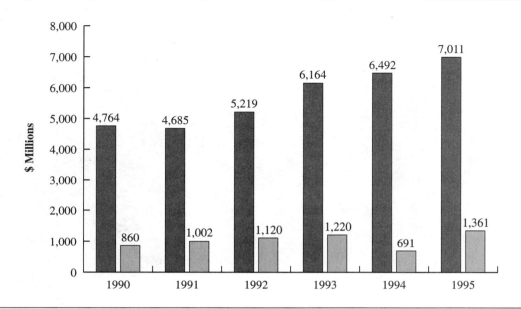

Source: Company reports.

its main geographic market, it also had sales in the Far East, Latin America, and the United States.

Almost half of Taisho's self-medication sales came from the Lipovitan line of mini-drinks. In fact, one particular product, Lipovitan D, accounted for almost 7 percent of sales in the entire Japanese OTC market. Taisho had the top or one of the top products in all categories in which it competed. Pabron, a cough and cold remedy, was another strong product for the company. Taisho was a leader in Rx-to-OTC switching in Japan, having done over eighteen switches in its history. Most of the switches were the result of agreements with other companies. Future possible switch ventures included the H_2 antagonist Zantac and a minoxidil product for hair loss treatment.

Perrigo

Perrigo was the leading private label manufacturer of nonprescription drugs in the United States. Sales in

1995 reached U.S.$717 million. Sales and profit growth were historically solid, although earnings dipped a bit in 1995 (refer to Exhibit 36). Unlike the other competitors profiled previously, Perrigo did not generate any sales in the prescription sector. That, coupled with the fact that its products could not command a premium price for being national brands, meant lower gross margins for the company. Still, Perrigo saved immensely on R&D and selling costs, which made its bottom line competitive with other industry players. Its sales were split between OTC, personal care, and vitamins (refer to Exhibit 37). Perrigo stuck to its core competency of selling its products in the U.S. market.

Perrigo's main products were in the analgesics, cough and cold, gastrointestinals, skin treatments, and vitamins markets, although it had a presence in almost every category (refer to Exhibit 38). Access to new products depended on whether or not companies still had a patent or if it had been granted an exclusivity by the FDA. In some cases Perrigo was offered licensing

Exhibit 24 ● SmithKline Beecham Sales Breakdowns by Geography and Activity, 1995

Exhibit 25 ● SB/Sterling OTC Sales by Region, 1993

Geography

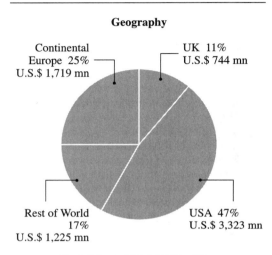

Total Sales in U.S.$ 7,011 million

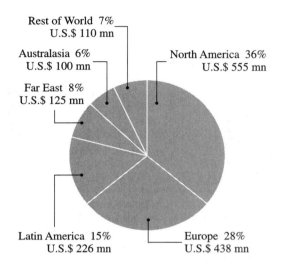

Source: Nicholas Hall & Co. estimates.

Activity

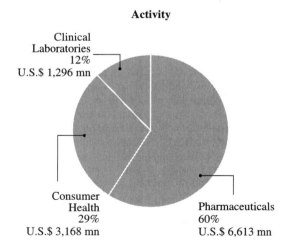

Total Sales in U.S.$ 11,077 million

*Includes OTCs, nutritional health care, and oral health care.
Source: Company reports; *Nonprescription Drugs USA 1995.*

arrangements from other pharmaceutical companies. A good example of this was the marketing agreement Perrigo had with Sandoz to market a private-label version of Tavist and the future promise to market Aleve in 1997.

In the United States, private labels were taking more and more market share away from branded products. This was in part due to the increased education of consumers about health care. In 1994, U.S. private label OTCs grew 10.2 percent over the previous year, compared to only 3.4 percent growth for the overall OTC industry. Private labels accounted for 18.2 percent of all OTC sales, up from 16.8 percent in 1993. This trend was expected to continue.

Pharmavite

Pharmavite was a wholly owned subsidiary of Otsuka America, which was, in turn, a wholly owned sub-

Exhibit 26 ● Rhône-Poulenc Rorer Sales and Earnings Growth

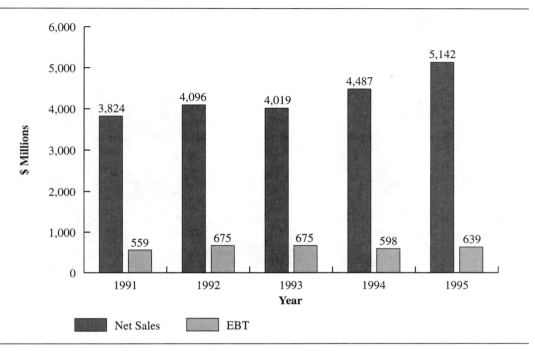

Source: Company reports.

sidiary of Otsuka Pharmaceutical of Japan. It was acquired by Otsuka in 1989. Estimated 1994 sales of U.S.$140 million made it the smallest of the competitors analyzed. Roughly 96 percent of the company's sales came from vitamins and minerals, with personal care products making up the difference. The United States was Pharmavite's primary market, although through the parent corporation, access to Japan and other markets was possible.

Nature Made was Pharmavite's most-well-known product line, accounting for 10–12 percent of company turnover in 1994. Nature Made was the leading brand in most individual vitamin categories in the United States, and was also sold in Japan. Pharmavite introduced a line of homeopathic products in May 1994 called Nature's Resource. The herbal line had U.S.$3.6 million in sales during its first year. In addi-

tion to its own lines, Pharmavite manufactured some private label products for other companies.

Pharmavite's strategy was to develop a strong relationship with retailers and support it with magazine advertising. The company would go into retail outlets and set up full displays and train the sales forces. Traceable media expenditures in 1993 were $3.1 million, or roughly 2 percent of total OTC sales. This was a much lower figure than for other companies (e.g., P&G at 26.4 percent in 1995). However, the average for the vitamins, minerals, and nutritional supplements market segment in the United States was only 3.5 percent in 1993. Thus, Pharmavite was only a little below average. Advertising and promotional spending in the category was dominated by big brands such as Centrum (American Home Products) and One-A-Day (Bayer).

Exhibit 27 ● Rhône-Poulenc Rorer Sales Breakdowns by Geography and Activity, 1995

Geography

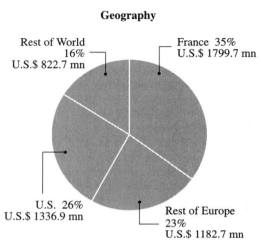

Rest of World
16%
U.S.$ 822.7 mn

France 35%
U.S.$ 1799.7 mn

U.S. 26%
U.S.$ 1336.9 mn

Rest of Europe
23%
U.S.$ 1182.7 mn

Total Sales in U.S.$ 5,142 million

Source: Datamonitor, Company report.

Activity

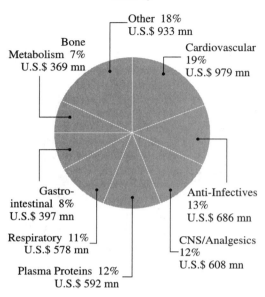

Other 18%
U.S.$ 933 mn

Bone
Metabolism 7%
U.S.$ 369 mn

Cardiovascular
19%
U.S.$ 979 mn

Anti-Infectives
13%
U.S.$ 686 mn

Gastro-
intestinal 8%
U.S.$ 397 mn

CNS/Analgesics
12%
U.S.$ 608 mn

Respiratory 11%
U.S.$ 578 mn

Plasma Proteins 12%
U.S.$ 592 mn

Total Sales in U.S.$ 5,142 million

Glaxo Wellcome

Glaxo Wellcome (Glaxo) was not an OTC company in the traditional sense of the word; however, it had strong ties to the OTC industry. Sales in 1995 were U.S.$11,264 million, mostly generated by pharmaceutical products. Glaxo used joint ventures and licensing agreements to market its products in the OTC market. Due to its prescription product portfolio, Glaxo had the highest profit margin of any of the competitors (refer to Exhibit 39). The company's sales were relatively evenly split between the United States, Europe, and the rest of the world (refer to Exhibit 40). Glaxo reinforced its relationship with Warner-Lambert by purchasing Wellcome in 1995. Warner-Lambert already had a joint venture with Wellcome (Warner-Welcome) dating back to 1993. Glaxo used this relationship to market its Rx-to-OTC switches.

Gastrointestinals played a major role in annual turnover, generating 43 percent of corporate-wide sales in 1994 (refer to Exhibit 40). Zantac was Glaxo's main product in this segment, and a global switch to

OTC was in process. The cold sore treatment, Zovirax, had much OTC potential in the skin treatment segment, although it was only available OTC in Europe. Regulators in the United States had not approved it for sale in their nonprescription market. Beconase, which was an allergy remedy, was launched in Europe, but had not hit the U.S. market yet. It was not expected to be introduced in the United States until the patent neared expiration in 1999.

Glaxo decided to focus on its core competencies: bringing new drugs through the pharmaceutical process and selling them to professionals. As a result, the company relied on relationships with other companies for both development and OTC marketing. Unlike many of its competitors, Glaxo resisted the merger craze in the pharmaceutical industry for many years. Glaxo's deviation from this policy to purchase Wellcome was an effort to protect its competitive position through improved synergies and clout with customers. Glaxo was the number one pharmaceutical company in the world.

Exhibit 28 ● RPR's Leading European OTC Brands, 1994–1995

Country	Category	Brand	Rank	% share	Market ($mn)
France	Internal analgesics	Doliprane	1	25	260
	Sore throat pastilles	Solutricine	3	14	72
	Indigestion remedies	Maalox	4	9	117
	Vitamin C	Vitascorbol	3	18	21
	Antiseptics/disinfectants (pharmacy)	Hexomédine	1	10	119
	Hay fever remedies	Phénergan	5	7	6
		Théralène Sirop	7	6	
Germany	Cold remedies	Contramutan	4	6	52
	Cough remedies	Bronchicum	1	8	156
	Indigestion remedies	Maaloxan	2	19	57
	Tonics	Biovital	2	19	74
	Garlic	Ilja Rogoff	2	23	89
Italy	Chest rubs & inhalants	Calyptol Inalante	2	22	8
	Varicose vein remedies	Essaven gel	2	35	8
	Topical antihistamines	Calmogel	4	9	11
Netherlands	Cough remedies (syrups)	Bronchicum	2	16	13
	Indigestion remedies	Maalox	2	10	7
Spain	Antacids	Maalox Concentrado	6	8	18
United Kingdom	Topical analgesics	Oruvail Gel	5	6	21
	Antidiarrheals/ORT	Dioralyte	1	70	5
	Insect bites & stings	Anthisan	1	60	2
	SCG eye drops	Brol-eze	1	32	2
		Opticrom	2	31	

Source: OTC News based on trade estimates (MSP).

Exhibit 29 ● Schering-Plough Sales and Earnings Growth

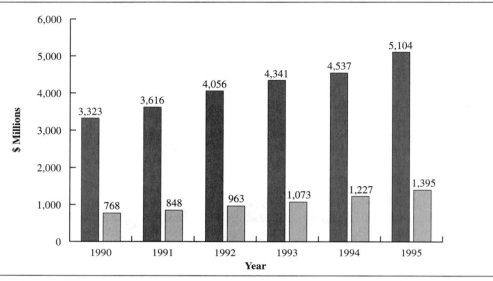

Source: Annual report, 1995.

Exhibit 30 ● Shering Plough Sales Breakdowns by Geography and Activity, 1995

Geography

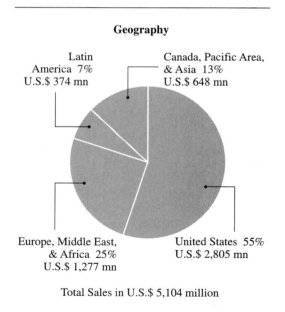

Latin America 7%
U.S.$ 374 mn

Canada, Pacific Area, & Asia 13%
U.S.$ 648 mn

Europe, Middle East, & Africa 25%
U.S.$ 1,277 mn

United States 55%
U.S.$ 2,805 mn

Total Sales in U.S.$ 5,104 million

Source: S-P Annual Report, 1995.

Activity

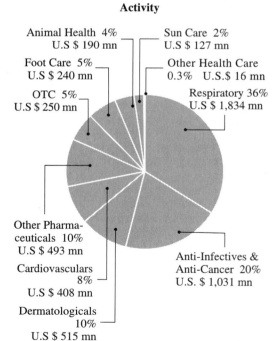

Animal Health 4%
U.S $ 190 mn

Sun Care 2%
U.S $ 127 mn

Foot Care 5%
U.S.$ 240 mn

Other Health Care 0.3%　U.S.$ 16 mn

OTC 5%
U.S $ 250 mn

Respiratory 36%
U.S $ 1,834 mn

Other Pharma-ceuticals 10%
U.S $ 493 mn

Cardiovasculars 8%
U.S $ 408 mn

Dermatologicals 10%
U.S $ 515 mn

Anti-Infectives & Anti-Cancer 20%
U.S. $ 1,031 mn

Total Sales in U.S.$ 5,104 million

Exhibit 31 ● Schering-Plough U.S. and European Brands

U.S. Rx-to-OTC Switches, 1951–1991

Brand	Category	Year
Coricidin	Cough & cold	1951
Tinactin	Topical antifungals	1971
Afrin	Nasal decongestants	1976
Chlor-Trimeton	Anti-allergy	1976
Drixoral	Cough & cold	1982
Lotrimin AF	Topical antifungals	1989
Gyne-Lotrimin	Vaginal thrush treatments	1990
DuoFilm	Wart treatments	1991

Source: Schering-Plough.

Leading European OTC Brands, 1994

Country	Category	Brand	Rank	% Share	Market ($mn)
France	Hay fever remedies	Polaramine	1	30	6
Italy	Topical antihistamines	Polaramin	1	35	10
	Hay fever remedies	Polaramin	1	57	4
	Antifungals	Tinaderm	4	19	1
Portugal	Cold remedies	Antigripe Asclepi	1	30	4
	Nasal decongestants	Constipal	4	9	5
Spain	Cold & flu remedies	Desenfriol	3	6	32
	Nasal decongestants	Respir	6	9	11
	Anti-itching products	Polaramine	4	7	1
	Antifungals	Tinaderm	3	3	2
United Kingdom	Hay fever remedies	Clarityn	5	8	12
	Athlete's foot treatments	Tinaderm	5	4	6

Source: OTC News based on trade estimates (MSP).

Exhibit 32 ● Angelini Sales and Earnings Growth

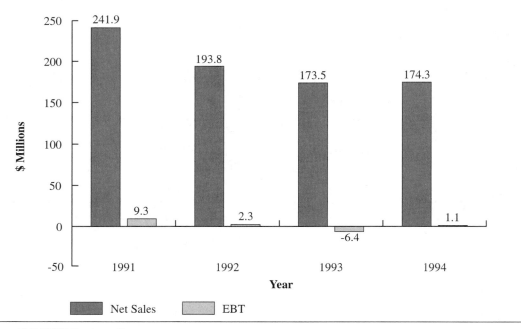

Source: AMADEUS Database, Company reports.

Exhibit 33 ● Angelini OTC Sales Breakdown by Product
Category, 1995

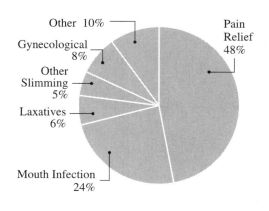

Source: OTC Review 1996.

Exhibit 34 ● Taisho Sales and Earnings Growth

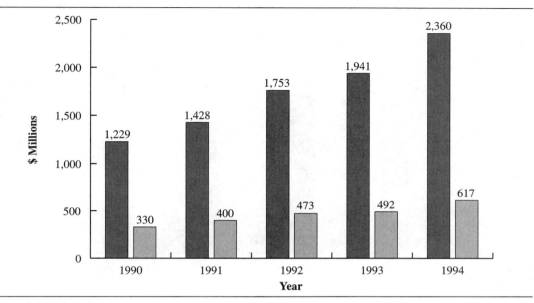

Source: Company reports.

Exhibit 35 ● Taisho Sales Breakdowns by Activity, 1994

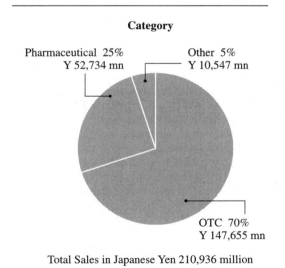

Category

Pharmaceutical 25%
Y 52,734 mn

Other 5%
Y 10,547 mn

OTC 70%
Y 147,655 mn

Total Sales in Japanese Yen 210,936 million

Source: Far East Focus, Company reports.

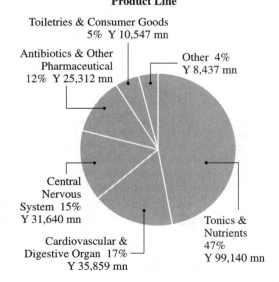

Product Line

Toiletries & Consumer Goods
5% Y 10,547 mn

Antibiotics & Other
Pharmaceutical
12% Y 25,312 mn

Other 4%
Y 8,437 mn

Central
Nervous
System 15%
Y 31,640 mn

Cardiovascular &
Digestive Organ 17%
Y 35,859 mn

Tonics &
Nutrients
47%
Y 99,140 mn

Total Sales in Japanese Yen: 210,936 million

Exhibit 36 ● Perrigo Sales and Earnings Growth

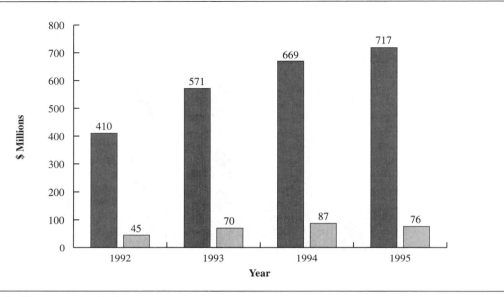

Source: Merrill Lynch Capital Markets Report.

Exhibit 37 ● Perrigo Sales Breakdown by Division, 1995

**Perrigo
Sales Breakdown by Division, 1995**

Vitamins 9%

Personal Care 28%

OTC 63%

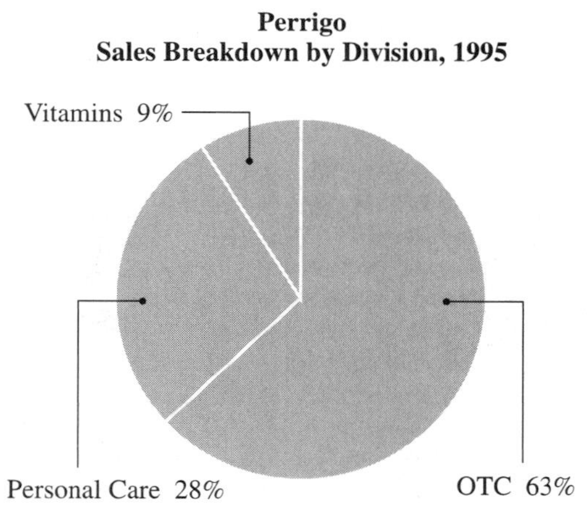

Source: Nonprescription Drugs USA 1995.

Exhibit 38 ● Sampling of Perrigo Nonprescription Drugs and Their National Brand Equivalents

Perringo Product	*National Brand Equivalent*
ACNE AIDS	
Medicated Skin Cream	Noxzema (Procter & Gamble)
ANALGESICS	
Aspirin	Bayer Aspirin (Bayer Group)
Extra Strength Pain Releiver	Tylenol Gelcaps (Johnson & Johnson)
Pain Reliever & Sleep Aid PM	Tylenol PM (Johnson & Johnson)
Ibuprofen Tablets and Caplets	Advil (American Home Products)
ANTACIDS AND ANTI-GAS	
Antacids Gelatin Caps	Mylanta Gelcaps (J&J/Merck)
Flavored Antacid Tablets	Tums (SmithKline Beecham)
Maldroxal	Maalox (Ciba)
ANTIDIARRHEALS	
Loperamide Hydrochloride	Imodium A-D Caplets &
Caplets & Liquid	Liquid (Johnson & Johnson)
ANTI-ITCH PRODUCTS	
Calamine Lotion	Caladryl (Warner-Lambert)
COUGH/COLD REMEDIES	
Dailyhist-1	Tavist-1 (Sandoz)
Diphedryl	Benadryl (Warner-Lambert)
Effervescent Cold Relief	Alka-Seltzer Plus (Bayer Group)
Nite Time Cough Syrup	NyQuil (Procter & Gamble)
Pseudoephedrine	Sudafed (Warner-Lambert)
DIET AIDS	
Diet Caplets	Dexatrim (Thompson Medical)
FEMININE YEAST INFECTION REMEDIES	
Miconazole-7 Cream	Monistat 7 (Johnson & Johnson)
HEMORRHOIDAL PREPARATIONS	
Hemorrhoidal Ointment	Preparation H (American Home Products)
LAXATIVES	
Milk of Magnesia U.S.P.	Phillips' Milk of Magnesia (Bayer Group)
Natural Fiber Laxative	Metamucil (Procter & Gamble)
VITAMIN AND NUTRITIONAL SUPPLEMENTS	
A-Shapes Chewables	Flintstones (Bayer Group)
Century IV vitamins	Centrum (American Home Products)
Multiple vitamins	One-A-Day (Bayer Group)
Ginseng	Ginsana (Sunsource)

Source: Nonprescription Drugs USA 1995.

Exhibit 39 ● Glaxo Sales and Earnings Growth

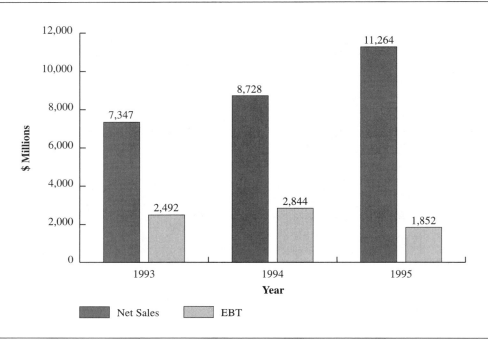

Source: Company reports.

Exhibit 40 ● Glaxo Sales Breakdowns by Geography and Activity, 1995

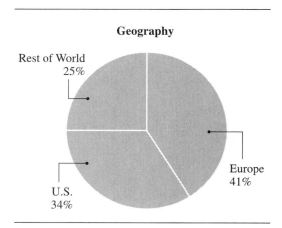

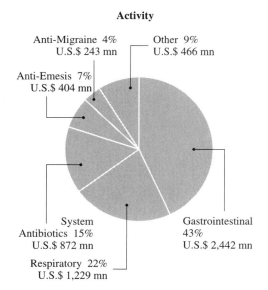

Source: Company reports.

Total Sales in U.S.$ 5,656 million

Case 4

Note on OTC Brands

OTC INDUSTRY BACKGROUND

The world market for OTC pharmaceutical products was estimated at $51.45 billion in 1995 and was expected to sustain a compound annual growth rate (CAGR) of 7 percent through the year 2004. Many factors were driving this growth: more educated consumers taking control of their health care, governments and managed care organizations trying to reduce health care expenditures, and pharmaceutical companies trying to expand the product life cycle of key brands.

Typically, the market was divided by geography and product segment. The biggest markets were the United States, Japan, Germany, the United Kingdom, and France. The largest product segments were cough/cold and upper respiratory, skin treatments, digestive remedies, vitamins, minerals, and nutritional supplements, and tonics and stimulants. Two growth categories were habit control and diagnostic kits. Exhibit 1 details the size of these segments and their respective growth rates.

The behavior of OTC consumers changed according to the particular medical situation: when suffering from an ailment, consumers either self-medicated, visited a doctor, applied a home remedy, or did nothing at all. Most people either self-medicated or visited a doctor. The choice depended on the ailment and how comfortable the consumer

●

This case was written by Kristi Menz and Shauna Pettit, MBA candidates at the F. W. Olin Graduate School of Business at Babson College, under the direction of Professor Jean-Pierre Jeannet. To be used in conjunction with Cases 2, 3, and 5. Copyright © 1996 by IMD—International Institute for Management Development, Lausanne, Switzerland. Not to be used or reproduced without written permission from IMD.

was with self-diagnosis. Consider two common ailments in the United Kingdom with OTC remedies available: headaches and vaginal yeast infections. For headaches, 86 percent of sufferers chose to self-medicate, compared to only 34 percent for vaginal yeast infections.

One could observe a development pattern in the OTC industry. In the early stages of the industry life cycle, consumer choice was limited to general purpose products. As the segment evolved, new competitors entered, niche products emerged, and new product segments were created. As a result, growth in developed countries with largely mature OTC markets came from introducing new products, or line extensions. At the same time, product life cycles of old products were extended by entry into developing countries. The drivers for this evolution were a combination of new medical technologies making their way to the OTC market and existing products needing to redefine the segment in order to remain competitive. Also, changes were happening with consumer products in general that created an atmosphere of more extensive segmentation and product specialization.

The most important demographic trends affecting the OTC industry were the aging populations of the United States, Japan, and Europe and the increasing buying power of consumers in developing countries due to rapidly advancing economies.

There were many participants in the OTC industry. The following were main players: chemicals suppliers, OTC manufacturers, distributors, retailers, consumers, medical professionals, governments and regulators, and managed care organisations. Exhibit 2 describes the forces in the industry.[1]

---

1. For more information on the OTC industry and competitors, see Case 3 and Case 5.

Exhibit 1 ● OTC Industry Product Classification and Sales Figures, 1995

Category	Major Therapeutic Segments	Share of Segment Sales[a]	Growth 1995–1998	Top U.S. Brands
World OTC	*Total Sales: U.S.$51.45 Billion*			
Pain relief	*Percent of total sales: 17%*		4.6%	
	General pain relievers	69.5%	4.2	Tylenol, Advil, Aleve
	Muscular pain	26.4	6.1	Ibuprofen (PL), Ben-Gay
	Migraine remedies	.25	5.8	Migraclear
	Mouth pain relief	1.97	3.9	Anbesol, Orajel
Cough, cold, and respiratory	*Percent of total sales: 17%*		7.7	
	Cough remedies	29.0	5.9	Halls, Robitussin DM
	Cold remedies	44.0	8.1	NyQuil, Alka Seltzer Plus C
	Sore throat	12.9	8.5	Chloraseptic, Sucrets
	Hay fever	11.5	9.4	Benadryl OTC, Tavist-D
	Asthma	2.6	9.2	Bronkaid, Primatene Mist
Digestive preparations	*Percent of total sales: 12%*		3.4	
	Stomach remedies	53.0	4.1	Pepcid AC, Pepto Bismol
	Laxatives	28.1	2.7	Metamucil, Milk of Magnesia
	Antidiarrheals	14.1	2.0	Imodium-AD, Pedialyte
	Liver remedies	4.2	2.1	Lipoflavonoid, Decholin
	Worm treatment	0.6	2.0	Combantrin, Pin-X
Skin treatments	*Percent of total sales: 12%*		7.6	
	Skin protection	28.3	8.7	Coppertone
	Skin irritation	18.2	8.8	Campho Phenique
	Antiseptics	11.2	8.2	Alcohol (PL), Campho-Phenique
	Antifungals	11.0	9.2	Lotrimin AF, Desenex
	Spot and blemish care	8.2	4.5	Clearasil, Oxy
	Antidandruff	5.7	7.7	Head & Shoulders
	Antiparasitics	3.1	2.2	Lice Treatment Kit
	Cold sore remedies	1.3	31.3	Zovirax, Blistex
	Antibaldness	0.7	17.3	Rogaine
Vitamins, minerals and nutritional supplements	*Percent of Total Sales: 10%*		8.1	Centrum, One-A-Day, Ensure
Diagnostic tests	*Percent of total sales: 5%*	–	15.5	One Touch, E.P.T.
Tonics and stimulants	*Percent of total sales: 4%*	–	6.5	Vivarin, No Doz, Ginseng
Eye care	*Percent of total sales: 4%*		4	Renu, Opti-Free, Aosept
Oral care	*Percent of total sales: 4%*		1.2	Listerine, Polident, Fixodent
Circulatory remedies	*Percent of total sales: 4%*		5.5	Preparation H, Tucks
Ear care	*Percent of total sales: 5%*	0.5	7.3	Murine Ear Drops
Bladder and genitals	*Percent of total sales: 2.5%*		–1.6	Monistat-7, Trojans
Habit control	*Percent of total sales: .3%*		21	Nicorette, Nicotinell
Other	*Percent of total sales: 7.7%*			

a. 1995 sales for ten countries: Belgium, France, Germany, Italy, Netherlands, Spain, United Kingdom, Canada, United States, and Japan.

Exhibit 2 ● OTC Industry's Five Forces

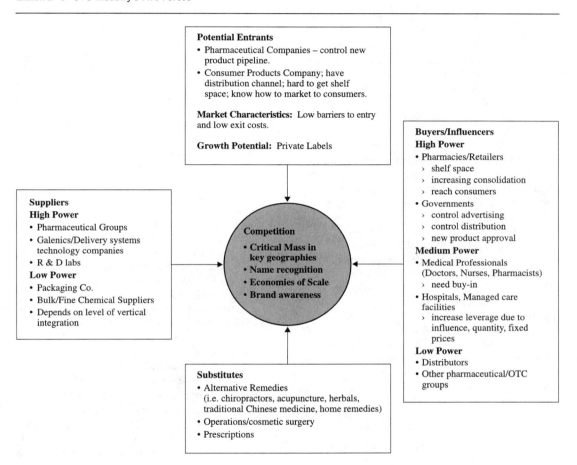

Potential Entrants
- Pharmaceutical Companies – control new product pipeline.
- Consumer Products Company; have distribution channel; hard to get shelf space; know how to market to consumers.

Market Characteristics: Low barriers to entry and low exit costs.

Growth Potential: Private Labels

Buyers/Influencers
High Power
- Pharmacies/Retailers
  › shelf space
  › increasing consolidation
  › reach consumers
- Governments
  › control advertising
  › control distribution
  › new product approval

Medium Power
- Medical Professionals (Doctors, Nurses, Pharmacists)
  › need buy-in
- Hospitals, Managed care facilities
  › increase leverage due to influence, quantity, fixed prices

Low Power
- Distributors
- Other pharmaceutical/OTC groups

Suppliers
High Power
- Pharmaceutical Groups
- Galenics/Delivery systems technology companies
- R & D labs

Low Power
- Packaging Co.
- Bulk/Fine Chemical Suppliers
- Depends on level of vertical integration

Competition
- **Critical Mass in key geographies**
- **Name recognition**
- **Economies of Scale**
- **Brand awareness**

Substitutes
- Alternative Remedies (i.e. chiropractors, acupuncture, herbals, traditional Chinese medicine, home remedies)
- Operations/cosmetic surgery
- Prescriptions

BRANDING IN THE OTC INDUSTRY

As mentioned above, the OTC industry evolved from a generalist market to a specialist-oriented market with an abundance of choices. Companies tried to grow in the OTC market through product differentiation based on product form (e.g., liquid versus tablets) and new product advancements (e.g., 24-hour relief, extra strength, improved taste, etc.).

New products were introduced as a result of new product or brand developments or through product line extensions. New products were created either from an existing substance from the prescription pharmaceutical market or from commonly available ingredients. Factors that influenced product rollout decisions included: prescription brand heritage, advertising regulation by governments and protection of other businesses such as prescription and/or semi-ethical business. Furthermore, if an OTC company obtained access to a new substance from another company, the licensing agreement may have contained limitations either on branding or geographic distribution.

Another strategy often used by OTC companies to grow product portfolios was to extend product lines by leveraging strong brand names across different therapeutic categories within existing segments or completely different product segments (e.g., a cold medicine brand migrating to include a cough medicine or a cold medicine brand migrating into the stomach remedies category).

As a product moved from the prescription arena to OTC, the target customer also changed. With prescription products, doctors and other medical professionals were targeted. With an OTC product, the consumers were the final decision makers. Therefore, it was not uncommon to see a change in presentation when the product switched from prescription to OTC (e.g., changing tablets to liquids, improvement in taste, etc.).

There was no uniform description of an OTC company. Likewise, there was no uniform method of competing. However, like most industries, there were classic examples of strategies that enabled companies to achieve their goals and strategies that did not.

SUCCESSFUL NEW BRAND LAUNCHES

Advil

Advil was first introduced in 1984 in the U.S. pain relief market segment by American Home Products (AHP). At the time, the pain relief segment was dominated by two brands, Bayer Aspirin and Tylenol, an acetaminophen.

Advil was the first ibuprofen switch in the United States. Six weeks after the launch of Advil, Bristol-Myers Squibb launched its own version of ibuprofen, Nuprin. Both products had a two-year patent protection.

As a prescription product, ibuprofen was sold under many brand names. In the United States, the best known was Motrin. Considered a breakthrough in pain relief, ibuprofen was in many ways superior to aspirin and acetaminophen. It was known to be more potent and exhibited fewer side effects than the other products. It was easier on the stomach than aspirin and, in the event of an overdose, safer than acetaminophen.

AHP had a ten-year licensing agreement for the ibuprofen substance with a U.K. pharmaceutical group, Boots. Production was initially carried out by Boots in its U.K. factories. This enabled AHP to launch the new brand more quickly and without the need for a production commitment. The company could instead focus on educating consumers and gaining support from the medical community.

The brand name Advil was completely new. It had neither a prescription nor consumer brand heritage. However, due to clever marketing it was able to create both by association. Advil was positioned as a new standard for the treatment of pain that was "the same as the prescription drug, Motrin."

To support its positioning, AHP implemented an integrated marketing campaign, investing significantly in consumer advertising and also launching an extensive professional campaign. This included dedicating an entire sales force of 650 people to call on doctors and hospitals. In addition, AHP unleashed an intensive pharmacist campaign lasting over six months and offering pharmacists education and training programs. Exhibit 3 shows a snapshot of Advil's advertising and promotion investment for the first three years of launch as well as its position in 1994.

Exhibit 3 ● Advil and Nuprin Advertising Expenditures at Launch

Indicator	1984		1985		1986		1994	
	ADVIL	NUPRIN	ADVIL	NUPRIN	ADVIL	NUPRIN	ADVIL	NUPRIN
Advertising ($mn)	$26	$20	$37	$29	$52	$37	$90	$0
A:S[a] ratio (%)	119	138	48	76	37	66	25	0
Share of voice (%)	13	10	16	13	21	16	24	0
Budget for professional campaign ($mn)	$1	$0	$2	$1	$5	$1	n/a	n/a

Note: n/a = not available

a. A:S = advertising-to-sales

As a result of this effort, AHP was able to gather medical testimonials for future advertisements.

In 1995, Advil was ranked behind Tylenol as the second-leading brand in the U.S. pain relief segment. (See Exhibit 4 for comparative shares of U.S. pain relief market.) Furthermore, it was the largest-selling OTC ibuprofen product in the United States, Canada, and France. This position was expected to be challenged as significant activity continued in the pain relief segment (Exhibit 5). New active ingredients, such as ketoprofen and naproxen, were beginning to be introduced to the market.

Aleve

In 1994, Procter & Gamble (P&G) launched Aleve as a new brand to the U.S. pain relief market. The active ingredient in Aleve was naproxen sodium. Aleve was originally a prescription product named Anaprox. Anaprox closely resembled the best-selling prescription brand, Naprosyn, which also contained naproxen sodium. Both Anaprox and Naprosyn were nonsteroidal anti-inflammatory drugs (NSAIDs), which were known as effective treatment for chronic pain such as arthritis. Like ibuprofen ten years earlier, naproxen sodium was a new substance to the OTC market. P&G licensed the U.S. marketing rights for the product from Syntex, a pharmaceutical company.

Aleve's major competitors were Advil, Tylenol, and Bayer. P&G invested in clinical studies to show that Aleve provided stronger relief than Advil and Extra-Strength Tylenol. In addition, the cost for a full day of pain relief was about half that of Advil and Tylenol. The product targeted heavy users of pain relief, for example, consumers with arthritic or muscular pain. Its slogan was "All Day Strong. All Day Long." Its position as a value-oriented product was supported by the 150- and 250-unit packages, compared to many other analgesics which came in units of less than 100. The image of Aleve as new and different was reinforced through the introduction of a new Safety Squeeze cap which was easier for adults to use than the traditional child-resistant packaging.

In 1994, Aleve reached $65 million in sales and surpassed the first year results of Advil in terms of sales, market share, trial, and brand awareness (refer to Exhibit 6). By 1995, Aleve accounted for 5.2 per-

Exhibit 4 ● Share of U.S. Pain Relief Market

	1984	1994
Acetaminophens	45%	44%
Ibuprofen-based	2	29
Aspirin	53	27

Source: James Dudley, *Winning Strategies*, pp. 1–2.

OHIO CHRISTIAN UNIVERSITY

Exhibit 5 ● U.S. Market Share (%) and Advertising Expenditures for Major Analgesic Brands

Brand	Market Share		Measured Advertising ($mn)	
	1993	1992	1993	1992
Tylenol	24.5%	25.2%	$74.9	$56.9
Private label	19.0	17.3	0	0
Advil	13.7	13.5	74.7	68.2
Extra Strength Excedrin	3.8	4.1	15.9	4.3
Motrin IB	3.7	3.6	27.2	28.5
Tylenol PM	3.7	3.2	15.4	13.1
Genuine Bayer	2.9	3.3	8.2	1.6
Anacin	2.4	2.8	13.2	38.0
Nuprin	2.0	2.6	6.0	11.5
Ecotrin	2.0	2.2	0.1	5.5

Source: Advertising Age, September 1994.

cent of the highly competitive internal analgesics market. Company officials credited Aleve's success to the growing analgesics category and said 45 percent of Aleve's volume came from increased usage and new analgesic consumers. To help prevent retailer stockouts, P&G established a "Fast Start" program which guaranteed customer delivery on day one for any orders placed three weeks prior to the start of shipments. More than 1 million cases were shipped within the first two weeks.

P&G was able to leverage its joint venture rela-

Exhibit 6 ● Sales and Advertising Expenditures for Aleve

	1994	1995
Sales ($mn)	$65	$125
Advertising ($mn)	$37	$69
A:S ratio (%)	57	55
Share of voice (%)	9.7	14.5

tionship with Syntex to fill in for its weak position in the prescription pharmaceutical industry. While P&G focused on its strength, marketing to consumers, Syntex targeted doctors and other health care professionals.

Imodium

Johnson & Johnson's (J&J) Imodium was first switched to OTC status from prescription-only in the United Kingdom in 1983 and in other major markets over the following eight years (refer to Exhibit 7). Based on the active ingredient loperamide, Imodium was the prescription leader for antidiarrheal treatments (refer to Exhibit 8A). J&J achieved sales with Imodium of U.S.$92.4 million in the twelve months to July 1995. The biggest market for Imodium was the United States with a 53 percent share of the antidiarrhea remedies market in 1994. Kaopectate was ranked second with a 30 percent share. Other competitors were Pepto-Bismol from P&G and Maalox A-D from Ciba.

As a prescription product, Imodium was sold in tablet form. Studies showed that consumers preferred liquid formulas. J&J changed the dosage at switch

Exhibit 7 ● National Brand Names and Market Share for Imodium

Country	Brand Name	Year of Switch	1993 Market Share (%)
United Kingdom	Arret, Imodium	1983	33%
United States	Imodium A-D	1988	62[a]
Belgium	Imodium	c. 1988	n/a
France	Imossel	1992	10
Germany	Imodium Akut	1993	6
Netherlands[b]	Diacure	1986	n/a
Japan	Marupi Geridome	1990	n/a

a. In the twelve months ended 8/93.
b. Comarketing venture with Taxandria.

time. Later in 1990, caplets were introduced as a convenience for travelers' diarrhea. A big campaign accompanied this new product formulation, with the tag line "When all you've got is one week, even a morning of diarrhea is too much." This campaign helped grow the category significantly for J&J.

J&J launched the product in many major markets with a strategy that best fit each market. In the United States, J&J adopted a three-pronged marketing strategy which included consumer advertising, a professional campaign, and a pharmacist campaign. In some European markets, J&J opted for a dual brand strategy, enabling them to target both consumers and medical professionals. In Japan, the company chose to license loperamide to Dainippon

In the United States, campaign budgets for the first three years of launch are listed in Exhibit 8B. Twelve months after launch, Imodium A-D was the most highly recommended antidiarrhea brand by pharmacists. It received a pharmacist recommendation 88 out of 100 times, whereas its challenger, Kaopectate, only received 7 out of 100 recommendations. In general, the product was positioned as "Imodium A-D. The original prescription for one dose relief." This tag line helped J&J to leverage its prescription heritage.

In the United Kingdom, Imodium was a semi-

Exhibit 8A ● Prescription Heritage of Imodium in the Global Market

Country	Market Share (%)	Rank
United States	44%	1
France	86	1
Germany	87	1
Italy	35	1

Exhibit 8B ● U.S. Imodium Promotional Spending

	1988	1989	1990
CONSUMER CAMPAIGN			
Advertising (mn)	$9	$16	$17
A:S ratio %	144%	108%	52%
Share of voice	32%	46%	32%
PROFESSIONAL CAMPAIGN ($mn)			
Imodium A-D	1	1	2
Imodium Rx	3	2	1

ethical.[2] As a semi-ethical, sales were driven by doctors rather than consumers. Doctor prescriptions were considered an important driver for the brand's overall success. The reason for selecting a dual brand strategy in the United Kingdom was to avoid alienating health care professionals. In 1985, J&J launched Arret, an identical product, with an identical pricing structure and heavy consumer advertising. Arret directly targeted consumers and was positioned for travelers' diarrhea. At the same time, the Imodium brand continued to be marketed to doctors to treat general diarrhea throughout the year. Sales were disappointing and there was little brand awareness.

In 1994, Imodium had 24 percent of the U.K. market compared to Arret's 21 percent. J&J used this dual brand strategy to exploit the seasonality of the market.[3] Imodium gradually lost share to Arret, until J&J stopped advertising support for Arret in 1991. With the two brands combined, J&J's share of the U.K. market went from 41 percent in 1988 to 45 percent in 1994. After 1990, Arret trailed Imodium (the original switched brand) in sales volume. Virtually no consumer brand investment was ever expended on Imodium in the United Kingdom.

Nicotinell

Nicotinell was Ciba's smoking cessation product first switched to OTC in 1992 in Sweden, Denmark, and Italy. Approval was obtained for several other European countries in 1993 and 1994 (refer to Exhibit 9A).

Nicotinell's first major launch was in the United Kingdom, followed by Germany. In the United Kingdom, key OTC competitors with similar products were Nicorette by Pharmacia-Upjohn and Nicabate by Marion Merrell Dow.

It was government rather than industry which drove this OTC product launch. Pharmacia's Nicorette gum was first to market in the United Kingdom in 1991. The Nicorette patch went OTC in the United Kingdom in November 1992. However, its competitive advantage was nullified when the Depart-

2. "Semi-ethical" refers to a non–prescription-bound product that was reimbursed if prescribed by a doctor.

3. Travelers on vacation often suffered from diarrhea as a result of changes in diet. The sales were correlated with the cycles of the travel industry.

Exhibit 9A ● OTC Availability of Nicotinell

Country	Brand Name	Launch Date
Sweden	Nicotinell	1992
Denmark	Nicotinell	1992
Italy	Nicotinell	1992
United Kingdom	Nicotinell	late 1992
Germany	Nicotinell	1994
Austria	Nicotinell	1994
United States	Habitrol	1997[a]

a. Expected. Johnson & Johnson's Nicotrol patch was given approval in 1996.

ment of Health forced all transdermal patches into the OTC market. Pharmacia, Ciba, and Marion Merrell Dow were expecting to introduce their products as prescription-only medicines but ended up obtaining OTC status. Ciba was able to move in quickly and help establish the new sector by the end of 1992, although it had to use its prescription package for the first several months.

European OTC sales for smoking cessation products experienced a decline after the initial launch years. The concept of a transdermal nicotine patch was both new to consumers and considered to be scientifically advanced in comparison to the existing gum product. The newness of the product produced a high degree of interest and trial when first introduced. When the newness wore off, the sales for Nicotinell decreased with the market from $24.2 million in 1993 to $19.7 million in 1995. However, Nicotinell maintained its market share.

In 1993, European pharmaceutical sales for Nicotinell were $62 million. This gave the brand a number one rank and a 52 percent share of the European market. Of these sales, 60 percent came from doctor prescriptions. As a prescription product in the United States (brand name Habitrol), Germany, France and Italy, Nicotinell was one of the category leaders. Key competition came from Nicoderm in the United States and Nicorette in Europe (refer to Exhibits 9B and 11).

In the United Kingdom in July 1995, Ciba introduced a 2 mg nicotine gum that had been originally

Exhibit 9B ● Total Pharmaceutical SOM (%) for Smoking Cessation Products: Major Markets, 1993[a]

Brand	Company	United States	France	Germany	United Kingdom	Italy
Nicotinell Patch	Ciba-Geigy	—	37	54	42	32
Habitrol	Ciba-Geigy	32	—	—	—	—
Nicorette Patch	Pharmacia	—	—	—	27	4.6
Nicorette Gum	Pharmacia/SmithKline Beecham[b]	20	18	23	22	31
Nicoderm	Marion Merrell Dow/ SmithKline Beecham	31	—	—	—	—
Nicabate	Marion Merrell Dow	—	—	—	6.5	—
Nicotrans	Recordati	—	—	—	32	—
Nicotrol	Johnson & Johnson	9.5	—	—	—	—
Nicopatch	Pierre Fabre	—	39	—	—	—

a. Includes both prescription and nonprescription sales.

b. SmithKline Beecham had the license to market Nicorette Gum in the United States.

introduced as a transdermal nicotine patch.[4] One of the key differentiators for Nicotinell was that it was better tasting than the brand leader, Nicorette, and available in two flavors: original and mint.

Smoking cessation products were expected to support a price level similar to cigarettes. However, this resulted in a higher price level per purchase than for other OTCs. The average daily treatment cost for Nicotinell was competitive with Nicorette and Nicabate. The cost for the Nicotinell patch was $2.10. For Nicorette, the gum was $1.99 and the patch was $2.17. Nicabate's patch was $2.06. It was estimated to take three months to complete a full cycle of Nicotinell's smoking cessation schedule. In the United Kingdom, Ciba spent £4.1 million on consumer advertising, of which £1.5 million was for print. This was more than the promotional spending by both Nicorette and Nicabate (refer to Exhibit 10). In addition, in the United Kingdom, Ciba invested a large amount of resources into trade directed activity in comparison to the competitors. The Ciba U.K. office had a field force of over 200 people whereas Pharmacia and Marion Merrell Dow had fewer than 50 people each.

Ciba positioned Nicotinell as not just another

patch but a complete smoking cessation aid. One of Nicotinell's key competitive advantages was its twenty-four-hour effectiveness as opposed to sixteen hours for Nicorette. It was positioned as a product that would be able to help the consumer all day long. By lasting twenty-four hours, Nicotinell freed the consumer from having to suffer through hours when the product was ineffective. Hence the U.K. campaign slogan was "It needn't be hell with Nicotinell."

Ciba targeted heavy smokers with the patch and lighter smokers with the gum version. By segmenting the consumers, Ciba hoped to keep cannibalization to a minimum. By being offered both a patch and a gum, consumers had a choice and could change their smoking habits at their own pace.

Recognizing that consumer counseling was a very important aspect of product usage and success, Ciba used help lines, charts, audio tapes, and relaxation techniques as part of the program. To promote the product, heavy TV and point-of-sale advertising were used. Doctors were heavily detailed[5] since this was a new delivery system and since doctors had some responsibility for counseling patients. Educa-

4. Two mg of nicotine was the equivalent of one cigarette.

5. *Detailing* was an industry term which referred to the education and promotion of pharmaceutical products to medical professionals.

Exhibit 10 ● Smoking Cessation Promotional Spending in the United Kingdom (£mn)

Brand	1992	1993
Nicabate Patches	£0.0	£0.5
Nicorette Patches	0.3	0.6
Nicorette Gum	1.5	2.8
Nicotinell Patches	1.4	4.1
Nicotinell Gum[a]	n/a	n/a

a. Launch spending of Nicotinell Gum in the United Kingdom was £1.6 mn in 1995.

tional material was given to pharmacists and pharmacy sales assistants.

Despite being beaten to the market by Nicorette and Nicobate patches, Ciba won the battle for the pharmacists' support through higher levels of trade-directed activity and by capitalizing on the twenty-four-hour effectiveness. Not recognized by consumers as a benefit, the twenty-four-hour aspect was accepted by the trade. With all brands called "Nico-something," consumers had no brand affinity and asked pharmacists for recommendations.

Zantac 75

Zantac 75 competed in the stomach remedies product segment, which was a subcategory of the larger digestive remedies category. The global market for stomach remedies was $3.2 billion in 1995.

Originally a prescription product created and marketed by Glaxo Wellcome, the OTC version, Zantac 75, competed against Pepcid AC and Tagamet 100. Glaxo developed joint venture agreements to handle the OTC marketing of the product. Glaxo made this strategic decision so that it could focus on its prescription pharmaceuticals business. OTC partners were Warner-Lambert in Europe and the United States, and Taisho Pharmaceuticals in Japan.

One of the last H_2 antagonists to switch, Zantac 75 was introduced in the United Kingdom in January 1995, nearly a year later than competitors Pepcid AC and Tagamet. Final FDA approval for Zantac was not granted for an OTC launch in the United States until 1996.

The three major H_2 antagonists were based on different active ingredients,[6] although the way they interacted with the body was similar. Consequently, each active ingredient had to go through its own approval process.

As a prescription product, Zantac was the world's biggest-selling drug and accounted for 45 percent of Glaxo's sales. The OTC version of Zantac was approximately half the strength of the prescription formula. Doctors typically prescribed Zantac as a general stomach remedy, or as a treatment for peptic ulcers. The U.S. patent for Zantac was expected to expire in 1997.

When Warner-Lambert launched Zantac in the United Kingdom, it targeted both consumers and medical professionals. The professional campaign included a support package with training materials for pharmacists and pharmacists assistants, reference manuals and a training video, and a suggested pharmacy prescription protocol. Zantac achieved approximately $2.2 million in sales in its first year. This was about twice as much as Pepcid AC and Tagamet 100 during the same time period (Exhibit 20). Although better than the competition, it was considered a marginal success.

Warner-Lambert targeted the larger market of antacid consumers, particularly Gaviscon users. J&J and SmithKline Beecham, owners of Pepcid and Tagamet, were more careful not to infringe upon the position of their other stomach remedy products, Mylanta and Tums.

To reaffirm Zantac's position as the number one prescription product, Glaxo advertised the brand name prior to launch in the United States. Because it was not yet an OTC product, it managed to escape the big marketing battle between Pepcid AC and Tagamet 100. Both J&J (Pepcid AC) and SmithKline Beecham (Tagamet 100) engaged in heavy comparison advertising and slightly exaggerated claims. The matters were eventually resolved in court. Glaxo focused on its prescription business and preparation for the OTC launch.

6. Zantac 75 was based on the active ingredient ranitidine; Pepcid AC was based on the active ingredient famotidine; and Tagamet 100 was based on the active ingredient cimetidine.

Exhibit 11 ● The Race for Smoking Cessation Leadership: OTC Market Share by Country

	1993	1994	1995
GERMAN SMOKING CESSATION MARKET SALES			
(U.S.$ THOUSANDS)	$899	$13,896	$19,836
Nicotinell	0%	23.5%	53.9%
Nicorette	0	63.1	32.2
Nicotin	0	5.7	8
Nikofrenon	0	2.4	3.2
Nicobrevin	87.9	4.6	2.3
U.K. SMOKING CESSATION MARKET SALES			
(U.S. $THOUSANDS)	$56,241	$33,756	$27,368
Nicorette	48.7%	54.4%	61.2%
Nicotinell	42.4	35.2	31.4
Nicotrol	.7	6.3	3.9
Stoppers	1.2	2	2.6
Logado	0	0	.5
Nicabate	>5	1.7	.01
FRENCH SMOKING CESSATION MARKET[a] SALES			
(U.S.$ THOUSANDS)	$275	$389	$290
Nicoprive	67.7%	56.6%	49.4%
Berthoit	0	14.2	35.8
Valerbe	18	10.2	7.4
Pastabe	13.7	17.4	5.9

a. In France, Nicotinell, Nicorette, and Nicopatch were not OTC products but were still prescription-bound.

Zovirax

The cold sore treatment Zovirax was a product of a joint venture between Glaxo Wellcome and Warner-Lambert. Zovirax was categorized as a skin treatment and created a new therapeutic category for cold sore prevention. It was estimated that the switch of Zovirax added a million new users to the market. Exhibit 12 shows the results of this category growth in the United Kingdom.

Zovirax was first introduced on an OTC basis in New Zealand in 1991. Its first major market was Germany in 1992, followed by the United Kingdom in 1993. At the end of 1995, Zovirax was available on an OTC basis in Europe (Germany, United Kingdom, Austria, Denmark, Finland, Ireland, Belgium) with OTC status pending for the United States and Japan. It was ranked number one in the United Kingdom and Germany with primary competition coming from Blisteze and Cymex in the United Kingdom, and Lomaherpin and Lipactin Gel in Germany. Both the U.K. and German markets saw similar growth and success with the switch of Zovirax, taking over half the market (refer to Exhibits 12 and 13).

Zovirax contained the active ingredient acy-

Exhibit 12 ● Growth of Cold Sore Market in United Kingdom after Launch of Zovirax

	Before Zovirax, 1992	
Total Market	$1.9 mn/yr.	
Brand	*Market Share (%)*	*Sales (U.S.$mn)*
Blisteze	52%	$.99
Cymex	12	.23
Boots Cold Sore	12	.23
Lypsyl	9	.17
Brush Off	9	.17
Others	6	.11

	After Zovirax, 1994	
Total Market	$7.1 mn/yr	
Brand	*Market Share %*	*Sales (U.S.$mn)*
Zovirax	78%	$5.54
Blisteze	11	0.78
Cymex	3	0.21
Boots	3	0.21
Others	5	0.36

Exhibit 13 ● Market Share (%) Before and After Launch of Zovirax in Germany

	Before Zovirax	
Brand		*SOM*
Lipactin Gel		31%
Lomaherpin		35
Virudermin Gel		22
Others		12

	After Zovirax	
Brand		*SOM*
Zovirax		49%
Lomaherpin		35
Lipactin		13
Others		11

clovir and was available in cream, tablet, or liquid form. A top-selling prescription product, Zovirax was primarily used to treat genital herpes, shingles, and chicken pox. The OTC version had the same dosage as the prescription product but positioned itself as a treatment and preventative medicine for cold sores. As a result, there was little threat to the still important and existing prescription business.

As with many switches, Zovirax was introduced while it was still under patent. This allowed Glaxo Wellcome to establish an OTC market for the product under patent protection. When launched in the United Kingdom, it had three years left on the patent. In Germany, Glaxo Wellcome only had twelve months left to establish the OTC market. It comarketed Zovirax with the German pharmaceutical company, Hoechst. Germany's market was strongly semi-ethical, with several cold sore treatments that had a strong prescription heritage. Zovirax was initially marketed as a semi-ethical for six months.

Distribution of Zovirax was limited to pharmacies.[7] In Germany, the launch price was $15.70, but at the start of 1995, the retail price was cut in half to $7.80[8] for a 2 gm tube. Two generic manufacturers entered in 1994. They competed on consumer advertising and on price.

Zovirax held a unique position as the only really effective treatment for the prevention of cold sores. Warner-Lambert tried to move customer expectations from cold sore treatment to cold sore prevention. The campaign message was "Early use can stop a cold sore."

Warner-Lambert used the Zovirax name whenever possible throughout Europe. To promote the product to consumers, Warner-Lambert used TV advertising and print media with a "be kissable" catch line. Due to differences in regulatory procedures, Zovirax could not be launched at the same time in all European countries; however, Warner-Lambert tried to use a formula and to maintain the same look and feel in each country (i.e., used the same name, posi-

7. This was true of most medicines in Europe. In general, it was easier to get prescription products approved for OTC sale in Europe than in the United States, but distribution and merchandising were restricted, whereas they were not in the United States.

8. Prices were converted from DM at an exchange rate of U.S.$1 = .5186 DM.

Exhibit 14 ● Advertising Spending at Launch ($mn)

Brand	United Kingdom (1993)	Germany (1992)
Zovirax	$7	$3.5
Blisteze (United Kingdom)	0.36	n/a
Lypsyl (United Kingdom)	0.47	n/a
Lipactin (Germany)	n/a	0.4
Virudermin (Germany)	n/a	0.3

tioning, pack design, etc.). Consumer research indicated that consumer knowledge, awareness of, and attitudes toward cold sores and their treatment were fairly similar throughout Europe.

Zovirax ad spending was far beyond what was typical for that product category (refer to Exhibit 14). The high levels were expected to continue as pressure from generics played an important role. In addition to advertising, Warner-Lambert added an educational and merchandising program for pharmacists and pharmacy sales assistants.

However, not everything was kept the same. Some aspects, especially pricing and competition, were attacked on the national level, but as many common elements as possible were applied (with local adaptation to regulations, pharmacists, etc.). The launch for the U.S. market[9] began on a different course than in Europe. Warner-Lambert was trying to register an indication for genital herpes in the United States instead of for cold sores as in Europe. However, since final approval for this indication had not been granted yet, the final launch strategy was still unclear.

UNSUCCESSFUL OTC LAUNCHES

Efidac/24

Ciba's Efidac/24 was a nasal decongestant available in the United States. Sales reached $23 million and $17 million in 1994 and 1995, respectively. The product held a 1.6 percent market share in the U.S. cold remedies market (1995). Efidac's major competitors

were Sudafed and Contac, with 7.8 percent and 3.3 percent share of the market respectively.

Efidac was launched in 1993 as a breakthrough in cold relief by offering twenty-four hours of relief, compared to only four to six hours offered by competitors. Efidac used an osmotic delivery system which controlled the release of the medicine. Ciba obtained exclusive rights for the OROS delivery system developed by Alza. It had been difficult to obtain FDA approval because of the high dosage in each tablet and because the product was not based on an existing monograph. Consequently, Ciba could not change the product without undergoing a full review with the FDA.

Efidac was based on one single ingredient, not a combination of ingredients like most other products in its category. At the time, a majority of consumers preferred a combination product (e.g., a decongestant and analgesic or a decongestant and antihistamine).

Leveraging the time release technology, Efidac's marketing message was "Get consistent 24-hour cold symptom relief in just one tablet." The campaign was supported by a $27 million advertising budget in 1994. In addition, Efidac used extensive detailing and sampling programs, in-store displays, and mail-in rebates. However, studies showed that the majority of first-time users did not purchase the product again. Sales in the first two quarters were strong, but by the third quarter, sales began to drop. Exhibit 15 shows the sales and media spending for Efidac and two of its major competitors, Sudafed and Contac.

Gyne-Lotrimin

Schering-Plough's (S-P) Gyne-Lotrimin was a vaginal yeast infection product that was the first of its kind to be switched from prescription to OTC in the United States. Exhibit 16 illustrates the sales and market share of the brand from 1991 (the year of launch) to 1995. Gyne-Lotrimin's major competitors were Monistat 7 from J&J and Mycelex-7 from Bayer.

The prescription version entered the U.S. market in 1976 and achieved about 1 million prescriptions per year in 1990. However, the prescription version only had 6 percent market share[10] and was given little

---

9. The U.S. patent for Zovirax was expected to expire in 1997.

10. Compared to approximately 30 percent held by Johnson & Johnson's Monistat 7.

Exhibit 15 ● Sales and Advertising Spending for Efidac ($mn)

Brand	1993		1994		1995	
	Sales	*TME[a]*	*Sales*	*TME*	*Sales*	*TME*
Efidac/24	$10	$19	$23	$27	$17	$11.5
Contac	—	—	40	—	36	8.2
Sudafed	91	22.7	86	23.8	85	30.6
Cold Medication Category Total	1,085	283	1029	247	1,090	237

a. TME = Total marketing expenses.

marketing attention. Gyne-Lotrimin did not fit with S-P's focus on respiratory and derma products, which comprised the majority of the company's prescription pharmaceutical product mix.

When the FDA was reluctant to switch Gyne-Lotrimin, S-P agreed to make marketing and labeling concessions. It would only market the product to women with recurrent vaginal yeast infections, and it would use the term self-recognizable instead of self-diagnosable. To help with the application process, S-P sought support from women's groups and professional organizations. Finally, J&J, whose Monistat was also ready to go OTC, joined forces with S-P to lobby the FDA. Initially, J&J was reluctant to risk its highly profitable prescription version by coming to market with an OTC version, but acted quickly when it realized S-P might succeed with its switch of Gyne-Lotrimin.

Both Gyne-Lotrimin and Monistat were well-known prescription products, but Gyne-Lotrimin's brand heritage was weaker than that of Monistat. It only had about 20 percent of the prescriptions of Monistat. Despite this, when Gyne-Lotrimin was launched, S-P tried to leverage its prescription heritage with the consumer. When Monistat entered three months later, it capitalized on its stronger prescription heritage and quickly became the market leader.

Consumer promotion of Gyne-Lotrimin included heavy advertising, money-off coupons, and rebates. For retailers, S-P offered rapid shipment of stock directly to retailers via couriers. Detailing of medical professionals was also a part of the marketing

strategy. In fact, Schering-Plough's professional marketing campaign had a larger budget than J&J's Monistat (refer to Exhibit 17). Despite this difference in spending, Monistat received almost three times the doctor recommendations of Gyne-Lotrimin.

Nicabate

Nicabate was developed by Marion Merrell Dow as a smoking cessation product. Its only market was the United Kingdom, where it competed side by side with Pharmacia's Nicorette and Ciba's Nicotinell. Pharmaceutical sales[11] share for Nicabate accounted for 3.2 percent of the total European market for smoking cessation, compared with 52 percent for Nicotinell and 35 percent for Nicorette.

Similar to Nicotinell, Nicabate was marketed as a twenty-four-hour transdermal nicotine patch. However, Nicabate was the third product to enter the growing smoking cessation market.

Marion Merrell Dow put relatively more effort and resources on doctors than on pharmacies and less attention was given to consumer advertising. Press was the only medium used (refer to Exhibit 10).

Marion Merrell Dow was one of the major manufacturers of the nicotine patch but chose to license the technology to other companies for launch under their own brand names (i.e., Nicoderm in the United States, marketed by SmithKline Beecham). As a re-

11. Includes prescription-bound and non–prescription-bound products.

Exhibit 16 ● U.S. Sales of Vaginal Yeast Infection Products ($mn)

Brand	1991		1992		1993		1994		1995	
	Sales	SOM %	Sales	SOM %	Sales	SOM %	Sales	SOM %	Sales	SOM %
Gyne-Lotrimin	$57	—	$77	31%	$37	22%	$24	17%	$18	12.7%
Monistat 7	82	—	155	65	86	52	73	49	68	48.2
Mycelex-7	—	—	—	—	23	14	21	14	22	15.5
FemCare	—	—	—	—	12	7	7	5	2	1.4
Others	—	—	—	—	8	5	24	15	31	22

sult, the brand Nicabate had no prior prescription heritage, whereas its competitors, Nicotinell and Nicorette were the top-ranking prescription brands in Europe (refer to Exhibit 9B).

Nuprin

The second ibuprofen product (after Advil) to enter the analgesic market in 1984, Bristol Myers Squibb's (BMS) Nuprin failed to make inroads in the marketplace. As a joint venture between Bristol Myers Squibb and Motrin owners Upjohn, Nuprin should have been able to draw on the prescription heritage of Motrin, the original ethical drug, but AHP beat them to it in advertising Advil.

BMS allocated promotional dollars to a program targeted to health care professionals (Exhibit 3). In

1988, BMS changed the look of the product by coloring the pills yellow. This coincided with a new campaign whose tag line was "Little. Yellow. Different. Better."

The market for ibuprofen products grew and invited several other competitors (Exhibit 4). However, Nuprin was never able to capture enough market share to be considered a player (Exhibit 5). As sales continued to fall, BMS invested less and less in the brand. By 1994, there was no major media advertising support.

Nurofen

The ibuprofen product, Nurofen, was developed by Boots PLC of the United Kingdom, and launched by its consumer marketing group, Crookes. Boots held

Exhibit 17 ● Promotional Budgets: Gyne-Lotrimin and Monistat-7 ($mn)

	1991	1992	1993	1994	1995
GYNE-LOTRIMIN					
Ad spends	32	18	18	10	2
A:S ratio (%)	60	42	49	40	11
Professional campaign	3	2	n/a	n/a	n/a
MONISTAT-7					
Ad spends	n/a	n/a	36	31	27
A:S ratio (%)	n/a	n/a	42	42	40
Professional campaign	1	1	n/a	n/a	n/a

the original rights to the substance ibuprofen and used licensing agreements with other companies to develop the product in regions where it was weak.[12] Discovered in 1969 by Boots Research, ibuprofen was introduced to the prescription market under the brand name Brufen in most countries, and Motrin in the United States. It was one of the top three NSAIDs[13] prescribed around the world.

The only European markets where ibuprofen, as a prescription product, was unsuccessful were Germany and Spain. This carried over into the OTC market. For example, in Spain the total market share of all ibuprofen products in the pain relief segment was less than 2 percent from 1991 to 1995, compared with 17 percent in Italy and 14 percent in the United Kingdom.

The application for an OTC switch began in 1980 in the United Kingdom under the brand name Nurofen. Final approval was received in 1983. By 1990, Nurofen had achieved OTC analgesic leadership in the United Kingdom, among all pharmacy-only pain relievers.[14]

Distribution was limited to pharmacies only and Nurofen obtained 100 percent penetration of pharmacy outlets in the United Kingdom and benefited from the special relationship with Boots the Chemist.[15]

After initial success in the United Kingdom, Boots wanted to turn Nurofen into a pan-European brand. To accomplish this, Boots applied the same launch strategy to the Italian and Spanish markets. However, differences in each country as well as resistance from competitors such as Angelini and Bayer made this goal unachievable. Exhibit 18 illustrates these differences.

12. Boots licensed ibuprofen to other companies in the United States, Germany, and Japan all countries where it had limited market presence.

13. Nonsteroidal anti-inflammatory drugs (NSAIDs) were analgesics in the pain relief category They were considered a major scientific breakthrough since they provided powerful pain relief without the side effects of aspirin and acetaminophen.

14. In the United Kingdom, some aspirin-based analgesics were available mass market. New substances such as ibuprofen were limited to pharmacy-only distribution.

15. Boots the Chemist was the retailer division of Boots PLC and accounted for approximately 30 percent of all pharmaceutical sales in the United Kingdom.

In 1987, Boots launched Nurofen in Italy. A few weeks before launch, there was an advertising ban on NSAIDs. Boots went ahead and launched the product without any means of consumer education except through pharmacists who knew that the ban on advertising was due to speculation about NSAIDs safety.

When the ban was lifted, Angelini, a local Italian company, launched its ibuprofen brand, Moment. The campaign included heavy TV advertising and pharmacy promotion. Within two years, Moment took second place in the OTC general analgesic market. Boots failed to reassert Nurofen once the advertising ban was lifted (refer to Exhibit 19).

Nurofen was launched in Spain in 1989. Three years later, Bayer introduced its own ibuprofen, Dorvial. Targeted to menstrual pain and supported by a strong brand name and heavy advertising and promotion dollars, Dorvial outsold Nurofen. Boots had positioned Nurofen as a general pain relief product. Even though Dorvial was the leader for ibuprofen products in Spain, the substance as a whole never captured more than 2 percent of the pain relief market. A focused position and a well-funded consumer and professional campaign would have been necessary to educate the consumer about the benefits of ibuprofen.

Tagamet 100/Tagamet HB

The H_2 antagonist Tagamet (SmithKline) was known in the prescription world as an anti-ulcerant treatment. In 1989, Denmark was the first market to issue OTC approval. Later, in April 1994, Tagamet 100 was switched to OTC in the larger U.K. market.[16] It was not until 1995 that it received approval from the FDA to be marketed as OTC in the United States.

Other H_2 antagonists were Pepcid AC (J&J) and Zantac 75 (Warner-Lambert). The entry of H_2 antagonists threatened the market position of existing heartburn remedies. Reckitt & Coleman launched a preemptive attack for Gaviscon declaring that Tagamet had a slower onset of action and more potential for dangerous interactions.

Post-launch sales of Tagamet met the company's expectations in the United States, but fell far short in Europe (refer to Exhibit 20). Worldwide sales of Tagamet were more than $74 million in 1995. The

16. In the U.S. the brand name was Tagamet HB.

Exhibit 18 ● Comparison of Nurofen Launch in Europe

	United Kingdom	*Italy*	*Spain*
Product position	General Analgesic	General Analgesic	General Analgesic
Competitive share of voice	Yes	No	No
Ibuprofen share of pain relief market	14%	17%	2%
Major competing brands	Anadin (American Home Products)	Bayer (Bayer AG) and Moment (Angelini)	Bayer (Bayer AG)
Primary source of distribution	Pharmacy chains	Independent pharmacies	Independent pharmacies
Sales and marketing infrastructure	Complete field force utilized, home country	Dependent on third-party relationships	Dependent on third-party relationships

U.S. sales for Pepcid AC were upward of $200 million in less than a year after its launch. Significant competition was expected to continue as Warner-Lambert prepared its launch of Zantac 75, another H_2 antagonist.

It took four years for Tagamet to receive final FDA approval in the United States. First, there was a question of efficacy as a heartburn treatment (Tagamet was primarily used as an anti-ulcer remedy prescription product). Second, there were concerns over negative drug interactions. Final approval was received in 1995. Again, as in Europe, Pepcid beat Tagamet to the U.S. market by several weeks.

Indigestion remedies fell under the broad umbrella of digestive remedies. Chalk-based tablets, such as Tums and Rolaids, were frequently used treatments for fast relief of mild indigestion and heartburn. For more serious cases, more powerful liquid remedies, such as Gaviscon, were used.

At the time Tagamet was launched, there were no obvious gaps in the indigestion market. Research in the United Kingdom showed that heartburn happened to a concentrated number of people. Those who did suffer exhibited a fairly high level of brand awareness and did not exhibit any dissatisfaction with their brands.

SmithKline's communications strategy leveraged Tagamet's successful prescription heritage and referred to the product as "superior" to the less potent remedies. It also differentiated itself as not only a heartburn treatment but also a heartburn preventative. J&J chose a different position for Pepcid. Coming from an inferior prescription heritage than both Tagamet and Zantac, it targeted a specific user group: the heavy and frequent heartburn sufferer. This strategy was supported by research that showed that 84 percent of all heartburn attacks were suffered by individuals who suffer heartburn once or more per week.

In comparison to other H_2 antagonists, Tagamet

Exhibit 19 ● Ibuprofen Market in Italy

	Launch of Ibuprofen in Italy		
Brand	*Year of Launch*	*Entry Costs*	*1991 SOM*
Nurofen	1987	$1 mn	15%
Moment	1989	$7 mn	43%

Ibuprofen Share of Pain Relief Market			
1991	*1992*	*1993*	*1994*
13%	15%	17%	13%

offered six hours of relief and Pepcid 9 hours. The product also came in either 16-, 32-, or 64-count packages. According to SmithKline, on a per dose basis, Tagamet was less expensive than Pepcid. For the consumer, it appeared more expensive than other H_2s available and far more expensive than the chalk brands, such as Rennie and Tums. Tagamet was four times more expensive than Rennie because the active ingredient was more expensive than chalk.

The U.K. launch included a professional campaign that targeted pharmacists and doctors. The pharmacist portion of the campaign included a support package with training materials for the pharmacists and their assistants, reference manuals, a training video, and a suggested pharmacy-counter–prescribing protocol. Despite this effort, pharmacists were four times more likely to recommend Pepcid AC than Tagamet.

H_2s were subject to restrictions on sale, contraindications, and side effect warnings, while no other competing brands, such as Rennie or Gaviscon, faced the same level of scrutiny. For example, Tagamet and Pepcid had to be displayed behind the sales counter. This restriction was put into effect to protect consumers from misusing the product. In contrast, all the other leading heartburn brands had approval to be displayed in self-select areas and were merchandised accordingly.

SUCCESSFUL PRODUCT LINE EXTENSIONS

Clearasil

Clearasil was a global brand created by Richardson-Vicks. In 1985, P&G acquired Richardson-Vicks and took over the marketing responsibility for the brand. It had a significant market presence in the United States, Europe, and Japan.[17] What started as an anti-acne product in the skin treatment category evolved into a franchise of products covering an entire skin care regime.

In 1995, US sales for Clearasil acne treatment products had reached $53 million (Exhibit 21A) resulting in a 23 percent market share. Key competitors

17. In Japan Clearasil was ranked eleventh in the entire skin treatment industry in 1995, and it was the only non-Japanese skin treatment product to be ranked.

were Oxy, Neutrogena, Sea Breeze, Stridex and private labels (refer to Exhibit 21B).

P&G often grew its products via line extensions, particularly with its major brands. Clearasil followed this pattern. The product was sold in many different forms: cream, stick, moisturizer, medicated pads, and lotion. It was also offered in many different strengths: regular, ultra, and Clearasil for sensitive skin (refer to Exhibit 22).

Although Clearasil was a global brand, P&G approached each country differently. In Germany, Ultra Clearasil was marketed only in pharmacies, whereas standard Clearasil was in the mass market. When the pharmacy market declined. P&G refocused its attention on the mass market and spent $8.2 million[18] on advertising in 1993. Also in 1993, P&G tried to improve Clearasil's performance in the French market by relaunching the product and introducing the Clearstick. Sales increased by 80 percent.

In addition, the product line was differently distributed depending on the country. In Germany, most of the product line competed in the mass market acne remedies category. Only Clearasil Ultra was restricted to pharmacies. In contrast, the entire product line was restricted to pharmacy-only in Italy. In the United Kingdom, the product line was sold equally through both pharmacy and grocery outlets. Mass market entries tended to have greater pressure to spend more on advertising than pharmacy products because they could not count on prescription driven sales (refer to Exhibit 23).

The traditional target for Clearasil products was teenage girls. However, when the teenage population began to decline, the company expanded its market by targeting teenage boys and adults. P&G created a product to treat adult acne. Advertising and promotional campaigns targeted both of these groups.

Gaviscon

Gaviscon was owned by Reckitt & Coleman and marketed in Europe. SmithKline Beecham marketed the product in the United States. Gaviscon was an antacid OTC product that provided-relief for acid-related stomach ailments such as heartburn, acid indigestion, and sour stomach.

18. Converted from DM using an exchange rate of U.S.$1 = .588 DM.

Gaviscon was launched as a prescription product in 1970. Slowly it evolved into an OTC product in Europe, although in some countries, it maintained a semi-ethical status. Gaviscon's primary market was Europe, with sales ranging from $67.3 million to $77.7 million from 1993 to 1995. The antacid category as a whole grew 5.9 percent in Europe during this time (Exhibit 20).

Traditionally, Gaviscon ranked as one of the most powerful OTC antacids available. As the product moved away from semi-ethical status, it faced severe competition from new OTC brands in the nonpharmacy sector (e.g., Tums). Furthermore, its position as the strongest available antacid was threatened with the switch of new H_2 antagonists. These were expected to enter the U.K. OTC market in early 1994 and target Gaviscon users.

As a semi-ethical, the product was sold in liquid form. As the product moved to OTC, it was apparent that some consumers preferred a tablet form. Reckitt & Coleman launched Gaviscon 250 in 1993 as a range of flavored tablets aimed at competing with the mass market antacids such as Tums.

By differentiating the dosage (tablet versus liquid) and modifying the brand name, Reckitt & Coleman was able to compete against both the mass market chalk-based tablets and the more potent, doctor-recommended, liquid formulas. Gaviscon 250 competed against mass market products. It was positioned as fast, effective, and long-lasting relief from heartburn and acid indigestion, which was safe enough for pregnant women to use. Flavor and merchandising support were competitive issues. The original Gaviscon formula maintained its position as a semi-ethical, doctor prescribed remedy.

Reckitt & Coleman launched a press campaign in 1991 to promote both to doctors and consumers. An unprecedented amount of advertising was spent at that time (refer to Exhibit 20). Unaided brand awareness increased from approximately 20 percent to 40 percent from 1990 to 1991. In Europe, the distribution of Gaviscon was kept to the self-select areas of pharmacies even though it had received approval to distribute in nonpharmacy outlets.

Prior to the switch of the H_2 antagonists, Gaviscon launched a preemptive trade campaign and pharmacy sales missions aimed at showing Gaviscon's strength in comparison to H_2 antagonists. This was executed ahead of H_2 launches in early 1994. Reckitt & Coleman subtly used the pharmacy displays of Gaviscon to remind pharmacists of H_2 antagonists' contraindications and warnings of side effects.

Tylenol

Johnson & Johnson's Tylenol line of pain relievers and cough/cold products were strong players in their market segments and achieved a top position in overall global sales. However, this success was attributed to the Tylenol line's strong position in the United States, since it was not very common in other parts of the world.

The original Tylenol was an acetaminophen product which was introduced to the OTC market in the 1970s as the first alternative to aspirin. By 1995, the brand franchise had grown to over $857 million in the United States with over twenty-five line extensions. (Refer to Exhibit 24.)

The pain relief category had seen much activity through the years as new medical technologies made their way into the OTC sector.[19] To respond to these changes, J&J employed two different strategies. First, it strengthened the Tylenol product line through line extensions. Second, when it seemed that ibuprofen was going to be a strong therapeutic alternative in the pain relief category, J&J decided to introduce its own product, but not under the Tylenol brand name. Instead J&J adopted a multibranding strategy and introduced Medipren to the U.S. market.[20]

Product Line Extension   For product line extensions, Tylenol was introduced in new dosages, new delivery systems, and new combinations of ingredients. All major extensions attained leading positions in their respective subcategories (refer to Exhibit 25).

For new dosages, J&J introduced an extra strength formula (to compete with the ibuprofen products) and a children's formula. Both were leaders in their categories. As technology advancements in delivery systems[21] became available, Tylenol offered

19. The activity refers to the switch of NSAIDs such as ibuprofen in 1984 naproxen in 1995, and ketoprofen in 1996.

20. In contrast, Bristol Myers Squibb's extended its acetaminophen brand, Excedrin, to include an ibuprofen product which it called Excedrin IB.

21. Delivery systems, or galenics, referred to the way a drug was introduced into the body.

Exhibit 20 ● European Sales and Advertising Expenditures for Antacids, 1993–1995 (U.S. $mn)

| | 1993 | | 1994 | | 1995 | |
Bramd	*Sales*	*Ad Spends*	*Sales*	*Ad Spends*	*Sales*	*Ad Spends*
Gaviscon	$67.3	$3.0	$73.4	$3.6	$77.7	$3.2
Rennie	39.7	20.5	38.3	23.9	38.0	16.6
Tums[a]	2.2	0	2.1	1.9	2.0	1.8
Maalox	57.1	.6	59.5	6.3	63.1	9.3
Almax	36.2	.004	39.0	0	42.2	0
Talcid	18.7	2.1	19.9	2.6	19.6	4
Tagamet 100	0	0	1.1	3.6	1.0	3.7
Pepcid AC	—	—	—	7.0	.95	2.6
Zantac 75	—	—	—	—	2.2	n/a
Antacid Total	415.5	48.5	427.0	74.6	440.1	60

a. Tums a top player only in the United Kingdom and United States, not in France, Germany, Italy, Belgium, or Spain.

US Sales and Media Expenditures for Antacids and Antigas, 1993–1995 (U.S. $mn)

| | 1993 | | 1994 | | 1995 | |
Brand	*Sales*	*Ad Spends*	*Sales*	*Ad Spends*	*Sales*	*Ad Spends*
Gaviscon	$23	$0	$25	$3.9	$33	$10.7
Tums	135	28	143	22.8	144	27.8
Maalox	98	19	90	20	80	23.9
Mylanta	132	32	135	33	129	36.0
Tagamet HB	—	—	—	—	54	42.1
Pepcid AC	—	—	—	—	107	62.8
Zantac 75	—	—	—	—	—	—
Antacid Total	813	135	834	145	981	275

new options. For example, there were gelatin-coated capsules and tablets which made the product easier to swallow. Also, there was a liquid formula for those who could not swallow pills and, most recently, an extended release formula which offered a higher dosage that was released into the body slowly. This product was introduced as a direct response to the launch of Aleve, a new product offering all-day relief.

New combinations of active ingredients also added new products under the Tylenol umbrella. This allowed Tylenol to extend into new product segments. Tylenol introduced a line of cold and flu medicines,

Exhibit 21A ● Sales and Advertising Ratios for U.S. Acne Treatment Brands

Brand	1993 Sales ($mn)	A:S Ratio	1994 Sales ($mn)	A:S Ratio	1995 Sales ($mn)	A:S Ratio
Category Totals	$219	11%	$227	16%	$234	24%
Clearasil	56	14	54	16	53	25
Oxy	49	27	46	31	39	11
Stridex	14	2	17	5	17	20

cough formulas, and a nighttime product which combined acetaminophen with a sleep aid. Children's Tylenol was also expanded into the cough/cold segment. All of these line extensions achieved a top rank in their respective categories.

Advertising support for the different Tylenol products was not distributed evenly. Some products received more than others. Extra Strength Tylenol received the most (refer to Exhibit 24).

Multibranding Strategy   Medipren was launched in the United States in 1986 in an attempt to avoid cannibalizing the Tylenol brand. J&J positioned

Medipren for muscular aches and pains. It was launched only in the United States. Exhibit 26 illustrates sales for the product from 1986 to 1990, the year the product was discontinued.

Medipren's main competitors were other ibuprofen products that existed at the time (Advil, Nuprin, and Motrin). Exhibits 3 through 5 show sales and continued growth of each of the major pain relief brands and the ibuprofen market as a whole since ibuprofen was switched in 1984.

J&J was uncertain how to position the product so that it would benefit from the Tylenol heritage but not hurt Tylenol sales. J&J decided to position Medipren as a muscular aches and pain product and keep the headache and fever reduction indications for Tylenol.

Exhibit 21B ● U.S. Acne Treatment Shares (RSP), 1995

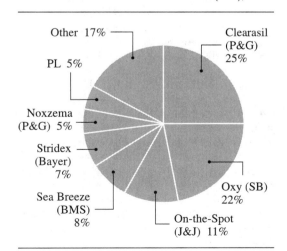

Other 17%
PL 5%
Noxzema (P&G) 5%
Stridex (Bayer) 7%
Sea Breeze (BMS) 8%
On-the-Spot (J&J) 11%
Oxy (SB) 22%
Clearasil (P&G) 25%

Exhibit 22 ● The Clearasil Brand in Europe, 1995[a]

Country	Sales (U.S. $mn)	SOM %	A:S Ratio
Germany	$27	44%	34%
France	6	20	7
Spain	2.5	32	59
Italy	3.1	31	35
United Kingdom	3.9	16	69

a. Sales figures and share of market figures used the following exchange rates: U.S.$1 = .64887367DM; U.S.$1 = .877 GHF (used for Italy sales figures); U.S.$1 = .00771861 pesetas; U.S.$1 = .1868633FF.

Exhibit 23 ● The Clearasil Brand Franchise in the United States

Segment	Brand	Sales ($mn)	% of Segment	% of Total Market
NONBENZOYL PEROXIDE CLEANSERS				
	Clearasil Daily Face Wash	$8	11.6%	3.4%
	Clearasil Moisturizer	2	2.9	.9
	Clearasil Moisturizer— Fragrance Free	—	—	—
NONBENZOYL PEROXIDE MEDICATED PADS				
	Clearasil Double Textured	4	6.9	1.7
BENZOYL PEROXIDE SPOT TREATMENTS				
	Clearasil Vanishing	15	28.8	6.4
	Clearasil Tinted	7	13.5	3.0
NON-PEROXIDE BAR SOAPS				
	Clearasil	4	16.7	1.7
NON-BENZOYL PEROXIDE SPOT TREATMENTS				
	Clearasil Clearstick	8	42.1	3.4
	Clearasil Adult Care	5	26.3	2.1

Introductory print advertising had the following copy: "Who makes Medipren? Medipren, brought to you by the makers of Tylenol products, so you know its a product you can trust. But Medipren is very different from Tylenol. Tylenol is widely used for headaches, fever reduction, and general pain. However, Medipren contains ibuprofen, ideal for relieving body aches and pains." But the TV ads, which could not go into much detail, only said "New Medipren. From the makers of Tylenol." Company officials later found this to be too confusing for consumers and discontinued the ads. Other advertising copy tried to position ibuprofen directly against aspirin. Meanwhile, the other ibuprofen products such as Advil, Motrin, and Nuprin were including a headache claim and were positioning the product against aspirin and Tylenol.

Medipren was subsequently launched in the United Kingdom and Germany under different brand names. In the United Kingdom, it was launched in 1990 as Inoven, and in Germany as Dolormin in 1992. Exhibit 27 illustrates sales and volumes from 1991 to 1995.

Tylenol was not known in Europe. When J&J decided to enter the European pain relief market, it started with a fresh slate. In the UK, the most opportunity in pain relief seemed to be with an ibuprofen product since that was the fastest-growing subcategory. The major U.K. competitor was Boots with Nurofen. In Germany, the market for ibuprofen was not large and, other than Dolormin, there were no strong entries. Germany was Bayer's home market, and so Bayer had an advantage over the classical pain relievers such as aspirin.

Exhibit 24 ● Traceable Media Expenditures for Tylenol Brands

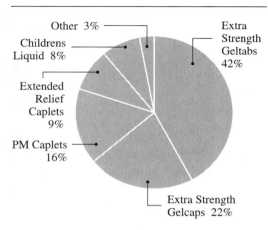

Other 3%
Childrens Liquid 8%
Extended Relief Caplets 9%
PM Caplets 16%
Extra Strength Geltabs 42%
Extra Strength Gelcaps 22%

Total Budget: $132.4 million

Vicks

The Vicks brand franchise had been managed by P&G since 1985.[22] The first product, Vicks VapoRub was introduced into the OTC market more than twenty-five years ago. All Vicks products were in the cough/cold and upper respiratory market segment.

Vicks was a global brand, with strong sales in the United States, France, Germany,[23] Italy, Spain, and the United Kingdom. In 1994, global sales of the Vicks range was $703 million, which made it the world's largest cough and cold brand. Exhibit 28 illustrates the brand's market share in these regions. Competitors tended to change with both the geographic market and the particular therapeutic category within the cough, cold, and upper respiratory segment. Major competition came from Tylenol, Alka Seltzer, Bayer Select, Afrin, Otrivine, Robitussin, and Sucrets.

Vicks was the leading cold remedies product in

22. In 1985, Procter & Gamble acquired Richardson-Vicks, founder of the Vicks brand.

23. For pronunciation reasons, Vicks was spelled Wicks in Germany.

the U.S. market. In Germany, it held 25 percent of the cold and flu market and approximately 30 percent of the medicated confectionery market. Vicks Sinex was the leading nasal decongestant in Italy and the United Kingdom. Vicks VapoRub dominated the chest rubs category in the United States, the United Kingdom, Italy, and Spain.

Through the years, the Vicks product line was extended with the introduction of new delivery systems and new combinations of products. For example, LiquiCaps was a major addition to the Vicks NyQuil cold medicine brand to improve the taste. With Liqui-Caps, the product could be administered orally without the need to taste it.

Vicks was considered to be a company name and, as a result, enabled P&G to use Vicks as an umbrella name for all products, regardless of ingredients used or product category. P&G focused on its core brand, Vicks VapoRub. Through a positive association with Vicks VapoRub, the customer would buy other Vicks products. Exhibit 29 illustrates the positioning of the major brands.

The latest introduction to the Vicks family was Vicks Action in the United Kingdom in 1994. This was a revolutionary multisymptom cold and flu remedy containing a combination of ibuprofen and the decongestant pseudoephedrine. It was available only in pharmacies and was priced at £2.29 for twelve tablets and £3.65 for twenty-four tablets. Its main competition in the market was Nurofen Cold & Flu. P&G intended to support this brand with £4 million in advertising.

In 1993, the Vicks Formula 44 brand extended its line and upgraded its packaging to create a megabrand look and feel. This was in direct response to extensions made by Robitussin.

OTC BRAND MANAGEMENT FAILURES

Bayer Select

Bayer Select was launched in the United States in 1992 by Sterling Health, then a division of Eastman Kodak, which had acquired the North American OTC business of Bayer during WWII.[24]

24. Bayer's U.S. assets were confiscated during World War II by the U.S. government and sold to U.S. companies.

Exhibit 25 ● Tylenol Products: U.S. Sales and Media Expenditures, 1995

Product	Market Share (%)	Sales ($mn)	TME ($mn)
TOTAL GENERAL PAIN RELIEVERS		*$2,245*	*$477*
Extra Strength Tylenol (Gelcaps, Caplets, Geltabs)	16.5%	$370	$91
Tylenol PM	3.7	84	25
Children's Tylenol (Elixir, Drops, Jr., and Chewable formulas)	6.3	140	12.4
Tylenol Extended Relief	1.6	35	28.5
Tylenol	1.5	33	
Tylenol Headache Plus	.3	6	.165
COLD MEDICATIONS		*$1,090*	*$237*
Tylenol Cold	3.6	39	1.8
Children's Tylenol Cold	3.2	35	2
Tylenol Flu Maximum Strength	2.5	21	13.6
Tylenol Cold & Flu	.3	3	—
ALLERGY MEDICATIONS		*$351*	*$82*
Tylenol Allergy Sinus and Tylenol Severe Allergy Caplets	11.7	41	18[a]
SINUS MEDICATIONS		*$159*	*$28*
Tylenol Sinus	29.6	47	11.3
COUGH SYRUPS		*$340*	*$40*
Tylenol Cough Maximum Strength	.9	3	—

a. $11.7 million was for Tylenol Severe Allergy Caplets.

Exhibit 26 ● Medipren Advertising Expenditures and Sales Figures, 1986–1989

	1986	1987	1988	1989
Market share (%)	1.5	2.1	NA	1.3
Advertising expenditures (U.S. $mn)	12	36	29	6

Bayer Select was intended as a remedy for every type of pain and every type of cold. In other words, "Not all pain is the same." Sterling envisioned that the consumer would see a display of all Bayer Select products and then "select" the best one for his or her ailment. The line was initially launched with five nonaspirin pain relievers. A year later, the company added six cold and flu products. The pain relievers addressed headache pain, back pain, period pain, night time, and sinus pain. The cold and flu remedies offered choices for treating head cold, a chest cold, head and chest cold, flu relief, nighttime cold, and allergy and sinus.

Unfortunately, the retailers did not envision the product layout the same way. First of all, not all products in the Bayer Select line were stocked. Second, those stocked were separated and placed with other brands with similar indications.

Consumers did not respond as favorably to the product as the company had expected. First of all, there was evidence that consumers misunderstood the concept and were combining products themselves and overdosing. Second, there was scepticism about the true differences between the versions. For example,

Exhibit 27 ● Sales and Advertising Expenditures for Medipren Brands in Europe, 1991–1995

(UK)	*1991*	*1992*	*1993*	*1994*	*1995*
INOVEN (U.K)					
Sales (U.S.$ thousands)	690	222	162	83	49
Market share (%)	—	—	0.1	almost 0	almost 0
Advertising expenditures (U.S.$ thousands)	—	—	—	—	—
A:S ratio	n/a	n/a	n/a	n/a	n/a
Share of voice (%)	n/a	n/a	n/a	n/a	n/a
Budget for professional campaign	0	0	0	0	0
DOLORMIN (GERMANY)					
Sales (U.S.$ thousands)	Product not available	741	7,402	8,282	10,100
Market share (%)	n/a	—	2.1	2.5	3.1
Advertising expenditures (U.S.$ thousands)	n/a	—	11,258	9,627	6,042
A:S ratio (%)	n/a	—	152	116	60
Share of voice (%)	n/a	—	12	9	8
Budget for professional campaign	n/a	—	0	0	0

Consumer Reports reported that ". . . with some of the products, one purportedly specific remedy differs from another only in packaging and price: Bayer Select Head Cold is identical to Bayer Select Sinus Pain, save for the colour of the caplet and the price. The lime-green head-cold caplets cost us 17 cents each; the dark green sinus-pain caplets 10 cents each." Finally, with a cold and flu, it was not uncommon for symptoms to start in one area and migrate to other areas as the ailment progressed. To expect that the consumer to be willing to purchase a different product for each stage of the cold required far more out of pocket expenditures than the consumer was accustomed to.

Unlike the Tylenol extensions, which always included their core ingredient acetaminophen, Bayer Select versions were not always aspirin-based.

For the allergy/sinus launch, Sterling used a direct mail campaign and radio during allergy season (July–September). Further support was given with a consumer rebate offer through three national free-standing inserts.

The entire Select line was advertised on national TV and print ads in women's magazines. Sterling announced that it would spend more than $100 million in advertising support. In reality, the only traceable media expenditures added up to approximately $50 million. Similarly, when the cold remedies line was launched a year later, the company announced that it had committed to a larger media investment than was actually the case.

Stridex

Stridex, created by Sterling Health, was an anti-acne treatment marketed in the United States. Sales in 1994 were $17 million, and the brand had a 7.3 percent market share, ranking fifth overall (refer to Exhibit 21B).

Stridex was best known for its unique packaging. It was the first to offer presoaked medicated pads for consumer convenience. This differentiation did not last because Clearasil and Oxy followed suit immediately. Stridex was still the leader in the medicated pads segment with a 29.3 percent share of the market.

Exhibit 28 ● Top Ranking Vicks Products Worldwide, 1993–1994 (MSP)

Country	Category	Brand	Total Marketing Expense ($ mn)	Rank	% MS	Market Size ($ mn)
Belgium	Chest rubs/inhalants	Vicks VapoRub	0.5	1	60	2
France	Chest rubs/inhalants	Vicks VapoRub	1.2	1	23	20
Germany	Cold & flu remedies	Wick MediNait	6.8	1	25	88
	Chest rubs/inhalants	Wick VapoRub	3.7	1	18	51
	Cough remedies	Wick	17.9	5	3.1	243
Italy	Cold & flu remedies	Vicks MediNait	1.9	2	12	21
	Nasal decongestants	Vicks Sinex	1.9	1	29	31.5
	Chest rubs/inhalants	Vicks VapoRub	1.6	1	58	9
Netherlands	Nasal decongestants	Vicks Sinex	n/a	2	13	7
	Chest rubs/inhalants	Vicks	n/a	1	24	3[a]
	Medicated confectionery	Vicks	n/a	1	40	21[a]
Spain	Nasal decongestants	Vicks Sinex	1.4	1	19	10
	Chest rubs/inhalants	Vicks VapoRub	8.7	1	77	3
United Kingdom	Chest rubs/inhalants	Vicks VapoRub	0.08	1	33	10
United States[b]	Cold remedies	Vicks NyQuil[c]	25	1	11	1029
		DayQuil	14[d]	12	2.7	1029
	Cough remedies	Vicks Formula 44	12.5	2	18	307
	Chest rubs/inhalants	Vicks VapoRub	10.9	1	65	44
	Sinus medications	DayQuil Sinus	—[e]	6	4	169
	Nasal decongestants	Sinex	1.7	2	8	207

a. 1992.
b. 1994 sales and advertising figures.
c. Includes all line extensions for NyQuil: liquid cold remedy, capsules, cold remedy, liquid children, liquid hot therapy, and cold formula for children.
d. Includes DayQuil line extensions which were: Liquid, LiquiCaps, and Cold & Sinus.
e. Most of advertising was done for all brands of DayQuil line: "More complete anytime relief from your cold, flu, sinus or allergy symptoms."

When the teenage population reached a low point in the 1980s and 1990s, players in the acne treatment category started to redefine the market to maintain sales. One trend was to enlarge the definition of a brand name beyond one product and redefine the brand to encompass an entire skin care regime. Another trend was to target adult women, a significant portion of whom suffered from acne. Neutrogena, Clearasil, and Oxy took significant steps in this direction.

The majority of Stridex's product line extensions focused on adding new versions of the pads (refer to Exhibit 30). The goal was to offer different pads to different members of the same household. The company eventually added an antibacterial soap and a gel formula to its product line. However, it was not nearly as extensive as offerings from Clearasil, Oxy, and Neutrogena.

Acne treatment consumers exhibited little brand loyalty. In 1994, Stridex's packaging was updated and a new logo was introduced to help the product stand

Exhibit 29 ● Product Positioning for Leading Vicks Products

Brand	Positioning	Product Forms
Vicks VapoRub	Targeted to parents for use on children. The medicated cream was applied directly to the skin, which helped to create a bond between parent and child.	Available in either a cream or ointment.
Vicks NyQuil (MediNait)	The all-inclusive medicine that relieves all cold and flu symptoms and enables the user to get a good night's sleep.	Available in liquid, liquid gel caps, and powder to make a hot therapy.
Vicks DayQuil	The all-inclusive medicine that relieves all cold & flu, sinus, and allergy symptoms but does not make you drowsy.	Available in liquid, liquid gel caps, multisymptom (cold, flu, & sinus), and allergy relief tablets, and allergy & sinus tablets and capsules.
Vicks Sinex	Nasal decongestant.	Available in nasal spray and a topical formula.
Vicks Formula 44	All-inclusive cough syrup that cures all kinds of coughs.	Available in regular strength, extra strength, pediatric, and combination cough & cold formulas.
Vicks Action	Revolutionary product combination to provide the most effective cold relief.	Available in tablets.

out on the shelf. In addition, the added versions Sensitive Skin, Super Scrub, and Dual-Textured used visible icons to convey added benefits.

Stridex spent about 2 percent of sales on advertising when under the management of Sterling. The average for the category was 11 percent (refer to Exhibit 21A).

Exhibit 30 ● Stridex Brand Franchise

NON-BENZOYL PEROXIDE MEDICATED PADS
Stridex Medicated Pads Total
Stridex Medicated Pads
Stridex Big Pads
Stridex Dual Textured Pads
Stridex Maximum Strength
Stridex Maximum Strength Big Pads
Stridex Maximum Strength-Single
    Textured Pads
Stridex Oil Fighting Formula
Stridex with Aloe Vera for Sensitive Skin

NON-BENZOYL PEROXIDE BAR SOAPS
Stridex Antibacterial Cleansing Bar

NON-BENZOYL PEROXIDE SPOT TREATMENTS
Stridex Clear Gel Antiacne Treatment

NON-BENZOYL PEROXIDE CLEANSERS
Stridex Anti-bacterial Face Wash

OHIO CHRISTIAN UNIVERSITY

Case 5

Ciba Self Medication

Roland M. Jeannet had been in his position as president of Ciba Self Medication for only six months when he arranged for a full strategy review in November of 1994. (In 1997, Ciba merged its health business with Sandoz to create Novartis. The Ciba self-medication operations are now under Novartis Consumer Health.)

Ciba Self Medication, although ranked tenth worldwide, is still a relatively small player compared with industry leaders. We need to think about a strategy that strengthens our global position in line with the realities of the industry. As a next step, the division needs to develop a strategy for presentation to the Ciba Group management. This strategy, among other issues, needs to articulate the type of global strategy we intend to pursue, where to place the emphasis both geographically and in segments, and how to structure our business organizationally.

COMPANY OVERVIEW

Ciba Self Medication was a division of Ciba-Geigy Limited, a Swiss-based chemical company. Formed in 1970 by the merger of two Swiss chemical companies, Ciba and Geigy, Ciba-Geigy had three operating segments: Healthcare, Agriculture, and Industry. Exhibit 1 shows the main business segments and their

fourteen autonomous divisions which resulted from a reorganization in the early 1990s. The move toward decentralization showed Ciba-Geigy's commitment to getting closer to the customer, encouraging cost-consciousness in the divisions, and providing a climate to encourage individual initiative.

Ciba-Geigy's financial performance was heavily dependent upon the cyclical chemical industry. In 1994, the chemical industry was in a downturn. Thus, Healthcare contributed only 40 percent of turnover but accounted for over 50 percent of operating profits (refer to Exhibit 2). On an after tax basis, Healthcare contributed upward of 70 percent to profits. The appreciation of the Swiss franc in recent years had considerably depressed Ciba-Geigy's profitability.

Self Medication was created as a segment within Ciba-Geigy's healthcare area in 1983. It gained status as a separate division in 1992 as a result of the consolidation of Zyma SA[1] and Ciba's self-medication activities. Self Medication had two autonomous business units, Ciba US, located in New Jersey and responsible for the U.S. OTC business, and the Zyma, based at Nyon, Switzerland, and responsible for all other geographies (refer to Exhibit 3). In 1994, Ciba Self Medication's (Ciba) sales of U.S.$823 million ranked it tenth in the world with a 2 percent market (refer to Exhibit 4). Geographically, Ciba generated the majority of its OTC sales in Europe (refer to Exhibit 5). Germany was its biggest European market, generating 17 percent of sales, with the United Kingdom second largest at 7 percent of sales, followed closely by Switzerland.

Historically, Ciba had a limited R&D pipeline for its prescription products. To compensate, the company entered into numerous joint ventures with biotechnical companies and other small, research-based pharmaceutical companies. In addition, Ciba

This case was prepared by Kristi Menz and Shauna Pettit, MBA candidates at the F. W. Olin Graduate School of Business at Babson College, under the direction of Professor Jean-Pierre Jeannet. This case was written for class discussion purposes only. This case is to be used in conjunction with Case 2, Case 3, and Case 4. Copyright © 1996 by IMD—International Institute for Management Development, Lausanne, Switzerland. Not to be used or reproduced without written permission directly from IMD.

1. At the time, Zyma SA was a wholly owned subsidiary of Ciba-Geigy.

Exhibit 1 ● Ciba Corporate Organization 1994

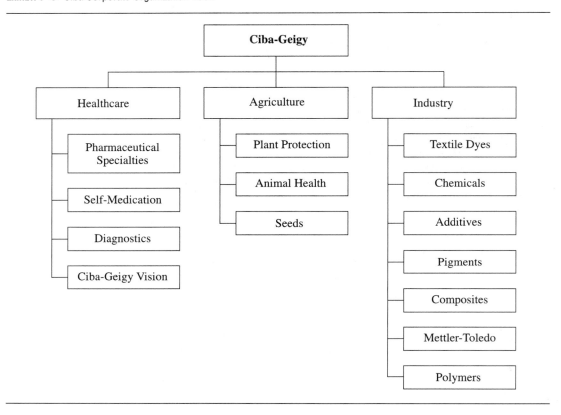

Exhibit 2A ● Financial Overview of Ciba Group ($mn)

	1990	1991	1992	1993	1994
Net sales	$16,254	$17,387	$18,317	$18,683	$18,189
R&D costs	1,692	1,803	1,939	1,817	1,774
Operating profit	852	1,056	1,254	1,949	2,251
Profit after tax	852	1,056	1,254	1,468	1,578
Total assets	21,572	23,460	25,243	26,204	26,270
Shareholders funds	12,749	13,464	14,910	14,090	12,770
Cash	3,061	3,521	4,345	5,950	6,739
Short-term debt	2,851	2,916	2,706	2,843	2,928

Exhibit 2B ● Ciba-Geigy 1994 Sales and Profits by Division

Division	% of Sales	Operating Profits % of
Healthcare	40%	51%
Agriculture	22	21
Industry	38	28

Exhibit 2D ● Financial Results of Healthcare Group ($mn)

Segment	1993	1994
Pharmaceuticals	$5,789	$5,355
Self Medication	826	823
Ciba US		226
Zyma		597
Diagnostics	578	534
Ciba Vision	895	960
R&D	1,936	1,891

Exhibit 2C ● Ciba-Geigy Sales and Operating Profits by Division, 1994

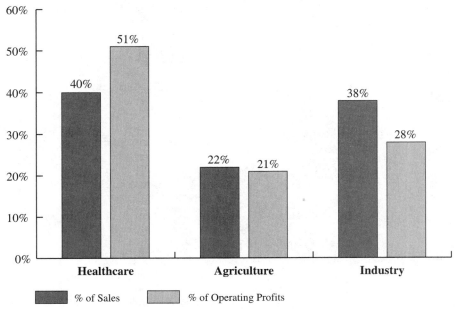

Ciba-Geigy Sales and Operating Profits by Division, 1994

Exhibit 3 ● Ciba Self Medication Division

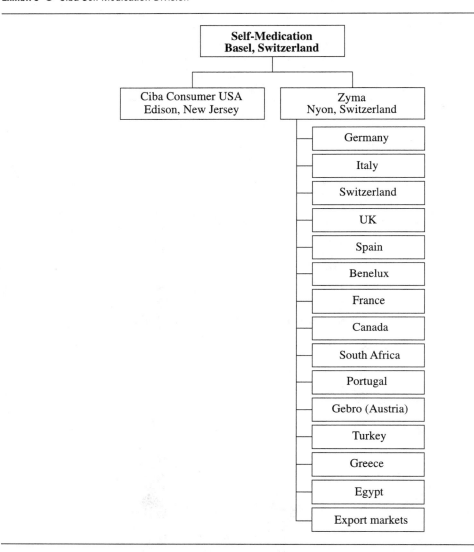

acquired several businesses to strengthen its OTC portfolio (refer to Exhibit 6). The pharmaceutical division as a whole increasingly concentrated on R&D for cardiovascular disease, central nervous system (CNS) disorders, cancer, inflammation, allergy, and bone disease. R&D did not concentrate solely on finding new chemical entities. Ciba also actively explored new delivery systems. This effort yielded such innovations as transdermal patches used for smoking cessation (Nicotinell).

Exhibit 4 ● OTC Company Rank, 1994

Rank	Worldwide	SOM %	United States[a]	SOM %	Europe	SOM %
1	J&J/Merck	5.4%	Johnson & Johnson	11.0	Rhône-Poulenc Rorer	3.6
2	American Home Products	4.9	American Home Products	9.0	Sanofi/Sterling	3.2
3	Warner Wellcome	4.7	Procter & Gamble	7.6	Bayer	3.2
4	Procter & Gamble	4.2	Warner Wellcome	7.5	Warner Wellcome	2.7
5	Bayer	3.1	Bristol-Myers Squibb	4.0	Boehringer Ingelheim	2.4
6	Sanofi/Sterling	2.8	SmithKline Beecham	3.5	Roche	2.2
7	Bristol-Myers Squibb	2.8	Schering-Plough	3.3	SmithKline Beecham	2.2
8	SmithKline Beecham	2.7	Abbott Laboratories	3.2	American Home Products	2.1
9	Rhône-Poulenc Rorer	2.6	Bayer	3.0	Pierre Fabre	2.1
10	Ciba-Geigy	2.0	Sanofi/Sterling	2.3	Servier	2.0
11					Ciba-Geigy	1.9

a. Ciba's purchase of Rhône-Poulenc Rorer's North American OTC business at the end of 1994 placed them in the top ten U.S. OTC companies.

Source: OTC Review 1994.

MARKET SEGMENTS

Ciba's OTC products covered a range of product categories (refer to Exhibit 7). Ciba's strongest categories were cough/cold, gastrointestinal, circulatory, and skin treatments (refer to Exhibit 5). Ciba also had a growing presence in the smoking cessation market. In common with other OTC manufacturers, Ciba's product portfolio in Europe contained semi-ethical products,[2] making the company vulnerable to government cost-reduction measures.

Cough/Cold and Other Respiratory

The global cough/cold segment generated sales of U.S.$7.1 billion in 1994. Ciba's estimated revenues were about U.S.$198 million, or 3 percent share of the

market. Products in this segment treated ailments related to cough, cold, sore throat, hayfever, and asthma. Ciba focused mainly on the cold remedies subcategory with several products in the cough and sore throat remedies categories, as well.

Ciba's only pan-European OTC brand[3] was Otrivin,[4] a nasal decongestant. Otrivin's competitive positioning as "The most advanced and effective nasal decongestant you can buy" helped it achieve the top position in that category in Belgium, Germany, Netherlands, and the United Kingdom. It was ranked second in Switzerland. Otrivin was also available in Italy, Spain, the United States, and Canada (refer to Exhibit 7). Otrivin was Ciba's second-largest brand

2. Semi-ethical products are those that are non–prescription-bound but are still prescribed by some doctors (and thus reimbursed).

3. A pan-European brand was one that spanned numerous European countries and to which the same base marketing strategy was applied.

4. Also known as Otrivin and Otriven, depending on the country.

Exhibit 5A ● Ciba's Expected OTC Sales by Region, 1995

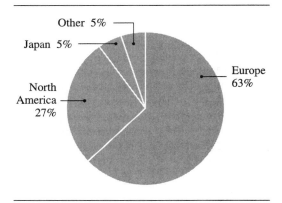

Other 5%
Japan 5%
North America 27%
Europe 63%

Source: Datamonitor.

Exhibit 5B ● Ciba's Expected OTC Sales by Category, 1995

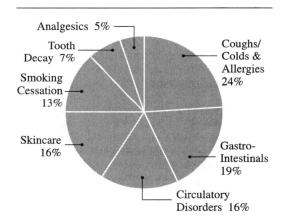

Analgesics 5%
Tooth Decay 7%
Smoking Cessation 13%
Skincare 16%
Circulatory Disorders 16%
Coughs/ Colds & Allergies 24%
Gastro-Intestinals 19%

Source: Datamonitor.

with 1994 SFr. 63.8 million[5] (refer to Exhibit 8). Otrivin was Europe's fourth-largest self-medication cold remedy behind Vicks, which held the top three rankings. In the nasal decongestants category, Otrivin ranked second, giving way only to Vicks Sinex.

Ciba marketed Otrivin with slightly different

---

5. Includes all sales of Otrivin, prescription and nonprescription, except those in the United States.

names in different markets, making it difficult to advertise with a pan-European approach. As such, Ciba used national campaigns to market the product, including different pack designs in each country. Direct promotion accounted for 18 percent of sales in 1993. In Germany and Belgium, Otrivin was the top advertiser in the nasal decongestants category, achieving 24 percent and 60 percent share of voice (SOV) in those markets.[6] The second-biggest advertiser in the German market, Sinex, had 20 percent SOV. In Belgium, Rhinospray achieved an SOV of 20 percent. In all other markets, Otrivin's consumer advertising spends did not rank it among the top three brands. Across Europe, Otrivin's advertising to sales ratio of 18 percent ranked it second to Sinex with an A/S ratio of 50 percent. Ciba's goal was to leverage Otrivin more widely across the cough/cold market with line extensions into, for example, oral decongestants.

Another nasal decongestant, Efidac/24, was launched in the United States at the end of 1993. Its main attraction was its innovative delivery system, which allowed the medicine to be released into the body gradually over a twenty-four-hour period. At launch, Ciba spent over U.S.$30 million to promote this new technology. It achieved first-year sales of U.S.$28.7 million. Ciba believed twenty-four-hour coverage would appeal to consumers, since most other medicines in this category lasted four to six hours only.

The Fisons acquisition in 1992 added two allergy and sinus relief products, Allerest and Sinarest, to Ciba's U.S. portfolio. Prior to the acquisition, Allerest commanded a 7 percent share of the U.S. allergy relief market, placing it third in 1991 behind Benadryl and Chlor-Trimeton. Allerest's nondrowsy formulation made it attractive to consumers who were wary of products causing drowsiness, such as Tavist. Both Allerest and Sinarest lost share as new, more innovative products were introduced to the market.

Digestive and Other Intestinal Remedies

Digestive remedies was an important OTC market for Ciba with 1994 sales of approximately U.S.$156 million translated into a 3 percent share of the global

---

6. Total advertising spending on nasal decongestants in Germany was SFr. 19.3 million compared to only .9 million in Belgium.

Exhibit 6 ● Historical Development of Ciba and Its OTC Operations

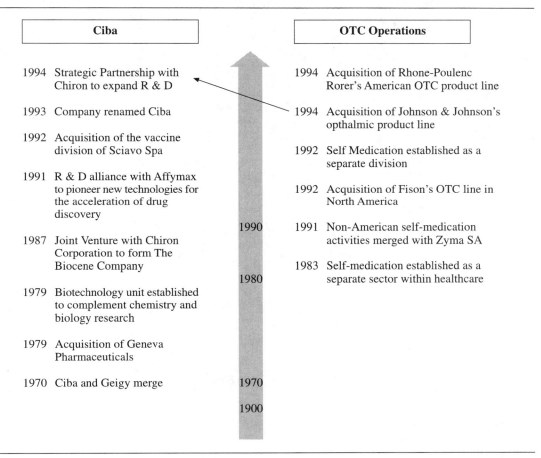

Ciba		OTC Operations
1994 Strategic Partnership with Chiron to expand R & D		1994 Acquisition of Rhone-Poulenc Rorer's American OTC product line
1993 Company renamed Ciba		1994 Acquisition of Johnson & Johnson's opthalmic product line
1992 Acquisition of the vaccine division of Sciavo Spa		1992 Self Medication established as a separate division
1991 R & D alliance with Affymax to pioneer new technologies for the acceleration of drug discovery		1992 Acquisition of Fison's OTC line in North America
1987 Joint Venture with Chiron Corporation to form The Biocene Company		1991 Non-American self-medication activities merged with Zyma SA
1979 Biotechnology unit established to complement chemistry and biology research		1983 Self-medication established as a separate sector within healthcare
1979 Acquisition of Geneva Pharmaceuticals		
1970 Ciba and Geigy merge		

Source: Datamonitor.

digestive remedies market. Digestive and other gastrointestinal medications treated such ailments as constipation, diarrhea, heartburn, and indigestion. Most of Ciba's sales in this segment were generated from laxatives treating constipation. The acquisition of Maalox from Rhône-Poulenc Rorer in 1994 gave Ciba a stronger entry point into the U.S. antacid market for indigestion.

Importal was perhaps the backbone of Ciba's gastrointestinal segment. Launched as a semi-ethical laxative in France in 1990, the brand quickly moved into several other European countries. Italy, Belgium, and Spain were other high sales markets for Importal, although it was not ranked in the top ten in any of those countries. Importal was ranked among the top five in France only. Importal was one of few products marketed in France that had reached such rank.[7]

Promotion of Importal accounted for 18 percent

7. The French market is much different from other European markets in terms of government regulation and the attitudes of doctors, pharmacists, and consumers.

Exhibit 7 ● Ciba Self Medication Key OTC Brands, 1994

	France	Germany	Italy	Spain	United Kingdom	United States	Japan	Other
ANALGESICS								
Systemic		Eu-Med		Neo-Cibalgina[f]	Librofem	Ascriptin Doan's Q-Vel		Voltaren
Topical					Proflex[m]	Eucalyptamint Myoflex		Emulgel: Belgium Switzerland[z]
COUGH/COLD								
Cold remedies		Otriven[c] Vibrocil	Otrivine	Otrivin[k]	Otrivine[n] Do-Do Mu-Cron	Otrivin Privine Allerest Sinarest Efidac/24		Otrivine: Canada Belgium Netherlands Vibrocil: Belgium
Cough/sore throat remedies			Sinecod Resyl		Bradosol	Delsym		Delsym: Canada Sinecod: Turkey
Allergy remedies						Efidac/24		Orofar: Belgium
DIGESTIVE REMEDIES								
Antacid/indigestion remedies				Bicarbonato Torres Munoz[l] Fructosel		Maalox[r]		
Laxatives	Importal[b]	Neda- Fruchtewurfel[d] Biolax	Importal	Importal		Dulcolax[s]		Importal: Belgium
Antidiarrheal						Fiberall Perdiem[t] Maalox A-D		Netherlands Switzerland
DERMATOLOGICALS								
Acne remedies					Tri-Ac Cepton			
Antifungals						Desenex[u] Cruex[v] Ting		
Antihemorrhoidals			Proctidol			Nupercainal Americaine		

Anti-itch products	Eurax	Fenistil[e]	Eurax Fengel[f,g]	Fenistil	Eurax[o]	Caldecort	Eurax Fenigel: Belgium
Therapeutic				Halibut			
Moisturizers							
Wound care			Bialcol[h]		Savlon / Very Dry Savlon[p]	Caldesene	
Medicated shampoo			Neril[i]				
Lip treatment					Lypsyl		
DIETARY SUPPLEMENTS							
Vitamins						Sunkist	Webber: Canada
Minerals					Slow Fe	Slow Fe[w]	
Fish oil			MaxEPA				
SLIMMING AIDS						Acutrim	
HABIT CONTROL[n]							
Smoking cessation			Nicotinell[j]		Nicotinell[q]		
EYE CARE[a]							
Contact lens solution						Aosept[x] Quick Care	
Artificial tears						HypoTears[y]	
Decongestant						Vasocon A	

a. Sales and profits for eye care are accounted for in the Ciba Vision division's financial statements.

b. Ranked 5th with 3% share of U.S.$105 mn market.

c. Ranked 1st with 22% share of U.S.$54 mn market.

d. Ranked 4th with 5% share of U.S.$98 mn market.

e. Ranked 4th with 7% share of U.S.$26 mn market.

f. Ranked 3rd with 8% share of U.S.$87 mn market.

g. Ranked 3rd with 13% share of U.S.$10 mn market.

h. Ranked 6th with 6% share of U.S.$35 mn market.

i. Ranked 4th with 7% share of U.S.$21 mn market.

j. 15% share of U.S.$4 mn market.

k. Ranked 6th with 9% share of U.S.$11 mn market.

l. Ranked 6th with 4% share of U.S.$33 mn market.

m. Ranked 4th with 7% share of U.S.$19 mn market.

n. Ranked 1st with 55% share of U.S.$8 mn market.

o. Ranked 2nd with 39% share of U.S.$4 mn market.

p. Ranked 1st with 50% share of U.S.$6 mn market.

q. Ranked 1st with 55% share of U.S.$8 mn market.

r. Ranked 4th in U.S. Antacid market.

s. Ranked 4th in U.S. Non-Fiber Laxatives market.

t. Ranked 4th in U.S. Fiber Laxatives market.

u. Ranked 3rd in U.S. Foot Powder market and 4th in U.S. Athlete's Foot Remedy market.

v. Ranked 1st in U.S. Jock Itch Treatment market with 36% share of U.S.$23.9 mn market.

w. Ranked 2nd in U.S. Iron market.

x. Ranked 3rd in U.S. Contact Lens Solution market.

y. Ranked 2nd in U.S. Artificial Tears market.

z. Ranked 1st with 25% share of U.S.$26 mn market.

of 1993 sales. Another 30 percent went to field force allocation for promotion to the medical profession. Importal was available in sachet form. Ciba intended to further build Importal's brand equity through line extensions and new delivery systems (e.g., cubes and liquid). Importal was still highly semi-ethical, and the company hoped to position the brand more as a consumer product in the future.

In 1991, Dulcolax and Fiberall competed in the U.S. laxatives market for Ciba. Dulcolax accounted for over half of the gastrointestinal sales for the company. In 1994, Dulcolax ranked fourth in the U.S. market for nonfiber laxatives. However, the brand's sales represented less than 5 percent of the U.S. laxatives market. Marketing rights for the U.S. sale of Dulcolax were licensed from Boehringer-Ingelheim in 1990. Boehringer-Ingelheim retained marketing rights outside the U.S. market. Fiberall generated less than one-third of the sales of Dulcolax. It was given little advertising support and was repositioned as a value brand[8] by Ciba. Fiberall was available in chewable tablets, wafers, and powder form.

Maalox was the main reason for Ciba's acquisition of Rhône-Poulenc Rorer's North American OTC business in 1994. As an antacid, it faced tough competition from the introduction of H_2 antagonists. Maalox had a strong image, which was used to launch two line extensions in 1993: Maalox Anti-Gas and Maalox Antidiarrheal. Original Maalox ranked fourth in the U.S. antacid market in the twelve months to July 1994 with sales of U.S.$58.7 million (11.4 percent share of market).

Circulatory Remedies

Circulatory remedies achieved a 4 percent share of the global OTC market. Hemorrhoidal treatments were the most well-known products in this segment. Although Ciba's portfolio did not contain any strong products with this indication, Ciba had about 8 percent of the circulatory remedies market due to Venoruton, a medication used to improve circulation in the veins. Venoruton was used mostly by women as a night medication to prevent restless, achy legs. If left untreated, poor circulation could lead to varicose veins.

Venoruton was available worldwide in seventy

countries throughout Europe, Latin America, Africa, Australia, and New Zealand. The drug was semi-ethical in all markets. Sales were highest in Germany at SFr. 56 million in 1993. Spain, Italy, Belgium and the United Kingdom rounded out the top five, but sales in those four countries combined were less than the total for Germany. Venoruton's different pricing strategies in many of the countries, causing parallel importing in some instances.[9] Venoruton was available in two forms, systemic and topical. The systemic version tended to have a higher price and thus was less likely to be offered OTC. The topical version, however, was more likely to be taken without prescription by consumers.[10]

The company's intention was to switch the brand to OTC status in as many markets as possible, thus building OTC sales through direct consumer promotion. In 1994, government-imposed classification changes in Italy changed Venoruton to a nonreimbursable, nonprescription drug, but did not automatically grant consumer advertising approval. Ciba did not immediately apply for OTC with advertising status. Venoruton enjoyed a good reputation among pharmacists and was generally considered effective. Ciba hoped to continue support of the product to medical professionals in those countries where the product was still reimbursed, while branching out with new forms in those markets where the product could become completely OTC.

Skin Treatments

Skin treatments were the fourth-largest product segment worldwide, with a 12 percent share of the global OTC market. Products in this segment treated a broad range of ailments, including dry skin, dandruff, athlete's foot, jock itch, cold sores, and cuts and scrapes. Ciba offered several brands for skin treatments. Perhaps the two most important were the Desenex family of foot care products in the United States and the anti-itch remedy, Fenistil, in Europe. Ciba generated approximately 16 percent of its 1994 OTC sales in the skin treatments segment.

Desenex was another US brand acquired in the

---

8. A value brand was generally priced lower than other brands in the same segment.

9. Parallel importing occurred when products were cheaper in one country than another, making it financially attractive for a wholesaler to buy the products in one country and sell them at a much higher price in another.

10. *OTC News Company Monitor,* June 1995, p. 190.

Exhibit 8 ● Ciba Self Medication Sales of Top Zyma Products (SFr. mn)

Product	1992	1993	1994
Venonuton	156.6	115.4	109.8
Otrivin	52.2	50.1	63.8
Fenistil	46.2	44.0	50.5
Importal	31.8	30.2	34.4
Nicotinell	N/A	N/A	29.2
Zymaflour	19.1	21.8	24.7
Vibrocil	18.7	18.9	17.5
Neda	14.3	13.0	13.9
Savlon	12.8	12.6	13.4
Voltaren/Emulgel	10.8	11.4	11.7
Total Zyma	700.8	667.0	681.1

Note: These figures include all sales of the products, both prescription and nonprescription. Top products for U.S. operation were not available.

Source: Ciba Self Medication.

Fison's purchase in 1992. It was considered Ciba's most important skin care brand. Ciba invested heavily in the line. In 1994, Desenex was ranked fourth in the U.S. athlete's foot remedy market and third in the foot powder market.

Zyma's third-largest brand was Fenistil, an anti-itch remedy.[11] It was offered in several dosage forms, such as tablets, drops, syrup, injectable phials, and gel. Only the gel was OTC-approved; all other forms were still prescription–bound.[12] The gel accounted for 38 percent of overall sales in 1993 at SFr. 16.7 million. Germany was by far the most important market for the product, where it commanded a 7 percent share of the anti-itch market. Its sales in Switzerland,

11. Also called Fenigel, in Italy and Belgium.

12. Except in Germany, where the oral forms were available without a prescription.

13. Total sales for Fenistil were SFr. 44 million, of which SFr. 12.7 million came from prescription-bound sales. The direct promotion ratio includes promotion for both the prescription- and non–prescription-bound versions of the product.

Portugal, and Benelux were also important. As an OTC, Fenistil competed mostly as a topical antihistamine in the skin irritation market against Parfenac and Polarmine. Eurax, another Ciba product, competed in markets where Fenistil was not available (e.g., France and the United Kingdom). Fenistil's systemic, prescription-bound version competed with antihistamine products like Clarityn, Hismanal, Teldane, and Zyrtec.

Promotion of Fenistil accounted for 13 percent of sales.[13] Fenistil (Fenigel) was the only advertised anti-itch brand in Belgium, where Ciba spent SFr. .05 million in 1993. The brand had 52% SOV in Germany, making it the biggest advertiser in its category. Fenistil was generally positioned as a cooling gel with antihistamine (effects for the relief of mosquito bites and sunburn. It had previously been marketed more as a hay fever medication, but its drowsy side effects were seen as a disadvantage by consumers. As a skin treatment, on the other hand, its drowsiness was more desirable to consumers because it got them through the night without itching.

Smoking Cessation

Habit control represented a relatively small portion of the global OTC market, but it was expected to grow at a compound annual growth rate of 21 percent from 1993–1998. Ciba entered the rapidly growing smoking cessation market on the ground floor with its transdermal nicotine patch, Nicotinell.

At the end of 1994, Nicotinell was available as OTC in six European markets, generating sales of SFr. 29 million, with SFr. 11 million of direct promotion. Germany and the United Kingdom were Nicotinell's top markets, with sales of SFr. 13.9 and 13.4 million, respectively. It ranked second in Europe to Nicorette, which came in both gum and patch forms.[14] Habitrol, as the product was known in the U.S. market, had not been approved for OTC status as of the end of 1994.

Nicotinell's key feature was its slow-release mechanism which gradually allowed nicotine into the system for a twenty-four-hour period. Nicorette's patch, on the other hand, lasted for sixteen hours. Ciba was also working to develop a gum it expected to introduce in 1995.

Analysts expected Ciba to eventually market Nicotinell with a pan-European approach. Ciba chose to package the OTC version of the product in a completely different fashion from the Rx version. Advertising in 1994 centered on building brand recognition and promoting the benefit of twenty-four-hour effectiveness. It's tag line in the United Kingdom was "It Needn't Be Hell With Nicotinell." In Germany and the United Kingdom, Ciba used extensive TV advertising with good initial success.

Oral Care

Oral care accounted for approximately 4 percent of global OTC sales. It included products for tooth decay, bad breath, dentures, and so on. Ciba was not a big player in oral care but offered a very solid product in this category with Zymaflour.

Zymaflour had been introduced as a prescription-

only more than forty years before. Its indication was as a fluoride supplement tablet for babies and children. Sales in 1993 were SFr. 21.8 million, mostly from France and Germany. It ranked second in the overall European fluoride supplement market.

Zymaflour was the only pan-European brand in its category. It was highly semi-ethical—mostly prescribed by doctors to strengthen children's teeth during development. Because it was semi-ethical, Ciba could not do any consumer advertising for the product. Zymaflour built up strong consumer awareness with its standard pink packaging. Pricing of the product varied by country. In Belgium, Ciba attempted to market a toothpaste version of the product as a pure OTC but was unsuccessful in developing a substantial market presence.

Pain Relief

Pain relief was the largest product segment in the world OTC market, with 1994 sales of U.S.$7.3 billion. This segment was very dynamic, with many new product introductions and line extensions by leading players such as Johnson & Johnson (Tylenol) and American Home Products (Advil). Pain relief was generally divided into four therapeutic segments: general pain, muscular pain, migraine, and mouth pain. Ciba generated only 5 percent of its OTC sales in this category, giving them less than a 1 percent share of the total pain relief market.

Ciba marketed several pain relief products in the United States and Europe. Most notable in the United States were Doan's and Ascriptin, neither of which were ranked in the top ten. In Europe, Ciba achieved top-ten rankings with Proflex cream in the United Kingdom and Neo-Cibalgina in Italy.

Voltaren Emulgel, a topical nonsteroidal anti-inflammatory drug (NSAID) for muscular pain relief, was believed to have much potential as a future Rx-to-OTC switch[15]. It had achieved success as an OTC in Switzerland, the only market where it was available on a nonprescription basis. For 1994, Voltaren Emulgel achieved sales in Switzerland of SFr. 7.5 million, 25 percent of the market for muscular and arthritic pain remedies. The oral prescription version of

---

14. Nicorette had 51 percent of the European market (43 percent gum and 8 percent patch), while Nicotinell had 32 percent (patch). The next closest competitor was Nicopatch, at 10 percent.

15. Emulgel was a trademark of Ciba-Geigy; its galenic presentation was in between a cream and a gel.

Voltaren was the single most important product in Ciba's pharmaceutical portfolio. More switches to OTC status of Voltaren Emulgel were discussed.

Ciba acquired the distribution rights to Doan's in 1987. The product possessed a strong brand name and was positioned specifically as a backache medicine. Sales dropped 5 percent in 1994 to U.S.$21 million. Products such as the Bayer Select line offered by Sterling Health also targeted niche markets such as backaches. Doan's PM, a line extension for relief of pain during sleep, gained slightly in 1994 to reach U.S.$5 million in sales.

The RPR acquisition gave Ciba its top-selling analgesic, Ascriptin. Sales of aspirin products had been relatively flat or declining in recent years, and Ascriptin held an insignificant share of the market.

Vitamins, Minerals, and Nutritional Supplements

The global OTC segment, vitamins, minerals, and nutritional supplements (VMS), was broadly defined, and there were discrepancies between countries as to what products were included. Even so, approximately 10 percent of global OTC sales occurred in VMS.

Ciba had few offerings in this category, its strongest being Sunkist and Slow Fe in the U.S. market. Vitamins accounted for roughly 4 percent of the U.S. operation's total OTC sales in 1994.

Ciba's Sunkist Vitamin C product was the fourth-ranking product in its category in the twelve months to March of 1995. It held a 5 percent share compared to Pharmavite's 19 percent share with its Nature Made Vitamin C tablet. The U.S. market for vitamin C was approximately U.S.$135.5 million at retail selling price. In the U.S. iron category, Slow Fe ranked second behind Geritol. Ciba's product claimed 14 percent of the U.S.$64.9 million dollar market (retail selling price).

MANAGEMENT STRUCTURE & DECISION-MAKING

In 1992, when Ciba Self Medication became a separate division, Ciba US and Zyma were two separate OTC organisations. Both reported to Pierre Douaze, who headed both the Pharmaceutical and Self Medication divisions at Ciba's corporate headquarters in Basel, Switzerland. The relationship between the OTC operations and corporate headquarters was very much at arms length, according to Eric Decosterd, head of Markets & Marketing at Zyma during this period. Even between the Pharmaceutical and Self Medication divisions very little information sharing occured.

At Zyma, located in Nyon, Switzerland, a few miles from Geneva Airport, the *Committee de Direction* (CD) made all key decisions. Its chairman, Remo Denti, also served as president of Zyma. Reporting to Denti were five committee members: Business Development, Production, Markets & Marketing, Research & Development, and Finance. This committee, along with its subcommittees, was the coordinator for all of Ciba's OTC operations outside of the United States.

"Product decisions funneled through the CD and were basically on a country-by-country basis, because it was mainly Europe," said Decosterd, explaining that Ciba's Self Medication business outside of Europe and the United States was almost nonexistent.

As far as business decisions were concerned, planning input meetings (PIM) were held each May or June, which gave countries the chance to explain to CD members what they foresaw happening in their market in the upcoming year. The CD came to the meeting with its own preconceived forecast. The purpose of the meeting was to reconcile the two views and build a business strategy for the next year. Individual meetings were held with each country. Once all of the meetings had taken place, it was up to the head of Markets & Marketing to consolidate the information and see what the global strategy looked like and then go back to the countries with corrective measures. Ciba management described this as a "bottom up, top down" approach to decision making.

Product development decisions were handled differently from the overall business strategy. For those types of decisions, an International Product Committee (IPC) composed of the CD chairman, the heads of Development and Markets & Marketing, and representatives from the five biggest countries, met two or three times a year to discuss product development ideas. Development for major brands was done at the Zyma facility in Nyon, with local brand development done in the countries.

Each country's management team was structured similarly to the CD, with a general manager (GM) at the head and production, marketing, field force, and finance managers reporting to the GM. Financial reporting was done on a country-by-country basis. While each country had control of implementing its own strategy, it was not allowed to introduce new products without the approval of the CD, even if the brand was to be sold only in that market.

INTERNATIONAL CATEGORY MANAGEMENT

Ciba did not have a clear international marketing strategy it applied to all OTC brands. In addition, marketing was performed separately for its U.S. and Zyma operations. At Zyma, each country took control of its own marketing. Until 1992, there was loose coordination of international brands. When Self Medication became a division in 1992, an international category manager (ICM) system was created. Each market segment had its own ICM, who coordinated the strategies of products that were offered in more than one country.

Philip Cross, head of Strategic Marketing Management, and his team began setting up the ICM structure by looking at the portfolio for each segment. With the help of the three lead countries for the particular segment, they developed a category strategy. Cross explained, "This involved identifying Ciba's key brand and geographic strengths by market segment, defining realizable midterm brand share objectives, and focusing marketing and product development resources accordingly." Once the strategy had been put in place, it was up to the countries to implement it. Cross and his team had no direct authority to mandate the individual countries to adopt any given strategy.

Implementing the ICM system was Ciba's first real attempt at a more coordinated approach to international OTC marketing. Six group brands evolved, which were offered across Europe. A proactive approach was taken in marketing these products. Ciba's ten key multilocal brands, which were offered in several countries only, were looked at in a more reactive fashion by the ICM.

OTC PORTFOLIO STRATEGY

Cross described Ciba's European OTC portfolio:

None of Ciba's brands could be considered block-busters. Like most of today's successful OTCs, they hadn't been launched as consumer brands but, through doctor prescription and pharmacist recommendation, had evolved over the years to become familiar names. Today, however, the pace needed to be accelerated and the brands more actively shaped and managed.

Ciba generally used acquisitions and some licensing agreements to fuel product growth, in addition to switches from the pharma division. According to Raja Rajagopal, head of Business Development, "Part of Ciba's acquisition strategy was a natural response to the consolidation of the fragmented OTC industry."

"We set ourselves on a course to get into new markets or to build to a certain size in markets like the United States. So our strategy then was driven by the need to gain some respectable business volume in that market." The quality of the products purchased was not the main criteria. Rather, emphasis was placed on gaining critical mass in a specific geography. This strategy was used to get a start in the United Kingdom, Germany, Spain, and the United States, for example. There were bigger, higher quality acquisitions available in the early 1990s, but corporate headquarters in Basel chose not to take advantage of them. "They could not be justified financially," said Rajagopal.

A prime example was the sale of Sterling Health in 1994, which Ciba initially took an interest in. There were executives within Ciba, such as newly appointed head of the Self Medication division, Roland Jeannet, who tried to convince Ciba-Geigy executives to place a competitive bid. However, he could not convince them to take such a huge step in their OTC business. "To put it into perspective, Sterling sold for U.S.$3 billion. Several months later, we purchased RPR's North American OTC business for U.S.$400 million," stated Jeannet.

GEOGRAPHIC SETUP

The largest Ciba Self Medication manufacturing facilities were in the United States and at the Zyma

Exhibit 9 ● Ciba Self Medication: Operating Units, 1994

OPERATING UNITS IN:		Marketing/Sales	Production	Development
EUROPE				
Switzerland	Headquarters		X	Complete
Austria	Affiliate	D[1]		MR
Benelux	Affiliate	D P		MR
France	Affiliate	D		MR
Germany	Affiliate	D P	X	MR G
Greece	Division	P		MR
Italy	Affiliate	D P	X	MR
Poland	Division	D P		MR
Portugal	Affiliate	D P		MR
Spain	Affiliate	D P	X	MR G
Switzerland	Affiliate	D P		MR
Turkey	Division	D P		MR
United Kingdom	Division	P S		MR G
NORTH AMERICA				
USA	Division	P S	X	Complete
Canada	Division	P S	X	MR G
AFRICA, ASIA, AND PACIFIC RIM				
Egypt	Division	D P S	X^2	MR
South Africa	Division	D P S		MR

Field force visiting: Doctors: D   Pharmacists: P   Supermarkets: S

Development: Medical/Regulatory: MR   Galenical: G

1. Joint Venture Zyma/Gebro
2. Joint Venture Ciba/Sandoz

headquarters in Nyon, Switzerland. Production centers were also located in Canada, Egypt, Germany, Hungary, Italy, and Spain (refer to Exhibit 9). Country subsidiaries sourced products in different ways. Basically, they could either produce locally, source them from Nyon, buy from a Ciba operation in a third country, or purchase from a Ciba pharmaceutical manufacturing site in their own country. Products sourced from Nyon were generally those that were considered international brands (e.g., Venoruton). Countries with their own manufacturing sites did not necessarily produce all of their own products, and they sometimes opted to get them from Nyon or from another country. Government regulation in countries such as Egypt and Hungary forced at least some local production to be done. The U.S. operations sourced largely locally.

COST STRUCTURE[16]

Ciba obtained most of its OTC products through switches from its pharma division or by acquiring other company's products. Most of its R&D was spent on reformulating Rx versions of drugs or developing new delivery systems. R&D was generally 5–10 percent of sales (refer to Exhibit 10).

Cost of goods sold for Ciba was comprised of variable and period expenses and usually amounted to 30–35 percent of wholesale price. Period expenses included: direct labor, equipment (depreciation and repairs & maintenance), quality control, and production overhead. Raw materials and packaging costs were the variable part of the manufacturing costs.

Active ingredients, or raw materials, used in Ciba's manufacturing process were less expensive than those for the pharma division. This was mainly due to the fact that ingredients used in OTC products are more commonly available. Together, the active ingredients and the excipients accounted for one-third of the variable materials cost, with packaging accounting for the other two-thirds.[17] Packaging was much more complicated than processing and much more labor-intensive. Each country required different packaging, resulting in small batch sizes and frequent changeovers for packaging equipment. Packaging equipment tended to be much more expensive than processing equipment.

Direct labor ran from 4–7 percent of cost of goods sold, with equipment and quality control at less than 2 percent. Production overhead was another 8–13 percent and included personnel administration, information systems, and other plant infrastructure costs.

Transportation and rebates to wholesalers added another 5–9 percent to the final cost of the product.

Marketing and sales was a major expense for Ciba, averaging 35–45 percent of the wholesale price. Ciba marketed to the trade, to medical professionals, and to consumers. Also included in this percentage were brand management and sales force expenses, which ran at about 5–9 percent and 7–11 percent, re-

16. Actual data disguised. Ciba's cost structure was broadly similar to industry-wide averages. Data cited in case reflects OTC industry averages.

17. Excipients are the components other than the active ingredients that comprise the final form of the drug.

Exhibit 10 ● Ciba Self Medication Cost Structure

Business Operaton	Proportion of Wholesale Price
RESEARCH & DEVELOPMENT	5–10%
COST OF GOODS SOLD	30–35%
Variable Expenses	
Raw Materials (⅓)	4–6%
Packaging (⅔)	8–12%
Period Expenses	
Direct Labor	4–7%
Equipment	1%
Quality Control	1%
Overhead	8–13%
TRANSPORTATION & REBATES	5–9%
MARKETING & SALES	35–45%
Brand Management	5–9%
Sales Force	7–11%
Customer Service	2–5%
General Advertising	10–15%
Trade Promotion	4–8%
Consumer Promotion	2–5%
Medical Promotion	2–5%
GENERAL & ADMINISTRATIVE	5–10%
PROFIT	10–20%

Note: Cost structure shown represents average values for OTC industry.

spectively. In addition, Ciba included its customer service expenses under marketing and sales, which averaged 2–5 percent.

General advertising expenditures accounted for 10–15 percent of sales. Promotion to the trade and to both medical professionals and consumers averaged 4–8 percent respectively. Consumer and medical advertising were at about 2–5 percent, respectively.

General and administrative expenses for Ciba

Self Medication ranged from 5–10 percent, allowing Ciba to earn a profit margin of 10–20 percent.

DEVELOPING A CIBA SELF MEDICATION STRATEGY

With the strategy review in full swing at the end of 1994, Jeannet expected that a complete proposal to the Ciba Group would have to be made by early spring 1995. The review process would take two steps. First, Jeannet and his team would need to get the support of the Ciba Health sector, where the Self Medication Division reported. Secondly, the plan would be presented to the Ciba Group executives for final approval.

Case 6

Interactive Computer Systems Corp.

In September 1990, Peter Mark, marketing manager of Interactive Computer Systems Corporation,[1] was faced with a perplexing conflict between his company's USA sales group and the European subsidiaries. The USA sales group had begun to sell a display controller which had been developed in Europe. The product had been selling in Europe for several years, and sales were relatively strong. Now, however, several major European customers had begun to purchase the product through their USA offices and ship it back to Europe. The Europeans were complaining that the U.S. pricing was undercutting theirs and that they were losing sales volume which was rightfully theirs. Both the U.S. and European groups claimed that their pricing practices followed corporate guidelines and met the profit objectives set for them.

INTERACTIVE COMPUTER SYSTEMS CORP.

Interactive Computer Systems Corporation (ICS), headquartered in Stamford. Connecticut, was a large, multinational manufacturer of computer systems and equipment. The company made a range of computer

●

This version of this case was prepared by Professor Jean-Pierre Jeannet based on an earlier version by Mark Uhrich as a basis for class discussion rather than to illustrate either effective or ineffective handling of an administrative situation. Copyright © 1996 by IMD, Lausanne, Switzerland. The International Institute for Management Development (IMD), resulting from the merger between IMEDE, Lausanne, and IMI, Geneva, acquires and retains all rights. Not to be used or reproduced without written permission from IMD, Lausanne, Switzerland.

1. Names and data are disguised. All prices are stated in U.S. dollars.

systems and was best known for its workstations. ICS was considered one of the industry leaders in that segment of the computer industry, which included such companies as Digital Equipment, Hewlett-Packard, and Sun Microsystems.

The company was primarily a U.S.-based corporation, with the majority of its engineering and manufacturing facilities located in the eastern United States. In addition, ICS had manufacturing facilities in Singapore, Germany, Brazil, and Taiwan, and a joint venture in South Korea.

Sales were conducted throughout most of the world by means of a number of sales subsidiaries with sales offices located in Canada, Mexico, Brazil, Argentina, Chile, Japan, Australia, and most European countries. Elsewhere, sales were conducted through a network of independent agents and distributors.

PRODUCT LINE

The ICS line of products was centered around a family of powerful workstations. *Workstation* was the popular term referring to small to medium-sized computer systems, which were used in a wide variety of engineering applications including industrial control, telecommunications systems, laboratory applications, and small business systems.

In addition to the computer central processing units (CPUs) and memory units, ICS produced a line of peripheral devices required for making complete computer systems. These included devices such as disk storage units, printers, video and hard-copy terminals, display units, and laboratory and industrial instrumentation interface units. These various peripherals were used as appropriate and combined with the final computer systems to meet the specific customer's requirements. ICS produced most of these products in-house, but some, such as printers, were purchased to ICS specifications from companies specializing in those products.

ICS manufactured several central processing units, which were positioned in price and performance to form a product family. They all had similarity of design, accepted (executed) the same computer instructions, and ran on the same operating system (master control programs). The difference was in speed, complexity, and cost. The purchaser was able to select the model which economically met the performance requirements of the intended application.

This family of CPUs, together with the wide range of available peripheral devices, formed a family of computer systems offering a considerable range of price and performance but with compatible characteristics and programming.

MODEL 2000 COMMUNICATIONS INTERFACE

A communication interface was a peripheral device used for transmitting data to or from the computer system. The specific product in question was the model 2000 communications interface, a multiline programmable multiplexer.

The 2000 provided the interface for many separate communications lines, which were connected by means of specially designed connectors on the module. Such multiline interfaces were typically called multiplexers after the manner in which they worked internally. They offered the advantages of more efficient space utilization and lower per-line costs compared with the normal alternative of a separate single-line interface per line. Depending on the computer vendor, multiplexers come in various sizes such as 2, 4, 6, 8, 16, 32, and 64 lines.

ICS already had multiplexers in its line of high volume standard products. The specified advantage of the 2000 was its programmable nature. It could be loaded with software to handle any of several different protocols directly in the interface, using its own microprocessor on the module. Since these functions had previously all been performed by a program running in the computer, the 2000 relieved the computer of this load and freed it up to do other work. The result was a net improvement in system speed and power.

The model 2000 was designed in 1987 at ICS's small European engineering facility assigned to its German subsidiary, Interactive Computers GmbH, in Frankfurt and was manufactured there for shipment worldwide to those ICS subsidiaries who were selling

the 2000. Sales had initially started in Europe and then spread to other areas. Sales volumes are given in Exhibit 1.

INTERSUBSIDIARY TRANSACTIONS

With the exception of the Korean joint venture, all of ICS's subsidiaries were wholly owned, and products moved freely between them. ICS had set up its procedures and accounting systems in line with the fact that it was basically a U.S.-based company manufacturing a uniform line of products for sales worldwide through various sales subsidiaries. For the major product lines, the only differences by countries were line voltages and some minor adaptations to comply with local government regulations.

Although the subsidiaries in the various countries were essentially sales subsidiaries functioning as sales offices to sell products in those countries, they were separately incorporated entities and wholly owned subsidiaries, operating under the laws of that particular country. Careful accounting of all transactions between the parent company and the subsidiaries had to be maintained for the purpose of import duties and local taxes.

When a customer ordered a computer system, the order was processed in the subsidiary and then transmitted back to the parent company (ICS) in the United States to have the system built. The order paperwork listed the specific hardware items (CPU, memory size, disk units, etc.) wanted by the customer,

Exhibit 1 ● Model 431 Sales Volume (Units), Selected Countries

	1987	1988	1989	1990
Germany	30	100	110	100
U.K.	5	40	60	70
France	10	20	50	40
Canada	0	0	5	5
Switzerland	3	20	30	15
Australia	0	0	10	30
United States	0	2	80	200

and each system was built specifically to order. The component pieces were built by ICS in volume to meet the requirements of these specific customer systems orders. Like most companies, ICS expended a great amount of effort attempting to accurately forecast the mix of products it would need to meet customer orders.

When the customer's system, or any product, was shipped to the subsidiary, the subsidiary "bought" it from the parent at an intercompany discounted price, or "transfer price," of list minus 20 percent. The level of subsidiary transfer price discount was established with two factors in mind:

- It was the primary mechanism by which Interactive repatriated profits to the U.S. parent corporation.

- The 20 percent subsidiary margin was designed to give the subsidiaries positive cash flow to meet their local expenses such as salaries, facilities, benefits, travel, and supplies.

Import duties were paid on the discounted (list minus 20 percent) transfer price value according to the customs regulations of the importing country. Some typical import duties for computer equipment are shown in Exhibit 2.

Most countries were quite strict on import/export and customs duties and required consistency in all transactions. Therefore, all shipments were made at the same discounted transfer price, including shipments among subsidiaries and shipments back to the United States.

PRICING

ICS set prices worldwide based on U.S. price lists. which were referred to as "Master Price Lists," or MPLs. Prices in each country were based on the MPL plus an uplift factor to cover the increased cost of doing business in those countries. Some of these extra costs were:

- Freight and duty, in those countries where it was included in the price (in some countries, duties were paid for separately by the customer).

Exhibit 2 ● Import Duties for Computer Equipment for Selected Countries[a]

United States	5.1%
Canada	8.8
Japan	9.8
Australia	2.0
European Union countries	None between EU countries; 6.7% from outside EU countries

a. These are typical amounts only. The topic of customs duties is quite complex. It varies with the type of goods, even within an industry (computer systems may be one rate, while computer terminals may be another, higher rate and parts a third rate), and by country of origin.

- Extended warranty: in some countries, the customary warranty periods were longer than in the United States, for example, one year versus ninety days.

- Cost of subsidiary operations and sales costs, to the extent that they exceed the normal selling costs in the United States.

- Cost of currency hedging: in order to be able to publish a price list in local currency, ICS bought U.S. dollars in the money futures market.

Uplift factors were periodically reviewed and adjusted if needed to reflect changes in the relative cost of doing business in each country. Typical uplift factors for some selected countries are shown in Exhibit 3.

Each subsidiary published its own price list in local currency. The list was generated quarterly by use of a computer program which took a tape of all the MPL entries and applied the uplift and a fixed currency exchange rate which had been set for the fiscal year. This price list was used by all salespeople in the subsidiary as the official listing of products offered and their prices.

SPECIAL PRODUCTS

In addition to its standard line of products which were sold worldwide in volume, ICS had a number of lower

Exhibit 3 ● Typical Country Uplift Factors: Local Price = Master Price List + Uplift %

United Kingdom	8%
Germany	15
France	12
Switzerland	17
Sweden	15
Australia	12
Brazil	20
Canada	5

volume, or specialized, products. The model 2000 communications interface was considered one of these. Specialized products were typically not on the MPL, and prices were set locally by each subsidiary wherever they were sold. They were either quoted especially on request for quote basis or added to a special price list supplement produced by each country. This was a common procedure in the computer industry.

To support the sales of the specialized products, ICS had a separate team of specialists, with one or more specialists in each subsidiary. They were responsible for the pricing of their products and had a high degree of independence in setting prices in each subsidiary. The specialist or team in each subsidiary was responsible for all aspects of the sales of their assigned products and essentially ran a business within a business.

For the purposes of internal reporting to management, the specialists were measured on achieving a profit before tax, or PBT, of 15 percent, which was the ICS goal. The results were shown on a set of internal reports which were separate from the legal books of the subsidiary. The purpose of the internal reports was to give ICS management more information on the profitability of its various product lines. These reports took the form of a series of profit and loss statements of operation by line of product with overhead and indirect costs allocated on a percentage of revenue basis. For these internal P&L reports, the cost of goods was the actual cost of manufacture (in-ternal cost) plus related direct costs instead of the discounted price paid by subsidiaries and shown on their official statements of operation.

2000 SALES IN EUROPE

The model 2000 communications interface was designed in 1987 by the European engineering group in Frankfurt as a follow-up to some special engineering contracts for European customers. It was introduced in the European market in 1988, where it grew in popularity.

The 2000 was produced in Frankfurt only on a low-volume production line. The manufacturing and other direct costs amounted to U.S. $1,500 per unit. Because there were no tariffs within the EU and shipping costs were covered by allocated fixed costs, there were no other direct costs. The allocated fixed costs in Europe were running at 47 percent of revenue. Thus, a contribution margin of 62 percent was required to achieve a 15 percent PBT. Based on these costs, a list price of U.S. $3,900 had been set within the EU. The resulting P&L is shown in Exhibit 4.

Because of the popularity of this product, it had been listed on the special products price list in most European countries. Within the EU, the price had been set at the same level, with any variation due only to local currency conversions. In European countries outside the EU, the price was increased to cover import duties.

At the above price, the 2000 had gained market acceptance and had grown in popularity, especially in

Exhibit 4 ● Model 2000 European Profit Analysis (in U.S. dollars)

European List Price	U.S. $3,900
Manufacturing and Other Direct Costs	1,500
Contribution Margin	2,400
	62%
Allocated Fixed Costs (47%)	1,833
PBT	U.S. $567
	14.5%

Germany, the United Kingdom. and France. Its customers included several large European based multinational companies of major importance to ICS in Europe. These customers designed specific system configurations and added programming to perform specified applications and shipped the systems to other countries, either to their own subsidiaries for internal use (for example, a factory) or to customers abroad.

2000 SALES IN THE UNITED STATES

The 2000 was brought to the attention of the U.S. sales group in two different ways. In sales contacts with U.S. operations of some European customers, ICS was told of the 2000 and asked to submit price and availability schedules for local purchase in the United States. U.S. customers expressed irritation at being told that the model was not available in the United States.

Secondly, the U.S. sales force also heard of the 2000 from their European counterparts at sales meetings, where the Europeans explained how the 2000 had been important in gaining large accounts.

As a result of this pressure from customers and the sales force, the U.S. special products specialists obtained several units for evaluation and in 1989 made the 2000 available for sale in the United States.

Originally, the U.S. specialists set the price equal to the European price of $3,900. However, it became obvious that the U.S. market was more advanced and more competitive, with customers expecting more performance at that price. As a result the price had to be reexamined.

The 2000 was obtained from Frankfurt at the internal cost of $1,500. Transportation costs were estimated at $200. In the U.S. accounting system, import duties and transportation were not charged directly and were absorbed by general overhead. This came about because ICS was primarily an exporter from the United States, with very little importing taking place. Consequently, it was felt that import costs were negligible. Thus, the only direct cost was the $1,500 internal cost. Overhead and allocated fixed expenses in the United States averaged 35 percent.

The result was, as shown in Exhibit 5, a revised price of $3,000 with a contribution margin of 50 per-

Exhibit 5 ● Model 2000 U.S. Profit Analysis

U.S. list price	$3,000
Manufacturing cost	1,500
Contribution margin	1,500
	50%
Allocated fixed costs (35%)	1,050
PBT	$450
	15%

cent and a PBT of 15 percent—the ICS goal. Following this analysis, the U.S. price was reduced to $3,000. The 2000 was not listed on the main U.S. price list but was quoted only on an RPQ basis. Subsequently, this price was also listed on special products price list supplements which were prepared by the U.S. product specialists and handed out to the sales force in each district.

CURRENT SITUATION

The repricing of the 2000 to $3,000 was instrumental in boosting U.S. sales. The sales volume continued to grow, and some large customers were captured. These customers included existing ICS customers who previously used other, lower-performance communications interfaces or had bought somewhat equivalent devices from other companies who made "plug compatible" products for use with ICS computers. Also, a good volume of sales was being obtained from the U.S. operations of European multinationals who were already familiar with the product. ICS's U.S. group, who had first viewed the European designed product with suspicion, was now more confident about it.

But the Europeans were not entirely happy with the situation. Recently, they had started complaining to ICS management that the U.S. pricing of the 2000 was undercutting the European price. This was causing pressure on the European subsidiaries to reduce the price below the $3,900 they needed to meet their profitability goals. Pressure was coming from customers who knew the U.S. price and from European salespeople who, as a result of travel to the United

States or discussions with U.S. colleagues, knew the U.S. price and what the uplifted European price "was supposed to be."

The price difference had also been noticed by several of ICS's larger European multinational customers. They started buying the 2000 through their U.S. offices and reexporting it, both back to Europe and to other countries.

So far, three customers had done this, two German firms and one French customer. Several additional customers were showing definite signs of "shopping around."

This loss of customers to the United States was particularly painful to the Europeans. They had invested considerable amounts of effort into cultivating these customers.

In addition, the customers still expected to receive technical and presales support from their local ICS office (that is, European) as well as warranty and service support, regardless of where they placed the purchase order. Attempts to discuss this with the customers or persuade them to purchase in Europe had not been successful. Typical reactions had been "That's ICS's problem" (U.K. customer) and "But are you not one company?" (German customer).

In brief, the ICS European subsidiaries were complaining that they were "being denied the prof-itable results of their own work" by the unfair pricing practices of the U.S. parent company.

In the eyes of the U.S. team, however, they were pricing in accordance with corporate guidelines to achieve a 15 percent PBT. They also maintained that the market did not allow them to price the 2000 any higher. Furthermore, they felt that they were simply exercising their right to set their own country prices to maximize profits within their specific country market.

The U.S. group was so pleased with the U.S. market acceptance of the 2000 that they wanted to begin an aggressive promotion. As an important part of this, they were now planning to add the 2000 on the official ICS U.S. price list. This was viewed as a key to higher sales since, especially in the United States, products tended to be sold from the regular price list, and the sales force tended to lose or ignore special price list supplements.

At this point, both the European and U.S. specialists were upset with each other. Both sides maintained that they were following the rules but that the actions of "the other side" were harming their success and profitability.

It had been a long day, and it was time to go home. As he turned his car out into the traffic on High Ridge Road, Mark was still feeling confused about the issues and wondering what should be done.

Case 7

ICI Paints (A): Strategy for Globalization

"We at ICI Paints aspire to the number one position globally in the paint business. Our goal is to make ICI Paints the first choice among paint suppliers to whom a customer anywhere in the world would turn if he were seeking a long-term supply relationship," said Herman Scopes, PEO (principal executive officer) of ICI Paints. "Now, we are already the world's leader if measured in market share, sales volume, or liters of paint produced. However, we have not yet been able to translate this position into superior financial performance. To get there, we will have to become much better at learning from each other and at transferring best practice from one operation to another."

INDUSTRY PROFILE

The world paint market was estimated at some £20[1] billion at ex-factory level and some 12 billion liters. Growth was expected to average 2–3 percent through the next decade.

North America accounted for 31 percent of the market by volume, followed by Europe (29 percent), Japan (13 percent), Asia Pacific (11 percent), and the rest of the world (16 percent). In the more mature paint markets of North America and Europe, annual growth was expected to be below GNP growth, whereas in the newly industrializing countries growth was expected to be in line with GNP growth. Long term, the three principal paint user areas of Europe, North America, and Asia Pacific were expected to become of equal size and account for 75 percent of the world market (refer to Exhibit 1).

Major application segments included decorative uses (50 percent), industrial uses (37 percent), coatings for cans (3 percent), automotive OEM (6 percent), car repair and refinishing (4 percent). (See Exhibit 2).

There were approximately 10,000 paint manufacturers worldwide. Leading paint companies, aside

This case was prepared by Jean-Pierre Jeannet, Professor of Marketing and International Business at Babson College and Adjunct Professor at IMD, as a basis for class discussion rather than to illustrate either effective or ineffective handling of a business situation. Copyright © 1990 by IMD, Lausanne, Switzerland. The International Institute for Management Development (IMD), resulting from the merger between IMEDE, Lausanne, and IMI, Geneva, acquires and retains all rights. Not to be used or reproduced without written permission from IMD, Lausanne, Switzerland.

1. In 1988, £1.00 = $1.50.

Exhibit 1 ● World Paint Industry Profile by Region (12,000 ML[a] worth $35 billion at suppliers' prices)

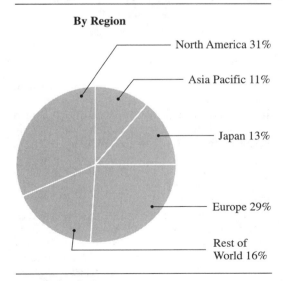

By Region

North America 31%

Asia Pacific 11%

Japan 13%

Europe 29%

Rest of World 16%

a. ML = million liters.

Exhibit 2 ● World Paint Volume by Market Segment

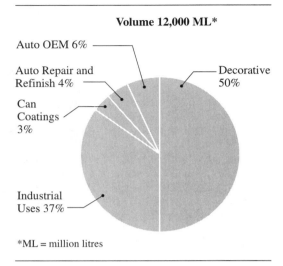

Volume 12,000 ML*

Auto OEM 6%

Auto Repair and
Refinish 4%

Can
Coatings
3%

Decorative
50%

Industrial
Uses 37%

*ML = million litres

a. ML = million liters.

from ICI, PPG, and BASF, were Sherwin-Williams (United States), Akzo (Netherlands), Nippon (Japan), International-Courtaulds (United Kingdom), Kansai (Japan), Du Pont (United States), and Valspar (United States). The top ten companies shared 30 percent of the world paint market in 1988. That share was expected to increase over the next decade.

COMPANY PROFILE

ICI Paints was the world's largest paint manufacturer, with a sales volume of £1.5 billion, or 8 percent of the world market, and an annual output of 800 million liters, or 7 percent of world volume. The company operated some sixty-four manufacturing plants in twenty-nine countries. Licensees operated in another fourteen countries (refer to Exhibit 3). ICI was about 70 percent larger than its next biggest competitor, PPG Industries.

ICI Paints was part of the Consumer and Specialty Products sector of ICI. The division accounted for about 12 percent of total ICI turnover and 7 percent of its trading profit. Sales in 1988 (excluding sales by related companies) had reached £1.363 billion, with a trading profit of £98 million resulting in a

return of 7.2 percent of sales. ICI Paints' profitability was on a par with BASF, its leading European competitor, and about twice that of its Japanese competitors. ICI Paints had been a consistent performer in an industry that had been characterized by considerable restructuring (refer to Exhibit 4).

ICI's market position varied considerably by market segment. The company was the world leader in the decorative and can coatings areas, a major player in automotive refinishes, one of the smaller automotive OEM players, and also held positions in powder, coil coatings, and other industrial coatings. ICI was absent from the marine paints sector (refer to Exhibit 5).

Decorative Paint Segment

About 57 percent of ICI Paints' business was accounted for by the decorative segment, which included paints and coatings used for the protection and decoration of industrial, commercial, and residential buildings. ICI was the world's largest producer of decorative paints, both for professional and do-it-yourself (DIY) users. The company marketed its Dulux brands in the United Kingdom, Australia, New Zealand, and a few other Asian markets; the Valentine brand in France; Ducolux in Germany; and Glidden Spred in the United States, which was acquired as part of the acquisition of Glidden in 1986. Glidden was the inventor of waterborne latex paints for popular emulsions. Although trading under different brands, ICI was the leader in most of these markets, particularly in the premium end of the market.

Most decorative paint was used where produced, with little cross-shipping, due to its low value. ICI tended to meet different local players country by country.

The wholesaling structure and retailing industry as well as the role of the DIY market varied considerably from one country to another. Furthermore, there was little economy of scale effect in this business. Some 500 paint companies competed in this segment in Italy alone. Paint formulations also had to be adjusted to local use conditions such as prevailing surfaces, building materials, and climate.

Despite these local differences, some commonalities existed. "Attitudes to what consumers want are far more common than different," commented John Thompson, ICI Paints' planning manager.

Exhibit 3 ● ICI Paints Territorial Spread

ICI paints manufacturing companies	ICI minority holdings	Companies manufacturing under license
Australia	Botswana	Colombia
Canada	Malawi	Cyprus
Eire	Indonesia	Japan
Fiji	Nigeria	Jordan
France	South Africa	Kenya
India	Zimbabwe	South Korea
Italy		Portugal
Madagascar		Saudi Arabia
Malaysia		Sudan
Mexico		Trinidad
New Zealand		Turkey
Pakistan		Venezuela
Papua New Guinea		Yemen
Singapore		
Spain		
Sri Lanka		
Taiwan		
Thailand		
United Kingdom		
Uruguay		
United States		
West Germany		

"We have done market research in Turkey, Italy, and Columbus, Ohio, and the same overall pattern emerges: the woman in a household determines when a surface is to be painted, and she determines the color. The husband selects the brand, usually on the basis of price and technique, although women are increasingly also making this decision. In terms of paint application, it is about evenly split between husbands and wives."

Can Coating Segment

Although the can coating segment, with worldwide sales of £800 million, accounted for only 3 percent of the world paint market, it accounted for 11 percent of

ICI business, or £165 million, representing about 28 percent market share and giving it world leadership. Some 46 percent of the market was in North America, followed by Europe (24 percent) and Asia Pacific (22 percent). Major competitors were BASF, Midland, and Valspar.

The coatings were used on the inside of tin or aluminum cans for food or beverage containers, making them corrosion resistant. This thin layer on the inside of every can was a crucial part for a successful canning operation. Consequently, this part of the paint industry was viewed as a high technology application.

Customers were concentrated, with major use in the hands of four groups and their licensees: Continental Can, Pechiney-Triangle (included former

Exhibit 4 ● ICI Paints Financial Performance, 1985–1989

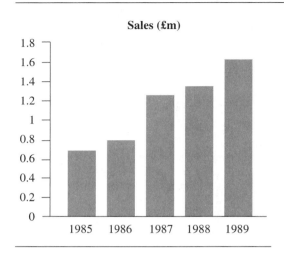

Sales (£m)

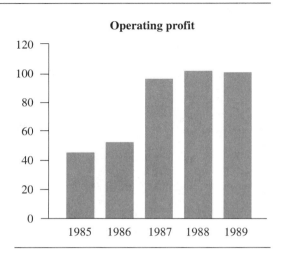

Operating profit

Exhibit 5 ● ICI Volume by Market Segment

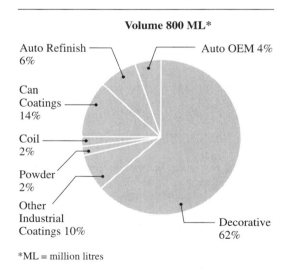

Volume 800 ML*

Auto Refinish 6%
Auto OEM 4%
Can Coatings 14%
Coil 2%
Powder 2%
Other Industrial Coatings 10%
Decorative 62%

*ML = million litres

American Can and National Can), Carnaud–MetalBox, and Crown Cork and Seal. These can manufacturers operated canning lines all over the world, and they expected the suppliers to follow them everywhere with a consistent product ensuring same tastes for globally marketed products such as Coca-Cola.

Coating products had to be developed for each application and depended on the particular food or beverage as well as on the type of metal or aluminum container used. Customers were increasingly looking for simplifications and tended to look for a narrower technology range.

In this business, it was important to be able to make the development effort go around. A new product for sardines might be developed in Portugal but might have applications for Norwegian packers as well. Success depended on avoiding duplication of effort in applications development. Although coatings were usually not identical, a considerable part of the concept development could be widely applicable to other customers with the same applications.

ICI had acquired some eleven coatings companies over the years, including Holden (Birmingham) with operations in Europe, Marsden (United Kingdom), Wiederhold (Germany), Attivilac (Italy), and Glidden (United States). In Europe, ICI had strong operations in Rouen, France, where its Holden operation was located near the Carnaud company. The French operation had thus always been strong in food applications. Glidden, on the other hand, enjoyed an 80 percent market share in the United States for beverage cans.

ICI had targeted the can coating segment for major growth and planned to increase its market share to

40 percent of the world market, up from 28 percent currently. A new production facility was planned for Taiwan. As part of this expansion strategy, the company combined all of its various can coatings businesses under the same leadership in a single packaging group. Prior to that change, can coatings had been part of the larger group for general industry coatings.

Major changes were also contemplated for development. Work was conducted to transfer Glidden's aluminum can coatings technology to steel and tin plate. Also under review was a decision whether or not to site a new development center in Singapore or Malaysia to service the growing Asia Pacific markets. Other research initiatives were considered on basic background chemistry and how to develop this for the canning industry.

Automotive OEM Paint Segment

The automotive paint segment consisted of paint sales made to automobile manufacturers for use in their assembly plants. Worldwide, this segment represented 5 percent of the paint market. Major markets were North America (31 percent), Europe (32 percent), and Japan (26 percent). Leading competitors were PPG, BASF, Kansai, Nippon, Du Pont, Hoechst, and ICI, in order of importance.

ICI's market share was about 6 percent worldwide, ranking it number seven out of eight international players. Most of its sales were in Europe, followed by the Asia Pacific area (exclusive of Japan) and North America, with major local markets in Malaysia, Australia, and Canada. ICI was considered technically good but commercially weak in this segment. The company was a leader in the initial development of electrolytic paint and in the development of water-based top coat paints (Aquabase) for automotive users. The latest product was first introduced by GM in Canada and was now being introduced by Volvo in Sweden. Other European manufacturers were testing it, and ICI had granted a license to a Japanese company.

"This is an incestuous industry," remarked John Thompson, ICI Paints' planning manager. The customer base was largely globally operating companies and technologically very demanding. The technical service requirements of customers required paint suppliers to station technical service personnel permanently on location. As a result, the automotive

companies preferred suppliers located at their doorsteps. This led to scattering factories close to assembly plants. In the United States, major paint companies would typically have several plants. Trends were away from multiple sourcing, which had kept local players alive, toward single sourcing and worldwide deals. Typically, a customer maintained a major supplier each for top coats and base coats, with a second supplier for smaller volume applications "to keep the big ones honest."

This segment was technically very demanding. PPG had reached segment leadership by developing electrolytic techniques key for the important base coating of car bodies. The initial development was actually made by ICI, but it was PPG which had made a commercial success out of the invention. At that time, PPG occasionally achieved single-source status through the installation of "hole-in-the-wall" plants, where the company was producing adjacent to the paint shops of the assembly plant.

Although the particular paint applications, such as color, were developed for each customer, a substantial part of the basic research had worldwide applications. Technical spinoffs were also possible for other paint segments, such as the refinish sector (with modifications in formulations due to the different paint applications methods), and for industrial components in areas such as the domestic appliance industry. This was one of the reasons why many players stayed in this segment despite low profitability or losses.

ICI had a very narrow geographic base in this segment and currently lacked platforms for major expansion. As a result, ICI engaged in a joint venture with Du Pont called IDAC, on a 50:50 basis, to supply the western European automotive market. Du Pont had most of its automotive paint business in the United States and was therefore relatively weak in Europe. Du Pont's area of strength was in the top coat business, with GM and Ford as major customers in the United States. The IDAC goal was to reach a 20 percent market share in Europe during the early 1990s.

Automotive Refinish Paint Segment

The refinish segment included paints and coatings for repairing automobiles. The segment accounted for 4 percent of world sales and had the highest price per liter (£3.34). It was considered the most profitable paint segment. North America accounted for 36 percent of the world market, followed by Europe (30 percent) and Asia Pacific (25 percent).

Only ten paint manufacturers competed significantly in the refinish sector. Among those, only Sherwin-Williams of the United States and Rock of Japan did not also compete in the automotive OEM market. No new competitor had entered since the 1950s.

The world leader was BASF as a result of its recent acquisition of Inmont in the United States, followed by Du Pont and ICI. ICI was the largest refinish supplier outside the United States. Its Autocolor brand led in the United Kingdom and was well known in Europe. In France, the company was the leader with its Valentine brand. ICI had a color inventory of some 30,000 formulas to match the stock colors of virtually all vehicle manufacturers. ICI's matching capability was developed in the U.K. market, where a wide variety of car models was on the road following the decline of the local U.K. car industry.

Customers were largely small paint shops that needed quick and frequent deliveries, typically on a daily basis. Paint manufacturers supplied their customers with mixing schemes through local distributors who would combine the basic colors and shades with solvents to obtain the correct color match. There were some 10,000 different shades and some sixty different colors to select from. For ICI, this resulted in some 30,000 different formulas, partly as a result of different application techniques for the same shades and colors. A recent trend was in the direction of color mixing at the end-user location, using color systems supplied by the paint manufacturer. Recently, ICI had placed a computerized management system at the disposal of its customers.

To compete in this business, a company had to have access to the color and paint shops of the car manufacturers to obtain the needed information. Automobile manufacturers wanted to make sure that their customers could get their cars repaired wherever they were marketed. As an example, a company like Toyota was interested in worldwide coverage. Refinish paint manufacturers profited if they could have access to all car manufacturers, wherever they were located, so that they could supply the widest possible color range in any geographic market.

Powder Paint Segment

Powder paints was the fastest growing segment and represented an alternative technology for traditional wet paint rather than a particular application segment. Growing 10–20 percent annually, the segment had attracted many large companies as well as smaller suppliers. Leaders were International-Courtaulds (United Kingdom), Ferro (United States), ICI, and DSM (Netherlands).

Powder coatings were a precisely formulated mixture of pigment and resin which was sprayed using electrostatic spray guns. The sprayed item, a metal object, was then heated for about ten minutes to cure the surface. Coatings had been developed for heat resistance or chemical resistance. The major benefits for users were the reduced emissions such as solvents used with wet paints and the reduced need for waste disposal. Major user groups were the automotive component suppliers, the metal furniture industry, and domestic appliance manufacturers. Powder paint could conceivably substitute up to 50 percent of the paint being applied to metal. In Europe, where the product was pioneered, the substitution already amounted to about 20 percent, compared to about 10 percent in the United States, an amount that was, however, growing rapidly.

While the technology itself had become basic, there was room to develop many applications. ICI had selected some specific applications for further development, such as domestic appliances and architectural components. ICI had concluded a joint venture with Nippon Oil & Fats of Japan in Malaysia. About half of ICI's powder volume was in the United States, about 40 percent in Europe, and the rest spread over many countries. In the United States, ICI was tied for first place with Morton but was only sixth in Europe.

General Industrial Paint Segment

Some £250 million of ICI Paints' business was part of the general industrial paint category, which included general industrial liquid paints, wood finishes, adhesives, ink, and others. Two-thirds of this segment was allied in some way to its four core business areas, such as adhesives in the United States or metal can printing. Another part consisted of stand-alone businesses, not necessarily connected to core sectors, such as inks for screen printing in Germany. In these segments, ICI did not compete consistently throughout the world and had only selected local pockets of excellence.

STRATEGY

ICI Paints aimed at world leadership and profitable growth. The company intended to concentrate on its key paint businesses on a global basis and wanted to exploit particular regional opportunities in the EU and Asia Pacific regions. ICI believed that a commitment to R&D and innovation was an essential part of industry leadership.

Organizationally, ICI aspired to become a marketing-driven organization that was quality and customer focused, health and safety conscious, and environmentally responsible.

ORGANIZATION

ICI management believed it was essential to have a global organization and management structure which would be both global and territory centered, support R&D centers of excellence in certain locations, and maximize resources and synergy between businesses, operations, and locations.

ICI Paints was organized along both geographic and business lines (refer to Exhibit 6). Reporting to the PEO were three regional heads (chief executives) for Europe, North America, and Asia Pacific. Each chief executive had P&L responsibility for the entire paint business in his area. The North American chief executive was also the head of Glidden, ICI Paints' major U.S. operating unit.

Reporting to each chief executive were several managers with country or territorial responsibility, called territorial general managers (TGMs) and business area general managers (BAGMs) for the four core sectors: decorative, can, automotive refinish and OEM, and powder. In some situations, BAGMs were identical with TGMs. In general, P&L results were a joint responsibility of BAGMs and TGMs.

At the territory or country level, BAGMs existed for the core business areas to the extent that each country had business in each of the four core sectors. Each territory also had other paint businesses. The percentage of sales in the latter category varied across territories, with higher percentages reported for some developing markets in Asia and lower per-

centages in the developed markets of Europe and North America.

DECISION-MAKING

Major decisions were always discussed and decided by the International Business Team (IBT) chaired by Herman Scopes, its PEO. Eight executives were members of the IBT, including the PEO and the three chief executives. The ICI Paints Group was led by Herman Scopes as its PEO and the seven members of the International Business Team (IBT). Part of the IBT were the three chief executives for North America, Europe, and Asia/Pacific/Australia regions, as well as four other executives with either functional or segment responsibility (refer to Exhibit 7). The IBT met six to eight times per year at various locations.

Executives were nominated to the IBT because of their ability to contribute broadly to the development of the ICI Paints Group rather than their specialties or specific skills. Once part of the IBT, members were assigned "portfolios" based on their own talents and experience, occasionally resulting in changes when the personnel constellation changed in the IBT.

An important aspect of the way ICI Paints operated was its use of international leaders (ILs). IL positions existed for each of its four core business areas (decorative, can coatings, automotive, and powder) as well as for five functional areas: finance, information technology, operations, R&D, and management development. The ILs for three of these five areas were members of the IBT.

The ILs of the core sectors had the roles of facilitators or coordinators. These international leaders did not have P&L responsibility. However, they were responsible for the development of global strategies for each of their assigned core sectors. Powder was coordinated out of the United States, decorative out of Europe (by the chief executive Europe), and automotive and can coatings from Europe (head of those sectors for Europe).

Strategies were developed at the business level by the international leaders and their teams and were then proposed to the International Business Team.

COORDINATING CORE BUSINESS SEGMENTS

The strategy making and coordination process differed considerably across the four core business areas.

Exhibit 6 ● ICI International Business Team Organization Chart

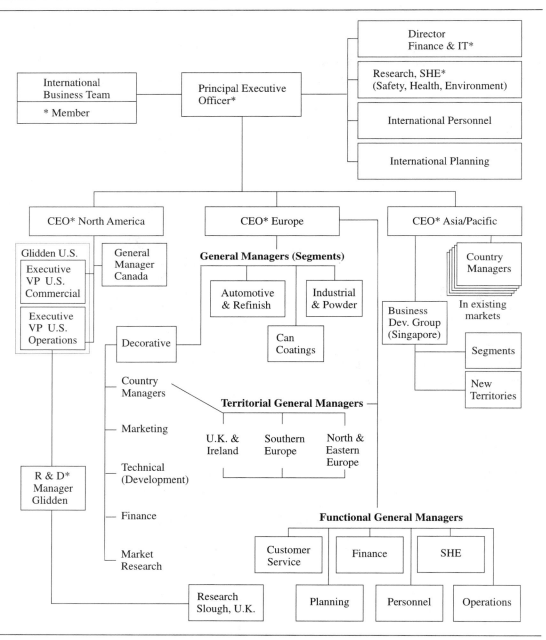

*Denotes IBT member.

Source: Company records.

Exhibit 7 ● Members of the International Business Team (IBT)

Herman Scopes	PEO ICI Paints
John Dumble	Chief Executive North America President Glidden
Doug Curlewis	Chief Executive Europe International Leader Decorative Paint
Richard Stillwell	Chief Executive Asia Pacific/Australia
John Danzeisen	Finance Director International Leader Powder International Leader Finance Function International Leader IT Function
Alex Ramig	International Leader R&D
Brian Letchford	International Leader Automotive Refinish and OEM (designated International Leader Can)
Quintin Knight	International Leader Can Coatings (retiring in March 1990)

INTERNATIONAL LEADERS NOT PART OF THE IBT:

June Thomason	Operations Manager Glidden International Leader Operations
Ian Cope	International Leader Management Development

The *decorative world strategy* consisted of three major elements. First, ICI Paints was to pursue quality leadership in all markets where the company was competing. It was understood that this meant setting the pace in the sector and pursuing a premium price. Second, there was to be a drive toward running a world brand, Dulux, the only world consumer paint brand in existence. This goal included having a consistent role for Dulux as the aspirational brand in all ICI decorative paint markets. Third, ICI was to use the fact that it was the largest paint producer worldwide and should thus be able to maximize its resources in key functional areas.

Coordination was hampered by the fact that local operating companies considered their competitive situations to be unique. Glidden in the United States did not compete in the premium sector at all, and its market share was only about 10 percent, compared to 40 percent in the United Kingdom, or the three-brand

product line in Australia. To launch Dulux as a premium brand in the United States would entail a marketing investment of about $50 million over four to five years with a seven-year payback period for a required 5 percent market share. Glidden executives were not convinced that this strategy would be successful in the United States.

Due to the differences encountered, the IL for the sector had pursued a "consultative mode," meeting about twice annually with the key executives from the various operating companies. In addition, the IL had frequent individual meetings with operating executives and territorial managers.

In the *automotive sector,* the IL positions for the OEM and refinish segments were combined. For refinishes, where ICI had major positions in Europe and Australia only, the strategy was fairly heavily led from the center. Involved were key managers from Europe and Australia, with others "mostly along for the ride." A major point of discussion was ICI's future strategy in the United States, where it had no position at that time. Glidden executives were very interested in entering the refinish sector. However, a "greenfield approach" (i.e., starting up with no previous capability) was considered difficult, and yet no ready candidates for acquisition existed.

In the automotive OEM segment, the IL role consisted largely of outside contacts with Du Pont, ICI's partner for Europe, and frequent negotiations with Japanese companies on technology transfers that might result in obtaining business for ICI from Japanese transplant operations in Canada, Australia, Southeast Asia, India, and Pakistan, all countries where ICI was active in the OEM business.

Coordination in the *can coatings sector* was very close and involved a formal business area review team under the leadership of the IL for can coatings. The team consisted of the key players worldwide in ICI Paints, who met several times each year. A major challenge here was to devise a strategy in view of the increased concentration among customers. Despite ICI's leading market position, the company could not dictate prices. The resulting squeeze on margins had reduced profitability, and a new strategy would have to be devised to lead the company out of this "commodity hole."

For the *general industrial paint sector,* no IL had been appointed. These businesses were led in various ways. Businesses that were closely affiliated with one of the four core areas were attached to the IL teams of those areas. Others were left under the direction of the territorial management. Some businesses not directly tied to the paint business were kept as long as they were meeting required profitability targets.

Coordinating at the Functional Level

The ILs for the five key functions undertook their roles in different ways. For all functional ILs, however, the objectives were similar. ICI wanted to transfer skills, experience, and best practice around its group operating companies. It also wished to accelerate the innovation process (as distinctly different from the invention process). And finally, the desire, as elsewhere in the business, was to simplify and focus on operational aspects, not just to "spin wheels."

For the *finance area,* this largely involved the enforcement of corporate guidelines and practice around the Paint Group. For *information technology* (IT), the mission was still vague. One of the jobs was to encourage and promote the use of IT where appropriate, often convincing chief executives to make the necessary investments. The coordinating activities had led to a policy of using DEC equipment for technical applications and IBM for commercial and operational tasks.

In *operations,* efforts were undertaken to spread efficient production procedures across the group. Here, ICI relied on Glidden's skill as a low-cost producer.

In the *R&D area,* there had been a long-held conviction that technology was driven by the automotive and industrial market, such as coil coatings. ICI Paints was now moving the emphasis of its R&D brainpower to new fields such as decorative, can coatings, and powders, which was beginning to yield exciting results.

Coordinating the various functions was a challenging task since many of its operating companies had different corporate origins, were acquired from various sources, and represented different nationalities and cultures.

Current Organizational Issues for ICI Paints Worldwide

Over the past years, ICI's organization had undergone considerable changes. Aside from its territorial focus, it introduced the idea of ILs for segments and functions. However, the company encountered a major obstacle in the fact that much of its production assets were shared. It was believed that some fifty of its sixty-four plants were common sites for a number of paint products and segments. This meant that the business segments were largely responsible for business volume, but the BAGMs did not have full asset responsibility. At this time, not more than 75 percent of the company assets could be clearly attributed to individual business lines.

Aside from the organization issues and the challenges faced by each of the four core sectors, ICI Paints needed to leverage the benefit of its being the largest global player into a superior financial performance.

OPPORTUNITIES FOR ICI PAINTS

ICI Paints faced a number of opportunities in different geographic areas and various paint segments. These opportunities had to be seen in relationship to its own resources. "Although ICI is a very large corporation with considerable financial resources, it is not realistic to expect that we can do everything," said Thompson. "We still need to keep in mind that our profitability, while on a par with the best paint competitors, is below average for ICI as a whole." Some typical opportunities (not an exhaustive list, however) were:

ICI Paints' Opportunities in Japan

ICI Paints, despite its world leadership, did not have a direct presence in the Japanese market. For some time, the company had been considering an opportunity to go beyond licensing but was unsure about the appropriate entry strategy. Considered were approaches ranging from exporting to joint ventures, making an acquisition, or even a greenfield start-up. Furthermore, which paint business to launch first in Japan was an unresolved question. Another question was how to relate any operation to the rest of ICI's business in Japan.

ICI Paints had virtually no direct sales in Japan. From time to time, decorative paint had been supplied by its Southeast Asian factories for sale as Japanese brands. Dulux Australia had supplied solid emulsion to be sold by Nippon Paints in the small Japanese DIY market.

The company's current presence in Japan consisted of two full-time ICI Japan employees—one long-serving and performing a liaison job with licensees plus color standards collection from Japanese automakers for ICI's refinish business, and the other recently appointed as a technical coordinator for submission of can coatings products for approval by the can manufacturers.

ICI had also concluded a series of licensing agreements, some granting technology to Japanese companies and others gaining access to Japanese technology. ICI granted automotive OEM licenses to Kansai, NOF, and Shinto, while obtaining licenses in the same area from Kansai and NOF. Furthermore, a powder coatings license was granted to Shinto while an industrial electrocoat license was obtained from

the same company. A flexible packaging refinish license was granted to Rock, which in turn granted ICI a refinish license. A can coatings license, due to expire in 1991, was also granted to Dai Nippon Inks.

ICI Paints considered it inopportune to enter the general paints business. Instead, an entry through one of its key segments was viewed as more promising. Best opportunities appeared in can coatings and powder paints.

Powder paints were viewed as having a major opportunity in Japan due to the high concentration of metal based industries (automobile, appliances) dominated by firms such as Matsushita, Hitachi, and Mitsubishi.

The market for powder coatings was estimated at about 18,000 tons, or 8 percent of the world market. This was equal to the U.K. market but smaller than the market for powder coatings for Italy. The cost of building a factory was estimated at about $3 million with breakeven volume of about 1,500 tons annually. Some $500,000–$750,000 of the original investment might be saved if the investment could be made together with ICI Films, another ICI international business, because the same buildings could be used. However, there were no production or marketing synergies between films and powder coatings.

In the can coatings sector, the opportunity was also tempting. Japan was a major market for metal cans, particularly in the beverage sector with three leading brewers, Kirin, Ashahi, and Sapporo, as well as international soft drink firms such as Coca-Cola and Pepsi-Cola. The soft drink firms were global companies which were already indirect customers of ICI Paints elsewhere.

The Japanese can-making market was dominated by Toyo Seikan (the second largest can maker in the world), Mitsubishi, and Daiwa. They supplied coated cans directly to major users. Can users. such as beverage companies, often looked for suppliers who could serve them on a worldwide basis. Can coatings were typically formulated to the specific requirements of a customer.

The Japanese market for can coatings was estimated at some 70 million liters, or about 17.5 percent of the world market. A greenfield investment would cost about $15 million. The annual breakeven point depended considerably on the particular product mix achieved. However, annual operating costs would be about $4 million, with another $1 million required for technical support. This would result in a breakeven volume of about 5 million liters. On the other hand, licensing fees averaged about 3 percent of sales, with a minimum annual payment of $150,000.

ICI Paints needed a presence in Japan as part of its strategy to reach its goal of 40 percent market share worldwide in the can coatings sector. Major risks were a drain on critical resources such as human resources, capital funds, and the need for "patient money" to do well in Japan.

Present suppliers for can coatings included Dainippon, an old ICI Paints licensee of an earlier generation of coatings technology. Market leaders were Toyo Ink and Dainippon (DNIC), which accounted for about 50 percent and 40 percent of the Japanese market, respectively. In the present Japanese market, ICI Paints could compete with superior technology. No other foreign company maintained a base in Japan for can coatings.

The major question remained on how to proceed. A joint venture with Toyo Sekan appeared possible. It was not clear, however, how to develop a local technology base, how to do the manufacturing and staffing. Another issue was how fast to proceed.

ICI Paints' Decorative Opportunities in the United States

ICI Paints had undertaken a recent attempt to investigate the possibilities of entering the premium paint segment in the United States. The difficulty of this strategy was underlined by the fact that such a premium segment was very small in the United States, amounting to about 12 percent of the market for DIY paint, compared to the United Kingdom, where it represented almost 40 percent of the decorative paint market. In the United States, regional companies such as Benjamin Moore and Pratt & Lambert were leaders in that segment.

Glidden, acquired in 1986, had pursued a low-price strategy that had resulted in enormous success. Sometimes described as "pile it high and price it low," Glidden was able to expand its business from just 4 percent market share to 17 percent currently in the DIY market, expanding its brand into national distribution and reaching the leading brand position in the

U.S. market. By contrast, Sears (supplied by De Soto) had dropped from 30 percent to just 16 percent market share in the same fifteen-year time period. Furthermore, Glidden also achieved a 10 percent share in the contractor market aimed at painters and professionals.

At first, ICI Paints in the United Kingdom believed it might pave the way for a launch of a premium decorative brand in the United States by sending one of its own people to the U.S. operation. The assignment was to investigate if ICI's premium brand Dulux might be launched in the United States at some time in the future. Actually selected by Glidden, this British executive was soon isolated and "cocooned," which rendered his situation untenable, and no progress was achieved in resolving the issue whether a premium strategy might work in the United States. "It was like sending a 'Brit' to the 'Colonials,'" commented Herman Scopes, ICI Paints PEO. "This experience taught us that some other approach would have to be chosen."

ICI Paints set up a study team consisting of both Glidden and ICI Paints executives. Scopes thought it might be helpful to "park" the idea of a position on global branding around Dulux and to look at the market more objectively. The output of the study was to be fed into a global review of ICI's decorative paint business. In the meantime, ICI's Canadian operation had agreed to launch a premium brand under the Dulux name.

Automotive Refinish Opportunity in the United States

The automotive refinish segment was a very stable market with only four major players: Du Pont, BASF/Inmont, PPG, and Sherwin-Williams. These top four accounted for 90 percent of the market. This segment was highly profitable, with return on sales ranging from 18 to 24 percent and return on net assets (RONAs) of around 40 percent. The market consisted of some 60,000 body shops supplied through local jobbers via company-owned warehouses. Warehouse distributors played a decreasingly important role as they were usually not specialized enough.

The refinish segment in the United States was subject to a number of changes. One major factor was the increase in car imports into the United States, which tended to increase the range of products requiring refinishing. New top coat technologies adopted by car manufacturers required new refinishes and continued technological improvements on the part of the paint manufacturers. More sophisticated body shop equipment, such as controlled environments to counter solvent emission into the air, constantly forced adjustment in the refinish formulas. Furthermore, there was a trend toward supplying body shops with color mixing schemes rather than factory-packaged colors, shifting the mixing forward into the body shop as each job required it.

In the opinion of John Thompson, ICI Paints' planning manager, key to success in this segment was color performance, followed by technical service to body shops, then environmental friendliness, training opportunities for paint sprayers, and finally delivery service. Price was viewed as much less important than any of the above five criteria.

Several theoretical entry options existed. The first was through a major acquisition. "Who would sell such a beautiful business?" John Thompson asked. Acquisitions of a smaller player would not be big enough to make a difference. A greenfield entry was likely to be slow. Akzo, the large Dutch paint manufacturer, had been working at it for ten years and had still only achieved a 3 percent market share. There was an opportunity to enter regionally, with expansion to national distribution later on.

The financial resources required to develop this segment were considerable. Depending on the approach chosen, the pace of expansion, and the company's skill and success, a maximum negative accumulated cash flow of about $30–$50 million for a national introduction would have to be considered. Thompson considered the necessary volume for breakeven to be 5 percent market share of a significant regional market and 4 percent market share nationally.

SELECTING A COURSE FOR THE FUTURE

ICI Paints management approached the future with some confidence. 1989 had been another good year for the paints business, with total sales of £1,628 million and a trading profit of £100 million. Volume in the major decorative DIY markets of the United States and the United Kingdom were affected by the depressed housing markets in both countries. Competitively, however, Glidden was able to assume clear brand leadership for decorative paints in the United States. Dulux Australia enjoyed record profits following the integration of an acquisition. Sales in Southeast Asia achieved strong growth with the successful introduction of new paint product lines and a joint venture in Hong Kong to develop business with China PRC.

In the can coatings segment, ICI was able to increase its world market share. Its position in Europe was strengthened through an acquisition in Spain (Quimilac SA). Powder paint continued to experience strong growth in Europe.

Case 8

ICI Paints (B): Considering a Global Product Organization

In the spring of 1993, Herman Scopes, chief executive officer (CEO) of ICI Paints, was having a discussion with the members of the company's International Business Team (IBT) about how the paint industry had changed over the past few years:

The passage of time has increasingly impressed upon us the rate at which markets are becoming international and global in nature. Over the past few years, ICI Paints has become an agglomeration of companies; global, but not necessarily globally managed. Moreover, as a result of past practices, we have an organizational structure that is, for the most part, based on geographic regions, not global product lines. As I look at the present business environment, however, I wonder whether that is the best arrangement and how the remainder of the IBT views the situation. Specifically, is our regional management structure, which has served us well in the past, appropriate for the rest of the decade?

In contrast to regional executives, who managed several of the company's products in one or more countries, some felt that ICI Paints should appoint worldwide business leaders with global product line responsibility. Doing so, however, raised all kinds of questions—such as the ability to maintain a local image in, say North America and Asia, with a product

●

This case was prepared by Robert C. Howard under the direction of Jean-Pierre Jeannet, Professor at IMD and Professor of Marketing and International Business at Babson College (USA), as a basis for class discussion rather than to illustrate either effective or ineffective handling of a business situation. Copyright © 1993 by the International Management Development Institute (IMD), Lausanne, Switzerland. Not to be used or reproduced without written permission directly from IMD.

manager based in the United Kingdom. Adopting an organization based on global product lines also raised communication issues; would people feel able to relate to a product line organization that was worldwide in scope? Despite the potential problems, a global product organization offered distinct advantages in terms of allocating resources, deciding priorities, and making investment decisions. For Herman Scopes and his colleagues on the IBT, the question was whether the company should move from a regional to a global product organization and if so, how.

IMPERIAL CHEMICAL INDUSTRIES PLC

The Imperial Chemical Industries (ICI) was formed in 1926 by the merger of Great Britain's four major chemical companies: Nobel Industries Limited, the United Alkali Company, the British Dyestuffs Corporation, and Brunner, Mond, and Company Limited. At that time, the newly formed ICI was divided into nine groups: alkalis, cellulose products, dyestuffs, explosives, fertilizers, general chemicals, rubberized fabrics, lime, and metals. Beginning in the 1930s, ICI's dyemakers used their knowledge of chemistry to diversify into plastics, specialty chemicals, and pharmaceuticals—higher-margin products that later became ICI's core businesses. In 1991, those core businesses were structured along product and geographic lines into four principal areas: Bioscience Products, Specialty Chemicals and Materials, Industrial Chemicals, and Regional Businesses. In the same year, the ICI Group reported a turnover of $22.1 billion, profits of $1.8 billion, and employed 128,600 persons around the world.

Sometime in the early 1990s, executives began considering breaking up ICI into smaller companies. In doing so, it was proposed, new companies would be better prepared to devote the amount of management attention and resources needed in an industry where the return on investment had gradually declined over the preceding twenty years. Had the reorganization occurred in 1992, ICI would have been split into two companies; one was to retain the company name with interests in industrial chemicals, paints, and explosives, while the other company—with the proposed name of Zeneca—was to include drugs, pesticides, seeds, and specialty chemicals. (Exhibit 1 gives financial data on how the two firms would have looked if they had been split in 1992.)

Organization of ICI Paints

In 1991, ICI Paints was the largest paint manufacturer in the world and accounted for $2.9 billion, or 13 percent, of all sales within the ICI Group of companies. In the same year, ICI Paints operated manufacturing plants in twenty-four countries, had licensees in an additional sixteen countries, all of which manufactured and marketed coatings in the company's main application segments: decorative, automotive OEM, automotive refinish, can, powder, and coil. (Refer to Exhibit 2 for a list of ICI Paints manufacturing companies, minority holdings, and licensees.)

Like other multinationals, ICI Paints traditionally structured its operations on the basis of individual

Exhibit 2 ● ICI Paints Territorial Spread

ICI PAINTS MANUFACTURING COMPANIES

Australia	Italy	Spain
Canada	Malaysia	Taiwan
Ireland	Mexico	Thailand
Fiji	New Zealand	United Kingdom
France	Pakistan	United States
India	Papua New Guinea	West Germany
Indonesia	Singapore	

ICI MINORITY HOLDINGS

Botswana	South Africa
Malawi	Zimbabwe

COMPANIES MANUFACTURING UNDER LICENSE

Brazil	Kenya	Sudan
Colombia	Korea	Trinidad
Cyprus	Madagascar	Turkey
Ecuador	Portugal	Venezuela
Japan	Saudi Arabia	Yemen
Jordan		

Exhibit 1 ● ICI-Zeneca Turnover & Operating Profit (Loss), 1992

Turnover ($mn)	Zeneca	Operating profit (loss) ($mn)
$228	Trading & Misc.	(18.2)
1,429	Specialties	39.5
1,961	Agrochemicals & Seeds	129.2
2,447	Pharmaceuticals	741.8
	New ICI	
$2,827	Materials	(38)
5,396	Industrial Chemicals	(25.8)
2,052	Regional Businesses	12.2
836	Explosives	89.7
2,402	Paints	174.8

markets. That is, executives had profit and loss responsibility for the full range of ICI products within a given market. Following the acquisitions of the 1980s, however, the management of ICI Paints felt that its customers could be better served by managers with a multicountry product line responsibility. To this end, ICI brought the management of Mexico, Canada, and the United States together under a regional CEO who reported to Herman Scopes in the United Kingdom. Similarly, regional constructs were devised for Europe and Asia. By 1990, the array of ICI Paints' subsidiaries and licensees was organized along geographic and business lines (as shown in Exhibit 3).

Within their respective regions, each regional CEO had profit and loss responsibility for the entire paint business. Also, within each region and reporting to the regional CEO, ICI Paints had country managers, territorial general managers (TGMs), and busi-

Exhibit 3 ● Previous Organization Chart, 1988–1990

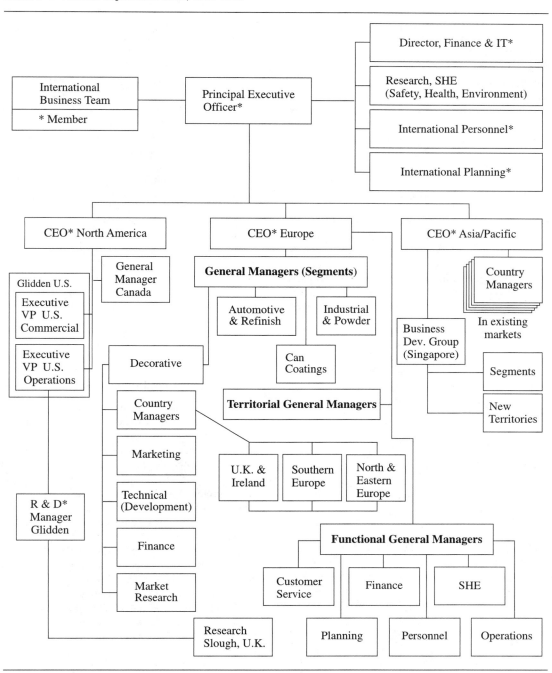

Source: Company records.

* Denotes International Business Team member.

ness area general managers (BAGMs). As the name implied, country and territorial managers supervised more than one of ICI Paints' product lines on a geographic basis, while business area general managers concentrated on the products of only one of ICI Paints' application segments. Because the latter were not required unless an individual segment reached a certain size, territorial general and business area general managers were sometimes one and the same person. In those areas where both existed, profit and loss results were a shared responsibility.

At ICI Paints, major decisions were always discussed and decided upon by an International Business Team (IBT), chaired by Herman Scopes. Additional members included the three regional CEOs, and four other executives with either functional or segment responsibility (as shown in Exhibit 4). Typically, executives were nominated to the IBT because of their ability to contribute to the development of the ICI Paints Group rather than their specialties or specific skills. Once part of the IBT, members were assigned "portfolios" based on their own talents and experience. Occasionally, these responsibilities changed

when there was a change in the composition of the IBT.

Yet another important aspect of the way ICI Paints operated was its use of international leaders (ILs), persons drawn from each of the company's core business areas as well as three out of five of the following functional areas: finance, information technology, operations, research & development, and management development. Typically, international leaders drawn from the core businesses acted as facilitators or coordinators. And though they did not have profit and loss responsibility, international leaders were responsible for developing global strategies in their respective application segment. Most recently, the company had appointed a worldwide safety, health, and environment (SHE) executive whose presence as an IL increased management's awareness of environmental issues.

Though the strategy making and coordination processes differed among ICI's application segments, in general, strategies were developed at the business, or operational, level by the international leaders and their teams. In turn, these strategies were proposed to the International Business Team which met six to eight times per year in various locations.

Exhibit 4 ● Members of the International Business Team (IBT)

Herman Scopes	CEO Paints
John Danzeisen	Chief Executive North America
Peter Kirby	Chief Executive Asia Pacific
Denis Wright	Chief Executive Europe International Leader Decorative
Adrian Auer	Chief Financial Officer
Nigel Clark	International Leader, Operations and Personnel
Brian Letchford	International Leader, Automotive and Can Coatings
Alex Ramig	International Leader, R&D
John Thompson	Chief Planner

THE WORLD PAINT INDUSTRY

In 1991, the world paints and coatings industry was valued at $46 billion at suppliers' prices, corresponding to a volume of 13.5 billion liters. Generally speaking, the industry included a range of products such as pigmented coatings, or paints, as well as unpigmented coatings like stain and varnish, used to decorate and/or protect different substrates. Analysts and participants alike divided coatings sales into two main classes: decorative or architectural paints, used in decorating buildings and homes,· and industrial coatings, which provided functional properties and added value to manufactured goods. Typically, decorative coatings were high-volume, low-priced goods and commanded low margins. Industrial coatings, on the other hand, were high priced and focused on niche markets. (Refer to Exhibits 5 and 6, respectively, for a breakdown of world paint sales by market sector and region.)

Exhibit 5 ● World Paints by Market Sector

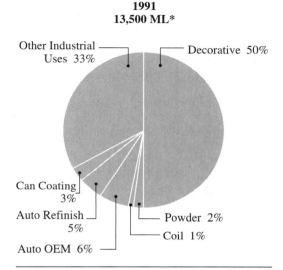

1991
13,500 ML*

- Other Industrial Uses 33%
- Decorative 50%
- Can Coating 3%
- Auto Refinish 5%
- Auto OEM 6%
- Powder 2%
- Coil 1%

*ML = million liters.

Note: Excludes central and eastern Europe, the Middle East, and Africa.

Decorative Paints

By far, decorative coatings was the largest single segment in the industry. Overall, the potential demand for decorative coatings in any country was influenced by climate, construction methods, and lifestyle, together with the collective successes of the local paint industry in presenting its offering to private and professional consumers in a readily accessible and attractive form. From this baseline, variations in demand were driven primarily by changes in real disposable income and in real interest rates, the latter already being an indicator of the level of construction activity and house moves.

In the decorative segment, paint sales were further classified according to two major user groups, each of which accounted for roughly half the sales in the segment. As the name implied, the professional market consisted of professional painters, further subdivided into restorers, new housing contractors, and

Exhibit 6 ● World Paint Markets by Region

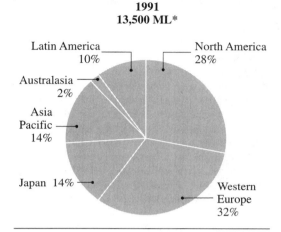

1991
13,500 ML*

- Latin America 10%
- North America 28%
- Australasia 2%
- Asia Pacific 14%
- Japan 14%
- Western Europe 32%

*ML = million liters.

Note: Region definitions are as follows:

1. Western Europe = The United Kingdom, France, Germany (including former East Germany), Italy, Spain, Portugal, Belgium, the Netherlands, Denmark, Finland, Norway, Sweden, Austria, Ireland, Greece, and Turkey.

2. North America = The United States and Canada.

3. Asia Pacific = India, Pakistan, Sri Lanka, Thailand, Malaysia, Singapore, Indonesia, Taiwan, Hong Kong, China, and Korea.

4. Australasia = Australia and New Zealand.

5. Latin America = Brazil, Argentina, Mexico, Ecuador, Uruguay, Colombia, and Chile.

6. Excludes Commonwealth of Independent States, eastern Europe, the Middle East, and Africa.

commercial contractors. Sales to the professional market were either through small independent stores or branches of manufacturers. The second segment consisted of individual do-it-yourself (DIY) users who bought paint through a variety of retail stores.

Retailing   Traditionally, decorative paints had been sold in small shops or hardware stores, but recent developments in the DIY segment were substantially changing the retailing process. In recent years, in fact, the DIY segment had increased its share to slightly over half the decorative market. In part, the increased share reflected a change in the way consumers viewed paint. Though once considered a lowly commodity, at the start of the 1990s, domestic paint was beginning to be seen as a household fashion accessory, adding value to the object it coated. In other words, the market for household paint, like that for beans, soap, and fish fingers, had become retail-led and susceptible to all the pressures which afflicted grocery producers. While the supermarket's rise to eminence in food and packaged goods took thirty years, the storming of the trade by DIY superstores happened in only ten years

Worldwide, these developments were most evident the in Anglo-Saxon countries—the United Kingdom, the United States, and Australia, to a lesser degree in northern Europe, and considerably less in southern Europe. To clarify, in the late 1960s and early 1970s specialist store chains like High Street in the United Kingdom and Sherwin-Williams in the United States replaced most small shops. Thereafter, variety department stores and supermarkets such as Woolworth, Sears, JC Penney, and Montgomery Ward in the United States, and Tesco in the United Kingdom took the lead in retailing decorative paints; at one point, it was reported that Sears had reached a 30 percent U.S. market share through its own branding. In concert with the growing popularity of variety department stores and supermarkets, however, DIY superstores—i.e., sheds—soon gained importance. In the United States, for example, the opening of stores like Home Depot cut Sears' market share in half. In the United Kingdom, the number of specialist stores declined from about 20,000 in 1979 to some 11,000 in 1988, and large DIY chains such as B&Q, Texas, and Pay Less accounted for 65 percent of all sector sales.

Throughout this retailing cycle, the marketing task of the paint manufacturer changed at each turn. In the first cycle, independent distributors and wholesalers gave way to manufacturer-owned stores and outlets. When the chains took over, increased buying power led to bargaining over shelf space. Thereafter, the supermarket or departmentalized variety stores brought private labels. Finally, the superstores narrowed the brand choice by typically carrying just one advertised brand and their own private label, and the reduced number of brands led to the disappearance of many retail paint suppliers.

In 1991, the decorative segment accounted for 50 percent of the value of all paint sold in the world, or roughly 6.67 billion liters. Geographically, North America accounted for 30 percent of these sales; western Europe, 32 percent; Japan, 9 percent; and the rest of the world, 29 percent. One analyst pointed out that despite the size of Japan's population and economy, decorative paints accounted for a surprisingly small share of the country's coatings sales. He attributed this to the fact that traditional, domestic architecture in Japan, with its paper partitions, meant that millions of square feet of walls were not painted.

Industrial Paints

In contrast to decorative coatings, demand for industrial coatings depended on a country's manufacturing profile, vehicles versus electronics or furniture versus textiles, for example. That is, industrial coatings tended to have more specialized uses than decorative coatings and included paint for cars, ships, planes, boats, white goods, cans, and thousands of other applications. In this segment, properties such as corrosion, abrasion resistance, and the ability to withstand high temperature or wet weather were important purchase criteria. To monitor the market, participants further classified industrial coatings according to application: automotive OEM (original equipment manufacturers), automotive refinish, can coatings, powder, and coil. Each segment had its own particular customer group and usually required its own technology and application base.

Automotive OEM   The automotive paint segment consisted of paint sales to automobile manufacturers—usually global companies—for use in their assembly plants. In this segment, users applied coatings by immersing an entire car body in a "paint bath" in which the paint carried an electric charge, opposite from that of the car body, resulting in a corrosion resistant finish. Because of the service requirements associated with maintaining electrolytic paint baths, as well as the desire to provide a consistent color wherever cars were assembled, automotive OEM customers preferred paint suppliers that were both local and global in nature. That is, customers favored suppliers able to provide a consistent color around the world yet, at the same time, deliver local service. As a result, paint manufacturers tended to locate their factories close to automotive assembly plants and stationed their personnel permanently at automotive sites. When purchasing coatings, automotive OEM customers usually maintained a major supplier for each top coat and base coat, and a second supplier for smaller volume applications "to keep the big ones honest." In 1991, the volume of paint sold to car manufacturers was roughly 791 million liters, or 6 percent of the industry volume, with sales distributed among North America, 22 percent, western Europe, 27 percent, and Japan, 34 percent.

Automobile Vehicle Refinishing The refinish segment included paints and coatings for repairing automobiles. Although the volume of paint sold in this market was smaller than the automotive OEM segment, it was a larger segment by value due to its higher sales price and was, in fact, the most profitable segment in the industry. Refinish customers were primarily small paint shops which needed quick and frequent deliveries, usually on a daily basis. Typically, paint manufacturers supplied these customers with mixing schemes through local distributors, who combined basic colors and shades with solvents to obtain a correct color match. Because there were some 10,000 different shades and some 60 different colors to select from, a refinish company had to have access to the color and paint shops of car manufacturers. And because automobile makers wanted to ensure that, if necessary, car owners could get their cars refinished wherever they were purchased, car manufacturers were interested in worldwide coverage. Not surprisingly, refinish paint manufacturers profited when they had access to all locations of a car maker because then they could supply the widest possible color range in any geographic market. Worldwide, the refinish segment accounted for 5 percent of industry sales, which were distributed among North America, 39 percent; western Europe, 23 percent; and Japan, 13 percent.

Can Coatings As the name implied, can coatings were applied inside tin and aluminum cans to make them corrosion resistant for use as food or beverage containers. In 1991, can coating sales were concentrated among four groups: Continental Can, Pechiney-Triangle (which included former American and National Can), Carnaud-MetalBox, and Crown Cork and Seal, as well as their licensees, all of which operated canning lines around the globe. Because these canning companies were expected to provide a consistent taste for globally marketed products such as Coca-Cola, they in turn expected their suppliers to provide local service at each of their canning sites. In 1991, the can coating segment accounted for only 3 percent of the world paint market, with sales distributed among North America, 41 percent; Europe, 27 percent, and Japan, 16 percent.

Powder Paints In contrast to other coatings, powder paints were 100 percent solids in the form of pigmented resin powders, usually electrostatically sprayed onto a grounded metal substrate and then cured by heat. Because powder paint could be applied in layers of 50–60 microns—five times as thick as wet paint, it was far more durable, retained its color longer, and resisted abrasions for up to twenty years. As a result, powder paint was ideal for coating domestic appliances such as washing machines or refrigerators, as well as metal surfaces on the outside of buildings which were subject to extreme weather conditions. Despite these advantages, powder paint had two limitations. First, because powder paint left thick layers, it could not be used in applications such as can coating where thin layers of coating were a must. Second, because powder coatings had to be cured by heat, there was an upper limit to the size of an object which could be coated.

In addition to the functional properties they imparted to a given substrate, powder paints had a major advantage over solvent-borne paints in that they released no toxic fumes into the atmosphere. As well as reducing emissions, powder coatings avoided the problem of waste disposal, as any stray powder was collected and reused. By contrast, wet paint always had a residual waste which had to be disposed of.

Worldwide, the market for powder coatings was growing 10–20 percent per year and was seen as a possible substitute for up to 50 percent of paint being applied to metal. In Europe, where the powder process was pioneered, the substitution already amounted to roughly 20 percent compared to about 10 percent in the United States. Although major user groups included automotive component suppliers, the metal furniture industry, and domestic appliance manufacturers, most powder makers were also looking into applying colored coatings to inferior grades of plastic, thus enabling them to compete with the attractive high-quality plastics used for chairs and garden furniture. As one analyst pointed out, the trick was to develop a paint that could be cured at relatively low temperatures, so that it did not melt the plastic. Other potential new applications included car engine blocks, baskets inside automatic washing machines, and the steel reinforcement bars used in concrete. One analyst commented that manufacturers were also experimenting with high-gloss powder finishes that could eventually be used for car body work. Worldwide, powder coatings accounted for only 2 percent of industry sales and were distributed among Europe, 54 percent; North America, 21 percent; and Japan, 10 percent.

Coil Coatings   The coil-coating segment derived its name from coiled steel or aluminum, which was given a decorative or industrial coating before the main manufacturing step or construction process. Typically, steel or aluminum coils were unrolled on automatic lines and the coating was applied by roller or spray. They were dried and hardened, and then the metal was coiled up again for shipment to manufacturers. Upon receipt, manufacturers could bend or stamp the metal into a required shape—such as a refrigerator cabinet or building cladding—without damaging the painted surface. In Europe, coil-coating customers included major metal producers such as British Steel, Sollac of France, Phoenix (part of the Belgian Cockerill group), Hoesch of Germany, Svenska Stal of Sweden, and La Magona of Italy.

In 1991, roughly 60 percent of coil-coated steel and 50 percent of coil-coated aluminum in Europe went to the building sector. Other important outlets were the automotive industry, domestic appliances, and packages. Also in Europe, it was estimated that, although manufacturers produced roughly 2.2 million tons of painted steel per year in the form of car and commercial vehicle bodies, 95 percent of that steel was painted after assembly. In other words, industry used only 110,000 tons of prepainted coil, and coil coaters hoped that more European manufacturers would follow the example of Nissan's Sunderland, United Kingdom, plant which used precoated car body panels. In terms of world paint sales, coil coatings represented less than 1 percent, or roughly 181 million liters, of industry sales. Geographically, these

sales were concentrated in Europe, 34 percent; North America, 33 percent; and Japan, 22 percent.

COMPETITION

Despite the takeover activity of the 1980s, in 1991, roughly 10,000 paint companies remained active around the world. In general, these competitors could be grouped into two categories: large multinational companies and primarily domestic manufacturers. In the first category, the ten largest companies accounted for 35 percent of industry sales, employed hundreds if not thousands of people, and were sometimes part of larger chemical companies. Typically, these players made and marketed coatings products in all, or almost all, of the industry's market segments, having attained their size by acquiring smaller companies. (Refer to Exhibit 7 for information on the top twelve paint companies.)

At the other end of the spectrum, small companies had sales under $10 million and employed fewer than ten persons. Normally, these smaller manufacturers concentrated production on one or only a few segments, usually in their home markets, and they sometimes augmented their sales by OEM relationships with other specialist paint companies.

ICI PAINTS' COMPETITIVE POSITION

Worldwide, ICI Paints' competitive position varied as a function of region and application segment (as shown in Exhibit 8).

Decorative

By far, decorative paints was ICI's strongest product line, accounting for 62 percent of the company's 1991 sales. Despite ICI Paints' worldwide strength in the decorative segment, however, it was not the biggest in some regional markets, and market shares varied considerably by country. In western Europe, for example, ICI had only a 5 percent market share, behind Akzo with 8 percent and Casco-Nobel with 7 percent. In the United Kingdom, on the other hand, ICI's Dulux product line accounted for an estimated 37 percent of all retail paint sales and included Dulux Vinyl Silk Emulsion, Dulux Matte Emulsion, Dulux Vinyl Soft

Exhibit 7 ● ICI's Principal Paint Competitors

	Coatings as % of group sales	1990 sales (million liters)	1990 sales ($ mn)	Average RONA 1987–1990	Key market sectors	Area of significant direct competition with ICI
INTERNATIONAL						
PPG	38%	515	$1,963	26%	Motors, Refinish, Decorative—U.S.	Refinish, Decorative—U.S.
BASF	7	485	c. 1,945	15	Motors, Refinish, Can	Refinish, Can
AKZO	23	485	2,160	15	Decorative—Europe, Refinish, Motors	Decorative—Europe, Refinish
Courtaulds	31	300	1,767	25	Marine, Can, Powders, Decorative	Can, Powders, Decorative—Australia
REGIONAL—AMERICAS						
Sherwin-Williams	100	535	2,338	26	Decorative, Refinish	Decorative
Dupont	3	265	c. 1,160	?	Motors, Refinish	
Valspar	100	230	539	24	Decorative, Can, Wood, Coil	Can
REGIONAL—EUROPE						
Casco Nobel	37	250	892	20	Decorative, Coil, Wood, General Industrial	Decorative—UK
Hoechst	4	220	1,160	c. 10	Motors, Refinish	Refinish
REGIONAL—ASIA						
Nippon	100	350	1,374	20	Motors, Refinish, Marine, Decorative, Coil	Decorative, Refinish, Motors
Kansai	100	275	1,080	19	Motors, Refinish, Decorative, Marine, Can, Coil	Refinish, Motors
ICI	13%	805	$2,927	17%	Decorative, Refinish, Can, Powders	

Sheen, Dulux Satinwood, Dulux Gloss Finish, Dulux Non-Drip Gloss, Dulux Definitions, Dulux Undercoat, Dulux Options, and Dulux Weathershed. Dulux was also known for its Natural Hints product line, consisting of nine or ten shades of off-white colors.

In North America, ICI Paints, through Glidden, its U.S. subsidiary, had an estimated 13 percent share of market, second only to Sherwin-Williams with 20 percent and well ahead of Benjamin Moore with 7 percent. And though ICI Paints had no decorative paint sales in Japan, it had a 5 percent market share in the rest of the Asia Pacific region, second only to Nippon Paint with 6 percent.

Industrial

Automotive Refinish   After the decorative segment, the automotive refinish segment was ICI Paints'

Exhibit 8 ● Breakdown of ICI Paints Sales by Region and Application Segment, 1991

	% Market Share by Region			*Application Segment's Share (%) of Total ICI Paint Revenues*
Segment	*Europe*	*N. America*	*Asia Pacific*	
Decorative	5%	13%	5%	62%
Auto OEM	4	0	15	3.4
Auto Refinish	11	1	14	13
Can	32	44	19	9
Coil	2	10	6	1.6
Powder	4	14	2	2

largest segment, representing roughly 13 percent of company turnover. Similar to the decorative segment, sales of paint in the automotive refinish segment varied by region. In western Europe, for example, ICI Paints had an estimated 11 percent market share, behind Hoechst with 19 percent; BASF, 18 percent; and even Akzo at 11 percent. In North America, ICI had only a 1 percent share of the refinish market, well behind Du Pont with 31 percent; PPG and Sherwin-Williams with 22 percent each; BASF, 13 percent; and Akzo, a 6 percent market share. Despite having no sales in this segment in Japan, ICI was in first place in the Asia Pacific region with a 14 percent market share, ahead of Korea Chemical with 13 percent; Kansai, 6 percent; and Kunsul and Nippon, each with 5 percent of the market.

Automotive OEM   With only 3.4 percent of ICI Paints' total sales, the automotive OEM coatings segment was among the smaller of the company's product lines. In western Europe, ICI had only a 4 percent share of this market segment, well behind PPG with 31 percent; Hoechst, 25 percent; BASF, 18 percent; and Akzo, 8 percent. In 1991, ICI sold the Canadian portion of its automotive OEM business to PPG. Thereafter, in North America and Japan, ICI was not present in the automotive OEM segment. In the rest of the Asia Pacific region, though, the company had a 15 percent market share in this segment, second to Korea

Chemical with 23 percent, but well ahead of Dong Ju with 9 percent; Goodlas Nerolac, with 7 percent; and Daihan and Shen Yan, with 5 percent each.

Can   Worldwide, can coatings accounted for roughly 9 percent of ICI Paints' sales. Geographically, ICI was a distant leader in western Europe with a 32 percent market share, well ahead of BASF with 16 percent, Dexter with 15 percent, and Courtaulds with 11 percent. ICI was also a formidable competitor in can coatings in North America with 44 percent of the market, more than twice the share of its closest rival— Valspar with 20 percent, and considerably ahead of BASF and Dexter with 12 percent and 10 percent of the market segment, respectively. Despite a strong presence in western Europe and North America in can coatings, ICI had no sales in this segment in Japan. It was, however, by far the leader in the rest of the Asia Pacific region with 19 percent of that market. In terms of market shares, its closest rivals in that part of the world were Courtaulds and Kunsul, each with a 9 percent share of market.

Coil   In 1991, sales of coil coatings by ICI accounted for a mere 1.6 percent of all sales; in western Europe, several competitors led in this segment. In decreasing order of market share, these competitors were Becker, 18 percent; Sigma 13 percent; Casco-Nobel, 12 percent; PPG, 9 percent; Akzo and Courtaulds, 7 percent each; Kemira, 3 percent; and BASF, Dexter, Grebe, Hoechst, Salchi, and ICI, 2 percent each. In the North American coil-coating segment, ICI was tied for fourth place with Lilly at a 10 percent market share; Valspar was the leader with 21 percent, followed by Morton, 19 percent; and Akzo, 16 percent. As with its other coatings, ICI had no sales in Japan but did have 6 percent of the Asia Pacific market for coil coatings, behind Nippon, 22 percent; Kansai, 17 percent; Korea Chemical, 13 percent; and Daihan, 10 percent.

Powder   Powder coatings represented approximately 2 percent of ICI Paints' 1991 sales and, in western Europe, accounted for 4 percent of all sales in that segment. Powder competitors with greater market shares were DSM, 13 percent; Becker, 11 percent; Courtaulds, 9 percent; and Hoechst, 6 percent. In North America, ICI's powder paints had a 14 percent market share, second only to Morton with 17 percent, yet still ahead of Ferro with 13 percent; Valspar, 12 percent; and Fuller O'Brien, 9 percent. In the Asia Pacific region, ICI's powder coatings had only a 2 percent share of market; there, leading competitors and their market shares were Daihan and Korea Chemical, 15 percent each; Jotun, 9 percent; Chokwang, 4 percent; and Kunsul, 3 percent. To bolster its presence in the powder segment, in 1991 ICI began merger discussions with Ferro. Though the deal was never concluded, a merger of Ferro and ICI would have made that company the worldwide leader in powder coatings.

DESIGNING AN ORGANIZATION FOR THE 1990S

At ICI Paints, management sought to have an organization in the 1990s that was both global- and territory-oriented, that supported R&D centers of excellence in certain locations, and maximized resources among the company's different operations and locations. At the same time, the company intended to concentrate on its key application segments on a global basis, and wanted to exploit opportunities in the European Union and Asia Pacific regions.

ICI Paints' organization had already evolved over time and, by 1992, several changes had been made (refer to Exhibit 9). In both the North American and European regions, territorial general managers

had been eliminated, moving the entire organization away from a territorial approach to a more brand-oriented structure.

Upon review, some of ICI Paints' executives felt that, in order to succeed in the future, the company needed to focus more directly on and better coordinate the activities of its main application segments. To this end, executives cited four advantages in moving toward a global product organization. First, it was believed that a global product organization would enhance ICI's ability to serve a customer base that was itself becoming increasingly global. For customers with global operations—such as can coating companies and automobile makers—a single product and service package that was applicable worldwide was bound to be appealing.

Second, executives cited the substantial cost benefits of standardizing ICI's products. To emphasize this point, it was mentioned that reducing the number of the company's refinish top coats from twenty-four to ten would save upward of $17 million on a product line with an annual turnover of approximately $300 million.

Third, executives believed that a global product organization would have additional benefits in terms of resource allocation. As an example, one manager mentioned that with increasingly expensive pollution abatement equipment, it did not make sense to have as many manufacturing plants. Rather, he stressed, the company should consider consolidating the number of plants and upgrading the remainder to world-class manufacturing standards. In fact, it was believed that some thirty of the company's sixty-four plants were common sites for a number of paint products.

Last, the executive mentioned that, in a truly global product organization, there would be a much greater chance to transfer experience from one market to another. For example, he described how an application developed for a can coating customer in North America, while not identical, had a number of parallels to the needs faced by can coating customers in Europe.

In contrast to these advantages, another group of executives pointed out that although some of ICI Paints' customer needs had become global, there were still substantial differences among individual markets. In the U.S. decorative segment, for example, Glidden had a 13 percent market share, was priced be-

Exhibit 9 ● Present Organization Chart, 1992

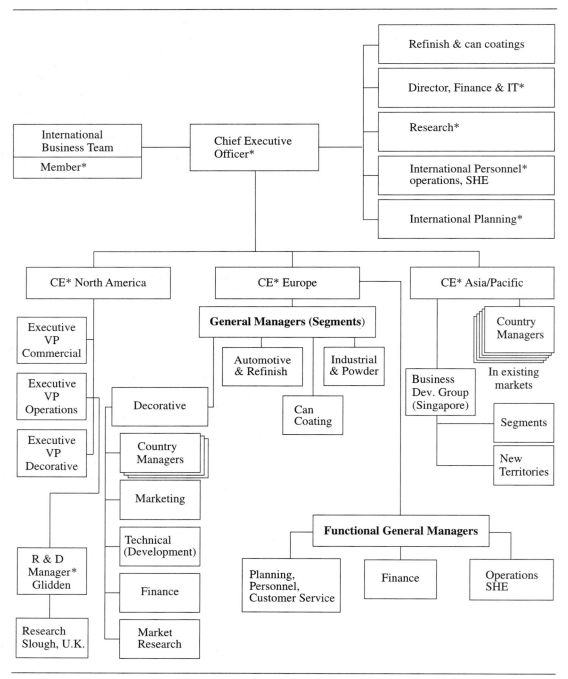

*Denotes IBT member.

low other brands, and distributed to DIY customers through mass merchandising outlets such as Wal-Mart. Because Glidden did not compete in the premium sector, it was seldom purchased by small-scale professional users like interior decorators. In contrast to Glidden in the United States, ICI's premium brand—Dulux—had a 37 percent market share in the United Kingdom. As a result, in 1993 ICI launched the Glidden brand in the United Kingdom, aiming it toward commercial contractors—a segment in which Dulux had been weak. John Thompson commented further:

To establish Dulux as a global brand, the U.S. market might be the next logical step. However, we estimated that a countrywide launch would cost ICI Paints $50 million over four to five years. An important issue would be not only determining the timing of such a large-scale project, but also resolving the positioning of Glidden versus Dulux.

In conjunction with trying to establish a global brand, the group went on to say that reducing the number of paint formulations and standards might well yield savings, but at the risk of jeopardizing ICI's sensitivity to local market conditions. "How would you feel," he asked, "if you worked at Anheuser-Busch and your 'local' can coating salesman was in fact based in the U.K?" Then too, the executives pointed out that, in theory, it was easy to reduce the number of manufacturing plants. In practice, however, local management and governments would hardly be receptive to the unemployment created due to such restructuring. As well, the executives men-

tioned that because many of ICI Paints' production assets were shared, business area general managers were largely responsible for business volume in an application segment, yet did not have full asset responsibility. In fact, no more than 75 percent of the company's assets could be clearly attributed to individual product lines.

SUMMARY

Before meeting with the IBT again, Scopes reviewed in his mind how his industry had changed and, in particular, what those changes implied for the organizational structure of ICI Paints. He recalled the words of one industry analyst, who said that the worldwide merger and acquisition activities of the 1980s were merely part of the ongoing globalization of the paint industry. At the start of the 1990s, the analyst believed that the globalization process was driven by three factors: first, the need to service customers with international manufacturing operations such as can makers, vehicle assembly, and domestic appliances; second, the need to service customers dealing with the aftercare of internationally traded products such as vehicles and ships; and last, the need to amortize the ever-growing costs of research, product development, and marketing over a broad volume base. With these thoughts in mind, Scopes turned to the IBT to renew the discussion on developing a new organizational structure at ICI Paints and the role of the territorial general managers, the business area general managers and, particularly, the international leaders in the 1990s.

Case 9

Gillette International's TRAC II

In mid-1972, Gillette International's management was considering the introduction of its new shaving system, the TRAC II, in some of its foreign markets. The blade had been introduced only nine months earlier in the U.S. market with considerable success. However, existing blade production capacity was limited, and the company could not serve all markets at the same time. Consequently, management was carefully evaluating which markets should get top priority for the TRAC II and how to combine this market selection process with an appropriate pricing strategy. In addition, the company was keenly aware of its main competitors, Schick of the United States and Wilkinson of the United Kingdom. The introduction of Gillette's newest product, the Platinum Plus, had been successful in most foreign markets; however, a number of executives believed the Platinum Plus's performance was below potential and wanted to avoid some of these negative experiences with the TRAC II introduction.

COMPANY BACKGROUND

The Gillette Company was a Boston-based consumer goods manufacturer with annual sales in 1971 of $730 million. The company was best known for its shaving

This case was prepared by Robert Howard under the direction of Jean-Pierre Jeannet, Visiting Professor at IMD and Professor of Marketing and International Business at Babson College. This case was prepared for class discussion rather than to illustrate either effective or ineffective handling of an administrative situation. This case was based on earlier work by Robert Roland, M.B.A. candidate at Babson College. Copyright © 1988 by IMD, Lausanne, Switzerland. The International Institute for Management Development (IMD), resulting from the merger between IMEDE, Lausanne, and IMI, Geneva, acquires and retains all rights. Not to be used or reproduced without written permission from IMD, Lausanne, Switzerland.

product line, which was marketed worldwide and where Gillette continued to be the major company both in the United States and abroad.

The company's main operating units were Gillette North America, Gillette International, and other companies under the Diversified Companies group (see Exhibit 1). Gillette North America included four product divisions: Safety Razor, Paper Mate, Toiletries, and Personal Care.

The Safety Razor Division was responsible for the Gillette shaving business within the United States. The Toiletries Division marketed such products as deodorants, antiperspirants, shaving creams, and hair grooming products for both men and women, including the leading brands Right Guard and Foamy.

The Personal Care Division marketed women's toiletry products such as hair sprays, cream rinses, home permanents, and hair conditioners, as well as a line of portable hair dryers (Max, Super Max, and Max Plus for Men). After only one year in national distribution, Gillette held second place in the competitive market for hand-held dryers.

Gillette's Paper Mate Division was responsible for marketing writing instruments in the United States and was the leader in porous point pens. The Paper Mate Division also sold ballpoint pens and refills, broadtip markers, and glue and had recently entered the lower price segment with a new line of ballpoint and porous point pens.

The Diversified Companies group included a range of recent acquisitions located both in the United States and abroad. Acquired in 1967, Braun AG of West Germany was a leading manufacturer of electric housewares. Its largest lines were electric razors, coffeemakers, digital clocks, and some photographic products. In electric shavers. Braun was the market leader in Germany and its products were distributed in many European markets. Shavers were not sold in the United States due to a licensing agreement signed with an independent company in

Exhibit 1 ● Gillette Organization Chart

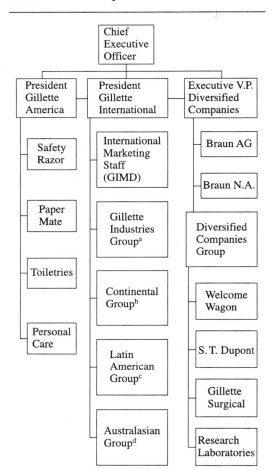

a. United Kingdom, S. Africa, and export departments to Ireland, Iceland, Greece, Eastern Europe, Near and Middle East, and African markets.

b. France, Germany, Italy, Spain, and affiliated sales companies in Scandinavia, Benelux, Alpine, and Portugal.

c. Argentina, Brazil, Colombia, Mexico, and Venezuela plus Latin American sales companies and export to Chile, Peru, Puerto Rico, Guatemala, Honduras, Costa Rica, Salvador, Nicaragua, Ecuador, Bolivia, Paraguay, Dominican Republic, Aruba, Curaçao, Guyana, Surinam, Barbados, and the Bahamas.

d. Australia, New Zealand, Japan, Hong Kong, and Southeast Asia.

Source: Company records.

1954 which was due to expire in 1975. Also part of this group was Welcome Wagon, a community service company acquired in 1971. Welcome Wagon was a service used by local businesses to acquaint new arrivals in the community with local companies and their services.

Safety Razor Division

The Safety Razor Division marketed Gillette's principal product line—shaving equipment and blades—in the U.S. market. Gillette was the world's leading blade manufacturer and the major factor in the U.S. market. The company marketed a full range of blades including double-edged stainless steel blades (Super Stainless Steel and Platinum Plus) as well as an older line of carbon steel blades (Super Blue, Blue, and Thin). Gillette sold its Techmatic Razor Blade and Lady Sure Touch on the band concept. In the United States, the Safety Razor Division also imported a line of disposable lighters under the name Cricket which was produced by Gillette's S. T. Dupont affiliate in France. Starting in the fall of 1971, the division began marketing the TRAC II, Gillette's latest shaving product based on a twin blade shaving system. 1971 had brought record sales and profits for the division, and the outlook for 1972 indicated another top performance.

International Division

Gillette International was responsible for marketing the majority of Gillette's products abroad. The company sold its products in more than 170 countries and territories, with shaving products accounting for most of the volume. International sales had been steadily increasing as a percentage of corporate sales and accounted for more than 40 percent of Gillette's volume. Because of the higher profitability of international operations, Gillette International accounted for half of the company's profits, as seen in Exhibit 2.

The president of Gillette International was also the executive vice president for international operations at corporate headquarters in Boston. The president was supported by a staff of international marketing experts located at Gillette's International Marketing Department (GIMD) in Boston. The staff was responsible for interacting with regional and

Exhibit 2 ● The Gillette Company Development of Sales and Profits, 1967–1971 (in millions of dollars)

Year	Total company		Blades and razors		Foreign operations	
	SALES	NET PROFITS	SALES	NET PROFITS	SALES	NET PROFITS
1967	$428	$57	$193	$38	$167	$20
1968	553	62	238	40	221	23
1969	610	65	250	44	256	29
1970	673	66	262	46	289	33
1971	730	62	270	41	327	33

country level managers on marketing, planning, and strategic issues and would set priorities for introduction when a supply of products was limited.

Reporting to Gillette International's president were four regional managers, each responsible for a group of markets. The Gillette Industries Group in London controlled Gillette operations in the United Kingdom and South Africa and export operations to Ireland, Iceland, Greece, eastern Europe, the Middle East, and Africa. The group's only manufacturing facility was located in the United Kingdom.

Also located in London was the Continental Group, with responsibility for subsidiaries in France, Germany, Spain, and Italy. The Continental Group also controlled the marketing operations of affiliated sales companies in Scandinavia, the Benelux countries, Portugal, Switzerland, and Austria. This group's plant facilities were located in Germany, France, and Spain.

Gillette International's other two regional operations were based in Boston. The Latin America Group headed subsidiary operations in Argentina, Brazil, Colombia, Mexico, and Venezuela and was responsible for export and sales in Chile, Peru, Puerto Rico, and all of the countries in Central America and the Caribbean area. The group's manufacturing plants were located in Brazil, Argentina, Colombia, and Mexico.

Gillette International's fourth regional group was the Australasian Group with responsibility for Australia, New Zealand, Japan, Hong Kong, and Southeast Asia. Its major plant facility was located in Australia.

THE DEVELOPMENT OF SHAVING TECHNOLOGY

Carbon Steel Blades

King C. Gillette, the company founder, introduced the first safety razor in 1895. The company was granted an exclusive patent in 1904 on an improved version of its blade, which was followed by the development of the double-edged blade. In the 1930s, Gillette introduced carbon steel blades under the brand name Gillette Blue. These blades were thinner than earlier blades, had lacquer applied to the surface, and offered an improvement in shaving comfort and blade life.

The introduction of the Super Blue blade in 1960 represented a quantum step in technology. The Super Blue came with a silicon coated treatment which was baked on to give it extra hardness. This new process significantly improved the quality of shaving, although the shave quality tended to decline more rapidly than with previous blades after reaching a certain point. The blade was priced at 6.9 cents per unit and quickly became the standard in the industry. Customers once accustomed to the more comfortable shave of the Super Blue found it very difficult to return to the older carbon blades. For about eighteen months, Gillette was able to exploit this product advantage before competitors could introduce similar products.

Stainless Steel Blades

In August 1961, another quantum leap in shaving technology occurred when Wilkinson Sword, a U.K. company, introduced a Teflon-coated stainless steel blade. The coating process was actually developed earlier by Gillette, and Wilkinson paid a royalty to Gillette for its use. Stainless steel was much harder than carbon steel and could absorb the high temperature generated in the Teflon coating process. However, because of this hardness, a stainless steel blade could not be sharpened as easily as a carbon blade. Stainless steel blades offered a high quality shave consistent over a relatively long time and were a considerable improvement for the user over carbon steel blades. Wilkinson introduced its new blade first in the United Kingdom and then launched it in the United States but did not have sufficient supply to satisfy the entire U.S. market. In response, both Gillette and Schick, the principal U.S. competitors, countered with crash development programs before Wilkinson could become fully established in major markets.

In 1963, Gillette introduced a Teflon-coated stainless steel blade under the brand name Stainless (Silver Gillette in Europe). The major hurdle to overcome was the manufacturing process, as the new blades required specially designed equipment. The Stainless blades were improved by a factor of 2 to 3 in blade life over the carbon, double-edged blades. Gillette was able to maintain market leadership in the United States because Wilkinson moved too cautiously with its product rollout and did not have a fully developed marketing function.

In 1965, Gillette introduced its first modern shaving system consisting of the Techmatic razor band technology. Rather than using single blades one after another, the Techmatic came equipped with a cartridge that contained a band of blades. The user would never have to touch a single blade; thus the Techmatic offered added convenience although blade quality was equal to the stainless steel blades. Techmatic's introduction was well timed and had a lead of six months over all competitors, resulting in a 2 percent gain in market share. The Techmatic was Gillette's first entry into shaving systems other than the double-edged blade.

Platinum Treated Blades

In 1969, Gillette made another improvement in its blades by adding a platinum chromium alloy. This new blade, marketed in the United States under the brand name Platinum Plus, further increased blade life and shaving comfort but was not considered a technological breakthrough. The blade was also introduced in European markets under various names which included the word *platinum.*

In 1970 it was once more Wilkinson of the United Kingdom reaching the market with an innovation. Wilkinson launched its Wilkinson "Bonded" blade, consisting of a single blade enclosed in a plastic casing. The term *bonded* meant that the blade remained permanently fixed in a cartridge. Although Gillette had been working on a twin blade cartridge, it was not ready for product launch at the time of the Wilkinson introduction. Fortunately for Gillette, Wilkinson did not have sufficient resources to make a major impact on the market.

In 1971, after combining Techmatic plastics knowledge with an innovative twin blade design, Gillette introduced the TRAC II. This was a major evolution from the single blade, double-edged razor and provided an entirely new concept in blade making. Although Wilkinson's Bonded razor gave the public its first experience with a cartridge product, the TRAC II represented the next step forward in cartridge design. Combined with Gillette's previous blade expertise, this shaving product was the most advanced in the industry in terms of quality and blade life (see Exhibit 3).

COMPETITION

Gillette Experience Prior to 1960

During the early development of the shaving industry, Gillette had almost no significant competition. The company got its first major break during World War I when U.S. soldiers were required to be clean shaven. By the end of the war, Gillette had sold some 3.5 million razors and about 52 million blades to the military forces, giving Gillette a substantial advantage over other razor companies. Another big step occurred in 1939 when Gillette spent 50 percent of its entire advertising budget to sponsor the U.S. baseball World Series. By World War II, Gillette had the dominant share of the blade market. Market shares reached an all-time high in the early 1940s with 55–60 percent in the double-edged segment and about 40 percent of the entire market. The advent of television gave Gillette another boost.

Exhibit 3 ● Blade Quality versus Blade Life

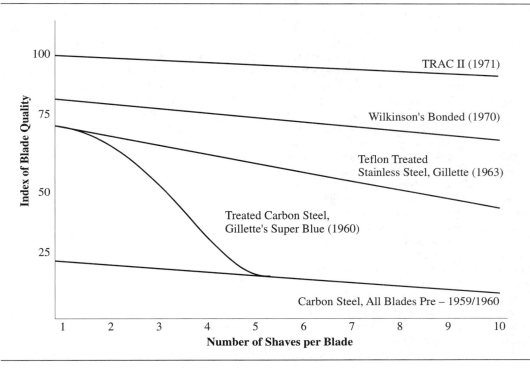

Source: Company records.

Gillette did not face real double-edged blade competition in the United States or abroad until the early 1960s. Before that time, Wilkinson of the United Kingdom was not a major factor and Schick was only of minor concern in the United States. Gillette was much more concerned with electric razors, particularly abroad, where the pricing of electric shavers tended to be lower than in the United States. With a smaller price gap between electric and wet shaving and with many customers preferring electric over wet shaving, Gillette was gaining market share in a stagnant or even declining segment.

Recent Developments: The Platinum Plus Experience

Gillette International's latest worldwide product introduction was the launch of Platinum Plus blades in early 1970. The Platinum Plus represented a product improvement and had been well received in the United States in the fall of 1969. In 1970, a number of key foreign markets were offered access to the Platinum Plus technology. However, because production machinery was only available in limited volume, Gillette had to introduce the product selectively. By 1972, all markets had been introduced to the Platinum Plus blade albeit with varied success.

From the outset, Gillette International gave its local managers considerable freedom in selecting the positioning strategy for the new blade. As a result, different countries chose different strategies. Some market introductions were unsuccessful by Gillette standards, and the company wanted to learn from these mistakes before introducing the TRAC II.

After reviewing the introduction of Platinum Plus in Europe, management came to a consensus on what had gone wrong. To gain further insight on the European scene, management looked closely at the U.K., German, and Brazilian experiences.

The U.K. subsidiary, faced with intensive competition in the U.K. market and a scarcity of retail shelf space, had decided to introduce Platinum Plus as its new top-of-the-line blade in place of Super Silver. Super Silver and Wilkinson's top blade had been similarly priced and selling at about the same volume. When Gillette withdrew Super Silver and introduced the higher priced Platinum Plus (with platinum coating), the company lost some of its share to Wilkinson because some users were unwilling to upgrade to the new product. As a result, Gillette lost overall market share and had not been able to regain it.

In West Germany, the Gillette subsidiary also faced intensive competition from Wilkinson. With a surplus of blade products in the retail trade, the German subsidiary opted to provide an improved product by adding a platinum coating to its top-of-the-line brand Super Silver and introduce the new product as Super Silver Platine. However, this variation brought only mixed success for Gillette.

By contrast, the Brazilian operation went ahead with the largely U.S. type strategy, by adding the new Platinum Plus to its existing product line, which included the Super Silver. This strategy proved successful. As a result of the Platinum Plus experience, management at Gillette International felt that local management should not decide on the introductory program. Rather than local companies proposing their own strategies, Gillette International's management preferred to give the local subsidiaries detailed instructions. If the decision did not suit the local market, then local management could argue its case. At the start, however, there would be a more standardized marketing and positioning strategy largely based on the U.S. experience.

Schick in the United States and Abroad

Schick, a fully owned subsidiary of Warner-Lambert, was Gillette's major competitor. Schick Safety Razor Co. manufactured injector and double-edged blades in the United States, Canada, Sweden, and the Netherlands as well as in Japan, where Schick was the dominant company in the wet shaving segment. Sales of Schick in 1972 were estimated at $47 million. In the United States and most other markets, Schick's market share was about one-third of Gillette's or less.

Schick's marketing strategy tended to emphasize print advertising or promotions such as free samples, in-store displays, or write-in offers. Schick was capable of introducing new blade types quickly and could be expected to react to Gillette within twelve to eighteen months after a new product introduction. But, like Gillette, Schick was constrained by the scarcity of machinery needed to introduce new products. In January 1972, Schick had entered Schick Super II, a product similar to TRAC II, into the shaving system market on the West Coast of the United States. By mid-1972, however, Schick Super II had still not reached full national distribution. Full-scale national television support had also not yet taken place. Most television exposure in the U.S. market was through partial sponsorship of the 1972 summer Olympics which were going on at the time.

Wilkinson on All Continents

Wilkinson, a British company, was not a serious competitor to Gillette until it introduced a treated stainless steel blade in 1961. Wilkinson had been marketing an untreated stainless blade since the mid-1950s with little success. Total sales for 1971 amounted to about £24 million ($60 million), of which the shaving portion accounted for about £18 million ($40 million). Wilkinson had experienced growth rates of 20 percent in recent years and had approximately 75 percent of its sales overseas.

Wilkinson operated its main manufacturing facilities in the United Kingdom, where it employed more than 1,300 people. The company's only other full manufacturing facility was in West Germany. Partial manufacturing and packaging were done in the United States, Australia, South Africa, and Spain.

When the treated stainless steel blade was first introduced, Wilkinson did not have sufficient capacity to satisfy demand, and the result was only a 20 percent erosion of Gillette's U.K. market share. After its introduction in the United Kingdom, Wilkinson moved into the West German market in 1962 and, on a limited basis, into the United States at the end of 1962. In addition to capacity constraints, Wilkinson did not have a fully developed marketing operation outside its key markets and, thus, could never capitalize on the Teflon-coated stainless steel blade. The only exception was the U.K. market, where Wilkinson's market share was larger than Gillette's.

Wilkinson's market share and market position differed considerably from market to market. As the major domestic producer, Wilkinson enjoyed a large share of the U.K. market. Its introduction of the "Bonded" razor ahead of Gillette had helped consolidate its market share further. It was estimated that Wilkinson's share was moving close to 50 percent for all blades sold in the United Kingdom. In Germany, Wilkinson continued to defend its share of about 30 percent. The same local subsidiary was also responsible for selling in Austria and Switzerland, where the company's market share had been increasing.

In Italy, Wilkinson had been able to increase its market share to about 20 percent as a result of introducing the Wilkinson Bonded system. Although Wilkinson maintained its own subsidiary in Italy, sales and distribution were handled by Colgate-Palmolive. In France, distribution and marketing were in the hands of Reckitt & Colman. In Spain, the company had started construction of full-scale manufacturing facilities which were expected to come on stream in 1974.

In other European countries, Wilkinson also relied on the distribution arrangements with established consumer products companies. In Denmark, Norway, Sweden, and Holland, Wilkinson products were marketed by Colgate-Palmolive. Wilkinson blades were marketed in Greece by Unilever, one of the world's largest consumer products companies, and in Ireland by Beecham, a U.K.-based personal products company. Distribution was also handled by Reckitt & Colman in South Africa, where Wilkinson's share had increased beyond 10 percent with the introduction of the Bonded blade. Wilkinson blades were also distributed in many Middle Eastern countries out of a Beirut office.

In Asia, Wilkinson blades were marketed in Japan, Australia, and New Zealand. The Australian market position improved considerably with the introduction of the Bonded blade. In Japan, Wilkinson was marketed through Lion, a major Japanese personal products company.

In the United States, where Wilkinson's share was about 10 percent, marketing had been handled exclusively since 1970 by Colgate-Palmolive, the large, U.S.-based multinational consumer products company. In Canada, where Wilkinson had a market share of about 20 percent, its blades were distributed by John A. Houston Ltd. Throughout Latin America, Wilkinson used independent distributors to market in Brazil, Colombia, the Dominican Republic, Haiti, Paraguay, Uruguay, and Venezuela.

THE TRAC II OPPORTUNITY

Manufacturing Overview

The manufacturing process of the TRAC II system consisted of three distinct phases: the manufacturing of the blade, the manufacturing of cartridge parts, and the assembly of these blades and cartridge parts into the TRAC II system. Each one of these stages offered particular challenges to Gillette. The key problem, however, had turned from making the system work to adding sufficient capacity. Although it was difficult to forecast exactly how much blade capacity would be available for Gillette International, it was felt that each gain in annual volume of 150 million units would take twelve to eighteen months.

Blade Manufacture

The blade manufacturing process alone consisted of six stages. In the first stage a continuous strip of soft steel, purchased in coils the width of one blade, was mounted on a wheel for perforation. Perforations in the steel served as guides for additional blade cartridge components and also enabled soap and water to pass through. Oil used in cutting these perforations was removed before the steel passed into a hardening furnace with three temperature zones. The hardening gave the blades an extended life of eleven to fourteen shaves. After leaving the furnace, the steel was cooled in an annealing process before being rewound onto a wheel for sharpening.

In the sharpening process, the perforated and hardened steel strip was ground to remove rough steel from the blade's cutting edge, followed by rough sharpening and honing (refined sharpening process). Once the honing process had put a cutting edge on the blade, the steel strip was cut into individual blade lengths and the individual blades airblown onto blade holders. Blade holders transferred stacks of razor blades to blade magazines, which passed through a washing cycle before vacuum phase sputtering.

The contents of each magazine were automatically unloaded onto a sputtering knife. Twelve sputtering knives were positioned around a sputtering post of chromium and platinum with the cutting edge of the razor blades facing the sputtering post. Using a technique known as ion deposition, chromium and platinum were transferred from the sputtering post to the blades' cutting edge.

In the final step, the blade edges were coated with Teflon and passed through a sintering furnace which baked the Teflon onto the blade and enhanced the bonding of chromium and platinum to the razor's cutting surface.

Cartridge Assembly

Each TRAC II cartridge contained two individual razor blades, as well as several plastic and metal parts. Cartridge assembly began with black plastic guard caps that were fed from a bowl of caps into a chute, with each cap positioned so that its plastic alignment studs were face up.

The first razor blade in the cartridge assembly was set on a guard cap, with the plastic alignment studs passing through the blade perforations. A spacer was set on top of the first blade, followed by a second blade and, lastly, the top plastic guard cap. This was a very delicate operation since the relationship of the two blades to the cartridge was critical to providing shaving comfort. A slight pressure was applied to seal the assembled cartridge before it was moved to an automated inspection stage.

If the automated scanning device verified that all parts were included and properly aligned in the cartridge assembly, the cartridge was relayed to a dispenser tray. A plastic cartridge dispenser was positioned over the dispenser tray and five TRAC II cartridges pressed into place. Once assembled, these dispensers were transported to another area for final packaging. (For an overview of the manufacturing process, see Exhibit 4.)

Equipment as Bottleneck

Manufacturing equipment for the production of razor blades had specific requirements and was not purchased on the open market. Instead, Gillette produced its own equipment in company-owned tool shops in Boston, the United Kingdom, and France. For TRAC II production, new equipment was needed for blade perforation, hardening, and sharpening. New equipment was also needed for the production of plastic elements such as guard caps and dispensers as well as for assembly and loading operations. The longest lead times (twelve to eighteen months) were for the procurement of sharpening equipment. For plastic parts production, molds had to be produced which also required high-precision tools.

For years, Gillette tool shops had been operating at full capacity. In recent years, Gillette had suffered from undercapacity in production, with output often a step or two behind actual demand for Gillette blades. As a result, Gillette's top management decided to add to existing capacity so that manufacturing capacity would always exceed demand by 10 percent. Consequently, just when the tool shops were busy providing this additional equipment, TRAC II increased the burden even more. It was estimated that Gillette was able to add about 150 million units of TRAC II (dispensers containing five cartridges) every twelve months, or about 12.5 million units per month. The Boston plant was using all its output to satisfy demand in the United States, and the North American division wanted still more products out of the newly planned capacity expansion. Given the nature of tool production, there was no short-term solution for expanding total output beyond the rate of 12.5 million units per month.[1]

PRICING ISSUES

Pricing was a main consideration in the launch of TRAC II abroad. Gillette International viewed pricing as the key to increasing market share and to maintaining or improving margins in each market. Pricing was dependent on a number of factors, any one of which could be used as a basis for selecting a final price policy. These factors were production costs, marketing costs, and competitor pricing.

---

1. The 150 million dispensers refer to annualized capacity increase; for example, after twelve months, the annualized output for the next twelve months would be increased by 150 million units (or 750 million blades).

Exhibit 4 ● Gillette TRAC II Manufacturing Overview

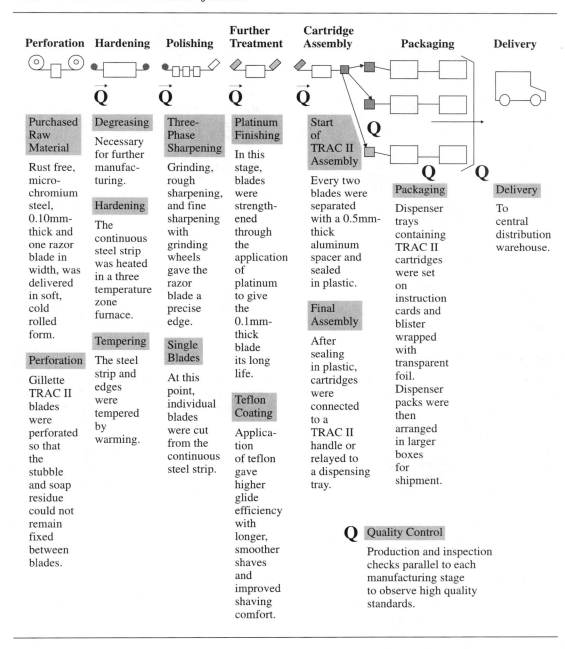

| Perforation | Hardening | Polishing | Further Treatment | Cartridge Assembly | Packaging | Delivery |

Purchased Raw Material

Rust free, micro-chromium steel, 0.10mm-thick and one razor blade in width, was delivered in soft, cold rolled form.

Perforation

Gillette TRAC II blades were perforated so that the stubble and soap residue could not remain fixed between blades.

Degreasing

Necessary for further manufac-turing.

Hardening

The continuous steel strip was heated in a three temperature zone furnace.

Tempering

The steel strip and edges were tempered by warming.

Three-Phase Sharpening

Grinding, rough sharpening, and fine sharpening with grinding wheels gave the razor blade a precise edge.

Single Blades

At this point, individual blades were cut from the continuous steel strip.

Platinum Finishing

In this stage, blades were strength-ened through the application of platinum to give the 0.1mm-thick blade its long life.

Teflon Coating

Applica-tion of teflon gave higher glide efficiency with longer, smoother shaves and improved shaving comfort.

Start of TRAC II Assembly

Every two blades were separated with a 0.5mm-thick aluminum spacer and sealed in plastic.

Final Assembly

After sealing in plastic, cartridges were connected to a TRAC II handle or relayed to a dispensing tray.

Packaging

Dispenser trays containing TRAC II cartridges were set on instruction cards and blister wrapped with transparent foil. Dispenser packs were then arranged in larger boxes for shipment.

Delivery

To central distribution warehouse.

Q Quality Control

Production and inspection checks parallel to each manufacturing stage to observe high quality standards.

Pricing Based on Production Costs

Production costs at Gillette were classified into two parts: manufacturing costs and initial investments costs. Manufacturing costs were defined as the sum of direct material, direct labor, and variable manufacturing overhead. The manufacturing costs of the new TRAC II were about twice the cost of the Platinum Plus blade, which averaged $.03 per unit. Initial investment costs for new processes at Gillette were normally 20 percent higher than prior blade processes. Added capital investment for the TRAC II, however, was substantially higher than for previous blade manufacturing processes because of the technology level and amounted to $10 million per 100 million units (dispensers at five blades each). As with the older line of blades, these investment costs would be reduced over time as volume increased and added equipment depreciated. A typical depreciation period was about six years. If the TRAC II were priced on the basis of total production costs, Gillette's typical ex-factory price for blades would give the company a gross margin of 70 percent. Out of this gross margin, the company would have to cover all direct marketing and general administrative expenses.

Pricing Based on Marketing Costs

Gillette's marketing costs tended to be higher for a new brand since the bulk of advertising expenditures would shift to the latest product. At the time of the TRAC II introduction, advertising expenditures for overseas markets were concentrated on Techmatic and Platinum Plus. If these expenditures were to be shifted to the TRAC II, management needed to decide on the changeover rate. Under ideal circumstances, these expenditures could be shifted at the same rate as customers upgraded brands. In the United States, the Marketing Research Group had charted trade-up patterns since 1960. When the Super Blue was introduced, it cannibalized Blue Blade sales, enabling Super Blue to achieve predominant market share after only eighteen months. Similarly, when Platinum Plus was added to Gillette's product line, customers traded up from the stainless steel blade at roughly the same rate. This type of data was not available for countries other than the United States, but management felt it could use these data as an estimate for trends in the European marketplace.

Initial interest in and purchase of the TRAC II was particularly dependent on two things. One was the newness of the product. Management in Boston felt that once the TRAC II was launched, there would be a certain period of vulnerability because of its level of sophistication. Whether trading up from a previous Gillette product or switching brands, a consumer would have to spend an initial $1.50 for a TRAC II handle to accommodate TRAC II cartridges. Secondly, therefore, the potential for cartridge sales was dependent on the number of TRAC II handles. The only experience Gillette had had with such a sophisticated trade-up was the Techmatic. Excluding the Techmatic, all of Gillette's other successor blades were compatible with the same razor handle. Hence, the level of advertising had to be sufficient to generate early sales of the sophisticated TRAC II while at the same time balancing demand with a limited supply in each key market.

Pricing to Gain Market Share

The pricing policy chosen to cover production costs and advertising expenses would certainly influence market share. In the past, a new product would be priced at a certain premium over its predecessor. The size of this price premium would have varying effects on resulting market share. Given Gillette's pricing strategy with country by country differences, adding a 10–20 percent premium for a sophisticated new product such as TRAC II could result in success in some markets and low performance in others.

Past new product introductions served as an example. On average, Gillette's Super Blue sold at a 38 percent premium over Gillette's Blue. The first stainless steel blade, marketed as Super Silver in most European markets, was sold at about twice the retail price of the Super Blue.

The Gillette Techmatic was marketed at a substantial premium over the Platinum Plus. The amount of this price premium depended on the various competitive factors and differed from market to market. In 1971, the premium was about 50 percent over the Stainless Steel in both Germany and the United Kingdom. However, the price base was not identical, and actual retail prices for the two markets differed.

Given the key market data in Exhibits 5 and 6, Gillette management was concerned with creating a

Exhibit 5 ● Size of Key Markets

Market	Estimated blade sales (1972) (in millions of blades)
United States	1,772
United Kingdom	361
West Germany	296
France	429
Italy	266
Spain	160
Canada	170
Argentina	250
Brazil	500
Mexico	310
Sweden	35
Holland	50
Japan	1,300

Source: Company records.

pricing policy that would lead to intracompany trade-up as well as intercompany brand switching.

Options for Gillette International

Having reviewed the manufacturing costs and anticipated demand patterns. Gillette management considered three pricing strategies: (1) in accordance with production cost differences, (2) at a constant premium over the now top Platinum Plus, or (3) at a uniform world price for all countries.

Pricing in relation to production costs would allow Gillette its existing margin structure and would take into consideration the new equipment investment. On the other hand, there were some markets where margins were lower than desired, and a constant margin would not increase margins in these countries.

If management chose to price at a constant premium, there would be a real potential for price dif-

ferences between markets. Such price differences between markets would not be easy to equilibrate once a product had been established at a certain price level. Furthermore, the differences could lead to product arbitrage (parallel imports).

The threat of parallel imports had always been a problem for Gillette and encouraged some managers to support the world pricing policy. Although this policy would alleviate parallel imports, it could put the TRAC II price out of reach in some markets, which would affect market share. And, although this policy would reduce product arbitrage, a uniform price would open up doors to competitors with various lower cost products and with identical products priced at a lower level.

Whichever policy was chosen, Gillette's management constantly had to keep the competition in mind. Gillette had to continue and increase its TRAC II supply with one-third of all new output going to the U.S. market. The decision to go international had been made, but only the remaining two-thirds of new output could be spread among those key markets.

Gillette had to move rapidly to reach its overseas markets before Schick introduced its Super II and before Wilkinson had a replacement for its own Bonded blade. The importance of getting to a market first was reinforced by the Marketing Research Group's findings on timing and market share. That meant, all things being equal regarding pricing, quality of product, and distribution, that the market share potentials to the second, third, and fourth entrants would be no more than 30 percent, 18 percent, and 12 percent, respectively, of the market leader.

Based on previous experience, the window of opportunity for the TRAC II would last twelve to eighteen months. Given that this time lead represented the number of months Schick and Wilkinson needed to invest several million dollars to achieve production capability, management had to make its decisions soon. Furthermore, the precise combination of pricing policy and selected target markets had to match and preserve Gillette's image as world leader in the shaving industry.

Exhibit 6 ● Key Market Shaving Data

	MALE POPULATION (IN MILLIONS)	% OF WET SHAVERS	Share of market			Manufacturing		
			G	S	W	G	S	W
United States	67.6	73%	58	23	10	X	X	
United Kingdom	19.7	72	40	3	42	X		X
W. Germany	21.7	40	59	6	31	X		X
France	17.4	50	65	23	5	X		
Italy	17.2	74	65	3	19			
Spain	11.7	48	70	17	4	X		X
Canada	7.4	58	55	23	19	X	X	
Argentina	8.1	75	95	1	0	X		
Brazil	21.5	97	85	3	4	X		
Mexico	10.0	95	80	5	0	X		
Sweden	3.1	39	54	45	1		X	
Holland	4.6	32	60	30	3		X	
Japan	40.0 (approx.)	n/a	14	64	n/a			

Source: Company records.

*Share of male wet shavers.

Note: n/a = not available; G = Gillette; S = Schick; W = Wilkinson.

Case 10

Alcon Laboratories

In the Spring of 1997, Ed Schollmaier, president and CEO of Alcon Laboratories, Inc. returned from a major meeting with senior management of Nestlé S.A., Alcon's shareholder. At Alcon's headquarters in Fort Worth, Texas, Schollmaier provided the executive management team with a recap of his discussion with Peter Brabeck, Nestlé's recently appointed CEO.

Peter has made it clear that he wants to intensify growth from within the Nestlé company, rather than just through acquisition. He realizes that much of Nestlé's brand portfolio is concentrated on mature products. For increasing growth, Nestlé will have to spend much more than in the past on market development and research. This will cost money and requires a higher profitability for the company. As a result, Alcon has a chance to remain a major strategic element for Nestlé, returning superior profits and thus helping the food company to achieve its overall growth objectives. To make this strategic contribution to Nestlé's corporate growth, we will have to continue to grow at 8% annually over the next decade, turning Alcon from the $2.0 billion business it will be in 1997 into a $5.0 billion company by 2010. And all of this against a world market that cannot be expected to grow more than 4% annually.

Alcon Laboratories was the global leader in a $7.3 billion ophthalmic industry with strong market positions in ophthalmic pharmaceuticals, surgical supplies, and vision care products. A member of Nestlé's corporate family since 1977, Alcon had been a strong contributor to its parent's growth and profitability over the years, an especially noteworthy feat given the competitive environment of the 1990s.

Health care reform in the United States had brought particular challenges to the industry and, in 1994, Schollmaier had considered revising Alcon's growth targets to adjust for expected negative impacts. With a sharply defined strategy and good execution, however, Alcon had thrived, growing from $1.2 billion in sales to nearly $2 billion over the past six years. In contrast, Allergan, Alcon's closest competitor in all three segments, had fallen from being a company of nearly equal size to Alcon in the late 1980s to only 60 percent, and it had reported a 1 percent decline in sales for the first quarter of 1997. Far from abating, however, the storm clouds of health care reform persisted, and it remained unclear what the alphabet of managed care—HMOs (Health Maintenance Organizations), PBMs (Pharmacy Benefits Management Companies), PPMCs (Physician Practice Management Companies),[1]—would eventually spell. Who would wield the most bargaining power and what would be the impact on companies that supplied products to the market?

In addition to managing the impacts of health care reform on the ophthalmic industry, Alcon also had to confront potential new competitive threats, both from established pharmaceutical companies and from innovative technologies. In response to the growing promise of the global ophthalmic market, several multinational drug companies were in the process of developing dedicated sales infrastructures to compete more effectively against the industry leaders. Although Alcon had excellent access to new tech-

This case was prepared by Sam Perkins under the supervision of Professor Jean-Pierre Jeannet as a basis for class discussion rather than to illustrate either effective or ineffective handling of a business situation. "Alcon Laboratories" Copyright © 1998 by IMD—International Institute for Management Development, Lausanne, Switzerland. Not to be used or reproduced without written permission directly from IMD.

[1]Please refer to the "Ophthalmic Industry Note" (GM 717) for more information on these organizations.

nologies, such as laser surgery, through its industry relationships, the path of eventual commercialization and impact on existing markets and products was unknown.

The challenges of dynamic marketplace reform and competitor initiatives, coupled with the projection of lackluster overall industry growth, promised to severely test Alcon's ability to achieve the targeted levels of both growth and profitability that Nestlé required. Looking back on his long career as CEO, Schollmaier was proud of what Alcon had accomplished and was eager to ensure that his company would play a critical role in Nestlé's strategy for the twenty-first century.

COMPANY BACKGROUND

Founding and Early Growth

Robert D. Alexander and William C. Conner combined the first syllables of their last names to found Alcon Prescription Laboratories, a pharmacy in Fort Worth, Texas. The two pharmacists, who made and sold their own sterile injectable vitamins, saw an opportunity to manufacture ophthalmic pharmaceuticals on a mass production basis employing sterile and consistent techniques. Ophthalmology as a medical specialty was in a period of transition, moving from a demesne that included eye, ear, nose, and throat, to a concentration solely on the eyes. At the time, no major pharmaceutical company was significantly engaged in ophthalmic compounds, which were usually prepared as individual orders in local shops, often leading to contamination that could cause eye infections. Within several years of Alcon's founding, however, at least ten other small firms recognized and pursued the market potential of ophthalmic drugs. Of those early entrants, only Alcon and Allergan remained as identifiable companies by the 1990s, the rest having long since either been bought out and consumed or withered away.

Alexander and Conner incorporated in 1947 to raise funds and started actively marketing their products to pediatricians, selected GPs (General Practitioners), ENTs (ear, nose, throat) and ophthalmologists. Ten years later a thirty-person salesforce was promoting Alcon eye-care products throughout the United States, and revenues reached the $1 million

mark. Ed Schollmaier joined the Alcon sales division straight out of Harvard Business School in 1958 and quickly started his ascent up the management ranks. At the request of Bill Conner, Schollmaier undertook a two-week special assignment in 1960 to define Alcon's mission, determine its future business potential, and develop a strategic plan for the company. Schollmaier's research convinced him that Alcon's pharmaceutical business had the potential to grow to $25 million within a reasonable period, a projection that Conner thought somewhat optimistic, given existing sales of $2 million.

Schollmaier articulated what were to be the five key components of Alcon's strategy over the next decade.

1. *Fill in the blanks.* Concentrate on the needs of ophthalmologists. Develop and sell products for every identified segment of the ophthalmic pharmaceutical market, the initial target market.

2. *Enlarge the market.* Increase market size by developing new products for new segments and actively pursue the acquisition of compounds from other companies.

3. *Pursue nonpharmaceutical ophthalmic needs.* Identify ophthalmic opportunities outside the pharmaceuticals, such as lenses and surgical products.

4. *Explore nonophthalmic medical specialties.* Explore opportunities in other subspecialties which share technology or market similarities with Alcon's basic ophthalmic business.

5. *Initiate international expansion.* Start selling in foreign markets.

Alcon undertook all elements of the articulated strategy, increasing its own research and development efforts, securing drug compounds with ophthalmic potential from other pharmaceutical firms, and opening sales offices abroad, first in Latin America and then in Europe. The company made numerous small acquisitions to obtain technology, enter new fields, and especially to expand internationally. Within a few years Alcon had launched operating divisions focused on the specialties of urology, allergy, dermatology, radiology, and pediatrics. By 1967, sales reached $10 million, and the strategic initiatives laid out by Schollmaier, with the exception of the move outside ophthalmology, were well established. The effort to expand into new specialties placed significant demands on the company that threatened to derail the success of the core ophthalmic business, which was growing more rapidly and showed more potential than the other specialties. The separate divisions required too much organization-building and consumed more management time than was justified by their prospects. It was also not feasible for Alcon to provide the technology support required to keep all the segments on the leading edge in innovation. By 1970, Alcon abandoned the effort to build the nonophthalmic business and gradually sold them all off except for its dermatological skin-care products.

Ed Schollmaier was promoted to president in 1972, assuming leadership of Alcon from its founders. Investment in research and development, small acquisitions, and international expansion all continued to provide the basis for strong growth, and by 1977 Alcon had 22 manufacturing facilities in the United States and overseas, and sales from 100 countries neared $100 million. Alcon had been a public company since the late 1940s, but had not received much investor notice until the late 1960s when its growth and profitability attracted attention. In 1972, the company was listed on the New York Stock Exchange and enjoyed favorable recommendations, but Schollmaier also vividly recalled the downside to Wall Street exposure.

One time Morgan Guaranty dropped us from their list of recommended stocks because they wanted to shift their allocation away from mid-cap companies, and they decided simply to cut out five or six names. Alcon was one. It had nothing to do with how we were doing or with any particular problem, and all of a sudden the price of Alcon stock dropped from the low 30s to 18. Then everybody started to worry about how we were going to get the stock price back up. We were consumed with the need for quarterly performance.

Nestlé's Acquisition and Management of Alcon

Nestlé, a multinational food company based in Switzerland, acquired Alcon in 1977 after an extensive investigation of investment opportunities in the United States. Nestlé had excess cash at the time and had set a goal of having 60 percent of its excess cash invested in the stable U.S. economy. The Nestlé acquisitions of U.S. food companies Libby and Stouffer had led to a consent agreement with the FTC, barring it from further immediate food industry purchases, and it redirected its interest toward other sectors. The cosmetics business was appealing, but Nestlé's investment in L'Oréal, a large international French cosmetics firm, reduced the value of making other U.S. cosmetics acquisitions. The growth prospects in health care, and the possibility of marketing synergy with its existing infant formula business, also attracted the Swiss firm.

Nestlé avoided the first-tier pharmaceutical firms, deeming them too expensive, and found most of the second-tier firms lacking management talent and R&D competence. Then, according to Schollmaier, Nestlé "stumbled on to Alcon. We were the right size, had good R&D and marketing, and they liked the management." Part of the rationale for a pharmaceutical acquisition was related to Nestlé's partial ownership of L'Oréal. The CEO of L'Oréal at the time suggested to Nestlé: "You buy your own pharma company, and we at L'Oréal will buy ours. If we eventually merge our firms, we will combine the businesses."

Alcon had a somewhat different perspective on the acquisition. According to Schollmaier:

We at Alcon were looking for a safe haven. With our founders interested in liquidating their investment, we wanted to avoid becoming subject to the tyranny of quarterly profit pressures. We also had no interest in getting acquired by a large pharmaceutical company. For us, Nestlé was the perfect match despite the fact that there was no technology or market synergy between our businesses. We saw them as providing us with management stability and investment funds to grow the business.

Characteristic of most of the then Nestlé-owned companies, Alcon management retained substantial autonomy for developing and implementing strategy yet benefited substantially from its parent's strong financial resources. Nestlé helped fund the building of new plants in the United States and other countries, including a facility in Puerto Rico, and enabled Alcon to expand its research program to a scale that Alcon's size as an independent company could not have supported. More important than providing actual cash, Nestlé enabled Alcon to adopt a long-term approach (Schollmaier banished the word "quarter" from Alcon's corporate lexicon) and to undertake initiatives sooner than it otherwise could have justified. Shortly after Nestlé's acquisition, Alcon purchased Burton Parsons and constructed a $26 million R&D building expansion. In 1989, the support of Nestlé also permitted Alcon to acquire Coopervision Surgical, a promising but problem-plagued company that Allergan considered too risky to buy.

The purchase of Coopervision for roughly $350 million provided major benefits, expanding Alcon's presence in surgical instrumentation and intraocular lenses and enabling it to offer a complete, leading-edge surgical product line. Alcon had traditionally been a pharmaceutical company, and, although it offered surgical products, it trailed Cooper, which pioneered foldable lenses and technologically advanced ophthalmic surgical equipment. Alcon was able to resolve Cooper's production difficulties and improve its operations, and the Cooper products contributed substantially to the development of Alcon's international surgical business, its fastest growing segment. Cooper had a good second-tier management and within a few years the company had been successfully merged into Alcon. According to Schollmaier:

For Alcon, the Cooper acquisition was a turning point. It represented quite a risk since their products were not really ready for the market and, although representing breakthrough ideas, they were below the required quality and reliability which we considered essential for success in this market. Without the support of top Nestlé management at that time, we might have stepped back from this opportunity.

Following its acquisition of Alcon, Nestlé never took the next step of acquiring additional pharmaceutical businesses. Under the leadership of its then newly appointed CEO, Helmut Maucher, Nestlé focused on a series of acquisitions in the food industry that led to substantial external growth. Schollmaier recalled:

Alcon continued to grow, however, with Nestlé's financial assistance, and we became Nestlé's most profitable business segment with average operating earnings of 24% compared to 10% for the food business.

Growth accelerated sharply in the late 1980s and early 1990s, propelled by the amply-funded R&D, well-defined focus on eye-care, and strategic acquisitions *(refer to Exhibit 1)*. In spite of Alcon's growth, however, in the early 1990s Nestlé corporate management was increasingly confronted with questions at annual shareholder's meetings and from security analysts on the future of its eye-care subsidiary. Many observers felt that Nestlé could easily divest Alcon since the intended buildup of a pharmaceutical business and potential combination with L'Oreal had never materialized. As Schollmaier articulated, however, Alcon could easily justify its position in Nestlé's corporate family.

During the early 1990s, our own superior profitability was key. Nestlé top management could always point to our superior results. We had established a track record that we have come to call the 10-11-12-13% "magic" formula: We planned for a 10% sales growth, 11% growth in operating profit, a 12%

Exhibit 1 ● Alcon Sales ($U.S. million)

Year	Sales
1947	Start
1957	1
1967	10
1977	100
1987	500
1991	1,050
1992	1,200
1993	1,300
1994	1,500
1995	1,700
1996	1,900
1997	2,000+ projected

Source: Alcon

growth in profit before tax, and a 13% growth in net profit. With this type of performance, we were looking forward with confidence towards continued success.

Impact of U.S. Health Care Reform

As health care reform gathered momentum in the United States, there was widespread consensus that the twin forces of stricter government policies and growing leverage of managed care would have a detrimental impact on health care companies. Reflecting this concern, the share prices of many large pharmaceutical firms were sharply lower in 1993 and 1994. Schollmaier commented on the situation:

As a result of all this change, health care companies started merging and restructuring. Operations were streamlined and costs were cut. Everyone became used to the idea of providing more for less. Margins became reduced as companies had to pass discounts on to managed care firms.

It was at this time that Schollmaier and his management team thought about the need to possibly change Alcon's strategy and reduce the performance expectations of Nestlé.

With the changes in health care taking place, Nestlé management told us that they would understand if the magic formula would be reversed. For some time, we spoke of 10-9-8-7% sales and earnings growth. In early 1994, we at Alcon debated intensively whether we should lower the goals and Nestlé's expectations. In the end, we not only kept it, but we actually improved the performance through several strategic moves.

Strategic Response to U.S. Health Care Reform

Schollmaier understood that even though Nestlé might be willing to accept lower performance for a few years, if Alcon's profitability lagged it would be forced to reduce its commitment to R&D. Without sufficient investment in new product development to drive growth, Alcon would struggle to return to its former level of profitability and possibly jeopardize

its position with its corporate parent. He also understood that with change came opportunity, and Alcon's response to the cost and competitive pressures of health care reform included new initiatives designed to address specific aspects of managed care as well as enhanced attention to existing elements of the company's strategy. The key features of the strategy and its implementation included:

- *Narrow focus.* Concentrate on what the company knows and does best and can support technologically. A core precept since the early 1970s when it discontinued its efforts in other medical specialty areas, Alcon tightened its focus further by divesting the dermatology business to the Nestlé L'Oreal joint venture, Galderma Laboratories.

- *Full line approach.* Develop comprehensive product lines to maximize sales and marketing efforts and overhead efficiencies. Alcon filled in gaps in its segment offerings through acquisition, and product development. It also created a generic drug business to respond to the growth in that market and to provide a defense against new entrants.

- *Low-cost producer.* Drive down manufacturing and other operating costs through continuous "noncrisis basis" evaluation of facilities and all functional activities. Alcon began to consolidate some of its manufacturing to achieve economies of scale and became the low-cost producer in the industry, a position that provided considerable flexibility when competitors sought to gain market share through price cutting.

- *Global presence.* Leverage U.S. experience internationally, seek to be first presence in new markets and to be in every country. Alcon sought to maximize the impact of every product by using its expertise in regulatory approval to introduce products into as many countries as possible. It also focused increased attention on the large and highly profitable Japanese market.

- *Organizational stability.* Promote management continuity, foster strong individual growth, and develop executive succession plan. In the mid-1990s Alcon achieved a workforce reduction through normal attrition and retirement, avoiding the layoffs that sapped management talent and energy from many health care industry participants. Turnover was very low among Alcon management, a limited number of whom had come from competitors.

- *Managed care division.* Alcon created a new division—Managed Care—to respond to the growth of managed care institutions and the emerging decision-making power of nonclinical customers in the United States.

- *R&D productivity.* Focus internal R&D for maximum result and leverage external resources: major pharmaceutical companies, industry relationships, and contacts.

Corporate Culture

Complementing Alcon's commercial strategies were a culture and philosophy that embodied a sense of corporate responsibility in the mission of preserving and restoring sight, as articulated by Tim Sear, executive vice president.

We have a role to play. In Sub-Saharan Africa there are 500 ophthalmologists for 500 million people. There are 30 million people blind to the world from cataracts whose sight could be restored in 20–30 minutes. Some have been blind for 10 or 15 years. We have to reinvest in ophthalmology. We have been successful, and we have to give something back. That's part of our mission.

Alcon gave back through direct charitable activities and educational programs. Every year it donated $10s of millions of free medical supplies to ophthalmologists in developing countries who were willing to provide their services free of charge. Alcon's educational initiatives included associations with ophthalmic centers of excellence around the globe, distribution of instructional videos, and sponsorship of "web labs," where leading ophthalmologists demonstrated new surgical procedures and treatments, and students had the opportunity to use new instruments and practice techniques.

Alcon's leading position in the ophthalmic arena was emblemized by the Alcon Research Institute, started in 1982. Alcon initiated the program by appointing a committee of external academic and industry leaders. Five honorees, each awarded $10,000, presented their papers at the first symposium. After ten years, the grants had grown to $100,000, and the annual symposia drew hundreds of the leading academic and practicing ophthalmologists in the world. Alcon Labs funded the awards and hosted the two-day event, considered to be the premier academic ophthalmic meeting in the world, but the company did not participate in committee selection or deliberation thereby preserving the Institute's independence.

The Institute, Alcon's reputation, and the longevity of its executive team enabled the company to develop relationships with many of the leading ophthalmologists in the world. Many at Alcon considered the extent and quality of those relationships to be "unique . . . when senior Alcon people travel they typically visit the top ophthalmologists in whatever country they happen to be in." These relationships, coupled with the recognition Alcon received from its association with the Institute and from its charitable and educational programs, as well as from its own research efforts and position as the largest dedicated ophthalmic company, provided significant benefits, according to Allen Baker, executive vice president:

Because of Alcon's reputation, people with new ideas, new inventions, new techniques, tend to come to us to get help in commercializing them. Thus Alcon gains a significantly greater amount of research knowledge than it actually has to fund.

DIVISIONS

In 1997, Alcon had four operating divisions: ***Ophthalmic, Surgical,*** and ***Vision Care,*** all reporting to Tim Sear, and ***International,*** headed by Allen Baker.

Ophthalmics

Ophthalmics accounted for just under a third of Alcon's 1997 sales, equally split between the United States and international markets, and represented 15 percent of the global ophthalmic drug industry *(refer to* **Exhibit**

2). Revenue growth had stagnated in the early 1990s but had been on an upward track over the past four years, rising from 4 percent in 1993 to 8 percent growth in 1995. Division plans projected 5 to 7 percent growth through the rest of the decade but were historically conservative. Approximately 60 percent of U.S. sales were under some form of managed care contract, with discounts ranging from 1 percent to 15 percent.

Marketing and Sales

The impacts of managed care and the newfound prescribing authority of the optometrists in the United States required changes in Alcon's sales structure and methodology to address changes in purchase patterns and the geometric growth of potential customers. A salesforce of 90 in the United States, overseen by 10 regional and national managers, called on the traditional clinical customer group, 12,000 practicing ophthalmologists. (There was relatively minor overlap between this group and the surgical ophthalmologists who were customers of the other segments.) While the educational aspects of the sales mission were unchanged, the salesforce increasingly did not engage in negotiations regarding price or order taking. These tasks were handled by the business side of the managed care organizations and were the focus of Alcon's new Managed Care division. Alcon developed a separate, fifty-person sales organization to call on the large numbers of managed care gatekeepers (primary care physicians and pediatricians). Additionally the

pharmaceutical division cross-trained the sixty Vision Care salespeople to sell pharmaceuticals to optometrists, although the top prescribers were also the responsibility of the regular drug sales group.

Generics—Falcon

The U.S. market for generic versions of drugs had grown into a major business over the past fifteen years, facilitated by FDA approval procedures and the elimination of antisubstitution laws, and propelled by pressures to reduce costs. By the mid-1990s generics accounted for 33 percent of the U.S. ophthalmic pharmaceutical market units, although growth had leveled off due to the pace of new product introductions. Internationally, generic markets were at various stages of development but tended to be much smaller than the United States. Alcon entered the generics arena in 1994 primarily as a defensive move to protect itself against competition on the low end. It created a dedicated subsidiary, Falcon, which offered products only in the United States. Within two years Falcon had captured 29 percent of the generics market, largely on the basis of a single product.

Surgical

In spite of Alcon's roots as a pharmaceutical company, by the mid-1990s, its surgical division had become its largest business, contributing 45 percent of sales and boasting the highest growth rate. Acquisition of Coopervision in 1989, the leading manufac-

Exhibit 2 ● Alcon Pharmaceutical Market Shares (1997)

	North America	Europe	Latin America	Japan	Rest of World	Totals
Glaucoma Products (roughly half of market)	21%	15%	28%	4%	12%	**15%**
Other Products* (roughly half of market)	29%	27%	40%	1%	18%	**22%**
Totals	**24%**	**21%**	**34%**	**2%**	**15%**	**18%**

Source: IMS/Management Estimates

*Other Products includes: steroids, antibiotics, steroid/antibiotic combinations, artificial tears, antiallergies, decongestants, and mydriatic/cycloplegies. Alcon has product entries in all these categories.

turer of ophthalmic instrumentation and intraocular lenses, augmented Alcon's position as the industry leader in surgical solutions and supplies. In almost every product line Alcon held the number one market share position in the United States and globally *(refer to Exhibit 3)*, and held about 50 percent of the total $800 million U.S. market in cataract procedures.

Products: Differentiation, Trends, Opportunities Alcon's surgical products conformed to its broad-line strategy, offering a one-stop shop that provided everything needed (including equipment financing) for a surgical procedure from instrumentation to disposable supplies to surgical pharmaceuticals and solutions.

- *Custom Packs.* Alcon developed the concept of the custom pack which provided in one sterile package all of the supplies needed for a surgical procedure. Alcon had attained a 60 percent share of the market. Advances in information technology had simplified the selling process and reduced the order cycle time from several weeks to three days. During an interview with a surgical nurse, a

salesperson could develop a prototype on a laptop, display the contents and packing order textually and graphically, and then download the specifications to the facility in Houston, Texas, that assembled all the components. Alcon was willing to include the offerings of any other suppliers but offered better pricing based on a higher percentage of its own products in the pack.

- *Instrumentation.* At the former Coopervision plant in Irvine, California, Alcon manufactured instrumentation for surgical procedures, such as the phacoemulsification system used in cataract operations, vitrectomy equipment, used for surgery on the retina, and eye-testing equipment. In response to customer dissatisfaction with the need to replace equipment every two or three years to keep pace with technological innovation, Alcon implemented the concept of upgradable technology platforms for its instrumentation products in 1993. A worldwide field technical services group of

Exhibit 3 ● Surgical Instrumentation and Supplies Segment Market Share (1997)

Segment	United States	Japan	Others*
IOLs	31%	38%	36%
Disposables	62%	47%	48%
Irrigating Sol	90%	56%	69%
Viscoelastics	44%	0%	34%
Cataract Equip	60%	65%	50%
Cataract Paks	52%	65%	50%
Vitrectomy Equip	40%	53%	20%
Vitrectomy Paks	50%	78%	61%
Refractive	2%	0%	19%
Access/StandAlone	54%	4%	6%
% of Total	**50%**	**37%**	**27%**
Total Sales	**440**	**114**	**214**

Source: Management Estimates

*Others in this instance encompasses Europe, Latin America, and Rest of World. No significant market share differences exist in these sectors.

over 300 factory-trained technicians maintained machines and installed hardware and software upgrades every few years or as required.

- *Intraocular lenses.* In 1995 Alcon introduced the first acrylic foldable IOL (intraocular lens), the *AcrySof,* a new technology that provided improved performance over silicone lenses. Alcon adopted a policy of not discounting its *AcrySof* lens, in spite of considerable pressure from large hospital groups. In the absence of enactment of the Medicare regulation specifying multiple reimbursement rates based on IOL technology, Alcon attempted to make its own market-driven, performance-based case for receiving its asking price. Sear saw a direct analogy to the pharmaceutical model: "New drugs that are superior and provide better outcomes command premiums. There's no reason that same logic shouldn't apply with IOLs." Some executives carried the pharmaceutical model further, suggesting the possibility of going directly to the end-user patient, as drug companies had increasingly done to promote their new offerings.

- *Office computer system.* Also housed in the surgical division was an office computer product that enabled large, geographically disperse networks of providers to manage their patient scheduling, financial records/billing, and electronic medical records. It also enabled the capability to streamline their supply ordering and track surgical and therapeutic clinical outcomes. The product was a losing cost center but was considered to have strategic value.

Marketing and Sales

Alcon responded to changes wrought by health care reform by segmenting the market and by understanding where best to focus its sales effort. Before managed care, Alcon's strategy was to supply superior quality merchandise and charge premium prices. To accommodate cost pressures and to protect its high-end business, the surgical division planned to intro-

duce new versions of products that were targeted at and priced for lower-end market tiers. For example, in addition to *Viscoat* and *DuoVisc,* its top-line viscoelastics, which were priced at $55 and $75, Alcon was going to offer *Cellugel* at $25–$30. The *Hydrosof* IOL, which would sell for $50–$100, offered a less expensive alternative to the $150 *Acrysof* lens.

In the United States, Alcon's 50 percent share of the cataract market was slanted toward the higher-margin hospital segment. Surgicenters (ASCs) tended to be more cost-conscious than hospitals and also to demand more value, such as help with marketing and other services. On the plus side, ASCs usually gave all the business for procedures to one supplier and were a much higher user of custom packs, whereas hospitals preferred to maintain their ability to mix and match different brands. Alcon lost some ASC business to competitors who were willing to win market share on price reductions. It was overwhelmingly successful in competing for hospital-based business, however, where physicians tended to have greater influence in the purchase decision. As Caldwell remarked: "When a physician controls product selection we win many more times than we lose." Moreover, Alcon was usually able to retain that business when it transitioned to an ASC. Thus, surgical division focused its resources on increasing its share of the hospital segment, with a goal of moving from 40–50 percent to 70–80 percent.

Alcon's U.S. surgical salesforce consisted of 100 people dedicated to surgical disposables, 50 to equipment, and 20 focused on the office computer product, all overseen by 20 managers. The 170 front-line salespeople generated over $500 million in sales, nearly three times the per capita industry average. The group focused on the 6,000 to 8,000 surgical ophthalmologists and also interacted with Alcon's Managed Care group who dealt with the managed care customers on the business side.

Vision Care

Alcon sold off several small European contact lens companies in the mid-1980s, citing unfavorable competitive conditions, but it kept and grew the lens care business. In 1995 Alcon carved out its U.S. Vision Care business from Ophthalmics and created a separate division with a dedicated sales force and management structure, and by 1996 the division represented

23 percent of sales. The evolution of contact lens technology had presented significant challenges to Alcon over the years, as it saw its 33 percent share of the U.S. market in the late 1980s dissolve under the onslaught of disposables and multipurpose solutions. Margins for products to care for conventional and planned replacement lenses, especially enzymes, carried much higher margins than multipurpose solutions. In spite of the differences between Vision Care and the other divisions, Alcon followed the same basic strategy, as articulated by Orlando Rodriguez, director of marketing:

As with the other segments, it's technology first, then marketing. We are a technology-driven company and we can use that to build competitive advantage in vision care as well as in surgical or ophthalmics. The aim is to provide both convenience and cost benefits.

Several new products in the mid-1990s sought to challenge the market leaders and offer novel methods for lens cleaning and care. To differentiate its multipurpose solution from Bausch & Lomb's Renu, which contained a surfactant (detergent), Alcon introduced *Optifree Express,* a surfactant-free cleaning solution that provided effective cleaning but didn't impair the quality of the lens. *SupraClens,* launched in 1996, offered a new approach to lens care. A drop on each lens in the case, following a cleaning with a multipurpose solution, enhanced lens performance, providing immediate gratification. A survey indicated that two-thirds of participants reported that using SupraClens was as easy or easier than using a multipurpose solution.

SupraClens is our attack on disposables. It makes planned replacement and conventional lenses achieve a level of comfort and vision quality that is closer to what disposables are designed to provide. It also makes disposables perform better and last their entire expected two-week lifetime.

Marketing Initiatives

Complementing its technology development, Vision Care was pursuing two marketing initiatives to gain market share in its core product lines and to push into new areas. Although Alcon no longer had its own lens business around which to build brand synergy, it was attempting to form alliances with other lens manufacturers to develop brand relationships. In late 1996, Alcon entered into an agreement to remunerate Wesley Jessen, a contact lens manufacturer, for its endorsement of Alcon's vision care products and was close to a similar deal with other lens manufacturers. The other initiative, recently underway, involved Vision Care's access to the retain channel. As the Over-the-Counter (OTC) arm of Alcon, Vision Care saw potential opportunities to introduce products from the pharmaceutical side into the OTC market, moving more extensively beyond lens care into other eye-care products.

International Division

Alcon entered markets outside the United States in the 1950s and by 1996 international sales accounted for just under half of total revenues *(refer to Exhibit 4)*. Increasing Medicare reimbursement pressures within the United States and less regulation on surgical costs in international markets led to a significant shift toward surgical sales within the International Division *(refer to Exhibit 5)*. According to Schollmaier:

For the past decade, a major technology wave swept the ophthalmology industry, such as how cataract surgery is performed, and the use of phaco, smaller flexible IOLs. This wave had its beginning in the United States and then moved to Europe, Latin America, and eventually Japan. We followed that wave with the best equipment and IOLs, teaching the surgeons everywhere how to use them.

Country organizations ranged from large manufacturing facilities to two-person sales offices and included wholly-owned subsidiaries, distributor arrangements, and scientific offices. The size and type of organization depended upon the size of the market, macroeconomic conditions, the developmental status, system of health care delivery, state of ophthalmic practice, and the manner in which Alcon's position had evolved.

In a typical scenario, Alcon initially filled mail orders from an ophthalmologist who had heard of the company, then arranged for a local distributor to handle its offerings and eventually moved to a direct or indirect salesforce. When sales reached a sufficient level, Alcon formed a legal entity—branch office or subsidiary—depending upon local conditions, and legal/regulatory requirements. Continued growth then dictated support staff, accounting, and other functions.

Alcon also made numerous small acquisitions to gain entry to new international markets, and it inherited a diverse array of products over the course of its early global expansion. Initially Alcon kept many of the local products and gave country managers responsibility for new product registrations. To streamline the regulatory approval process and to optimize the profitability of its product portfolio in the 1980s, Alcon centralized all product registration activity at headquarters. It adopted a global product strategy aimed at introducing the same products into as many markets as possible.

Pricing in foreign markets varied significantly, depending upon the degree of governmental cost control and the extent to which private health care systems had developed. In many countries the prices of pharmaceuticals was substantially lower than in the United States, though surgical supplies were less im-

Exhibit 4 ● International vs. Domestic Product Mix

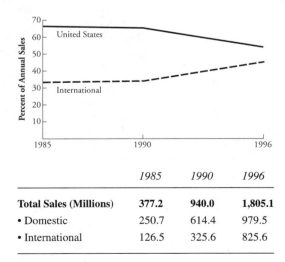

	1985	*1990*	*1996*
Total Sales (Millions)	**377.2**	**940.0**	**1,805.1**
• Domestic	250.7	614.4	979.5
• International	126.5	325.6	825.6

Source: Alcon

Exhibit 5 ● International Business Segment Mix

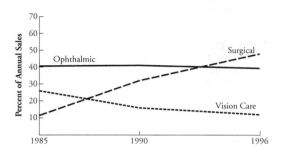

	1985	*1990*	*1996*
Total International Sales (Millions)	**126.5**	**325.6**	**825.6**
• Ophthalmic	50.8	133.4	326.3
• VisionCare	32.9	53.0	101.9
• Surgical	14.6	105.3	396.1
• Other*	28.2	33.9	1.3

*Mostly Galderma and Webcon in 1985 and 1990. Subsequently divested.

Source: Alcon

pacted and vision care products, not covered by national health plans, were entirely market-driven. Alcon's international strategy was to be everywhere with every product, regardless of pricing pressure and short-term obstacles to market development. The company invested considerably during the 1970s and 1980s in building a global infrastructure that, by 1997, it considered second to none. Sear commented:

You can't pick and choose which products you sell or which markets you're in. We have to be everywhere. As soon as a market opens up, we're there. When Latvia, Estonia, and Lithuania opened up in 1990 we had people there within a matter of weeks with a suitcase full of products to hand out. *Our man went to see the Minister of Health. Tell them we're Alcon and we'll be back. They'll always remember Alcon was first.*

Exhibit 6 shows a comprehensive picture of Alcon's global market share by region.

Managed Care Division

In April 1996, Alcon created a separate division in response to the growing importance and bargaining power of large managed care organizations in the United States. Except for one outside person from a large pharma company who was brought in to develop the organization, the Managed Care group was built internally and comprised sixteen up and coming and/or experienced salespeople drawn from sales management and national account positions in the other divisions. In late 1996, Cary Rayment, formerly comanager of the surgical division, was put in charge. Reflecting the differences in types of managed care institutions, account responsibility was grouped by customer segment, with HMOs and PBMs separate from PPMCs.

The mission of the organization was to establish Alcon as the preferred ophthalmic supplier by creating innovative contracting arrangements, providing services and developing relationships. Managed Care's goals were to ensure that Alcon sales representatives had access to decision makers, negotiate deals that maximized price consistent with optimal formulary inclusion, and to provide a single contact point representing Alcon to the business customer. Blaise McGoey, vice president U.S. Ophthalmics, offered a more pithy articulation of the objectives: "Managed Care gets us the hunting license to go sell our products. Excellent clinical selling is worthless today without good relationships with the business customers and the right formulary positions."

Ensuring inclusion in formularies involved both defensive and offensive strategies. A defensive measure was simply making sure that products were not excluded from a particular formulary through an NDC lock-out. Though sometimes forced into a defensive posture, Alcon preferred to develop offensive approaches that sought exclusive positions, preferred status in a formulary or a guaranteed market share. The levels of discount on drugs in a contract were tied to their status in the formulary and to a measure of market share performance.

Rayment attributed a good measure of Alcon's recent success to the resources the company had invested in Managed Care and to the division's role in helping to integrate the efforts of the other divisions. With some of its customers, the group was trying to develop comprehensive contracts that incorporated products from all three of Alcon's product areas. In its role as the single contact point, Managed Care had the

Exhibit 6 ● Alcon Share of Market 1990 and 1996

	North America		Europe		Latin America		Rest of World		Japan	
	1990	*1996*	*1990*	*1996*	*1990*	*1996*	*1990*	*1996*	*1990*	*1996*
PHARMACEUTICALS	23%	24%	12%	18%	30%	34%	12%	15%	0%	1.6%
SURGICAL	37%	54%	10%	25%	8%	30%	15%	30%	12%	37%
VISION CARE*	18%	31%	6%	12%	25%	37%	5%	13%	0%	1.4%
LENSES		n/a		n/a		n/a		n/a		n/a

Source: Alcon

*Soft Contact Lens Care

opportunity to cross-sell different products and create comprehensive performance incentive packages. The benefits of this contributed to a new attitude and perspective within Alcon, as Rayment described:

We used to have very much a stovepipe mentality here. I saw Blaise (McGoey) in the elevator but didn't really know or bother much about what he had going on. Now there is much more cross-functional communication than there used to be. I think it helps us as we deal with the needs and opportunities of integrated health care organizations.

Research and Development

New products and new technology were the lifeblood of pharmaceutical and health care companies, and Alcon had always devoted substantial resources to its research and development efforts, emblemized by the Alcon Research Center. Spending on research and development rose steadily as a percent of sales, reaching nearly 9 percent by the mid-1990s, equaling a total outlay of $160 million in 1997 *(refer to Exhibit 7).* R&D was projected to decrease to about 8 percent of sales by the year 2000, though there was a clear understanding that if emerging projects required additional funding, the money would be available. Nearly half of Alcon's 1996 sales came from products developed in the previous ten years.

Managed care stimulated the drive to develop new products whose value was augmented by an understanding of health economics. The clearest path to secure inclusion on formularies and premium pricing was to offer novel treatments that provided the best value in the context of integrated care. As McGoey succinctly stated about Alcon's strategy:

Technology drives the day. If I have the best product, I don't care what obstacles you put in front of me, I can win.

Alcon's R&D strategy combined narrowly focused internal efforts with external partnerships and alliances. As a niche pharmaceutical supplier, Alcon had fostered expertise in product development rather than in basic research. Historically it had licensed many of the compounds in its drugs from the major pharmaceutical companies and then fine-tuned the application and delivery vehicle. As big players grew reluctant to license compounds with substantial market potential and started to demand higher fees, Alcon moved more into basic research, which was closely targeted to areas where it had demonstrated competence. In the mid-1990s Alcon started to introduce products created completely in-house, such as Iopidine, a treatment for serious glaucoma cases.

A major goal of Alcon's R&D effort was to reduce the time it took to develop products, obtain regulatory approval, and get new products into the marketplace, especially in cases where a competitor had gained first mover advantages with an innovative treatment and was capturing market share. In addition to its technological expertise, Alcon developed strong competitor intelligence capability to understand what markets other industry participants were pursuing. It also recognized that it could create a competitive advantage by honing its ability to move quickly through the regulatory approval process.

Growth Opportunities

According to Schollmaier, Alcon needed to review its strategy of selective growth and determine whether this strategy is still appropriate in light of the changed corporate goals of Nestlé. Reviewing international opportunities, Schollmaier was careful to point out that the profitability of the various international markets had changed over time. Traditionally, the pharma business in the United States was significantly more profitable than elsewhere due to the fact that per unit

Exhibit 7 ● R&D Spending—1997

	$ mil	% Sales
PHARMACEUTICAL	100	13
SURGICAL	40	5
VISION CARE	20	4

Source: Alcon

prices outside the United States were only about one-third of the level in the United States. The profitability of the surgical division is about the same both internationally and in the United States, although the United States had traditionally had higher prices, and thus profits, than internationally. This was assumed to have been the impact of the U.S. health care reform. The surgical business although very profitable, was lagging behind the U.S. pharmaceutical business profitability.

The questions that are being posed to us are quite simple: Can we grow in our accustomed markets, or segments, or do we have to broaden our range or even diversify out of ophthalmology? Which business segments should we emphasize? Which geographies should we emphasize? To what extent should we rely on growth from industrialized countries vs. emerging economies? But we cannot play our strategic role within the Nestlé family if we stay still, thus the need to grow to maintain our importance.

Growth Options

Faced with Nestlé's challenge, Alcon's management team began to review and evaluate immediate and longer-term options for achieving the growth and profitability goals. In addition to the areas that Alcon currently targeted, the team considered paths that deviated somewhat from the narrow focus that had been one of the hallmarks of Alcon's strategy. Potential options included:

- *Market share growth.* Alcon held leading positions in most of the surgical segments, but had lost ground in some of the pharmaceutical product lines, notably antiglaucoma drugs.
- *Geographical expansion.* Demographic and economic trends dictated that significant future growth in ophthalmic markets lay outside the United States. Alcon's global product strategy and centralized regulatory approval process enabled it to introduce its product lines in most geographic areas. There were markets, however, such as

Japanese pharmaceuticals, where Alcon was underrepresented. Emerging markets, such as China, also offered substantial opportunity *(refer to **Exhibits 8, 9, and 10**).*

- *Market growth.* Technological advances and novel therapeutic treatments offered the potential to expand existing markets and create new ones. For example, the dramatic improvements in cataract removal and IOLs had spurred growth in a market projected at one point to decline. Similar possibilities in other areas invite continued research. New drugs or surgical procedures to treat ARMD (Age Related Macular Degeneration), CMV retinitis and diabetic retinopathy promised to generate significant sales where no markets currently existed. Additionally, there was potential for Alcon to increase its share of surgical markets it currently served by filling out remaining gaps in its product lines and thereby increasing its revenues per procedure.

- *Refractive market.* Alcon did not currently offer a line of refractive surgical products. The surgical technique was expected to evolve toward intraocular implants where Alcon's technological lead in the use of acrylic materials for IOLs gave it a possible long-term advantage. The procedure was expected to be commonplace, though expensive, in five years, with the lenses being a large portion of the cost.

- *Ear, Nose and Throat (ENT).* Concerned about the distraction of organization building and the challenge of providing R&D support, Alcon had discontinued its planned diversification into other medical specialties in the early 1970s. There were competencies, however, that Alcon possessed in 1997 that argued for reexamining that strategy. Several of Alcon's ophthalmic pharmaceutical compounds had potential applications in the treatment of ENT afflictions. Alcon had developed the ability to successfully

Exhibit 8 ● New Market Segments and Geographic Opportunities

	Potential Product Markets	*Geographic Markets*
PHARMACEUTICAL	CMV Retinitis	Japan, China, India, Indonesia,
	Diabetic Retinopathy	Russia
	Age-Related Macular Degeneracy	
SURGICAL	Refractive	Indonesia, Russia, Mexico,
	Office-Based Equipment	Middle East, Africa
VISION CARE	Contact Lenses	China, India, Middle East,
	Diagnostic Equipment	Africa, Eastern Europe
	OTC Products	
	Spectacles and Frames	

Source: Alcon

Exhibit 9 ● Alcon Sales in China and India ($U.S. thousands)

	1995	*1996*	*1997*	*Projected 1998 (2 x 6 m)*
China				
Pharmaceuticals	*500*	*1,000*	*1,650*	*2,000*
Surgical	*1,900*	*3,200*	*5,700*	*7,400*
VisionCare	—	*50*	*100*	*125*
TOTAL	**2,400**	**4,250**	**7,450**	**9,525**
India				
Pharmaceuticals	—	—	—	—
Surgical	*1,000*	*1,500*	*1,825*	*2,650*
VisionCare	—	—	—	—
TOTAL	**1,000**	**1,500**	**1,825**	**2,650**

Source: Alcon Internal Financials

Exhibit 10 ● Worldwide Eye Care Market—Present and Projected ($US factory sales in millions)

	North America	Europe	Latin America	Japan	Rest of World	Total
PHARMACEUTICALS						
Market Size 1996	1150	950	300	1150	300	3850
Market Estimate 2005	2300	1250	450	1800	450	6250
Growth 1990–1996	9%	2%	5%	5%	8%	5%
Growth 1997–2005	8%	3%	4%	5%	4%	5%
SURGICAL						
Market Size 1996	800	700	100	400	200	2200
Market Estimate 2005	1200	950	150	650	250	3200
Growth 1990–1996	2%	5%	8%	12%	9%	6%
Growth 1997–2005	4%	4%	4%	6%	4%	4%
VISION CARE						
Market Size 1996	600	450	140	350	160	1700
Market Estimate 2005	600	500	150	550	200	2000
Growth 1990–1996	2%	2%	2%	2%	2%	2%
Growth 1997–2005	NC	1%	1%	6%	2%	2%
SUB-TOTAL						
Market Size 1996	2550	2100	540	1900	660	7750
Market Estimate 2005	4100	2700	750	3000	900	11450
Growth 1990–1996	5%	4%	5%	6%	7%	5%
Growth 1997–2005	5%	3%	3%	5%	4%	4%
CONTACT LENSES						
Market Size 1996	1450	400	150	400	400	2800
Market Estimate 2005	1550	500	200	600	600	3450
Growth 1990–1996	4%	6%	7%	7%	7%	5%
Growth 1997–2005	1%	4%	4%	6%	6%	3%
TOTAL						
Market Size 1996	4000	2500	690	2300	1060	10550
Market Estimate 2005	5650	3200	950	3600	1500	14900
Growth 1990–1996	5%	4%	5%	6%	7%	5%
Growth 1997–2005	4%	3%	3%	5%	5%	4%

Source: IMS/Management Estimates

market to clinical specialists and the reputation of the Alcon brand was widely recognized among physicians. Additionally, in some countries ophthalmology was not a separate specialty from ENT, and therefore EENT (Eye, Ear, Nose and Throat) physicians represented one clinical customer.

As Alcon's management team examined these options, one executive, acting as the devil's advocate, challenged the premise of what the company was attempting to do.

We've been very successful by remaining tightly focused on a narrow band of technologies and markets and doing really well at what we do. Are we going to risk the foundation of that success by trying to push for growth and profit levels at a rate that we can't sustain? Are we going to change our strategy and veer off course, possibility destroying the golden goose we've built?

Case 11

Make Yourself Heard: Ericsson's Global Brand Campaign

In February 1998, Ericsson launched a major global communication campaign for its brand of mobile phones. This was the first time a leading telecommunication company had launched a brand campaign on such a scale. Inspired by "the simple fact that personal contact is the most important and powerful element in mobile communication," the management of Ericsson's mobile phone and terminals division had decided to launch the massive advertising despite reservations expressed by others that the focus on brand building could take resources and attention away from the increasing number of new products Ericsson was bringing into the mobile phone market. But in the words of Jan Ahrenbring, vice president of marketing communications:

The brand campaign is about Ericsson values, not just products. The brand platform is meant to convey a clear message about Ericsson's belief in the values of self-expression and ease of communication in relating to one another.

COMPANY BACKGROUND

Ericsson is a leading supplier of equipment and services for the telecommunications industry. The company produces advanced systems and products for wired and mobile telecommunications in both public

and private networks, sold to customers in more than 130 countries.

In 1997 Ericsson had 100,774 employees and 168 billion Swedish krona (SKr) in sales.[1] Close to 90 percent of its turnover was generated outside of Sweden, where it was founded more than 120 years ago.

Since early 1997 Ericsson's vast operations in virtually the entire telecommunications field had been organized into three business areas:

[1]In 1998: US$1=SKr 7.9

This case was prepared by Professor Kamran Kashani as the basis for class discussion rather than to illustrate effective or ineffective handling of a business situation. "Make Yourself Heard: Ericsson's Global Brand Campaign" Copyright © 1998 by IMD–International Institute for Management Development, Lausanne, Switzerland. Not to be used or reproduced without written permission directly from IMD.

Radio Systems. Mobile voice and data communication systems. 1997 sales: SKr78 billion.

Infocom Systems. Multimedia communications solutions for transmission of voice, data and images to network operators, service providers, and enterprises. 1997 sales: SKr48 billion.

Mobile Phones and Terminals. End-user mobile phones and terminals, such as pagers. 1997 sales: SKr42 billion.

*(Refer to **Exhibit 1** for a partial organization of Ericsson.)*

In 1996 a large strategy study was completed. Entitled "2005: Entering the 21st Century," it constituted the basis for Ericsson's future strategy:

Ericsson's mission is to understand our customers' opportunities and needs and to provide communications solutions better than any competitor. In doing

Exhibit 1 ● Partial Organization Chart, Ericsson Group and Mobile Phones and Terminals

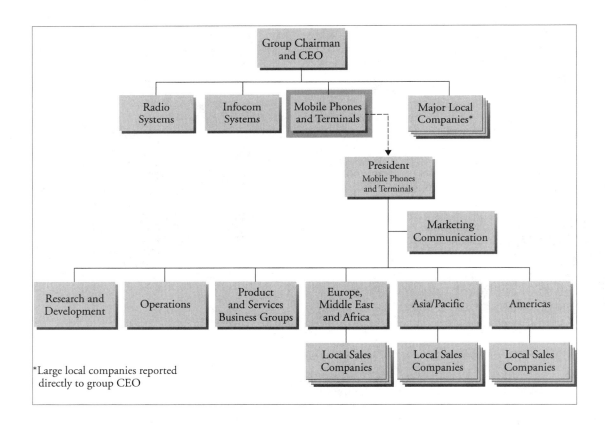

*Large local companies reported directly to group CEO
Source: Company Records

this, Ericsson can offer its shareholders a competitive return on their investments.

In recent years Ericsson's R&D budget exceeded 20 percent of sales. More than 18,000 employees in 23 countries were active in research and development. The management estimated that with the fast pace of technological development, its entire product portfolio would be completely renewed within two years.

In 1997 Ericsson's mobile phone *systems* were estimated to have served 54 million subscribers in 92 countries. With 40 percent of the world market for such systems sold to network operators, the company was the leader in this area.

Ericsson entered the market for hand-held mobile *phones* only in 1987. This was the first time the company marketed its products to consumers. The 1997 reorganization of Ericsson, which made mobile phones a separate division, was motivated by a recognition that, as an end-user market, mobile phones had their own "different business logic." The market share for Ericsson's mobile phones had strengthened recently compared with its two global rivals—Nokia and Motorola. *(Refer to market share data in Exhibit 2.)*

PAST ADVERTISING

Ericsson's advertising had been limited before it entered the mobile phone business. As a company targeting a few large telecommunication customers,

Exhibit 2 ● Mobile Phones: Global Market Shares

	1995	1996	1997
Nokia	23%	21%	21%
Motorola	31%	26%	22%
Ericsson	11%	12%	16%
All others* (Sony, Philips, Panasonic, etc.)	35%	41%	41%
Total	**100%**	**100%**	**100%**

*No single brand held a global share higher than 7%

Source: Company Records

typically large PTT organizations or business organizations, the management saw little need for advertising. Even after the introduction of its first mobile phone, the company abstained from heavy advertising. In the words of a senior mobile phone manager:

In a hot market for mobile phones we sold whatever we produced, and the assumption at the time was simply that if we made good products, we didn't need advertising.

Most early mobile phone ads were initiated by Ericsson's local sales companies around the world. In each ad, a phone product was introduced under a communication strategy that was decided by Ericsson's country management.

In 1995 Ericsson successfully implemented its first pan-European advertising campaign for a new phone line, GH337. Under headlines all starting with "It's about . . . ," the ads introduced the new product's features. *(Refer to Exhibit 3 for samples of press advertising.)*

Reflecting on the first pan-regional campaign, Goran Andersson, the marketing director for brand communications (reporting to Jan Ahrenbring), recalled:

The local management were not used to supporting such an initiative and, naturally, they were not very happy with the idea at the beginning. But that campaign showed us all that together we can do very useful things.

Following the reorganization of the mobile phone into a separate division, the management embarked on its first global communication initiative. In 1997 Ericsson entered into an agreement with United Artists Pictures to place its mobile phones in the James Bond movie *Tomorrow Never Dies*. The division's management saw the product placement as an opportunity to show that "Ericsson is the leading technological and style innovator . . . and to demonstrate its phones as part of everyday life." For a period of twelve weeks the company used the James Bond film theme for tie-in tactical ads for new products around the world. *(Refer to Exhibit 4 for a copy of local James Bond advertising in Austria.)*

It was estimated that in 1997 close to SKr2 bil-

Exhibit 3 ● Pan-European Press Advertising 1995

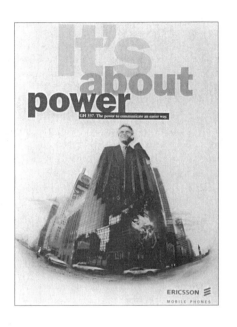

Exhibit 4 ● James Bond Tie-In Advertising: Austria 1997

lion was spent advertising Ericsson mobile phones worldwide. Of this total, 75 percent was spent by local organizations on product campaigns. The remainder was accounted for by pan-European or global product ads which appeared on such media as CNN, in-flight and business magazines.

BRAND BUILDING

The division management at mobile phone and terminals had closely monitored the forces that were fast changing the global mobile phone business. In the late 1990s the market was growing faster than ever, but becoming increasingly competitive. While in early 1997 there were 137 million mobile phone subscribers worldwide, this number was expected to grow to 590 million by 2002. The growth was ex-

pected to be fastest in Asia-Pacific, followed by Latin America, Europe, and North America. Meanwhile, there were an estimated twenty producers of mobile phones, a number that was expected to grow significantly in the near future.

Management had come to believe that future leadership in the mobile phone business was the privilege of those few companies that could build strong brands with the end-users. For division management the need for brands with differentiated consumer value was justified for a number of reasons:

1. Product differences among manufacturers were beginning to narrow down. Differentiation purely based on technology and features was becoming more difficult.

2. New products were witnessing ever-shrinking

life cycles. While a new Ericsson mobile phone introduced in 1992 was in the market for three years before being replaced by more advanced, and lower cost, models, the recent launches were expected to have life cycles of twelve to eighteen months. A proliferation of short-cycle models made product-specific communication expensive and possibly not effective.

3. The new generation of end-users was looking for different features in a phone than those who had entered the market early on. While the early adopters had been primarily business users who had looked for advanced features and small size, future growth was expected to come from non-business consumers who looked for different values in a mobile phone.

Furthermore, the management believed that in its competitive market, Ericsson could enjoy its traditional price premium (ranging for some models from 5 percent up to 30 percent over Nokia and Motorola) only if its reputation for technological leadership could be backed up with a strong brand. Goran Andersson commented:

While the network operators have tried to commoditize mobile phones by nearly giving them away to attract subscribers, we want the consumer to ask not just for a phone, but Ericsson's mobile phone—even if it costs more. Like the business buyers before them, we like the newcomers to the market to think of our products as something special, worth a premium.

While local market conditions differed widely, it was estimated that close to 60% of all mobile phones sold around the world was brought directly by consumers through a retail outlet. The rest was sold by network operators through their own promotional schemes. The share of retail sales was expected to grow.

MARKET STUDIES

In 1997 mobile phone division management commissioned a couple of studies the conclusions of which reinforced their own analysis of the trends in the mobile phone market, and the growing importance of brands in consumer choice. The first study, entitled

"Take Five," was a global segmentation effort aimed at better understanding the profiles of the mobile phone consumer. Researched in 24 countries in Europe, the Americas, and Asia, the study concluded that lifestyle and consumer values were better predictors of consumer behavior than traditional demographic factors. The study identified five global consumer segments, each with a different profile:

- *Pioneers.* Active individualists and explorers. Interested in and knowledgeable about technology. Motivated by innovation, they are impulsive buyers, attracted by strong brands and will pay for quality. Their loyalty is to technology, not brands.

- *Achievers.* Hard-working, competitive individualists. Willing to take risks, they are motivated by productivity, comfort, success, and advance technology that is also useful, time-saving, and visible. Care about appearance, but have limited brand loyalty.

- *Materialists.* Status seekers, they are attracted by well-known brands. Main motivations are recognition, status, and sense of belonging. They want trendy products and are attracted to known brands.

- *Sociables.* Convivial and community-oriented, they are highly rational, well-informed and buy products that are easy to use and attractive. They are loyal to brands.

- *Traditionalists.* Attracted to social harmony rather than change, they are attracted to established products with basic features that offer ease and reliability. Low prices and well-known brands are important to them. They tend to be brand loyal.

The study proposed that the five segments are measurable by size, penetration, and inclination to purchase. While in the early stages of market development in each country the pioneers were by far the largest group of mobile phone buyers, over time other segments entered the market and grew in both absolute and relative terms. The management believed that the global segmentation had the capacity of guiding action along a wide range of activities, from strategic planning and product development to brand marketing and sales. Future products were to be conceived, designed, and marketed with the values of different segment in mind.

The second international study, done in parallel with the first, was aimed at assessing Ericsson's current brand perceptions and defining directions for the future. The corporate "soul searching," as some members of the management labeled the study, revealed that Ericsson was perceived differently in different countries and by different segments. Nevertheless, the brand was commonly perceived as "cold, distant, conservative, and technology oriented." The study also revealed that the brand awareness and recognition was low in most markets, especially among the growing numbers of nonbusiness customers. For example, in the United Kingdom, which was typical of the more developed markets, spontaneous awareness among mobile phone users, and those who might purchase in the next twelve months, was 36 percent. This figure was at par with Motorola, but significantly below Nokia at 45 percent. In the United States, on the other hand, Ericsson's brand awareness was nil.

Among the second study's final conclusions, partly aimed at educating the management regarding the need for brand building, were the following statements:

1. For many people working in fast-moving technological fields at Ericsson, branding may be a concept which is difficult to accept. They like things to be concrete, technologically different; branding, though, is a product of the "mind and heart." But it would be a mistake to believe that branding is unimportant because good brands outlive any passing technological breakthrough.

2. The ultimate goal in branding is to cement a relationship with our consumers. Capturing a share of his mind . . . his imagination . . . his emotions. . . . It will generate sentiments like "The Ericsson mobile phone brand really understands what I am about—my hopes, my dreams." By creating a strong emotional and psychological bond, the Ericsson brand will give the consumers a reason to buy beyond price, features, or rebates.

3. Ericsson must work on two fronts simultaneously: Build a strong brand based on a consistent brand platform and pursue its traditional product innovation, which can quickly meet the ever-changing needs of consumers.

The study proposed a *brand platform* that was "not about cold technology, but about human contact . . . the contact that comes through human conversation, through people talking and listening." It defined Ericsson's *brand ambition* as "to be recognized as the brand that makes personal contact the most important element in mobile telecommunication."

COMPETITION

The growing mobile phone market was dominated by three players: Nokia, Motorola and Ericsson. Others with well-recognized brand names, such as Sony and Philips, were also present but held smaller market shares. Nokia was known for a constant stream of advanced new products. Its latest model, Nokia 9000 Communicator, combined voice, fax, E-mail and Internet functionality in a device that retailed at around $1000. Nokia's international advertising, using the slogan "Connecting People," had stressed these advanced features. Motorola, a leader in the field, had lost market share for lack of new models and poor marketing. After a recent reorganization, Motorola seemed to be fighting back. Its newest product, StarTAC, weighing 95 grams and selling at approximately $700, was the world's smallest phone, a claim stressed in the company's recent advertising. Before StarTAC, Ericsson's GH337, which sold to consumers for less than $200, had held the title of the world's smallest mobile phone.

Mobile phone prices had generally declined in recent years. In the United States, for example, the average consumer prices had dropped from $182 to $111 since 1994.

GLOBAL BRAND CAMPAIGN

In 1996, with a view to launching a global brand campaign, the mobile phone and terminals division hired Young & Rubicam, an advertising agency with an extensive international network. To maintain a degree of consistency in communication, local Ericsson organizations, long-accustomed to working with their own choice of agencies, were now required to work exclusively with Young & Rubicam.

In discussions that followed their appointment, the ad agency proposed two alternative platforms for a global brand campaign. Both platforms were seen by the agency as having the potential of fulfilling the brand ambition set out in the earlier study. The first proposal revolved around the slogan: "One Person, One Voice," but it was rejected for a number of reasons, including its political overtones, which limited its use in some countries.

The second platform was captured in the slogan: "Make yourself heard." The agency and the management both believed that this platform was true to the goal of projecting Ericsson as a human and compassionate company, thus setting it apart from all the other feature-oriented mobile phone brands. In the words of Ericsson's group chairman, Lars Ranqvist, "It is our belief that communication is between people—the rest is technology." The management also believed that the platform empowered people to communicate what is on their minds, and showed respect for individuals and what they had to say.

For press advertising the agency proposed a gallery of faces and a range of situations demonstrating shared thoughts, experiences, and ideas that would capture the spirit of communication between people around the world. The pictures were to be of ordinary people in everyday situations. Each ad would carry a statement in smaller print at the bottom giving Ericsson's credentials, including the fact that the company's products were used in "40 percent of all mobile communications around the world."[2] For TV, distinctive white-on-black TV commercials would feature a wordplay that would bring "Make yourself heard" to life. *(Refer to Exhibits 5 and 6 for samples of campaign billboards and TV commercial storyboards.[3])*

Unlike all previous Ericsson campaigns, the proposed ads did not show any mobile phone products. This unusual omission was thought to be the right ap-

proach, and for good reasons. First, the agency wanted to deflect attention away from specific products and their features towards the umbrella brand. Second, different models were being sold in different parts of the world, thereby limiting what could be shown in a standardized global campaign. Third, both the management and the agency wanted to leave the door open for the future use of Ericsson brand on non-phone products or services. Finally, in the words of Jan Hedquist, Young & Rubicam account executive, "The inclusion of a product would destroy the sense of intimacy we are trying to establish with the consumer. We would be seen as hawking something."

To ensure that the company was betting on the right campaign, "Make yourself heard" and its accompanying visual communication were pretested in nineteen countries, representing 85 percent of total mobile phone sales. The key findings were:

- Ads generated unusually consistent reactions across countries. The slogan "grew" on people, showing its long-term potential.

- The slogan was found to have a universal appeal. It was seen to be intelligent.

- Consumers found Ericsson as the brand that "will help you say what you need/want to say"; "cuts distance, mentally and physically, between people"; "knows about and is interested in people"; and "supports a global community."

The research agency conducting the pretest found the outcome so encouraging that it reported the following: "These are the most positive and consistent results we have seen in advertising research."

Early in 1998 a decision was made by the top management of the mobile phones and terminals to launch the proposed global brand campaign, starting in Europe. The Americas and Asia-Pacific markets were to follow later in the year. The budget for the first leg of the campaign was not publicly announced, but it was estimated to be in the SKr250–300 million range. Of this expenditure, 20 percent was to be financed by the head office, and the rest by the regions (25 percent) and local markets (55 percent). The media spread was different in different markets, but generally 70 percent was targeted for press, and the rest for TV and outdoors.

To assess the campaign's results, tracking stud-

---

[2]The full body copy of press ads read: *"Ericsson has been helping people share their thoughts for over 120 years. Today, Ericsson equipment is used in 40% of all mobile phone communications around the world. By mobile phone, data, pager or cordless phone—Ericsson gives you the power to be heard. Wherever you are, whenever you want."*

[3]In some markets, such as Sweden and the United Kingdom, the slogan "Make yourself heard" was to appear in English. In other markets it would be translated into the local language. The copy was in local language.

Exhibit 5 ● Global Brand Campaign Billboard Advertising 1998

ies measuring consumer awareness and brand image for Ericsson and its rivals were to be conducted weekly in twenty countries.

FUTURE DECISIONS

Barely a few weeks after its launch in mid-February 1998, the "Make yourself heard" campaign was generating reactions and raising new issues. Some observers were wondering if the company was putting its resources in the right place. A commentary in the U.K.-based *Marketing Weekly* called the global campaign a "courageous" move, but wondered if it "detracts from product advertising and, even more pertinently, from sales."[4]

[4]O'Sullivan, Tom. "Ericsson strives to make itself heard." *Marketing Week,* February 5, 1998.

Within the organization the campaign was raising other issues. One was whether the brand campaign should be coordinated with the product-oriented advertising sponsored by the regions and local operations. Goran Andersson explained:

As a brand campaign "Make yourself heard" isn't designed for any particular product or segment. It is about Ericsson and its values as a brand. On the other hand, more targeted product and segment ads are currently being run by the regional and local sales operations. The questions are whether or not the brand and the product campaigns should be coordinated and, if so, how.

Exhibit 7 shows a copy of a recent product advertising run by the European region for Ericsson's new GH688 model. Targeted at a segment the earlier

Exhibit 6 ● Global Brand Campaign TV Commercial Storyboards 1998

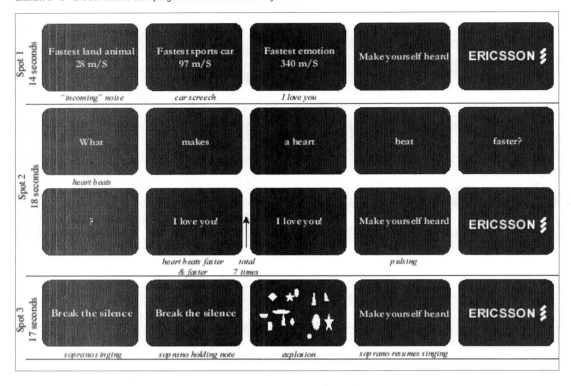

research had identified as "Achievers," the ad emphasized the product's features and carried the tag line "Made for business. Good for life." Product ads accounted for 80 percent of Ericsson's advertising budgeted for 1998; the rest was devoted to the brand campaign.

Andersson was aware of the fact that local and regional operations were jealously guarding their autonomy in deciding tactical product advertising. He also knew that the global campaign did not satisfy everyone in the local sales organizations. "Eighty-percent of the complaints I get from the field is about why we don't show a mobile phone in these ads," he noted.

Nevertheless, Andersson believed that the next phase of Ericsson's brand communication should address the growing number of new models that were coming out of development and which were targeting specific lifestyle segments. Five such models were expected to be launched in 1998 alone. "The question

is," Andersson commented, "how to connect and link your global brand campaign with hundreds of local advertising and promotions which are by their very nature tactical, product specific, and increasingly targeted at well-defined consumer segments." *Exhibit 8* shows a copy of the press ad for the launch of GF788, a product targeted at the "Sociables" segment.

Another related issue was the relationship between the mobile phone division's brand campaign and the communication strategies of other divisions. The recent publicity around the global campaign had made some members of the corporate management wonder if the message "Make yourself heard" was not equally appropriate for the other divisions of Ericsson. For Ahrenbring, vice president of marketing communication, a legitimate question was whether the brand campaign was an appropriate vehicle to promote a company dedicated to high technology.

Currently, Radio and Infocom Systems divisions were running limited press ads under different plat-

Exhibit 7 ● European Region's Product Campaign Press
Advertising 1998

Exhibit 8 ● Local Product Campaign Press Advertising
1997

forms. *Exhibit 9* shows a recent Radio Systems ad for
a new line of base stations targeted at mobile phone
network companies.

While flattered by the excitement the global
brand campaign had generated in other business areas, Andersson was more concerned with the future of
branding in his own division:

*If "Make yourself heard" becomes a corporate brand
platform, how can we in the mobile phone division
communicate those values which are so intrinsic to
our way of doing business? Doesn't that mean we
would be condemned back to product advertising?*

LATEST NEWS

On April 21 Andersson was to meet with the three
regional heads of mobile phone and terminals to discuss the future of the global campaign. The issues of

brand vs. product advertising were very much on
everybody's mind. Early campaign results from
around Europe indicated increased awareness for the
Ericsson brand among the general public: surveys
also showed a trend towards positive and long lasting
top-of-mind brand attributes. The first phase of the
European campaign was supposed to wind down by
the end of April.

Just a few days before the April meeting, Andersson came across a news item carried by the *Wall
Street Journal Europe* under the banner "Motorola
Launches New Image Campaign." The paper reported
that Motorola was about to launch a $100 million-
plus global advertising campaign, the largest in its
history, to "beat back rivals and change its image from
sturdy to contemporary."[5] The article explained that

[5]Beatty, Sally. "Motorola Launches New Image Campaign."
Wall Street Journal Europe, April 17–18, 1998.

Exhibit 9 ● Radio Systems Press Advertising 1998

Motorola's new campaign, under the theme of "Wings," was based on a year-long research that showed "consumers were looking for an inspirational, uplifting, high-utility relationship with communication devices." Against a background of Mick Jagger's music, the paper reported, the voice in TV commercials reassured the viewers that "Motorola gives you wings. Wings sets you free." An account executive for Motorola's ad agency, McCann-Erickson, was quoted as saying "Motorola is known but not preferred . . . Consumers tend to say 'good quality, durable,' but there is no real affinity for who the company is, what the brand is. It lacks personality." According to the paper, Motorola was trying to correct a situation in recent years in which it had lost market shares to both Nokia and Ericsson.

Case 12

Delissa in Japan

"We can maintain our presence in Japan or we can pull out . . ."

In the autumn of 1997, Bjorn Robertson, who had recently been named Managing Director of Agria, Sweden's leading dairy products cooperative, met with his team to review the international side of the business. The four men sat around a table piled high with thick reports, Nielson audits, film storyboards, yogurt cups, and a mass of promotional material in Japanese. Agria's "Delissa" line of fresh dairy products was sold all over the world through franchise agreements. Several of these agreements were up for review, but the most urgent one was the agreement with Nikko of Japan.

"In the light of these results, there are several things we can do in Japan. We can maintain our presence and stay with our present franchisee, we can change our franchisee, or we can pull out. But, let's look first at how badly we are really doing in Japan." Bjorn Robertson looked across the conference table at Peter Borg, Stefan Gustafsson and Lars Karlsson, each of whom had been involved with Agria's Japanese business over the past few years.

Robertson read aloud to the others a list of Agria's major foreign ventures featuring the Delissa yogurt brand: "U.S.A. launch date 1977, market share is 12.5 percent; Germany launch 1980, market share is 14 percent; U.K. launch 1982, market share is 13.8 percent; France launch 1983, market share is 9.5 per-

cent; Japan launch 1987, market share today is 2–3 percent." Robertson circled the figure with his marker and turned to look around at his team. "Under 3% after 10 years in the market! What happened?" he asked.

HISTORY

Agria was founded in 1973 when a group of Swedish dairy cooperatives decided to create a united organization that would develop and sell a line of fresh dairy products. The principal engineers of the organization were Rolf Anderen and Bo Ekman who had established the group's headquarters in Uppsala, near Stockholm. In 1980, after the individual cooperatives had been persuaded to drop their own trademarks, the Delissa line was launched. This was one of the few "national" lines of dairy products in Sweden. It comprised yogurts, desserts, fresh cheese, and fresh cream. In the two decades that followed, Agria's share rose from 3 percent to 25 percent of the Swedish fresh milk products market. Anderen's vision and the concerted efforts of 20,000 dairy farmer members of the cooperative had helped build Agria into a powerful national and international organization.

By 1997, more than 1.1 billion Delissa yogurts and desserts were being consumed per year worldwide. In fiscal year 1996, Delissa had sales of $2.1 billion and employed 4,400 people in and outside Sweden.

Industrial franchising was not very widespread in the 1980s, and few Swedish dairy products firms had invested money abroad. However, Ekman's idea of know-how transfer ventures, whereby a local license would manufacture yogurt using Swedish technology and then market and distribute the product using its own distribution network, had enabled Delissa to penetrate over thirteen foreign markets with considerable success and with a minimal capital outlay. In contrast, Delissa's biggest competitor

This case was prepared by Research Assistant Juliet Burdet-Taylor and Professor Dominique Turpin as a basis for class discussion rather than to illustrate either effective or ineffective handling of an administrative situation. All names and figures have been disguised. "Delissa in Japan ®. Copyright © 1998 by IMD—International Institute for Management Development, Lausanne, Switzerland. Not to be used or reproduced without written permission directly from IMD.

worldwide, Danone—a French food conglomerate marketing a yogurt line under the "Danone" brand name—had gone into foreign markets, mainly by buying into or creating local companies, or by forming regular joint ventures.

By the time Bjorn Robertson took over as European marketing director in 1991, the Delissa trademark—with the white cow symbol so familiar in Sweden—was known in many different countries worldwide. Delissa was very active in sponsoring sports events, and Robertson—himself a keen cross-country skier and sailor—offered his personal support to Delissa's teams around the world.

When he reviewed the international business, Robertson had been surprised by the results of Agria's Japanese joint venture which did not compare to those achieved in most foreign markets. Before calling together the international marketing team for a discussion, Robertson requested the files on Japan and spent some time studying the history of the alliance. He read:

Proposal for Entry into the Japanese Market
In early 1985, the decision was made to enter the Japanese market. Market feasibility research and a search for a suitable franchisee is underway, with an Agria team currently in Japan.

Objectives
The total yogurt market in Japan for 1986 is estimated at approximately 600 million cups (100mn ml). The market for yogurt is expected to grow at an average of at least 8% p.a. in volume for the next five years. Our launch strategy would be based on an expected growth rate of 10% or 15% for the total market. We have set ourselves the goal of developing a high quality range of yogurts in Japan, of becoming well known with the Japanese consumer. We aim to reach a 5% market share in the first year and 10% share of market within three years of launch. We plan to cover the three main metropolitan areas, Tokyo, Osaka, and Nagoya, within a two-year period, and the rest of the country within the next three years.

Robertson circled the 10 percent with a red pen. He understood that management would have hesitated

to set too high a goal for market share compared to other countries since some executives felt that Japan was a difficult market to enter. But, in 1993, the Japanese operation had not reached its target. In 1997, Delissa's share of the total yogurt market had fallen to 2 percent, without ever reaching 3 percent. Robertson wrote a note to the Uppsala-based manager responsible for Far Eastern business stating that he felt Agria's record in Japan in no way reflected the type of success it had had elsewhere with Delissa. He began to wonder why Japan was so different.

The report continued with a brief overview of the Japanese yogurt market:

Consumption
Per capita consumption of yogurt in Japan is low compared to Scandinavian countries. It is estimated at around 5.3 cups per person per year in Japan, versus 110 in Sweden and 120 in Finland. Sales of yogurt in Japan are seasonal, with a peak period from March to July. The highest sales have been recorded in June, so the most ideal launch date would be at the end of February.

Types of yogurt available in Japan—1986
In Japan, yogurt sales may be loosely broken down into three major categories:

- Plain (39% of the market in volume): Called "plain" in Japan because the color is white, but it is really flavored with vanilla. Generally sold in 500 ml pure pack cups. Sugared or sometimes with a sugar bag attached.

- Flavored (45% of the market in volume): Differentiated from the above category by the presence of coloring and gelifiers.
  Not a wide range of varieties, mainly: vanilla, strawberry, almond, and citrus.

- Fruit (16% of the market in volume): Similar to the typical Swedish fruit yogurt but with more pulp than real fruit.
  Contains some coloring and flavoring.

Western-type yogurts also compete directly in the same price bracket with local desserts—like puddings and jellies—produced by Japanese competitors.

Competition

Three major Japanese manufacturers account for about half of the total real yogurt market:

Snow Brand Milk Products is the largest manufacturer of dairy products in Japan and produces drinking milk, cheeses, frozen foods, biochemicals and pharmaceuticals. Turnover in 1985 was 443.322 million yens *($1 = ¥234 in 1985).*

Meiji Milk Products, Japan's second largest producer of dairy foods, particularly dried milk for babies, ice cream, cheese. Its alliance with the Bulgarian government helped start the yogurt boom in Japan. Turnover in 1985 was 410,674 million yens.

Morinaga Milk Industry, Japan's third largest milk products producer processes drinking milk, ice cream, instant coffee. It has a joint venture with Kraft U.S. for cheese. Turnover in 1985 was 301,783 million yens.

The share of these three producers has remained stable for years and is approximately: Yuki-jirushi (Snowbrand) 25%; Meiji 19%; Morinaga 10%.

The Japanese also consume a yogurt drink called "Yakult Honsha" which is often included in statistics on total yogurt consumption as it competes with normal yogurt. On a total market base for yogurts and yogurt drink, Yakult has 31%. Yakult drink is based on milk reconstituted from powder or fresh milk acidified with lactic acid and glucose. Yakult is not sold in shops, but through door-to-door sales and by groups of women who visit offices during the afternoon and sell the product directly to employees.

Along with some notes written in 1985 by Mr. Ole Bobek, Agria's Director of International Operations, Robertson found a report on meetings held in Uppsala at which two members of Agria's negotiating team presented their findings to management.

Selecting a Franchisee

We have just returned from our third visit to Japan where we once again held discussions with the agricultural cooperative, Nikko. Nikko is the country's second largest association of agricultural cooperatives; it is the Japanese equivalent of Agria. Nikko is a significant political force in Japan but not as strong as Zennoh, the National Federation of Agricultural Cooperatives which is negotiating with Sodima, one

of our French competitors. Nikko is price leader for various food products in Japan (milk, fruit juice, rice) and is active in lobbying on behalf of agricultural producers. Nikko is divided into two parts: manufacturing and distribution. It processes and distributes milk and dairy products, and it also distributes raw rice and vegetables.

We have seen several other candidates, but Nikko is the first one that seems prepared to join us. We believe that Nikko is the most appropriate distributor for Agria in Japan. Nikko is big and its credentials seem perfect for Agria, particularly since its strong supermarket distribution system for milk in the three main metropolitan areas is also ideally suited for yogurt. In Japan, 80% of yogurt is sold through supermarkets. We are, however, frustrated that, after prolonged discussions and several trips to Japan, Nikko has not yet signed an agreement with Agria. We sense that the management does want to go ahead but that they want to be absolutely sure before signing. We are anxious to get this project underway before Danone, Sodima or Chambourcy[1] enter Japan.

The same report also contained some general information on the Japanese consumer, which Robertson found of interest:

Some Background Information on the Japanese Consumer

Traditionally, Japan is not a dairy products consumer, although locally produced brands of yogurt are sold along with other milk-based items such as puddings and coffee cream.

Many aspects of life in Japan are miniaturized due to lack of space: 60% of the total population of about 120 million is concentrated on 3% of the surface of the islands. The rest of the land mass is mountainous. In Japan, 85% of the population live in towns of which over one third have more than half a million people. This urban density naturally affects lifestyle, tastes, and habits. Restricted living space

---

[1]Chambourcy was a brand name for yogurt produced and distributed by Nestlé in various countries. Nestlé, with sales of $52 billion in 1996, was the world's largest food company; its headquarters are in Vevey (Switzerland).

and lack of storage areas mean that most Japanese housewives must shop daily and consequently expect fresh milk products in the stores every day as they rarely purchase long-life foods or drinks. The country is fairly homogeneous as far as culture and the distribution of wealth is concerned. Disposable income is high. The Japanese spend over 30% of their total household budget on food, making it by far the greatest single item, with clothing in second place (10%).

The market is not comparable to Scandinavia or to the United States as far as the consumption of dairy products is concerned. There are young housewives purchasing yogurt today whose mothers barely knew of its existence and whose grandmothers would not even have kept milk in the house. At one time it was believed that the Japanese do not have the enzymes to digest milk and that, only a generation ago, when children were given milk, it was more likely to be goat's milk than cow's milk. However, with the market evolving rapidly towards "Westernization," there is a general interest in American and European products, including yogurt.

Although consumption of yogurt per capita is still low in Japan at the moment, research shows that there is a high potential for growth. When we launch, correct positioning will be the key to Delissa's success as a new foreign brand. We will need to differentiate it from existing Japanese brands and go beyond the rather standardized "freshness" advertising theme.

Distribution

Traditionally, Japanese distribution methods have been complex; the chain tends to be many-layered, making distribution costs high. Distribution of refrigerated products is slightly simpler than the distribution of dry goods because it is more direct.

The Japanese daily-purchase habit means that the delivery system adopted for Delissa must be fast and efficient. Our basic distribution goal would be to secure mass sales retailer distribution. Initially, items would be sold through existing sales outlets that sell Nikko's drinking milk, "Nikkodo." The milk-related products and dessert foods would be sold based on distribution to mass sales retailers. The objective would be to make efficient use of existing channels of distribution with daily delivery schedules and enjoy lower distribution costs for new products.

The Japanese Retail Market

The retail market is extremely fragmented with independent outlets accounting for 57% of sales (vs. 3% in the U.S.). With 1,350 shops for every 100,000 people, Japan has twice as many outlets per capita as most European countries. Tradition, economics, government regulations, and service demands affect the retail system in Japan. Housewives shop once a day on the average and most select the smaller local stores, which keep longer hours, deliver orders, offer credit, and provide a meeting place for shoppers. Opening a Western-style supermarket is expensive and complicated, so most retailing remains in the hands of the small, independent, or family business.

Japan has three major metropolitan areas: Tokyo, Osaka, and Nogaya, with a respective population of 11, 3, and 2 million inhabitants. Nikko's Nikkodo, with a 15% share of total, is market leader ahead of the many other suppliers. Nikko feels the distribution chain used for Nokkodo milk would be ideal for yogurt. Each metropolitan area has a separate distribution system, each one with several depots and branches. For instance, Kanto (Great Tokyo)—the largest area with over 40 million people—has five Nikko depots and five Nikko branches.

Most of the physical distribution (drivers and delivery vans) is carried out by a subsidiary of Nikko with support from the wholesalers. The refrigerated milk vans have to be fairly small (less than two tons) so that they can drive down the narrow streets. The same routes are used for milk delivery, puddings, and juices. Our initial strategy would be to accept Nikko's current milk distribution system as the basic system and, at the same time, adopt shifting distribution routes. Japan's complicated street identification system, whereby only numbers and no names are shown, makes great demands on the distribution system and the drivers.

The Franchise Contract

Robertson opened another report written by Ole Bobek, who had headed up the Japan project right from the start and had been responsible for the early years of the joint venture. He left the company in 1990. This report contained all the details concerning the contract between Agria and Nikko. In 1985, Nikko and Agria had signed an industrial franchise agreement permitting Nikko to manufacture and distribute Delissa products under license from Agria. The contract was Agria's standard Delissa franchisee agreement covering technology transfer associated with trademark exploitation. Agria was to provide manufacturing and product know-how, as well as marketing, technical, commercial, and sales support. Agria would receive a royalty for every pot of yogurt sold. The Nikko cooperative would form a separate company for the distribution, marketing, and promotion of Delissa products. During the pre-launch phase, Per Bergman, Senior Area Brand Manager, would train the sales and marketing team, and Agria's technicians would supply know-how to the Japanese.

By the end of 1986, a factory to produce Delissa yogurt, milk, and dairy products had been constructed in Mijima, 60 miles northwest of Tokyo. Agria provided Nikko with advice on technology, machinery, tanks, fermentation processes, and so forth. Equipment from the United States, Sweden, Germany, and Japan was selected. A European-style Erka filling machine was installed which would fill two, four, or six cups at a time, and was considered economical and fast.

Robertson opened another report by Bobek entitled "Delissa Japan—Pre-Launch Data." The report covered the market, positioning, advertising and media plan, minutes of the meetings with Nikko executives and the SRT International Advertising Agency that would handle the launch, analysis of market research findings, and competitive analysis. Robertson closed the file and thought about the Japanese market. During the planning phase before the launch, everything had looked so promising. In its usual methodical fashion, Agria had prepared its traditional launch campaign to ensure that the new Agria/Nikko venture guaranteed a successful entry into Japan for Delissa. "Why then," wondered Robertson, "were sales so low after nine years of business?" Robertson picked up the telephone and called Rolf Anderen, one of Agria's founders and former chairman of the company. Although retired, Anderen still took an active interest in the business he had created. The next day, Robertson and Anderen had lunch together.

The older man listened to the new managing director talking about his responsibilities, the Swedish headquarters, foreign licensees, new products in the pipeline, and so forth. Over coffee, Robertson broached the subject of the Japanese joint venture, expressing some surprise that Delissa was so slow in taking off. Anderen nodded his understanding and lit his pipe:

Yes, it has been disappointing. I remember those early meetings before we signed up with Nikko. Our team was very frustrated with the negotiations. Bobek made several trips, and had endless meetings with the Japanese, but things still dragged on. We had so much good foreign business by the time we decided to enter Japan, I guess we thought we could just walk in wherever we wanted. Our Taiwanese franchise business had really taken off, and I think we assumed that Japan would do likewise. Then, despite the fact that we knew the Japanese were different, Wisenborn—our international marketing manager—and Bobek still believed that they were doing something wrong. They had done a very conscientious job, yet they blamed themselves for the delays. I told them to be patient and to remember that Asians have different customs and are likely to need some time before making up their minds. Our guys went to enormous pains to collect data. I remember when they returned from a second or third trip to Japan with a mass of information, media costs, distribution data, socioeconomic breakdowns, a detailed assessment of the competitive situation, positioning statements, etc. But no signed contract. [Anderen chuckled as he spoke.] Of course, Nikko finally signed, but we never were sure what they really thought about us, or what they really expected from the deal.

Robertson was listening intently, so Anderen continued:

The whole story was interesting. When you enter a market like Japan, you are on your own. If you don't speak the language, you can't find your way around. So you become totally dependent on the locals and your partner. I must say that, in this respect, the Japanese are extremely helpful. But, let's face it, the cultural gap is wide. Another fascinating aspect was the rite of passage. In Japan, as in most Asian coun-

tries, you feel you are observing a kind of ritual, their ritual. This can destabilize the solid Viking manager. Of course, they were probably thinking that we have our rituals, too. On top of that, the Nikko people were particularly reserved and, of course, few of them spoke anything but Japanese.

There was a lot of tension during those first months, partly because France's two major brands of yogurt, "Yoplait" and "Danone" were actually in the process of entering the Japanese market, confirming a fear that had been on Bobek's mind during most of the negotiation period.

Anderen tapped his pipe on the ashtray and smiled at Robertson.

If it's any consolation to you, Bjorn, the other two international brands are not doing any better than we are in Japan today.

What About These Other European Competitors?

The discussion with Anderen had been stimulating and Robertson, anxious to get to the bottom of the story, decided to speak to Peter Borg, a young Danish manager who had replaced Bergman and had been supervising Agria's business in Japan for several years. Robertson asked Borg for his opinion on why "Danone" and "Yoplait" were apparently not doing any better than Delissa in Japan. Borg replied:

I can explain how these two brands were handled in Japan, but I don't know whether this will throw any light on the matter as far as their performance is concerned. First, Sodima, the French dairy firm, whose Yoplait line is sold through franchise agreements all over the world, took a similar approach to ours. Yoplait is tied up with Zennoh, the National Federation of Agricultural Cooperative Association, the equivalent of Sodima in Japan. Zennoh is huge and politically very powerful. Its total sales are double those of Nikko. Yoplait probably has about 3% of the total Japanese yogurt market, which is of course a lot less than their usual 15–20% share in foreign markets. However, Zennoh had no previous experience in marketing yogurt.

Danone took a different approach. The company signed an agreement with a Japanese partner, Ajinomoto. Their joint venture, Ajinomoto-Danone Co. Ltd., is run by a French expatriate together with several Japanese directors. A prominent French banker based in Tokyo is also on the board. As you know, Ajinomoto is the largest integrated food processor in Japan, with sales of about $3 billion. About 45% of the company's business is in amino acids, 20% in fats, and 15% in oil. Ajinomoto has a very successful joint venture with General Foods for "Maxwell House," the instant coffee. However, Ajinomoto had had no experience at all in dealing with fresh dairy products before entering this joint venture with Danone. So, for both of the Japanese partners—Ajinomoto and Zennoh, this business was completely new and was probably part of a diversification move. I heard that the Danone joint venture had a tough time at the beginning. They had to build their dairy products distribution network from scratch. By the way, I also heard from several sources that it was distribution problems that discouraged Nestlé from pursuing a plan to reintroduce its Chambourcy yogurt line in Japan. Japanese distribution costs are very high compared to those in Western countries. I suspect that the Danone-Ajinomoto joint venture probably only just managed to break even last year.

"Thanks, Peter," Robertson said. "It's a fascinating story. By the way, I hear that you just got married to a Japanese girl. Congratulations, lucky chap!"

After his discussion with Borg, Robertson returned to his Delissa-Nikko files. Delissa's early Japanese history intrigued him.

Entry Strategy

The SRT International Advertising Agency helped develop Delissa's entry into what was called the "new milk-related products" market. Agria and Nikko had approved a substantial advertising and sales promotion budget. The agency confirmed that, as Nikko was already big in the "drinking milk" market, it was a good idea to move into the processed milk or "eating milk" field, a rapidly growing segment where added value was high.

Bjorn Robertson studied the advertising agency's pre-launch rationale which emphasized the strategy suggested for Delissa. The campaign, which had been translated from Japanese into English, proposed:

Agria will saturate the market with the Delissa brand and establish it as distinct from competitive products. The concept "natural dairy food is good to taste" is proposed as the basic message for product planning, distribution, and advertising. Nikko needs to distinguish its products from those of early-entry dairy producers and other competitors by stressing that its yogurt is "new and natural and quite different from any other yogurts."

The core target group has been defined as families with babies. Housewives have been identified as the principal purchasers. However, the product will be consumed by a wider age bracket from young children to high school students.

The advertising and point-of-sale message will address housewives, particularly younger ones. In Japan, the tendency is for younger housewives to shop in convenience stores (small supermarkets), while the older women prefer traditional supermarkets. Housewives are becoming more and more insistent that all types of food be absolutely fresh, which means that Delissa should be perceived as coming directly from the manufacturer that very day. We feel that the "freshness" concept, which has been the main selling point of the whole Nikko line, will capture the consumers' interest as well as clearly differentiate Delissa from other brands. It is essential that the ads be attractive and stand out strikingly from the others, because Nikko is a newcomer in this competitive market. Delissa should be positioned as a luxurious mass communication product.

The SRT also proposed that, as Japanese housewives were becoming more diet conscious, it might be advisable to mention the dietary value of Delissa in the launch rationale. Agria preferred to stress the idea that Delissa was a Swedish product being made in Japan under license from Agria Co., Uppsala. They felt that this idea would appeal to Japanese housewives, who associated Sweden with healthy food and "sophisticated" taste. The primary messages to be conveyed would, therefore, be: "healthy products direct from the farm" and "sophisticated taste from Sweden." Although, it was agreed that being good for

health and beauty could be another argument in Delissa's favor, this approach would not help differentiate Delissa from other brands, all of which project a similar image.

In order to reinforce the product's image and increase brand awareness, the SRT proposed that specific visual and verbal messages be used throughout the promotional campaign. A Swedish girl in typical folk costume would be shown with a dairy farm in the background. In the words of the agency, "We feel that using this scene as an eyecatcher will successfully create a warm-hearted image of naturalness, simplicity, friendliness, and fanciful taste for the product coming from Sweden." This image would be accompanied by the text: "Refreshing nature of Delissa Swedish yogurt: it's so fresh when it's made at the farm."

Also included in the SRT proposal:

Advertising

To maximize the advertising effort with the budget available, the campaign should be run intensively over a short period of time rather than successively throughout the year. TV ads will be used as they have an immediate impact and make a strong impression through frequent repetition. The TV message will then be reinforced in the press. The budget will be comparable to the one used for launching Delissa in the United States.

Pricing

Pricing should follow the top brands (Yukijirushi, Meiji, and Morinaga) so as to reflect a high-class image, yet the price should be affordable to the housewife. The price sensitivity analysis conducted last month showed that the Delissa could be priced at 15% above competitive products.

Launch

In January 1987, Delissa's product line was presented to distributors prior to launch in Tokyo, Osaka, and Nagoya. Three different types of yogurt were selected for simultaneous launch:

- Plain (packs of 2 and 4)
- Plain with sugar (packs of 2 and 4)
- Flavored with vanilla, strawberry, and pineapple (packs of 2). (Fruit yogurt, Delissa's most

successful offering at home and in other foreign markets, would be launched a year or two afterwards.)

All three types were to be sold in 120 ml cups. A major pre-launch promotional campaign was scheduled for the month before launch with strong TV, newspaper, and magazine support, as well as street shows, in-store promotions, and test trials in and outside retail stores. On March 1, 1987, Delissa was launched in Tokyo, and on May 1 in Osaka and Nagoya.

1990: DELISSA AFTER THREE YEARS IN JAPAN

Three years after its launch, Delissa—with 2 percent of the Japanese yogurt market—was at a fraction of target. Concerned by the product's slow progress in Japan, Agria formed a special task force to investigate Delissa's situation and to continue monitoring the Japanese market on a regular basis. The results of the team's research now lay on Robertson's desk. The task force from Uppsala included Stefan Gustafsson (responsible for marketing questions), Per Bergman (sales and distribution), and Peter Borg (who was studying the whole operation as well as training the Nikko salesforce). The team spent long periods in Tokyo carrying out regular audits of the Delissa-Nikko operations, analyzing and monitoring the Japanese market, and generating lengthy reports as they did so, most of which Robertson was in the process of studying.

Borg, eager to excel on his new assignment, sent back his first report to headquarters:

Distribution/Ordering System

I feel that the distribution of Delissa is not satisfactory and should be improved. The ordering system seems overcomplicated and slow, and may very well be the cause of serious delivery bottlenecks. Whereas stores order milk and juice by telephone, Delissa products are ordered on forms using following procedure:

Day 1 A.M.: Each salesman sent an order to his depot.

Day 1 P.M.: Each depot's orders went to the Yokohama depot.

Day 2 P.M.: The Yokohama depot transmitted the order to the factory.

Day 2 P.M.: Yogurt was produced at Nikko Milk Processing.

Day 3: Delivery to each depot.

Day 4: Delivery to stores.

Gustafsson agrees with me that the delivery procedure is too long for fresh food products, particularly as the date on the yogurt cup is so important to the Japanese customer. The way we operate now, the yogurt arrives in the sales outlet two or three days after production. Ideally, the time should be shortened to only one day. We realize that, traditionally, Japanese distribution is much more complex and multilayered than in the West. In addition, Tokyo and Osaka, which are among the largest cities in the world, have no street names. So, a whole system of primary, secondary, and sometimes tertiary wholesalers is used to serve supermarkets and retailers. And, since the smaller outlets have very little storage space, wholesalers often have to visit them more than once a day.

I wonder if Nikko is seriously behind Delissa. At present, there are 80 Nikko salesmen selling Delissa, but they only seem to devote about 5 percent of their time to the brand, preferring to push other products. Although this is apparently not an uncommon situation in many countries, in Japan it is typical—as the high costs there prohibit having a separate salesforce for each line.

Borg's report continued:

Advertising

Since we launched Delissa in 1987, the advertising has not been successful. I'm wondering how well we pretested our launch campaign and follow-up. The agency seems very keen on Delissa as a product, but I wonder if our advertising messages are not too cluttered. Results of recent consumer research surveys showed only 4% unaided awareness and only 16% of interviewees had any recall at all; 55% of respondents did not know what our TV commercials were trying to say.

A survey by the Oka Market Research Bureau on advertising effectiveness indicated that we should stress the fact that Delissa tastes good . . . delicious. Agria's position maintains that according to the Oka survey, the consumer believes that all brands taste good, which means the message will not differentiate Delissa. Research findings pointed out that Delissa has a strong "fashionable" image. Perhaps this advantage could be stressed to differentiate Delissa from other yogurts in the next TV commercial.

DELISSA IN JAPAN: SITUATION IN AND LEADING UP TO 1997

In spite of all the careful pre-launch preparation, ten years after its launch in Japan, Delissa had only 3 percent of the total yogurt market in 1997. Although Agria executives knew the importance of taking a long-term view of their business in Japan, Agria's management in Sweden agreed that these results had been far below expectations.

A serious setback for Agria had been the discovery of Nikko's limited distribution network outside the major metropolitan areas. When Agria proposed to start selling Delissa in small cities, towns, and rural areas, as had been agreed in the launch plan, it turned out that Nikko's coverage was very thin in many of these regions. In the heat of the planning for the regional launch, had there been a misunderstanding on Nikko's range?

Robertson continued to leaf through Agria's survey of Japanese business, reading extracts as he turned the pages. A despondent Borg had written:

1994: The Japanese market is very tough and competition very strong. Consumers' brand loyalty seems low. But the market is large with high potential—particularly amongst the younger population—if only we could reach it. Nikko has the size and manpower to meet the challenges and to increase its penetration substantially by 1996. However, Nikko's Delissa organization needs strengthening quickly. Lack of a real marketing function in Nikko is a great handicap in a market as competitive as Japan.

Distribution is one of our most serious problems. Distribution costs are extremely high in Japan, and Delissa's are excessive (27% of sales in 1994

vs. 19% for the competition). Comparing distribution costs to production costs and to the average unit selling price to distributors of 54.86 yens, it is obvious that we cannot make money on the whole Delissa range in Japan. Clearly, these costs in Japan must be reduced while improving coverage of existing stores.

Distribution levels of about 40% are still too low, which is certainly one of the major contributing factors for Delissa's poor performance. Nikko's weak distribution network outside the metropolitan areas is causing us serious problems.

1995: Delissa's strategy in Japan is being redefined (once more). The Swedish image will be dropped from the advertising since a consumer survey has shown that some consumers believed that "fresh from the farm" meant that the yogurt was directly imported from Sweden—which certainly put its freshness into question! Ads will now show happy blond children eating yogurt . . .

Over time, the product line has grown significantly and a line of puddings has recently been added. Nikko asks us for new products every three months and blames their unsatisfactory results on our limited line.

By 1997, plain yogurt should represent almost half of Delissa's Japanese sales and account for about 43% of the total Japanese market. The plain segment has grown by almost 50% in the past three years. However, we feel that our real strength should be in the fruit yogurt segment, which has increased by about 25% since 1994 and should have about 23% of the market by next year. So far, Delissa's results in fruit yogurt have been disappointing. On the other hand, a new segment—yogurt with jelly—has been selling well: 1.2 million cups three months after introduction. Custard and chocolate pudding sales have been disappointing, while plain yogurt drink sales have been very good.

Robertson came across a more recent memo written by Stefan Gustafsson:

Mid-Year Results
Sales as of mid-year 1996 are below forecast, and we are unlikely to meet our objective of 55 million 120 ml cups for 1998. At the present rate of sales,

we should reach just over 42 million cups by year-end.

Stores Covered

In 1997, Delissa yogurt was sold mainly in what Nielsen defined as large and super large stores. Delissa products were sold in about 71% of the total stores selling Nikko dairy products. We think that about 7,000 stores are covered in the Greater Tokyo area, but we have found that Nikko has been somewhat unreliable on retailer information.

Product Returns

The number of Delissa products returned to us is very high compared to other countries. The average return rate from April 1996 to March 1997 was 5.06% vs. almost 0% in Scandinavia and the international standard of 2–3%. The average shelf life of yogurt in Japan is fourteen days. Does the high level of returns stem from the Japanese consumer's perception of when a product is too old to buy (i.e., five–six days)? The level of return varies greatly with the type of product: "healthy mix" and fruit yogurt have the highest rate, while plain and yogurt with jelly have the lowest return rate.

Media Planning

Oka's latest results suggest that Delissa's primary target should be young people between thirteen and twenty-four and its secondary target: children. Budget limitations demand that money be spent on advertising addressed to actual consumers (children), rather than in trying to reach the purchasers (mothers) as well.

However, during our recent visit to Japan, we found that Nikko and the agency were running TV spots—that were intended for young people and children—*from 11:15 to 12:15 at night.* We pointed out that far more consumers would be reached by showing the spots earlier in the evening. With our limited budget, careful media planning is essential. Nikko probably was trying to reach both the consumer and distributor with these late-night spots. Why else would they run spots at midnight when the real target group is children? Another question is whether TV spots are really what we need.

Looking at some figures on TV advertising rates in Japan, Robertson found that the price of a 15-second spot in the Tokyo area was between 1,250,000 and 2,300,000 yens in 1997 depending on the time it was run, which seemed expensive compared to European rates *($1 = ¥121 in 1997).*

Robertson continued to peruse the report prepared by Stefan Gustafsson:

Positioning

I'm seriously wondering whom we are trying to reach in Japan and with what product. The Nielsen and Oka research findings show that plain yogurt makes up the largest segment in Japan, with flavored and fruit in second and third positions. It is therefore recommended that regular advertising should concentrate on plain yogurt, with periodic spots for the second two categories. However, according to Nikko, the company makes only a marginal profit on plain yogurt, thus they feel it would be preferable to advertise fruit yogurt.

In light of this particular situation and the results of the Oka studies, we suggest that plain yogurt be advertised using the existing "brand image" commercial (building up the cow on the screen) and to develop a new commercial for fruit yogurt based on the "fashion concept." We also believe that, if plain yogurt is clearly differentiated through its advertising, sales will improve, production costs will drop, and Nikko will start making money on the product.

Last year, to help us understand where we may have gone wrong with our positioning and promotional activities, which have certainly changed rather often, we requested the Oka agency to conduct a survey using in-home personal interviews with a structured questionnaire; 394 respondents in the Keihin (Tokyo-Yokohama) metropolitan area were interviewed between April 11 and April 27, 1997. Some of the key findings are as follows:

Brand Awareness

In terms of unaided brand awareness, Meiji Bulgaria yogurt had the highest level with 27% of all respondents recalling Bulgaria first and 47% mentioning the brand without any aid. Morinaga Bifidus was in second place. These two leading brands were followed by Yoplait and Danone with 4% unaided awareness and 14% and 16% recall at any time. For Delissa, the unaided awareness was 3% and 16% for recall. In a photo-aided test, Delissa plain yogurt was recognized by 71% of all respondents with a score closer to Bulgaria. In the case of fruit yogurt, 78% recognized Delissa, which had the same level as Bulgaria. Awareness of Delissa was higher than Bifidus and Danone but lower than Yoplait. In the case of yogurt drink, 99% of all respondents were aware of Yakult Joy and 44% recognized Delissa (close to Bulgaria).

Interestingly, the brand image of Meiji Bulgaria was the highest of the plain yogurt brands in terms of all attributes except for "fashionability." At the lower end of the scale (after Bulgaria, Bifidus, and Natulait), Delissa was close to Danone and Yoplait in brand image. Delissa was considered less desirable than the top three, especially as far as the following characteristics were concerned: taste, availability in stores for daily shoppers, frequency of price discounting, reliability of manufacturer, good for health. Delissa's image was "fashionable." ["Is this good or bad?" Gustafsson had scribbled on the report. "Should this be our new platform??? We've tried everything else!"]

Advertising Awareness

In the advertising awareness test, half of all respondents reported that they had not noticed advertising for any brand of yogurt during the past six months. Of those who had, top ranking went to Bifidus with 43%, Bulgaria 41% and Delissa in third place with 36%. Danone was fifth with 28% and Yoplait sixth with 26%. Respondents noticed ads for Delissa mainly on TV (94%), followed by in-store promotion (6%), newspapers (4%), and magazines (4%); 65% of the people who noticed Delissa ads could recall something about the contents of the current ads, and 9% recalled previous ads. However, when asked to describe the message of the Delissa ads, 55% of the respondents replied that they did not know what the company was trying to say.

Consumption

77% of all respondents had consumed plain yogurt within the past month: 28% Bulgaria, 15% Bifidus, 5% Yoplait, 4% Danone, and 3% Delissa. The num-

ber of respondents who had at least tried Delissa was low (22%) vs. 66% for Bulgaria, the best scoring brand. In the plain category, Delissa was third of the brands mainly consumed by respondents. Bulgaria was number 1 and Bifidus number 2. In the fruit segment (under yogurt consumed with the past month), Delissa was in third place (5%) after Yoplait (10%) and Bulgaria (8%). Danone was in fourth place with 3%. ["So where do we go from here?" Gustafsson had scrawled across the bottom of the page.]

Robertson closed the file on Gustafsson's question.

Where Do We Go From Here?

Robertson looked around the table at the other members of his team and asked, "What happened? We still haven't reached 3 percent after ten years in Japan!" Bjorn knew that Borg, Gustafsson, and Karlsson all had different opinions as to why Delissa had performed badly, and each manager had his own ideas on what kind of action should be taken.

Gustafsson had spent months at Nikko, visiting retailers with members of the salesforce, instigating new market research surveys and supervising the whole Nikko-Delissa team. Language problems had made this experience a frustrating one for Gustafsson, who had felt cut off from the rest of the Nikko staff in the office. He had been given a small desk in a huge room along with over 100 people with whom he could barely communicate. The Japanese politeness grated on him after a while and, as no one spoke more than a few words of anything but Japanese, Gustafsson had felt lonely and isolated. He had come to believe that Nikko was not committed to the development of the Delissa brand in Japan. He also felt that the joint venture's market share expectations had been absurd and was convinced the franchise misrepresented the situation to Agria. He felt that Nikko was using the Delissa brand name as a public relations gimmick to build itself an international image. When he spoke, Gustafsson's tone was almost aggressive:

I don't know what to think, Bjorn. I know I don't understand our Japanese friends and I was never quite sure that I trusted them, either. They had a disconcert-

ing way of taking control right from the start. It's that extreme politeness. You can't argue with them, and then suddenly they're in command. I remember when the Nikko managers visited us here in Sweden . . . a busload of them smiling and bowing their way around the plant, and we were bowing and smiling back. This is how they get their way and this is why we had such mediocre results in Japan. Agria never controlled the business. Our distribution set-up is a perfect example. We could never really know what was going on out there because language problems forced us to count on them. The same with our positioning and our advertising, "We're selling taste; no, we're selling health; no, we're selling fashion—to babies, to grandmas, to mothers." We thought we were in control but we weren't, and half the time we were doing the opposite of what we really wanted.

Bjorn, the Japanese will kill Delissa once they've mastered the Swedish technology. Then, they'll develop their own brand. Get out of the joint venture agreement with Nikko, Bjorn. I'd say, get out of Japan altogether.

Robertson next turned his attention toward Borg, who had a different view of the problem. He felt that the Nikko people, trained to sell the drinking milk line, lacked specific knowledge about the eating milk or yogurt business. Borg—who had also taken over sales training in Japan after replacing Bergman—had made several trips a year to train the Nikko people both in marketing the Delissa brand, and in improving distribution and sales. He had also trained a marketing manager. Borg had worked closely with the Japanese at the Tokyo headquarters.

Borg said, "I understand how Stefan feels . . . frustrated and let down, but have we given these people enough time?"

"Enough time!" said Gustafsson, laughing. "We've been there for over ten years and, if you look at our target, we have failed miserably. My question is 'have they given *us* enough support?'" Turning to Gustafsson, Borg continued:

I know how you feel, Stefan, but is ten years that long? When the Japanese go into business abroad, they stay there until they get a hold on the market, however long it takes. They persevere. They seem to do things at their own speed and so much more calmly than we

do. I agree on the question of autonomy. It's their very lack of Western aggressiveness that enables them to get the upper hand. Their apparent humility is disarming. But, Bjorn, should we really leave the joint venture now? When I first went to Japan and found fault with everything we were doing, I blamed the whole thing on Nikko. After nearly six years of visits, I think I have learned something. We cannot approach these people on our terms or judge them as we would judge ourselves. We cannot understand them any more than they can understand us. To me, the whole point is not to even *try* and understand them. We have to accept them and then to trust. If we can't, then perhaps we should leave. But, Bjorn, I don't think we should give up the Japanese market so easily. As Stefan says, they can be excruciatingly polite. I wonder— beneath that politeness—what they think of us.

Lars Karlsson, the product manager, had been looking after the Japanese market only a short time, having been recruited by Agria from Procter & Gamble 18 months earlier.

Bjorn, for me, perhaps the most serious defect in our Japanese operation has been the poor communication between the partners and a mass of conflicting data. I came into the project late and was amazed at the quantity of research and reporting that had taken place over the last ten years by everyone concerned. Many of the reports I saw were contradictory and confusing. As well, the frequent turnover of managers responsible for Japan has interrupted the continuity of the project. And, after all the research we did, has anyone really used the findings constructively? How much is our fault? And another thing, have we been putting enough resources into Japan?

There are so many paradoxes. The Japanese seem to be so keen on the idea of having things Western, yet the successful yogurts in Japan have been the ones with that distinctive Japanese flavor. Have we disregarded what this means? Agria people believe that we have a superior product and that the type of yogurt made by our Japanese competitors does not really taste so good. How can this be true when we look at the market shares of the top Japanese producers? It obviously tastes good to the Japanese. Can we really change their preferences? Or should we perhaps look at our flavor?

It's interesting. Yoplait/Zennoh and Ajinomoto/ Danone's joint ventures could be encountering similar problems to ours. Neither has more than 3% of the Japanese yogurt market and they have the same flavor that we do.

Robertson listened to the views and arguments of his team with interest. Soon, he would have to make a decision. Almost ten years after launching Delissa with Nikko, should Agria cancel its contract and find another distributor? Or should the company renew the arrangement with Nikko and continue trying to gain market share? Or should Agria admit defeat and withdraw from Japan completely? Or was it, in fact, defeat at all? Robertson was glad that he had gathered his team together to discuss Delissa's future; their thoughts had given him new insights on the Japanese venture.

Case 13

tonernow.com:
A Dotcom Goes Global

It was the second week in April 2000. Dotcom euphoria gripped the U.S. economy and venture capital was flowing everywhere. Henry Kasindorf and Rich Katz, young founders of a New Jersey-based brick-and-mortar company recently turned dotcom, had received communications from all over the world soliciting their participation in licensing agreements, partnerships, and other similar relationships. Serious offers had come from Australia, Brazil, South Africa, Central America, and Europe. Their company, tonernow.com, was hot.

Kasindorf and Katz were facing a big question: should operations remain focused on the United States or should the company go global? The business was expanding and many issues required immediate attention. Globalization would inject even greater urgency into the situation.

tonernow.com was the e-commerce arm of IQ Computer Products, a company Kasindorf and Katz had founded in 1993. The brick-and-mortar segment of the business, not counting the Web site, was now selling approximately $5 million. Some two-thirds of this volume went to individual retail clients and one-third to wholesalers and distributors.

The tonernow.com Web site launched in beta format on September 15, 1999, now carried over 3,000 products at discounts of 30 percent to 70 percent off manufacturer list prices. The site also offered a proprietary line of compatible toner products.

●

This case was written by Martha Lanning, Research Associate, William F. Glavin Center for Global Entrepreneurial Leadership at Babson College, under the direction of Jean-Pierre Jennet, F.W. Olin Distinguished Professor of Global Business at Babson College. This case was written as a basis for class discussion rather than to illustrate either effective or ineffective handling of a business situation. Copyright © 2000 by Babson College, William F. Glavin Center for Global Entrepreneurial Leadership. Not to be used or reproduced without written permission.

Toner was a black, powdered, plastic substance contained in cartridges used in printers, copiers, and fax machines. Toner powder adhered to parts of a drum that had been properly charged for toner coverage. A fuser assembly within the printer or copier machine melted the toner to fuse it to the page, resulting in a sharp text that could not be smudged. When toner ran out, the machines could not function. Toner was critical for office productivity.

COMPANY HISTORY

Kasindorf and Katz had met as freshmen undergraduates at Babson College in 1987, the year Kasindorf achieved recognition for his successful launch of a condom vending machine business. Kasindorf described his rocky beginning as an entrepreneur:

I used all my professors. One in law helped me with the contracts, marketing helped me with the brochures. I was fascinated by all the resources that were available, some of the best in the world! I attended a student government meeting and brought the project up for approval, but the Assistant Dean shot me down. I stormed into the Dean's office and got it okayed. That business was fun, it got my feet wet. There were a lot of legal issues, such as liability if one of the condoms broke. Also, I was a freshman and in the middle of finals I got twelve voice mails from reporters!

Within months, Kasindorf had set up condom dispensers in college bathrooms throughout the Boston area. Two years later he sold the business for $25,000 and used the proceeds to start another venture. The partners laughed as they recalled their early collaboration:

Kasindorf. We didn't take much of a liking to each other.

Katz: We didn't hit it off.

Kasindorf: I needed a ride, I told him it would take five minutes, it took 40, and he liked me even less! Then we had a Human Communications class together. My only memory is that Rich got a 37 on the midterm and I got a 16.[1] We sort of bonded after that.

The T-Shirt Business

Kasindorf and Katz soon founded a screen-printed T-shirt company operating on campus. The shirts featured creative graphics using well-known consumer goods logos and sold like hotcakes. Kasindorf explained:

The copyright hounds had their bounty hunters looking for us. You do have to change 20% of the design so you're not infringing on someone else's mark. We had friends at other schools who started selling the T-shirts for us. Then U.S. News & World Report came out with the Babson ranking, and we launched a new T-shirt highlighting the No. 1 ranking during homecoming weekend.[2] In 1988–1989, our picture ran in the Babson College publication with the U.S. News & World Report ranking.

IQ Computer Products

After graduating from Babson College, Kasindorf and Katz briefly went their separate ways, each working elsewhere. However, in May 1993, they teamed up again, this time purchasing two small manufacturing companies with combined revenues under $300,000. According to Katz, "One was a sole proprietorship, a guy was making toner products out of his garage."

Based on this purchase, Kasindorf and Katz opened business activity in Spring Valley, New York, some forty-five miles from New York City. The new enterprise produced toner and employed four people in addition to Kasindorf and Katz: one in customer service, one to perform accounting and clerical tasks, and two in manufacturing. Operations included manufacturing, customer service, accounting, warehousing, and sales.

Recycling toner cartridges was encouraged on an industrywide basis. The two partners saw this as an

advantage, an aspect of the business that would aid in cost control and make the product "recession-proof."

Funding came entirely from cash flow, profits, and a small bank loan. In 1993 the partners held notes to the two original owners. Within two years the notes were paid off.

By 1994 business was exploding out of the 900-square-foot facility in Spring Valley. The young entrepreneurs consolidated the two original firms, named the new entity IQ Computer Products (IQCP), and moved the company to its present site in Englewood, New Jersey. Kasindorf discussed the decision to locate in Englewood:

We wanted to stay in New York, and so did the employees. We took it to the state to inquire regarding subsidies and incentives, but they laughed at us because we were under $1 million in sales. The next week I went to Trenton[3] to talk to the same department, but in New Jersey. They had a team of people assembled in a conference room. They offered training and incentives, and each one made a proposal to us on why we should locate in New Jersey. They welcomed us with open arms.

Growing the Business

During the period 1994–1998, the company added products and diversified as Kasindorf and Katz grew the business. They brought the repair division, previously subcontracted, in-house and hired their own technicians.

In 1994, IQCP sold in three states: New York, New Jersey, and Connecticut. IQCP also serviced a small number of other states by UPS.[4] In 1997 the company began using Federal Express to offer three-day delivery to California with standard ground rates. That same year, business expanded into Canada. By 1998, IQCP was selling in fourteen states, mainly in the Northeast but also in California and Colorado.

The partners elaborated on the importance of building customer relationships.

Katz: We felt we could sell products other than those we manufactured. Our customers told us they wanted other products. Our customers asked us because the

---

1. Out of a possible score of 100 on the midterm exam.
2. *U.S. News & World Report* ranked Babson College the No. 1 business school in the U.S. for entrepreneurial studies.

3. Capital of the state of New Jersey.
4. United Parcel Service, a delivery service.

level of service we offered was so far above what other companies offered.

Kasindorf: We hand-delivered the product, no matter how large or small the order. Our rep showed up with a nice shirt and our IQCP logo, offered to clean the printer and install the customer's cartridge so it would achieve optimal performance. People started to see the attention we gave.

Katz: When we started, quality was a major issue in the industry.

Kasindorf: People are leery of this industry. Therefore, it's important for us to appear as legitimate as possible. We advertise in the New York Times, *we bring large customers here to tour our facility.*

Katz: We encourage people to call our reference list. We've had long-standing relationships with our customers, and they rave about us. We are very, very careful here. It's a "razor blade" product, people come back and buy it again and again. We want people to have an experience second to none. If there's a problem, we replace it with no charge and we handle it quickly.

Kasindorf: We sell to some of the largest law firms in New York City. We are right there when their laser printers need repair. They rely on us.

Web Site Launch

In 1998, Kasindorf and Katz made the decision to go dotcom. They looked at what was necessary for their company to remain successful and determined that it would be essential to develop an e-commerce strategy and get on-line. As Kasindorf put it, "We knew we had to now or we'd be left behind."

Kasindorf and Katz knew what was successful *off-line,* and they wanted to translate that to *on-line.* They also wanted to avoid cannibalizing their existing business. The primary options were either to create on-line ordering for existing clients or to create an entirely new entity as the e-commerce solution.

Kasindorf and Katz decided to create a new entity. They would develop it as an e-commerce arm of the IQCP business. They needed to launch a Web site, and they would require it to be

- Serious and straightforward
- User-friendly

- Easy to navigate
- Fun with a couple of unique twists

The partners hired a full-service PR firm. In addition, they hired a freelance media consultant to do media planning.

Kasindorf: We knew we did not want to do this inhouse. We met with a lot of big communications companies and realized the budget we had to develop the site was low. We also realized we'd probably get lost in some of these companies. So we decided to look for more of a boutique-type Web developer. We found a great little company in Silicon Alley.

Katz: Henry really oversaw the process. We trust our vendors, but we really wanted to have a heavy hand in terms of how the site was developed. We knew how our customers wanted the experience to feel.

Kasindorf: For eight months, it was all I did. It was tremendously stressful! Even as good as the developers were.

Katz: We had to develop all the relational links. It was 3,000 products!

The staff in-house set about developing a large relational database that would allow prospective customers to shop four ways: by keyword, brand, product type, or product number. The project took six months and thousands of "man-hours" with five people dedicated full-time. The complete project cost approximately $200,000, half of which went to development alone.

The team designed the database to cross-sell and up-sell each product so that when a prospective customer input a product specification, the Web site would automatically offer helpful suggestions. The up-sell offered suggestions such as, "This printer also takes product so-and-so, we have these products at different prices, do you want to buy it/these also?" The cross-sell offered tonernow.com's own branded products once the customer had input a selection, for example, a compatible or related product version, some manufactured on a private label basis and others by tonernow.com.[5] The cross-sell also offered incentives such as double points for a rewards program.

Kasindorf described the complexity of the project:

[5]As an input example, product EPS-SO2-0089.

We had fantastic developers, but they did not know anything about product. It was up to us to develop the back-end issues. We learned through focus groups that most people really don't know what they need. Also, product numbers are long, and there's no apparent connection between the number and the product. We wanted to make the site user-friendly, for people to get what they wanted in two clicks or less. Most competitor sites require five clicks or more. There is nothing out there like our proprietary database, it's unique to the industry. We have people who want to license use of the database because of how powerful it is.

The Ambush Campaign

The next task was to develop a budget for the first three months after launch. An important part of this step was to look at the different vehicles for advertising. The budget would allocate money for various types of advertising such as banner ads, e-mail marketing, radio, TV, and billboard.

The partners examined many names for the new entity and finally found one they liked. It was owned by a cyber-squatter, so they bought it. The new name would be *tonernow.com*.

The original plan was to launch the Web site in June, but it quickly became apparent that June would be impossible.

Kasindorf: There was no way for June to work. September 15 was Internet World at the Javits Center.[6] We decided on an ambush campaign. No display at the expo. We had men dressed in white jumpsuits with the tonernow.com logo, in front of a giant tonernow.com billboard, handing out shopping bags with T-shirts to each person.

Katz (laughing): We really used our T-shirt expertise!

Dotcom Results

Once the Web site was launched, resulting activity was entirely new business. No activity migrated from the brick-and-mortar operation to the Web site. Kasin-

6. The Jacob K. Javits Convention Center, New York's premier trade show and convention venue with more than 814,400 square feet of exhibit space.

dorf and Katz had decided to maintain two separate profit centers and market to two separate databases. They would possibly migrate individual customers, two-thirds of the brick-and-mortar segment of the business, to the Web site at a later time. They had not publicized the Web site to their traditional customers in order to avoid cannibalization. Moreover, the Web site sold at lower margins, and significant customer migration would have reduced margins overall.

Gross sales rocketed upward. From initial sales volume of a few thousand dollars in December 1999, by January 2000 business had jumped 115 percent, by February 209 percent, and by March 118 percent.

Going for Venture Capital

The partners soon turned their attention to crafting a business plan.

Katz: Toward the end of the year was when we started to focus on VC. It had always been understood that at some point, we'd get venture capital and take the company public.

Kasindorf: We had first-mover advantage, we were more a "click-and-mortar" rather than e-commerce. Very appealing to the VC people. We'd shown we could grow in a brick-and-mortar way. It was more a question of how much equity we'd have to give up and who we'd go with, not if we'd go.

The partners expected to get exactly what they sought in the first round, but they were in for a few surprises. The first surprise was that profitability was not required.

Kasindorf: In our projections we were showing profitability after two years. Investment bankers, consultants, and VC people told us we were not showing a loss!

Katz: It just made sense to us, that we were in business to make a profit.

Kasindorf: Another thing! We'd walk into a VC meeting wearing business suits, not ripped jeans, wearing tattoos, and carrying our skateboards. The first meeting we ever had, we walked out of there with a $37 million valuation.

Katz: We began to get offers on the table. Then in spring the NASDAQ got hit hard.

THE TONER SUPPLIES INDUSTRY

The toner supplies industry was a highly fragmented segment within the larger office supplies industry. In 1999 the market for toner supplies was estimated at 30 billion. Players in the market included office equipment manufacturers (OEMS), office superstores, dealers of equipment such as copiers, printers, and fax machines, catalog distributors, and remanufacturers.

Customers were extremely sensitive to price and convenience. When toner ran out, the productivity of an office machine was placed on hold until new toner could be supplied. Thus, same-day delivery was a key to success.

Laser copying and printing had dramatically changed the industry in recent years. Developments such as color printing had placed new demands on paper quality. Paper needed to be able to handle black-and-white toner printing as well as printing that used the newer four-color toner technology. Color toner particles had recently been made smaller in order to improve print quality.

Competition

Toner cartridges and inkjet cartridges formed a highly specialized niche segment of the office supplies industry. Toner and other supplies carried a much higher margin than hardware. Within this segment there was no single dominant player. Several large companies held a major share of the toner supplies market: Hewlett-Packard (H-P), Lexmark, Xerox, IBM, Canon, and Ricoh, among other OEMs.

In early 2000, Konica Corp. and Minolta Co., both of Japan, announced an agreement in the areas of information technology equipment and printer toner production. The agreement involved a joint venture to manufacture toner.

In 1999, H-P had launched a new line of toner supplies, eliptica, to compete with Xerox. Two years earlier Xerox had begun to offer H-P-compatible laser printer cartridges, and the eliptica line was H-P's counterstrike response. After only eight months of operation, H-P surprised the industry in spring 2000 by announcing the end of the eliptica venture in order to refocus on other strategic growth opportunities.

H-P was the world's largest maker of printers, and China was the world's fastest growing market. Printer sales in China totaled some $900 million in 1999. H-P had been selling printers in China since the mid-1980s and now controlled almost one-quarter of the market.

Cartridge Recycling

The resale of toner and related products was highly profitable, with gross margins ranging from 20 percent to 70 percent. Empty toner cartridges that had been used could be returned to be recycled. The process ideally involved cleaning and refitting the cartridge as well as filling it with new toner. However, many remanufacturers used shortcuts and provided recycled cartridges of poor quality.

Industry Fraud

Fraud was a serious problem for the industry. Customers using counterfeit supplies risked poor equipment performance, low supply yields, inferior print quality, toner leakage, high cartridge failure rates, and increased equipment downtime.

Illegal operations typically contacted potential victims by telephone, misrepresenting themselves as having taken over the previous toner supplier's operation or as a firm that worked in tandem with the legitimate supplier. These "telemarketers" sold low-quality goods to unsuspecting customers. Advances in communications technology had increased the opportunity for this type of fraud.

Xerox had been working with federal authorities to crack down on counterfeit toner distributors. In 1999 federal agents raided a warehouse in Milwaukee, seizing 47,000 counterfeit supplies boxes estimated at a market value of $8 million.

BUILDING A STRATEGY FOR THE FUTURE

In spring 2000, Kasindorf and Katz had been marketing their company to venture capital people with the expectation of increasingly lucrative offers. However, the valuation of tonernow.com had tanked when the NASDAQ plummeted.

The deals now on the table were lower than the partners had previously considered desirable. Moreover, taking one of the deals would force them to relinquish at least some measure of control to their funding source.

Overview of the Current Business

Since 1994, tonernow.com had grown significantly. The firm employed thirty people and sold in all fifty states. Over 3,000 different products were offered, with approximately forty manufactured in-house. Some 10 percent the products covered 80 percent to 90 percent of the market. tonernow.com sourced OEM products from vendors and also provided 300 compatible products that were not OEM-branded. Compatibles were manufactured either by tonernow.com or by another firm and sold under the tonernow.com name.

The mission of tonernow.com was to become the best-known brand in the imaging supplies industry. The objective was to deliver high-end value through e-commerce while offering the following service elements:

- The Web's largest selection of toner products
- A superior Web site with built-in guidance tools and support designed for cross-selling and up-selling to products with superior margins
- Discounts from 30 percent to 70 percent lower than manufacturer's prices
- Service and maintenance programs for business equipment
- A rewards program with incentives for return customers
- Free next-day shipping with Federal Express
- E-mail reminders and an auto-ship program
- On-line and off-line ordering options
- National advertising

Customer Service: A Key to Success

The company had retained many of its original customers as a result of superior customer service.

Kasindorf: When we were just 23 and starting out, people saw the commitment we had to serving them.

Among our customers we have very low attrition rates. Companies we were doing business with in 1993 are still our customers.

Katz: We definitely benchmark other companies. We look at them to see if they're doing something right. And we learn from our customers.

Kasindorf: As we've grown, there have been a lot of internal pressures. The ability to have two partners running the business is unique in that we're able to feed off each other in certain ways. We're able to do that in a way that has really contributed to our growth. Our roles are not completely pigeonholed, we have insight into each other's areas, and that's beneficial.

Katz: When we first started, we were both into selling, selling, selling. We had no idea how things would develop. As you grow, there's always the issue of costs getting out of control. As a result, I am now more involved with the operations. Henry is more the outside guy who handles sales and marketing. He instituted the procedures of how we deal with customer relations. I've kinda stayed inside and developed cost-cutting measures. We run a manufacturing operation, and neither of us had any manufacturing or engineering background. Also, we have some very big competitors. They've put obstacles in our way, and we've had to figure out how to get around them.

Changing Realities

By spring 2000 tonernow.com had attracted attention from outside the United States. Katz remarked that the attention had been entirely unsolicited:

We got noticed through trade shows. But as soon as we became a dotcom, it added instant credibility. When people saw the functionality of the site, they were just wowed by it. International contacts were also wowed by it. Once they got into our site, they saw we had a great deal to offer.

A number of deals had been proposed, and the partners were now considering options for international expansion. They would need to examine every aspect of the business: from legal to operational, from inquiry handling to delivery process, including customer relationships and confirmation of shipping dates.

The move from small domestic player to globalization posed many challenges, among which might be any or all of the following:

- Licensing the technology
- Setting up licensing agreements
- Dealing with royalties
- Collecting payment via credit card
- Translating foreign currency into U.S. dollars
- Access to tonernow.com's proprietary database
- Restrictions to impose on Web site use run through other countries
- How to maintain control of the technology
- Cross-cultural revisions of Web site to make it readily understandable
- Legal requirements of setting up business activity
- Same-day delivery

Options on the Table

tonernow.com had received communications from Europe, Australia, Brazil, Central America, and South Africa (*Exhibits 1–3*). In some cases, a concrete business proposal had been offered. Suggestions included the following:

Gateway Page This element would enable a customer in a foreign country to log on to the tonernow.com Web site and then be directed to the specific site for his/her geographic region.

Localization Making cultural and linguistic changes in the Web site or gateway page in order to give the look and feel of the local country.

Licensing Making the Web site structure and content available in a non-U.S. setting, including templates, shipping, database, product information, and costing data, among other elements. Specifically, licensing would provide Web site content, brand relationships, and alternative revenue though co-op funds available with the brands. In addition, a licensing agreement would include:

- International contacts for global contracts
- Comprehensive collateral materials
- Outbound marketing material (bulk e-mail copy, promotions, on-line coupons)
- Launch support
- Development of local media affiliations
- Proprietary strategic information

The structure that would be required to handle business differed for each geography, and the partners did not want to undertake a different strategy for each region. Kasindorf saw this as a "monumental chore." He was also concerned about the level of service:

Who would send the second confirmation that confirms the ship date? C.O.D. orders and credit card orders on-line are an issue, because some people don't want to input their credit cards on-line. Who will handle customer service inquiries? Certainly you want someone local to do this.

Brazil The contact company had connections with all the major players, including the government. They had come to CEBIT, the major industry trade show in Hanover, Germany, looking for opportunities. For tonernow.com to go into Brazil as an aftermarket supplier might make sense because entry barriers were high. Katz stated,

We found there was only one licensee there for each manufacturer. To bring us in on a gray market basis would kill our margins. We would have to come in selling our own branded product because the distribution channels are so tight.

Australia tonernow.com had exhibited at a large print industry show in California where they met an Australian distributor of toner supplies. The partners recalled his offer:

He told us, "We want to use your site in Australia, how can we do this?" Licensing the technology would result in people getting access to our proprietary database. The alternative would be to set them up as licensees of the technology to use the site in their restricted geographic territory. We did the analysis, to look into running the site for them, and also collecting payment with credit cards in Australian dollars.

CONCLUSION

Conducting business internationally would require playing the game with more than one set of rules (*Exhibit 4*). Whether to globalize or remain domestic was the big question. tonernow.com was a small, new company. It shared little in common with firms running large global operations. The partners considered the ramifications of setting up business on an international scale:

Katz: In the U.S. when you shake on it, it's a done deal, but in other countries you're not sure. Also in some countries, to get a domain name is very expensive. Fraud overseas is a lot harder to combat than fraud in the U.S.

Kasindorf: We've started to question everything. Sales are very strong, site revenues are growing, but we're bleeding because of the costs associated with doing business in this manner: advertising, overhead, promotions "buy one, get one free" to gain market share. We are about eight months late with what we were trying to do because the landscape has changed so much. We've gotten into a difficult financial situation thinking we did not need to be as profitable as we had planned.

Katz: A lot of dotcom casualties have already happened. We want to be very careful.

Exhibit 1 ● Europe

E-MAIL FROM HENRY TO EUROPE

I enjoyed meeting you and discussing our mutual e-commerce interests. At this point we are in discussions with firms in various regions who are interested in forming alliances to build the tonernow.com brand on a global level.

It would be helpful if you could provide me with an understanding of your interest in working with tonernow.com and whether you are interested in pursuing further discussions. Many synergies exist between our firms, and a well-thought-out strategy of how we could work together would be mutually beneficial.

E-MAIL FROM EUROPE TO HENRY

Further to our recent telephone conversations and meetings, I have thought long and hard about how we could take this opportunity forward. The opportunities I see are as follows:

1. We could fulfill tonernow.com orders to customers within their countries and also fulfill a manufacturing role for tonernow.com.

2. We could bring on other companies in Europe who can also fulfill customer requirements in both.

3. We could introduce various OEMs to the tonernow.com distribution model.

I will call you tomorrow to discuss the above in more detail. I would like to work with you on these options but need to know whether they fit in with your plans. Other considerations are languages for Europe, software compatibility (i.e., order processing and stock system reconciliation), and dealer blind shipping time scales.

Exhibit 2 ● Brazil

E-MAIL FROM BRAZIL TO HENRY

As we talked about in Germany, one of the product lines we have interest to work with, and have been talking about, is the inkjet cartridges. So far it looks to us like it would not be good in Brazil to work with remanufactured cartridges, and we are evaluating the possibilities for importing compatible ones. We have received several proposals for that, mainly from European and Asian companies. One has a strong capability to give huge discounts on their lines, and we are about to receive some samples from them in order to test quality matters.

E-MAIL FROM HENRY TO BRAZIL

In terms of your market analysis for Brazil, I believe that a strategy with compatible products would be very effective for you. Please understand that there are many companies in the market producing and distributing "compatible" toner cartridges that are "remanufactured." Our firm produces and distributes both types of products.

I realize this may be a bit confusing, but packaging requirements enable us to use the term "compatible" if a certain amount of internal components are replaced during our production process. I realize that there are many companies throughout the world that would like to earn your business for the Brazil market, and I recommend that you proceed slowly and cautiously, as this can be very complex.

We can develop a comprehensive user-friendly Web site for you specifically for your market. The Web site can be a useful marketing tool for your sales reps, and your customers will appreciate the fact that they can access the information on-line, order product, or simply get product reference information. We can negotiate with the various suppliers on your behalf to produce products for your market under the brand name on a private label basis, therefore you will not be tied to any one manufacturer's brand except your own.

Exhibit 3 ● Central America

───

E-MAIL FROM HENRY TO CENTRAL AMERICA

We are currently undergoing our first round of venture capital financing. I have recruited some senior members for our senior management team, and one of the first steps we are taking is to partner with a major distributor in the European market. I am currently analyzing the possibilities for Latin America and the Caribbean in this market.

Currently the U.S. and European markets are highly fragmented and lack a dominant player. Our focus is to become the world leader in these markets via the Internet. We have relationships with many of the OEMs in each of the markets that we are targeting, and they will be working closely with us to achieve our objectives.

Please let me know if you have an interest in working with us, in what territories you can provide distribution, with which manufacturers you currently have relationships, and whether you have or are planning to implement an e-commerce strategy.

E-MAIL FROM CENTRAL AMERICA TO HENRY

Thanks for your continued interest. The opportunity to distribute the recycled toners is not as clear-cut for us as it would be for other companies. Let me explain. We have been approved to distribute (product xyz) in several countries of Central America. We will be investing a lot to open operations in each of these countries.

I know that some non-original supplies are being imported into these countries, and we certainly do not have 100% share of the original toner market, so there is room for growth. My main concern is that we may only substitute the (product xyz) toners for yours, thereby lowering our sales volumes and possibly the margin. The margin is the clincher.

I have no idea what your toners sell for and how much I can earn on each one. I'm sure you will have good news for me in this department. Please send me your price list and the credit terms we could work on. I'm sure we will be able to do something together.

Exhibit 4 ● Legal Advice

As you are aware, in many jurisdictions it is necessary to have some sort of local presence before a local domain name can be obtained. We can assist in helping you satisfy these local presence requirements, whether it be by setting up a branch office or a limited company, registering a trademark, or in some cases just providing a local address. We hope to be able to provide a seamless service.

As you will appreciate, setting up said alliance will involve a lot of work on our part and although we are some way down the line, it will inevitably take some time, possibly another couple of months, to put in place all the necessary arrangements and set up the technology. However, in the meantime, we have been approached by a number of clients of (company name) who wish to proceed more quickly.

We have already gathered a substantial amount of information and made contacts in most jurisdictions. In many we are in a position to begin offering our services. If you provide us with a list of the jurisdictions in which you are interested, we will forward to you further information regarding whether there is a local presence requirement in those jurisdictions, and if there is, the easiest option for satisfying this requirement.

In setting up this project, one of the most difficult issues to date has been ascertaining the costs of setting up local entities in each jurisdiction. Where it is possible to determine the actual costs, it is apparent that there are significant differences in costs. Therefore to simplify matters to date we have been suggesting a fixed fee per country. This gives you as the client a greater degree of certainty and makes it easier for us to manage the process and achieve consistency in the services we are offering.

However, if there is a relatively small number of countries, you may prefer to work individual fees for each country. We can discuss this with you in more detail when your exact requirements are known.

Excerpt from an entity in Europe.

Case 14

EURO RSCG Worldwide: Global Brand Management in Advertising

It was the first week of April 2000. Bob Schmetterer, chairman and CEO of Euro RSCG Worldwide (Euro RSCG), was conferring with his chief of staff and two members of the Network Development team at the headquarters office in New York. Formed in 1991, the new company had blazed ahead of competitors and by 1998 had reached the No. 5 global position among the world's top twenty advertising firms. Euro RSCG had set aggressive goals for the new millennium, and Schmetterer explained what this would mean:

We've set a vision for ourselves to be the leading network of the new century. We need to find new ways, better ways than our competition. We don't want just a level playing field. We want the playing field to be uneven.

The team was examining global brand management, a topic that had been the focus of a recent meeting in February. Agency leaders from the Euro RSCG network had convened in Florida to explore divergent models for handling global clients, with particular emphasis on the increasing demand for a broad array of integrated services.

The issue had become pressing for an important global client. In only the last six months, the client had approached Euro RSCG for a new solution. As Schmetterer put it,

●

This case was written by Martha Lanning, Research Associate, William F. Glavin Center for Global Entrepreneurial Leadership at Babson College, under the direction of Jean-Pierre Jeannet, F.W. Olin Distinguished Professor of Global Business at Babson College and Professor of Strategy and Marketing at IMD. This case was written as a basis for discussion rather than to illustrate either effective or ineffective handling of a business situation. Copyright © 2001 by **IMD**—International Institute for Management Development, Lausanne, Switzerland. Not to be used or reproduced without written permission directly from **IMD.**

They turned to us and said you've done some great creative advertising for us, but that's not what we need. We need something more.

It was critical for Euro RSCG to develop a comprehensive strategy for handling global clients. Several successful models existed or were beginning to emerge as the firm responded to client needs. The central question was how to balance customization and localization with high-quality global service. Schmetterer summed it up:

More and more companies are looking for one partner, or maybe two or three, that can work with them globally. How to handle these clients is really crucial. Probably only a dozen agencies all over the world can deal with multinational assignments. In the advertising and communications business, there are no models to follow. What has become clear to us is that it is not where on the map you have the dots, it's the lines between the dots that count. The key is our ability to deliver to clients a strategically coordinated set of activities that meet their needs.

COMPANY HISTORY AND BACKGROUND

In 1991 two French advertising agency groups, Eurocom and RSCG, merged to form Euro RSCG Worldwide. In April 1997, Bob Schmetterer was appointed CEO. One of his first strategic decisions, primarily to broaden geographic presence and exposure, was to move company headquarters from Paris to New York.

By 2000, Euro RSCG had become a leading global player in the advertising industry, operating 202 agencies with more than 8,500 employees in seventy-five countries (***Exhibit 1***). In over half of these countries, Euro RSCG was among the top ten advertising agencies. The corporate headquarters office used the name Euro RSCG Worldwide. Individual operating agencies used the name Euro RSCG plus the agency name, such as Euro RSCG BETC in Paris, and Messner Vetere Berger McNamee Schmetterer Euro RSCG in New York.

Exhibit 1 ● Euro RSCG Worldwide, January 18, 2000

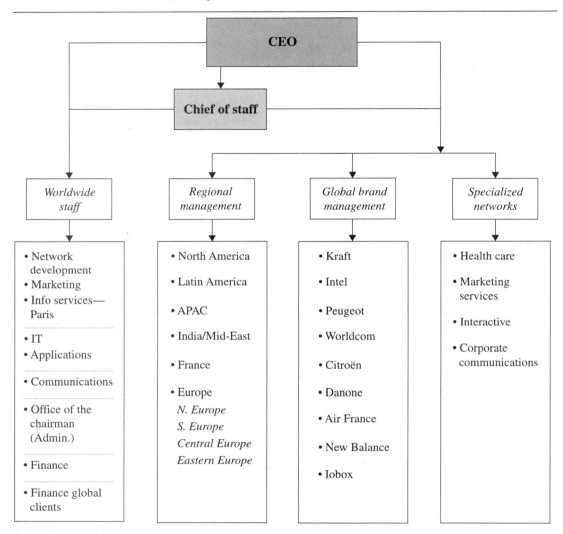

Source: Company information.

Euro RSCG Worldwide was a division of Paris-based Havas Advertising. Havas Advertising was 20 percent owned by Havas SA, also based in Paris. Havas SA was the oldest and largest publishing concern in France and ranked among the world's largest media companies. Havas SA was a subsidiary of French utility conglomerate Vivendi[1] (**Exhibit 2**).

Business Activity

Euro RSCG was a full-service advertising network. Business was divided into four geographic regions: Europe, North America, Latin America, and Asia/Pacific, which included India and the Middle East. Activity for 1999 is shown in the following table:

Region	Rank	Gross Income ($ millions)	Billings ($ billions)
Europe	1	781.3	5.178
North America	6	378.4	3.578
Latin America	8	74.9	587.5
Asia/Pacific	17	65.0	439.9

The four core business areas were advertising, marketing services, health care, and corporate communications. Euro RSCG used a matrix structure that incorporated a fifth core business area, interactive, throughout each of the other four. The service array included the following:

- *Advertising.* Integrated communications solutions utilizing television, print, radio, outdoor, and other media venues.

1. In early 2000, Vivendi was negotiating the acquisition of Seagram, the Canadian entertainment and liquor conglomerate. The deal was expected to go for $34 billion in mid-year and would transform Vivendi from a diversified conglomerate into one focused on environmental services and communications. The proposed company, Vivendi Universal, would become the world's second largest media group behind the pending union of America Online and Time Warner Inc. The new company would combine media, publishing, and entertainment content with fixed-line and mobile telephone and Internet access. Vivendi's strategy was to control the subscriber base in order to maximize revenue from services offered. The Bronfman family of Canada owned 24% of Seagram shares outstanding and had signed a binding commitment to vote in favor of the deal.

Also in early 2000, Havas Advertising Group was negotiating the purchase of Snyder Communications, a U.S.-based advertising and marketing services firm with operations closely tied to the Internet. The pure stock deal was valued at $2.1 billion.

- *The Sales Machine.* A branded marketing services network. Ranked No. 2 worldwide and comprising seventy-six agencies in forty countries. Consulting, direct marketing, sales promotion, event marketing, sales force motivation, database marketing, and interactive.

- *Euro RSCG Worldwide Health Care.* A network of forty-three agencies in thirty-eight countries, providing a full range of marketing and communications solutions to clients such as pharmaceutical companies in the health care industry. Ranked No. 3 worldwide.

- *Euro RSCG Corporate Communications.* A worldwide public relations network comprising more than eighty agencies in forty countries, providing corporate communications, reputation management, internal communications, marketing communications, public affairs, investor relations, employee communications, media relations, and institutional communications.

- *Euro RSCG Interaction.* A network of forty interactive agencies in eleven countries, providing consulting, interactive advertising and Web sites, e-commerce, interactive TV, and other activities. Euro RSCG Interaction was ranked No. 8 among all interactive networks and No. 1 among advertising company interactive networks.

Through 1999, Euro RSCG had grown and gained market share (**Exhibit 3**). Billings and income in all four geographic regions and all core business areas had increased. Margins and profitability had risen, making a favorable impression on Havas Advertising Group investors. Gross income had advanced 22 percent and operating profit 38 percent. By early 2000 marketing services, health care, and corporate communications offered potential for higher profit margins than traditional advertising, and Euro RSCG had begun to weigh advertising less heavily as demand grew for an expanded range of services.

Client Service Structure

Euro RSCG offered service through a "client-focused network," an integrated multidisciplinary matrix capable of providing both global and regional

Exhibit 2 ● Havas

Havas Advertising, based in Paris, operated both Euro RSCG and Campus, an ad agency network targeting smaller markets in Germany, Italy, and the U.K. Havas Advertising owned 45 percent of Media Planning, a media buying firm which provided service in fourteen countries. Havas Advertising was pursuing a strategy of acquisition in the multimedia segment and had divested outdoor advertising operations.

Havas SA, which owned 20 percent of Havas Advertising, had begun in Paris as a publishing company. The oldest and largest media company in France, Havas SA maintained holdings throughout Europe including periodicals, advertising, book publishing, and multimedia.

Havas SA was a subsidiary of Vivendi, a utility conglomerate formerly known as Générale des Eaux. Vivendi was a diversified global company based in Paris with operations in some ninety countries. In Asia, Europe, and the United States, Vivendi produced electricity through two subsidiaries and operated waste management, rail, and road transportation companies. Vivendi also held full or partial ownership of several television and telephone networks in Europe.

Havas Advertising, Havas SA, and Vivendi

	1999 Sales Revenues (€ millions)*	*No. of Employees*
HAVAS ADVERTISING	1,208	8,451
HAVAS SA	3,300	18,600
VIVENDI	41,623	234,800

* €1 = US$1.06.

The Four Divisions of Havas Advertising

Division	*Territory*	*Operations*
Euro RSCG Worldwide. A global advertising agency network	Europe, North America, Asia/Pacific, India/Middle East, Latin America	Global agency network
Media Planning. A worldwide integrated media resource	Europe, North America, Asia/Pacific, Latin America	Media specialist
Campus. A group of independent agencies	France, Germany, Italy, Spain, U.K., Brazil	Independent agency group
Diversified Agencies. A group of specialized communication companies	Europe, North America	Specialized communication services

Source: Public information.

Exhibit 3 ● Euro RSCG Worldwide Business Activity by Client Industry Segment, 1999

Rank by Growth Rate	Client Industry Segment	Growth % 1998–1999	Rank by % of Business Activity
1	Tourism/Travel	248.3	11
2	Financial services	87.7	7
3	Fashion/Clothing	76.0	12
4	Health care	67.2	1
5	Telecommunications	20.4	3
6	Food/Beverage	19.9	5
7	Retail	19.4	8
8	Industry/Energy	19.1	14
9	Hygiene/Beauty	16.9	9
10	Automotive	13.3	2
11	Media	11.5	10
12	Technology	4.2	4
13	Leisure/Household equipment	(19.4)	6
14	Household	(19.6)	13

Source: Company information.

brand management (***Exhibit 4***). The leadership, array, and level of services were based on actual client needs in all regions. A Euro RSCG executive commented,

The company is very decentralized to enable such a customizable service package. The upside is that there's a lot of flexibility for innovation and entrepreneurial action. The downside is that it's complicated to mobilize network level behavior. To resolve this, we rely on collaborative technology tools that bring us together to meet the needs of the client. Our client-focused approach to global services is also a part of this. We're starting to build these systems more and more, but we want to keep the organizational model open enough so we can still remain innovative. We are shaping a new kind of international structure, one that dynamically leverages the best of our local talent and worldwide resources.

Global Business Enablers

Schmetterer's strategy was to grow a network composed of entrepreneurial companies able to implement solutions in their own local markets. Much recent growth had come from acquisitions in all geographies and all core businesses. As a result, the network was composed of entrepreneurial agencies with local market strength. Euro RSCG was addressing the challenge of coordinating these agencies into a global network for client solutions through two major technology initiatives:

- *Euro RSCG StarLink.* StarLink was a secure, proprietary, Internet-based collaboration tool. Access was restricted to the client and the network agencies working on a given project. Multiple agencies could engage with the client. The tool allowed upload and download of work flow and corresponding approval via

Exhibit 4 ● Client-Focused Network

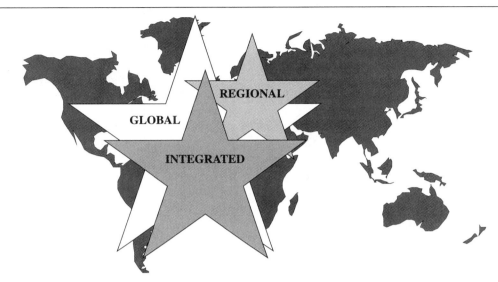

A Model for Global Client Service

Global Service

- **Brand Management**
  New York
- **Interactive** Lead Agency Salt Lake City
  *Paris – Hong Kong – Tokyo – São Paulo –
  Sydney – London – Amsterdam*
- **Consumer & Business**
  Lead Agency New York
  - **Advertising**
    Paris – Hong Kong – Tokyo – São Paulo
  - **Database & Direct Marketing**
    London – Hong Kong – Sydney

Regional Service

- **Brand Management**
  Paris – Hong Kong – Toyko – São Paulo
- **Advertising**
  Paris – Hong Kong – Toyko – São Paulo
- **Interactive** Lead Agency Salt Lake City
  *Paris – Hong Kong – Tokyo – São Paulo –
  Sydney – London – Amsterdam*
- **Database & Direct Marketing**
  London – Hong Kong – Sydney
- **Consumer & Business**
  Lead Agency New York
  - **Advertising**
    Paris – Hong Kong – Tokyo – São Paulo
  - **Database & Direct Marketing**
    London – Hong Kong – Sydney

Integrated Service

- **Marketing Communications**
  Markets Worldwide

Source: Company information.

PC, thus facilitating jobs containing creative work and media planning. StarLink provided an open link to all worldwide resources and a global approach to teamwork.

- *Euro RSCG StarNet.* StarNet was a company-wide, Web-based intranet. Euro RSCG used StarNet internally. It contained a news area, a database of contact information for all employees, community areas to bring together interest groups, and a resource center for sharing and storing materials. Employees could upload and download reports and other resources based on topic.

Euro RSCG expressed its vision for client service as "a commitment to applying new organizational concepts and information technology in ways that make us the leading network of the new century" (*Exhibit 5*).

Corporate Culture

Euro RSCG was by far the youngest company among the top global players. In 1998 the firm was seven years old, whereas the average age of the top ten competitors was eighty-one years old. Schmetterer viewed this as a key success factor:

Competing on the same playing field with brands that have been around for decades has challenged us to be different, to position ourselves as the most attractive global agency network for clients of the new century.

Euro RSCG as a global company had become a networked, multicultural family of agencies. Euro RSCG staff represented many cultural and linguistic backgrounds. The firm emphasized creativity and considered it a strength to be able to provide bold and innovative solutions for clients (*Exhibit 6*).

In autumn 1998, Schmetterer had summarized his thoughts about the organization as he introduced the first issue of *Star Magazine*, the company publication:

Euro RSCG is filled with dynamic people who are embracing innovation and creativity. It is one of our most important differences and it really sets us apart from other groups. I hope this new magazine captures some of the energy that I have felt in my visits with thousands of you over the past year. Together we made great

Exhibit 5 ● Euro RSCG Worldwide: Our Vision

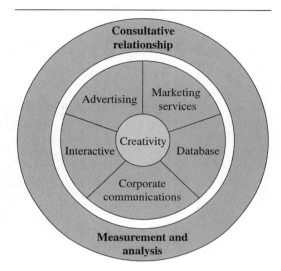

Source: Company information.

strides. Together we have begun to create a clarity of culture, to see ourselves as a multicultural network based on a clear, precise vision, clear leadership, clear organization, shared values, and shared trust. Our leadership isn't one person; it's groups of people having distinct responsibilities. You should be extremely proud of all that we have accomplished together.

THE ADVERTISING INDUSTRY

The advertising industry was characterized by extremely rapid change across every market, driven by global evolution of the consumer economy (*Exhibits 7* and *8*). Major worldwide trends in early 2000 overlapped one another and included the following:

- Advances in technology
- Consolidation of industry players
- Globalization of industry players and clients
- Changes in the nature of client relationship
- Media and communications advances, which affected all dimensions of the industry
- Expansion in the menu of services offered, in response to client demand

Exhibit 6 ● Creative Work by Euro RSCG

Exhibit 6 ● (continued)

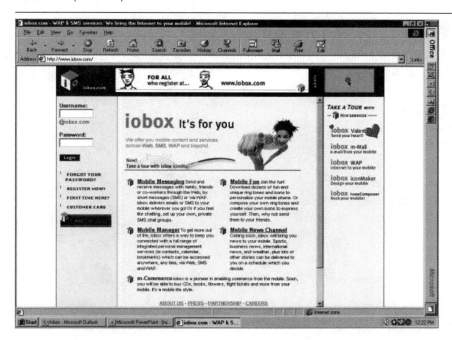

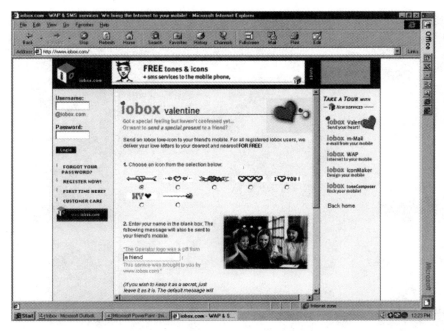

Exhibit 6 ● (continued)

Exhibit 6 ● (continued)

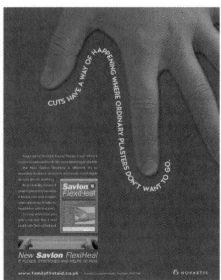

Source: Company information.

Competition

During the 1960s firms had begun to consolidate into holding companies. As service offerings expanded through the 1990s, it became expedient to merge or acquire. Geographic expansion in response to market growth and customer demand led to both globalization and consolidation, which were intertwined and often gave rise to one another. Many traditional agencies had grouped together into powerhouses with a global reach, and activity could no longer be viewed as limited by geography or service.

By the late 1990s the worldwide advertising industry was dominated by large holding company groups operating numerous agencies (***Exhibits 9*** and ***10***). Of the top 100 ad agencies worldwide, 90 ran international operations. Most were wholly or partially owned by a holding company and operated as subsidiaries or affiliates. The holding company structure allowed subsidiary firms to benefit from parent company support and resources (financing) while conducting business with product competitors.

The closeness of the traditional relationship between ad agencies and their clients, based on loyalty and confidentiality, had begun to constrain business growth for two reasons. Agencies declined to handle more than a single client in a given industry, and clients preferred not to share the same agency with a direct competitor. The holding company structure alleviated these issues.

The Regulatory Environment

In the United States, the advertising industry had long been subject to regulation by several entities: the Food and Drug Administration (FDA), the Federal Trade Commission (FTC), trade organizations such as the National Advertising Division of the Council of Better Business Bureaus, and numerous "grass-roots" and civic groups. Recently, controls on the advertising of pharmaceutical products had been relaxed, and drug firms such as Pfizer (Viagra) had moved forward with new ad campaigns.

In Europe, differing national regulations added a greater level of complexity. According to the Treaty of

Exhibit 7 ● Ad Industry Spending

Quick Facts:

- U.S. dominated ad industry with 62 percent of worldwide expenditures. Within United States, ad agencies concentrated mainly in New York. Japan held No. 2 worldwide position with 15 percent of ad expenditures. Markets in Germany, Brazil, and the U.K. experiencing rapid growth.

- 1999 spending: U.S. revenues $200.8 billion with 7.6 percent yearly growth. Worldwide revenues $417 billion, of which public relations and direct marketing composed $200 billion. Non-U.S. annual spending estimated over $112 billion. The top ten ad firms accounted for one-third of total sales.

- Largest customers: automobile industry $9.5 billion, retail $7.6 billion. Companies that spent the most: General Motors No. 1 ($2.173 billion in 1998), Procter & Gamble No. 2, and Philip Morris No. 3.

- Technology and Internet firms quickly gaining position as big spenders. This segment nearly tripled ad expenditures in five-year period 1995–2000. Estimated 1999 ad expenditures $2 billion, with firms such as Apple Computer, America Online, Intel, and Microsoft increasing ad budgets as sales rose.

- Media segments: No. 1 medium for advertising in United States was television. Other media included newspapers, radio, magazines, outdoor, telephone directories, direct mail, and the Internet. On-line and interactive advertising had most rapid growth.

- Industry predictions: On-line ad spending to hit $32 billion and compose 8 percent of total U.S. ad market by 2005. Internet ad spending to reach $2 billion in 1999 and subsequently experience extraordinary growth.

- Surveys in late 1999 indicated significant dissatisfaction with on-line advertising. Approximately 24 percent of executives contacted reported discontent with on-line ad campaigns.

- Japan: 1999 spending declined for traditional media but jumped 111 percent to $220 million for Internet advertising.

- China: 1994 to 1999 ad industry growth 45 percent. Over 3,500 ad agents in Beijing. Top ten firms were foreign ad companies targeting foreign customers. Increasing competition viewed as positive influence likely to raise professional standards and service quality of Chinese firms. Expenditures: No. 1 food, No. 2 cosmetics, No. 3 household electrical goods.

Source: Public information.

Rome, once a company had satisfied the laws of its own country, another state could not impose further restrictions unless specific conditions were met, such as overriding issues relating to the public interest. However, the regulatory impact on advertising was far from resolved, in light of conventions still in place such as the following:

- Greece banned TV toy advertising between 7:00 a.m. and 10:00 p.m.

- Some countries required candy advertising to feature a toothbrush symbol.

- Differing national rules on how much of the human body may be revealed; discounting,

special offers, free gifts, and promotions; promotion of alcohol, tobacco, financial services, and pharmaceuticals.

Service Array

The traditional service array of advertising, direct marketing, sales promotion, event promotion, and interactive had broadened to include PR, corporate communications, consulting, analysis, measurement, database services, and media buying and planning. The dividing line between advertising and PR had begun to disappear as agencies expanded from creating

Exhibit 8 ● Ad Growth by World Markets, 1999

Rank by Growth Rate	Country Market Area	Annual Growth Rate (%)	GDP 1999 (US$ billions)	Ad Spending as % of GDP	Estimated Total Ad Spending (US$ billions)
1	China	18.2	1,031.1	0.48	4.943
2	Portugal	16.0	107.4	1.49	1.601
3	Taiwan	10.7	296.3	1.56	4.637
4	Belgium	8.4	255.5	0.69	1.768
5	Philippines	7.2	85.2	0.89	0.760
6	South Africa	7.0	128.2	1.27	1.628
7	Greece	5.6	128.2	1.18	1.510
8	Czech Republic	5.5	50.5	1.01	0.511
9	Austria	5.2	217.9	0.80	1.741
10	India	5.0	435.6	0.39	1.702
11	Canada	4.7	648.8	0.81	5.286
12	Puerto Rico	4.6	33.5	4.06	1.360
13	Netherlands	4.1	384.7	0.93	3.587
14	Australia	4.0	420.0	1.27	5.331
15	Finland	3.9	129.5	0.88	1.139

Source: Public information.

an ad to creating and maintaining a brand. Most of the top agencies now ran PR divisions or subsidiaries.

Growth of the marketing services segment was fueling development and expansion of agencies dedicated to this niche alone. Clients were directing more money to promotions that produced visible return on investment for their marketing expenditures, for example sampling programs ("try it, you'll like it") both in stores and via direct mail. Also, new client categories were moving into promotional activity, in many cases clients whose industries had only recently been granted legal permission to advertise. Examples were utilities and health care as well as computers, software, electronics, automobiles, and retailers.

The broadening service array led to an increase in the number of niche service providers, with e-commerce players competing for advertising dollars, thus giving clients greater choice and negotiating leverage. Some insiders predicted that large advertising and marketing service firms would evolve into even larger professional service firms offering management consulting, software development, and venture capital. Others predicted the advent of agency boutiques with niche operations providing highly specialized services.

The media specialist had become a key player. Large global clients typically sought a single specialist to design a global media strategy. In some cases, the media specialist took precedence over the creative agency and dealt directly with large advertisers. Media specialists contributed profit margins averaging over 20 percent, whereas creative agencies generally contributed profit margins of approximately 15 percent. Many ad groups ran a media specialist subsidiary (StarCom of Leo Burnett and MediaVest of MacManus).

Exhibit 9 ● The Top Agency Networks Worldwide

Group	1995–1999 CAGR (%)	1999 Gross Income (US$ millions)	1998 Gross Income (US$ millions)	1997 Gross Income (US$ millions)	1996 Gross Income (US$ millions)	1995 Gross Income (US$ millions)
Dentsu	2.2	2,109	1,786	1,927	1,930	1,930
McCann-Erickson Worldwide	12.8	1,865	1,640	1,451	1,299	1,154
BBDO Worldwide	13.3	1,415	1,304	990	925	858
J. Walter Thompson	6.0	1,270	1,177	1,121	1,073	1,007
EURO RSCG Worldwide	**18.5**	**1,269**	**1,019**	**883**	**824**	**643**
Grey Advertising	11.3	1,193	943	918	842	777
DDB Needham Worldwide	8.2	1,078	1,007	920	848	786
Publicis Communication	13.6	1,009	765	625	677	606
Leo Burnett Co.	4.5	958	933	878	866	804
Ogilvy & Mather Worldwide	7.1	938	861	838	793	714
Young & Rubicam	13.0	905	879	781	707	556
FCB Worldwide	n/a	897				
Lowe Lintas & Partners Worldwide	11.8	888	656	621	606	568
Hakuhodo Inc.	−3.6	828	735	848	898	959
TBWA Worldwide	25.8	796	782	476	366	318
D'Arcy Masius Benton & Bowles	7.5	664	617	607	525	497

Source: Public information.

Exhibit 10 ● Agency Network Rankings Across Geographic Regions, March 2000

		United States	*Europe*	*Latin America*	*Asia/Pacific*
Seven truly global agencies*					
McCann-Erickson	IPG	3	2	1	4
J. Walter Thompson	WPP	2	10	2	5
Young & Rubicam	YNR	7	5	4	8
BBDO Worldwide	OMC	8	4	5	6
DDB Worldwide	OMC	9	7	9	12
Ogilvy & Mather	WPP	10	6	7	7
Grey Advertising	GREY	1	8	15	13
Four geographically lopsided agencies, within reach of truly global					
Euro RSCG	**Havas**	**6**	**1**	**8**	**19**
Lowe Lintas & Partners	IPG	13	9	10	15
Leo Burnett	BDM	5	13	6	11
Foote, Cone & Belding	TNO	4	16	3	18
Five quasi-global agencies					
Publicis	Publicis	25	3	14	16
DMB&B	BDM	11	12	11	20
TBWA Worldwide	OMC	12	11	17	17
Bates Worldwide	CDA	16	14	18	9
Saatchi & Saatchi	SSA	14	15	16	14

*This category represents the top ten firms in the United States and in Europe, and the top fifteen firms in Latin America and Asia/Pacific.

Source: Public information.

Service Delivery

Traditional delivery of service encompassed multiple stages of activity typically coordinated by an account executive: planning, design, media purchasing, and production. The agency and client first worked together to develop an advertising and marketing strategy. Next, a brief was produced for the creative team addressing specifics such as the message to be conveyed, definition of the target audience, and the medium for communication. Advertising text and images were then developed by art directors and copy-writers. The following stage, production, could require physical production of signage as well as photographic shoots for TV commercials. Photographic shoots could be costly and time-consuming. Media planning and buying staff chose outlets for the media mix, and traffic staff coordinated logistics. The final agency task was to ensure that the media did indeed publish or broadcast the advertisement as contracted.

Service delivery was changing rapidly, and the creation of an ad campaign could not be assumed to follow the traditional pattern. Increasingly, the goals of an agency were to redefine and redesign client and customer relationships. Expanding use of Internet advertising had begun to erase distinctions among marketing, sales, branding, promotions, and fulfillment. Dividing lines for budgetary allocation of expenditures had also become blurred, with funding drawn not only from advertising but also from sales, operations, and information technology budgets.

Branding

The concept of branding was evolving to meet changing global realities. No longer a single message for a single consumer, a brand spoke to multiple constituencies: manufacturer, distributor, consumer, corporate alliances, joint ventures, employees, investors, and analysts. The brand message needed to be easily understood by all constituencies including across geographic and cultural boundaries.

Models for branding had typically been driven by advertisers providing solutions to client problems through idea delivery. Branding was now reaching into personal belief systems to offer choices about personal identity. Concepts such as social responsibility and environmental sustainability were starting to play a role. According to one industry specialist, "the great brands will be driven by simple ideas bigger than advertising."

The quest for brand loyalty had generated new types of advertising and promotion. The ultimate goal was to capture market share. Database marketing allowed highly focused targeting of a specific customer segment. Loyalty marketing (direct mail, special values, and targeted communications) had become popular in consumer industries such as pharmaceuticals, hospitality, and toys.

EURO RSCG GLOBAL ACCOUNT MANAGEMENT

Euro RSCG served a broad range of clients in multiple industries (*Exhibit 11*). Although many clients operated globally, Euro RSCG did not necessarily serve a given client worldwide, often working in one or more regional or country market areas. Each client was handled differently, and service delivery was based on response to individual client needs. Clients operated at varying levels of internal profitability and globalization, and they ran differing strategies for expansion or retrenchment. Thus, service needs were by no means uniform, even among the larger multinational or global firms (*Appendix 1*).

Schmetterer and his team were addressing the issue of how the company should manage global clients. The key themes Euro RSCG emphasized were entrepreneurialism, innovation, technology, flexibility, and multiculturalism. Schmetterer believed Euro RSCG held an advantage over competitors: "Most of our competitors grew from a large central office with a fifty or sixty year heritage of working in a more homogeneous culture. We are a much more multicultural company." He saw the need to forge a new approach based on relationship management:

We have to take a global point of view about interactive advertising and marketing. We need to be part of our clients' future thinking. Part of showing them how to be heroes in their own industries. Part of many other things that in the traditional advertising world we're not so much a part of. We need to find a unique way of managing our global client relationships, not just account management.

However, for a variety of reasons, managing the relationship was not always easy. With one client, it seemed that by the time Euro RSCG established a good working relationship, the contact had either changed position or left the company. A Euro RSCG manager commented on staff turnover within this firm:

Every time they let the dust settle, there's a change. You work for somebody, then the person is gone. For an agency, this is difficult. It's not easy to build a relationship in a situation like this. You have to work constantly on building trust.

The Service Menu

Euro RSCG delivery of global client service was changing rapidly, influenced by growth and expansion of Euro RSCG itself, and also by growth and expansion of clients. Schmetterer viewed the company as a full-service, integrated organization (*Exhibit 5*). He recognized that as the industry moved toward an expanded range of services, the service array would be a key to success:

Exhibit 11 ● Euro RSCG Global Client Relationships

Company	Years*	Advertising	Media Services	Interactive	Corporate Communications
Air France	2	X	X	X	X
Airbus	4	X	X		X
Alberto Culver	1	X			
American Home Products	11	X			X
Auchan	3	X	X		X
Aventis	3	X	X		X
Bayer	31	X	X		X
BNP Paribas	3	X	X		X
Canal+	16	X	X	X	
UTC	1	X	X		X
Cartier	2	X			
Citroën	24	X	X	X	X
CNN	<1	X			
Dell	8	X	X		
Diageo	3	X	X		X
Elf	8	X	X		X
Eurofighter	3	X	X		X
Freemarkets	<1	X			
Ford (Volvo)	9	X	X	X	
GlaxoSmithkline	26	X		X	
Groupe Danone	29	X	X	X	X
Immarsat	1	X			X
Intel	10	X	X	X	X
JP Morgan	2	X			
Kraft Foods	22	X	X		
L'Oréal	25	X	X	X	X
LVMH / Louis Vuitton	10	X	X		X
Microsoft	6	X	X	X	
Nestlé	23	X	X		X
Novartis	8	X	X		X
P&G	20	X	X	X	X
Peugeot	19	X	X	X	X
Pfizer-Warner-Lambert	5	X	X		
Pharmacia	3	X			X
Sara Lee	5	X	X		
Schering Plough	16	X	X	X	
Skyteam	<1	X	X	X	
Union Chimique Belge (UCB)	2	X			
Vivendi	3	X	X		X
Worldcom	10	X	X	X	

* Years as Euro RSCG global client.
Source: Company information.

A much larger array of activities—that puts a whole different picture on how we organize ourselves in terms of global clients. There are so many activities we now deploy for the client. It requires much more of a team-based client approach.

Schmetterer noted that with some clients the question was how to deliver a full array of global services in each of the client's regions, whereas for others, Euro RSCG had already worked this out with some degree of success. A Euro RSCG executive addressed the complex issue of integrated service:

Portfolio management and integration are the centerpieces of our strategy today. They are at the heart of our acquisition and globalization efforts. The progression of our business from a stack of services, none of which work together, to an integrated set of services that provide seamless, media-neutral solutions to our clients—of course it's very easy to say this is what we do, but it takes a lot of attention to actually implement.

Euro RSCG's Model for Global Service

Considering which models had proved effective, Schmetterer noted,

We have thirty-some clients we are dealing with on a relatively global basis, but we have no one way of dealing with this. Over the last eighteen months, a new way of working has developed with Intel. We have appointed someone to work with that relationship who has a very strong way of handling it, and we have a twice-yearly face-to-face report card. There are also other models worth looking at but being managed in a different way. There seems to be a lot of positive feeling about how New Balance, a client much smaller than Intel, is being managed out of our New York agency, and there are probably about a dozen others. There's a new client, literally only a few weeks old. They contacted our agency in London to ask for help setting up in Europe, then our Hong Kong office to set up there.

The global service model Euro RSCG used for Intel was considered effective. Intel was seen as an exciting account and attracted the best people. George Gallate, Global Brand Manager for the Intel account, remarked

that "among people who work on it there's pretty high enthusiasm."

Intel global headquarters were located in Santa Clara, California (***Appendix I***). The company organized marketing on a global basis and split activity into two segments: business and consumer. Santa Clara led most programs, and strong regional operations matrixed to Santa Clara ensured locally relevant activity consistent with global direction.

Euro RSCG had won Intel's global business in 1996.[2] The service objective was to reflect client structure and style, and Euro RSCG had therefore created five geographic service regions: North America, Europe/Middle East/Africa, Asia/Pacific, Japan, and Latin America. The North American region took the global lead. Within this region there was a lead Euro RSCG agency for each part of the business they worked on: advertising, business interactive advertising, Internet content development, database marketing, and point of purchase (POP). This structure was replicated in each region.

The global lead agencies were MVBMS Euro RSCG[3] for advertising; FUEL NA, an integrated marketing services company attached to MVBMS, with a focus on interactive advertising, database marketing, and POP; and Euro RSCG DSW Partners (Salt Lake City) for interactive content.

Euro RSCG had established a brand management team to assure global integrated activity across each discipline. The team included a global brand manager (Gallate) based in New York and a brand manager for each region. The regional brand managers, based in Paris, Hong Kong, Tokyo, and São Paulo, held responsibility for the relationship with Intel in their geography. The global brand manager was responsible for the overall relationship and worked with lead agencies and regional brand managers in a client-focused partnership. Gallate elaborated:

The client does global integrated marketing. We have set up our network to do this. We provide client-focused networks to create a total brand experience. Each network reflects the unique structure and re-

2. Prior to winning the global account, Euro RSCG had managed the Intel account in Asia/Pacific and had also purchased the agency in the United States that serviced Intel.

3. Messner Vetere Berger McNamee Schmetterer Euro RSCG located in New York.

quirements of the client. Our mission is to improve the value of the network to Intel and the value of Intel to the network. Given our integrated structure, if we focus on this, we have a very successful relationship. We are their marketing communications partner. We act as an extension of the client. They operate in a highly competitive marketplace, and because of the prestige of the account, so do we. There are many agencies in many disciplines that covet the Intel account.

More than 350 people worked on the Intel account including a total of fifty-eight Euro RSCG agencies. Brand management facilitated a matrix structure wherein regional offices observed "dotted line" reporting to New York and local offices "dotted line" reporting to regional centers. Building and managing a network in this manner relied on three factors:

- A sense of partnership, shared responsibility, and shared success across the network, facilitated by regular face-to-face meetings and weekly teleconferences.

- Having the right people. Gallate phrased it "people networking as opposed to just a network of people." The prestige of the account attracted good people.

- Technology enablers. Euro RSCG had partnered with Intel to develop StarLink, which in addition to a range of other tools served to enhance speed, quality, and relevance of the work flow.

Gallate believed the requirements for success on the Intel account were

- Strength in understanding the client's brand, with a vision for their direction

- Strength in understanding the client's customers

- Ability to help position the client's products

- Speed facilitated through networking and technology

- Partnership within the network and with the client

- A global focus

Whereas the Intel service model was global in both aspects of the term (the client operated globally, and

Euro RSCG served the client globally), the service structures Euro RSCG had adopted for other clients operating in multiple markets differed considerably. Among multimarket service models, some exhibited varying stages of globalization while others remained international. Euro RSCG had found more than one model successful, and direct competitors offered examples of other service formats as well (*Appendix II*). Drivers that had typically shaped service models were

- Geographic locations in which the client operated

- Geographic market areas and/or service activities for which the client turned to Euro RSCG as opposed to competitors

- Client propensity for expansion

- Service array required

- Client budget

DEFINING THE RELATIONSHIP

Danone

Danone products fell into three categories: biscuits, dairy, and water (*Exhibit 6* and *Appendix I*). Euro RSCG worked with Danone in biscuits and water, handling the two differently as a result of how Danone had managed its own development. In water, Danone had internationalized its key brand, Evian. In biscuits, Danone had purchased leading brands in several countries.

Danone sold biscuits in many countries under different brands, having acquired the local market leader and retained its name, and in many cases its original recipes, in most geographic markets. Danone sold water internationally under mainly one brand name, Evian, and under a second brand name also positioned internationally, Volvic.

The challenge for Euro RSCG with Danone was to become more international. In order to gain influence at an international level, Euro RSCG had moved into a consulting relationship in addition to advertising. Euro RSCG had created an international brand platform for both water and biscuits, advised on portfolio organization in both segments, and worked on best practices in each country market.

Key issues had recently included the following:

- *Branding.* Developing a single worldwide brand platform for Evian.

- *New product launch.* Recommending the launch of a "slim water" to expand the Danone portfolio and to match a competitor.

- *Synergy.* Facilitating international synergies in the biscuit segment.

- *Organization.* Adapting to a group in a different stage of internationalization.

- *Impartiality.* Separating the international team from the French team.

Marianne Hurstel, an executive with International Brand Consulting and Coordination at Euro RSCG BETC, discussed the Danone account:

Danone is looking for a partner able to help them both define their future strategy and participate in its implementation. Danone is looking for a network that will complement their own international needs, one with strong authority over local agencies.

Iobox

Iobox was a small new company based in Helsinki, Finland. It specialized in mobile Internet services, Wireless Application Protocol (WAP), and other emerging communications technologies.[4] The firm had launched its first products in April 1999 and now operated with a pan-European strategy in Finland, Germany, Sweden, and the U.K. Iobox maintained of-fices in London, Helsinki, Munich, and Stockholm, and employed forty people.

Although Iobox was not yet a global player, the firm had established a strong base with stable financing and operations. A syndicate of international investors (U.K., Finland, U.S., Italy) led by Morgan Stanley Dean Witter Capital Partners contributed financing. The executive team combined experience in engineering, finance, and management.

Iobox had initiated the relationship with Euro RSCG in February 2000 (*Exhibit 6*). While considering expansion into Germany and the U.K., the firm had approached MHI/Euro RSCG, the agency office near Munich, which had in turn contacted Euro RSCG Worldwide in London. Euro RSCG had put together a comprehensive presentation outlining the industry, entry costs, competitor activity, and options for approaching the target market (a "guerrilla-type" approach vs. traditional advertising).

Iain Ferguson, CEO of Marketing Services in Europe at the Euro RSCG Worldwide office in London, and Ben Robinson, project director for the Iobox assignment, discussed the relationship. Ferguson described the early rapport:

The client was taken aback by the level of insight we presented. Decisions were made there and then, and they appointed us on the spot. There was strong synergy, and we were able to provide real insight into the marketplace. Iobox had no international structure, no people, no practices. Effectively they were building up from scratch. The relationship was developed largely by Ben. He moved around a lot, flying to the various markets. We've deployed a fast-track team. Ben di-

---

4. Iobox led the market for wireless Internet services in Europe with over 400,000 customers. Revenues came from user service fees, revenue sharing with content providers, vendors, and other partners (Yahoo!). Products included messaging services, personal management, information services, and other wireless applications. Iobox specialized in easy-to-use services from an Internet platform to mobile users (e-mail to mobile phone).

The wireless communications industry was expanding with unprecedented speed, and Iobox was well positioned to succeed. Currently Europe had 82 million mobile phone users, and this number was expected to reach 195 million within two years. Among world markets, Europe had the most rapid growth in the mobile phone segment. In addition, it was estimated that the number of Internet users in Europe would expand from 41 million to 136 million in the two-year period 2000–2002.

WAP was available globally and was expected to catch on quickly in Asia, where mobile phones had far higher market penetration than PCs. In spring 2000 the number of Internet users in Asia/Pacific excluding Japan was growing at an annual rate of 40%. E-commerce was growing at an annual rate of 109%. Cell phone penetration in Hong Kong was 60% of the total population. Telecommunications firms expected WAP services to become a major source of revenue as the technology caught on. Key attractions for customers were expected to be retailing, mobile banking, stock trading, and airline ticketing.

rects it totally, he is running the Euro RSCG end of the relationship and the Iobox business.

Robinson continued:

We have not handled this as a traditional account. A team was assembled for this project based on insight the team members have, on their intuitive level of understanding of the company, its target consumers, and the product.

Iobox required far more than the traditional array of advertising services. The fast-moving client looked to Euro RSCG for event creation, investor communications, database management, strategy advisement and formulation, and managing the corporate Web site. Euro RSCG had been able to use internal resources for most of the skill sets required, including direct consulting expertise.

Euro RSCG had taken the lead in strategy with the business model and timing, and also with internal and external communications. Decisions were approached jointly, and Iobox had the final word. Approximately four people in each of the four market areas, Finland, Sweden, Germany, and the U.K., worked on the assignment.

Communication played a key role in the success of the relationship. StarLink, the Euro RSCG proprietary communications tool, had been central to rapid decision making, an element absolutely critical for the client. StarLink provided nearly real time communication capability, and approval of advertising could be given via this system. Ferguson explained:

StarLink was one of the benefits we talked about at the very first meeting. The tool is sophisticated and takes some time to deploy, so we decided to create a mini-StarLink out of London. Concept development, notes on meetings—if a meeting was taking place in London, the guys in Germany would see it almost in real time.

Branding was pan-European. Globalization was not yet imminent, in spite of the fact that by spring 2000 market penetration had already reached the level anticipated for summer 2000. Ferguson and Robinson agreed that branding would be uniform and that prominent themes would be used as the client ex-

panded, but that messaging would need to vary according to individual markets. Since Iobox targeted both industry and consumer customers, language, especially "street" language, would require a customized approach.

The full importance of this client relationship would remain unknown at least for the near future. In financial terms, the relationship had been profitable from the outset, although the client did not yet represent a major portion of worldwide activity. Ferguson and Robinson considered the relationship and learning important especially because of the dynamic new sector. Ferguson addressed the element of unpredictability:

Where will this thing go? We don't really know. It's a narrow base on which to build a fast-growing relationship. We think we've done a good job. But it's bound to be a roller coaster.

In a comparatively short time, Euro RSCG had won a high level of trust based on performance and speed. The account had been conducted with transparency on both sides, and this fact had greatly facilitated problem resolution without conflict or misunderstanding. Ferguson commented on the shared trust:

Because of the core team Ben has put together, they turned to us to assume a broader role. Iobox tells us "this is what we could do, what should we do?" We give them recommendations. If we had made these claims on day one, we would not have been credible.

Robinson believed the defining moment was "the very first piece of work we did for them, the briefing in Helsinki." He recalled the event:

Getting approval from the client and also from the investor, and delivery of the material to San Francisco in less than seventy-two hours, that set the pace for the relationship. They come to us now and say, "These are the issues we're facing, how do you think we should handle them?" That whole process really did set the tone of trust.

New Balance

Euro RSCG had begun work with New Balance as a small U.S. client in 1989.[5] Euro RSCG began to serve the client in Europe in 1998. In 2000, full service was provided in the United States, France, Germany, and the U.K. Additional service was handled on request in the Netherlands, Italy, and Sweden with full service planned for these markets in the coming year. MVBMS Euro RSCG was the lead agency worldwide, and Euro RSCG in Paris oversaw activity in Europe.

Management of the New Balance account had progressed toward globalization in a unique way. Because of a limited budget, service had expanded through a "piggy-back" relationship with a New York–based account that had established representation throughout Europe. A total of twenty-five people in the United States and Europe worked on New Balance. Two were dedicated full-time, an account supervisor and an account executive.

Pamela Moffat, account director for New Balance at MVBMS Euro RSCG, described how the account was handled:

When the chance to partner with New Balance in Europe came up, we jumped on it. We had helped them grow from a small niche brand to a significant player in the United States and hoped to be able to do the same in Europe. What we didn't anticipate was that their small budget would demand finding a more creative, less traditional way of serving them. We were lucky to find a structure already established that allowed us to hit the ground running.

In Europe, local agencies had previously developed their own advertising for New Balance. Lack of a consistent position had caused New Balance to be seen

more as a fashion brand than a performance brand, a departure from its core identity. Euro RSCG had stepped in with a single message based on performance. According to Moffat, "We now have a coordinated message in Europe. Performance is all we talk about." The requirements for success on the New Balance account were

- Changing the brand image successfully in Europe
- Providing tactical support as the client expanded
- Maintaining the relationship as a partnership
- Serving the client effectively within a limited budget
- Communication, mainly by e-mail so that all shared the same expectations

Moffat discussed Euro RSCG strategy:

Our strategy was to take what we've learned from our success in the United States and translate that around the world. We needed to have one voice and one consistent position worldwide. To achieve that, we focused on the brand's heritage, running, to reestablish their performance credentials. We use the same tag line, "Achieve New Balance," around the world. Initially this proved difficult because of the play on words in English. However, the European team managed to find an effective translation. The tag line appears in both English and the local language in all countries. It was important for us to keep this tag line because it communicates both the physical and spiritual benefits of using the product.

Novartis

Swiss-based Novartis held the No. 4 position in the worldwide pharmaceutical industry. Novartis was a global company with worldwide business in three segments: health care (mainly prescription), consumer health (mainly known in the United States as over-the-counter, or OTC, also known in Europe as self-medication, or SM), and agribusiness (*Appendix I*). Euro RSCG worked with Novartis in prescription health care and OTC.

Novartis operations in each geographic market enjoyed a certain measure of autonomy in decision

---

5. New Balance Athletic Shoe, Inc., based in Boston (U.S.), manufactured performance-oriented athletic footwear. The company operated five production sites in the United States as well as facilities in other countries. Worldwide business activity in sixty-three countries was divided into the following geographic markets: Africa, Asia/Pacific, Europe, Middle East, Central America/Caribbean, North America, and South America. New Balance was one of the fastest growing athletic footwear brands in the United States and by early 2000 had risen to the No. 4 position. The brand was expanding rapidly in the United States, partly as a result of its orientation toward the serious runner.

making. Thus, Euro RSCG provided global service for Novartis in the U.K. but did not currently work with Novartis in the United States. Euro RSCG had handled the Novartis-U.K. assignment, in the consumer health segment with Voltaren 12.5 mg, as a European account only since February 2000. Service was centralized and covered advertising and marketing. Euro RSCG had previously worked with Novartis as a regional or local client in several countries. The client relationship had begun with Canada in 1992, the U.K. in 1996, France in 1997, and Switzerland in 1998. Although client headquarters were in Switzerland, the U.S. operations of Novartis wielded a strong influence everywhere.

Peter Koerfgen, European coordinator for the Novartis account, discussed the service structure:

The philosophy of Euro RSCG is to offer the best talent for the client, regardless of which country. A project champion is selected based on expertise. The project champion then selects the team members, choosing people from whichever agency and whichever country he wishes, based on expertise. It's very international and depends on who knows the therapeutic area, the competition, and the product.

Several issues had generated concern on both sides of the relationship. In one case, as a result of a particular incident, a U.S. agency in the Euro RSCG network had been excluded from working with certain areas of Novartis. Novartis in the United States had therefore declined to work with Euro RSCG, creating international repercussions. Koerfgen weighed the implications:

This is a very interesting point for global account management. You have to be a clean global network to work with these big global companies. One little mosaic in the network can destroy the entire relationship.

Novartis, the product of a 1996 merger between pharmaceutical firms Sandoz and Ciba-Geigy, had continued significant internal change including a December 1999 merger of its agribusiness with another company. Staff turnover after the merger had impacted the client relationship. According to Koerfgen, "We get assignments for projects, but the project sometimes gets abandoned according to the focus of the new managers."

Global branding would require future attention, and Koerfgen addressed this issue:

Novartis management identified global branding as a weakness, and significant efforts are now underway to make global branding stronger. In some countries, the product name and strategy are different. With some tactics, Novartis is very local, very decentralized. There is a debate going on about which is better in pharmaceutical marketing. Personally, I believe you have to have a global brand and present it globally, with minor adjustments for the local market. Novartis now has global brand teams, separate from their therapeutic areas. This is new at Novartis. We mirrored their organization when we put together our global teams.

CONCLUSION

Schmetterer and his team were now considering models for global brand management. The questions revolved around whether to adopt one service model as an overlay. Should the Intel model, or parts of it, be used with other clients? Should a matrix structure lead the organization? Should service be structured by brand rather than by geography or discipline? At recent meetings, a number of issues had been raised:

1. *Compensation was changing.* In some cases, commissions were being linked to performance. For example, some firms paid a fee for services plus an incentive tied to sales. Across Asian markets in general, commissions were simply being cut back, some as low as zero to five percent. Margins had been severely impacted by the recent economic downturn.

2. *Representation.* In early 2000, Euro RSCG internal analysis suggested that the company was

   • Underrepresented in PR

   • Underrepresented in the overall markets of Germany, Asia (specifically Japan), and the United States

   • Overrepresented in advertising

   • Overrepresented in France

3. *Targets for improvement.*
  - Pitching and attracting new global brands
  - Keeping and improving management of existing global brands
  - Financial accountability and control, improving results from global clients
  - More transparency in reporting
  - Centralization of some processes

Euro RSCG was now facing important strategy decisions. A key question was whether to copy other services or create something entirely new. Schmetterer believed the pace of change within the industry imposed a sense of urgency. He addressed the issues of change management and leadership for the new century.

Obviously we're not alone in understanding that the world is changing and that our place in it is changing. This is still an evolving medium and our issue needs to be how do we take a position as a leader that allows us to be the most attractive agency for clients in the new century. Most of the people who work in our organization have worked at one or more of our competitors and bring with them a heritage of understanding how others do it. There's a part of me that wants to say "O.K., let's look at who does it best and adopt their system." But on the other hand, systems have changed, communications and technology have changed. The speed of change is not fully appreciated. I know that what I say today is already six months behind the speed of change. We need to find a way to build in much more anticipation of client needs and a way to use speed to execute our response to client needs.

APPENDIX I
Euro RSCG Global Clients

A sample listing of multinational and global companies that either had been or were currently clients of Euro RSCG. Represented by Euro RSCG in multiple but not necessarily all markets of the client's operation. Equivalent information about activity with each client was not available. Companies listed in alphabetical order.

Citroën and Peugeot

Head Office	Sales 1998 (US$ billions)	No. of Employees	Products	Markets
France	39.425	156,500	Autos, parts, motorbikes, scooters, industrial machinery, light armored vehicles	France 35%, U.K. 14% Spain 12%, Germany 10%, Italy 7%, other EU 13%, other 10%

In early 1997, Citroën contracted Euro RSCG agencies in six European countries to spearhead the launch of a new automobile series in thirty-one countries of Europe, South America, and Asia. The Euro RSCG Paris agency coordinated activity with partners in Germany, Italy, Spain, the Netherlands, and the U.K. Numerous advertising commercials featured supermodel Claudia Schiffer, one a crash test from which Claudia emerged without a scratch, another with Claudia kissing a frog who turned into a handsome driver of a Citroën.

APPENDIX I (continued)

Danone

Head Office	Sales 1998 (US$ billions)	No. of Employees	Products	Markets
France	15.106	78,900	Bottled water, dairy (yogurts, cheese, dairy desserts), biscuits (cookies, crackers, snacks)	France 37%, other Europe 39%, other worldwide 24%

Evian, produced by Groupe Danone, was a natural spring water bottled exclusively at its source in the French town of Evian-les-Bains, scenically located on the shore of Lac Leman (Lake Geneva) in the Alps. Since the Middle Ages, the site had been renowned for the curative, rejuvenating effects of the natural waters. As a modern consumer product, the water was not treated or processed in any way. Bottles were filled, sealed, and shipped to over 120 countries.[1]

A key point for advertising, bottled water was known as low margin and difficult to transport. Moreover, any product was virtually indistinguishable from another once out of the bottle. Therefore, marketing expertise and the ability to reach the consumer with an impact were of great importance.

In 1999 a Euro RSCG advertising campaign for Evian created a sensation in France with twenty babies performing an aquatic ballet. The shoot required seventy babies, six nannies, as well as many parents, and was professionally choreographed. Because Evian, the market leader in bottled waters, had become known as a specialty water for babies, the company devised a strategy to motivate consumers to drink Evian at any age. The ad campaign chose the babies as a symbol of youth, demonstrating the mythical regenerative powers of Evian and communicating "a true sense of happiness, optimism, and rapturous well-being."

Intel

Head Office	Sales 1999 (US$ billions)	No. of Employees	Products	Markets
U.S.	29.389	70,200	Microprocessors, chips, networking, wireless, and branded products	North America 45%, Europe 28%, Japan 7%, Asia/Pacific 20%

1. In early 2000 the so-called "water wars" for the Asian market were just heating up. Market volume was estimated at $3 billion with a yearly growth rate of 10%. Over the next five years, bottled water sales were expected to grow 150% in China alone. Danone was estimated to hold a 25% market share in China and Indonesia as No. 2 in Asia overall behind Nestlé. The highly fragmented market had already attracted a large number of international and regional competitors. Since 1998, Danone had spent over $500 million to acquire controlling shares of the largest brand of bottled water in Indonesia and of a major brand of mineral water in China.

APPENDIX I (continued)

Louis Vuitton

Head Office	Sales 1998 (US$ billions)	No. of Employees	Products	Markets
France	8.126	33,000	Wines, champagnes, cognacs, cosmetics, perfumes, fashion apparel, luxury goods	France 18%, other Europe 19%, Japan 15%, other Asia 18%, U.S. 21%, elsewhere 9%

Novartis

Head Office	Sales 1999 (US$ billions)	No. of Employees	Products	Markets
Switzerland	19.979	81,854	Health care (prescription), consumer health (OTC & nutrition), agribusiness	Americas 48%, Europe 37%, Asia/Africa/Australia 15%

WorldCom

Head Office	Sales 1999 (US$ billions)	No. of Employees	Products	Markets
U.S.	37.1	77,000	Leading-edge Internet protocol services; a full range of advanced services such as local, long distance international, data, wireless, conferencing	U.S. 84%, Brazil 6%, other countries 10%

WorldCom had enjoyed a long-standing client relationship with Euro RSCG. Upon the 1998 merger of MCI and WorldCom, the new company chose Euro RSCG to develop a message assuring business customers that World-Com was now positioned to revolutionize communications and offer even better products, service, and value than either partner had been able to offer before the merger. In part because of Euro RSCG's successful television commercial and twelve-page advertising insert to the *Wall Street Journal* on the merger closing date, WorldCom lost no customers and the stock price rose dramatically.

Source: Public information.

APPENDIX II
Competitor Models for Global Service

Young & Rubicam   (New York). The Key Corporate Account (KCA) program, developed to coordinate service delivered globally and to integrate solutions, used client teams from separate disciplines and offered incentives based on service quality. The strategy was to increase penetration of KCAs by winning new assignments and by increasing the service array. Y&R guided brand development through a highly quantified process using measurement tools. Y&R had committed to serving global branding needs by electronic linkage of agency offices and by creative idea and resource sharing.

DDB Needham Worldwide   (New York). One position, the worldwide director, managed the global account relationship providing centralized leadership and added value. Specific responsibilities were to develop the worldwide business plan, to grow revenue and increase market penetration, and to manage profit and loss of the global account. Within each region, a secondary role, the regional account director, was designated to identify opportunities or problems, defend local and regional profit and loss, and lead regional account directors in preparing the business plan.

J. Walter Thompson   (New York). Corporate executives managed the global accounts. They oversaw worldwide profit and loss, client/agency relationships, and the quality of creative work. Corporate executive responsibility took precedence over that of local and regional managers. The structure allowed limited local initiative. A comprehensive service, Thompson Total Branding, aimed at local, regional, and global clients to provide tools and methodologies for enhancing creativity. Service consistency was a strength.

D'Arcy   (New York). D'Arcy Masius Benton & Bowles operated under the shortened name D'Arcy. A Worldwide Management Team known as the "Loop Team" ran global accounts. The objective was to manage each global brand with the fully integrated synergy of all disciplines. A senior worldwide management supervisor reporting to the CEO led the team, which included senior people from marketing services, strategic planning, and corporate PR, plus a senior creative director and a senior media director.

Leo Burnett   (Chicago). Global service was delivered by a team that provided fully integrated service structured according to management of a given brand. The brand team was centralized. Special strengths lay in integration and media planning.

McCann-Erickson   (New York). The firm delivered global brand management through a subsidiary. Service included both management and building of global brands. Operational objectives covered service to local and regional clients. A company within the McCann network, FutureBrand, was dedicated to brand consulting. It was believed that the top five clients made up 30 percent of the firm's income and 50 percent of profit. Integration was considered a weakness.

Ogilvy & Mather Worldwide   (New York). The firm provided fully integrated services. Traditional and new services, as well as media marketing, were offered to all clients. The integrated service package was offered regardless of whether the client played globally. Ogilvy placed strong emphasis on branding in all markets.

Source: Public information.

Case 15

Deloitte Touche Tohmatsu International, Europe

In February 1993, Tom Presby, Chief Executive Officer (CEO) at Deloitte Touche Tohmatsu International, (DTTI) Europe and Managing Partner of Deloitte & Touche Eastern Europe[1] in Paris, was reviewing a report entitled "Barriers to Integration." The report summarized the findings of a task force that had been asked to identify what DTTI's West European partners saw as barriers to integration among national practices, an issue that had become increasingly important in the accounting profession as a result of global consolidation. In Western Europe, that consolidation coincided with a variety of legal and regulatory changes brought on by the European Community's (EC) 1992 program. As DTTI's multinational clients implemented more pan-European-based strategies, management believed that it was only a matter of time before these same clients began expecting more pan-European services from their respective accounting and auditing firms.

To that end, there were at least four examples within the DTTI organization where partners had defined the scope of their services not on the basis of individual national markets, but on the basis of an expertise that was outside the traditional audit and tax fields. In the first example—the New York Financial Services Center—Tom Presby created a mix of services geared to the fast-paced Wall Street financial community. Contrary to company norms, the Financial Services Center was set up within the jurisdiction of a previously established office. In Europe, another area of expertise was established outside the traditional audit and tax fields in 1988 with the opening of Deloitte & Touche Europe Services in Brussels. Unlike practices in national markets, Deloitte & Touche Europe Services aimed to help the DTTI network by serving EC institutions and advising clients on changes and policies led by the EC. Similarly, in 1991, D & T Corporate Finance Europe was established in London to assist clients on cross-border merger and acquisition activities.

Recently, the national practice guideline had been bypassed by the creation of Deloitte & Touche Eastern Europe—a multilateral joint venture with a regional scope. Deloitte & Touche Eastern Europe was unique in that, unlike other parts of DTTI, which had independent national practices, all the national practices in Eastern Europe were contained within a single holding company. Moreover, the regional scope of that holding company's business was underscored by frequent meetings among all those active in the region. Yet another component of Deloitte & Touche Eastern Europe's regional focus was its "practice centers," which provided their expertise in banking, valuation, and insolvency throughout Eastern Europe.

Though the activities of the Financial Services Center were provided to only one market, they were similar to the three examples in Europe; that is, all four differentiated their services from those being provided by existing practices. More important for DTTI Europe was the fact that the regular cross-border activity among these East European practices might be able to provide some insight on how to coordinate and integrate the activities of its many West European practices. In the West European countries,

This case was prepared by Robert C. Howard, under the supervision of Professors Robert S. Collins and Jean-Pierre Jeannet, as a basis for class discussion rather than to illustrate either effective or ineffective handling of a business situation.

Copyright © 1993 by the International Management Development Institute (IMD), Lausanne, Switzerland. Not to be used or reproduced without permission directly from IMD.

1. Throughout the case, the term Eastern Europe is used to collectively refer to the countries of Bulgaria, the Czech Republic, Slovakia, Hungary, Poland, Romania, and the former territories and republics of Yugoslavia and the Soviet Union/Commonwealth of Independent States (CIS).

partners tended to provide DTTI's accounting and au-diting, tax, and management consultancy services to clients within the borders of their respective markets. That is, with a few exceptions, the staff from an office in a particular market seldom worked with staff from a practice in another one. Aside from Deloitte & Touche Europe Services and the practice centers in Eastern Europe, partners participated in cross-border engagements only when a multinational client re-quested an audit. Typically, a lead client service part-ner was designated as the liaison for practices in other countries that the partner visited during the audit process. Alternatively, partners sometimes worked in other countries when a practice lacked the expertise in a particular discipline such as telecommunications, utilities, or health care.

After the report on "Barriers to Integration" was complete, Presby was eager to see whether the expe-riences in Eastern Europe, and the creation of a multi-lateral joint venture with practice centers in particular, might serve as an example of how to achieve cor-porate objectives in Western Europe. That is, some believed that the construction of a regional organi-zation with practice centers could be a model for ways to provide a more pan-European service offer-ing in the Western portion of the continent. Turning to John Christie, Deputy Regional Director, Presby commented,

Here in Eastern Europe, we have an organization that did not exist just a few years ago, incorporating both national practices and practice centers. In those mar-kets where the national practices request their ser-vices, the practice centers have succeeded in building up the national practices' expertise in banking, valua-tion, and insolvency. In Western Europe, however, where we have pockets of expertise spread throughout our many offices, that expertise tends to be shared only when a joint opportunity arises—for example, when a client requests services in two or more coun-tries simultaneously. With those few exceptions, our West European offices still tend to work as national entities. As I look at the practice centers in Eastern Europe, though, I wonder if we can't take a more proactive approach in sharing our expertise through-out Western Europe. Are practice centers exemplary of one way we can manage the barriers to integration we face in Western Europe?

DELOITTE TOUCHE TOHMATSU INTERNATIONAL

Although Deloitte Touche Tohmatsu International was not established as an independent legal entity un-til 1989, the company's origins could be traced to three firms: Deloitte, Haskins, and Sells; Touche Ross; and Tohmatsu. Despite the success of each of these firms in North America, Europe, and Asia, com-petitive pressures in the United States and the emer-gence of a global economy during the 1980s had placed new demands on the accounting and auditing profession. That is, as client companies expanded their operations around the world, these same clients sought accounting firms that offered their services on a global basis. To meet the needs of such clients, ac-counting firms found it expedient to merge with firms already established in the world's leading economic areas. Thus, in October 1989, Deloitte, Haskins, and Sells merged with Touche Ross and affiliate Tohmatsu & Co. to form Deloitte Ross Tohmatsu (DRT) Inter-national.

Though the majority of local offices accepted the merger, there were some exceptions. Namely, in En-gland, the Netherlands, the Channel Islands, Belgium, and Austria, representative Deloitte, Haskins, and Sells offices joined Coopers & Lybrand, while the Australian office merged with KPMG Peat Marwick. Largely because a disagreement over the use of the Deloitte name in the U.K. at the time of the merger, it was decided to use the initials DRT (for Deloitte Ross Tohmatsu) to represent the new organization. Shortly thereafter, however, Coopers & Lybrand, Deloitte in the U.K. and DRT International reached an agreement on using the Deloitte name, and in 1992 management changed the name from DRT International to Deloitte Touche Tohmatsu International.[2] Although the change of name by local offices to Deloitte & Touche or De-loitte Touche Tohmatsu would not be completed for several years, management nonetheless believed that a single name used worldwide—like all its Big Six

---

2. Strictly speaking, the name Deloitte Touche Tohmatsu In-ternational was used to refer collectively to all of the prac-tices in the Deloitte Touche Tohmatsu International network. At the national level, however, various names were still used around the world. In Europe, the European Board was press-ing to have all practices use Deloitte & Touche, subject to minimal conflict of statutory and legal restrictions.

competitors—would more effectively communicate the global nature of the company's capabilities.

In 1992, DTT International was the world's fifth largest (based on head count and revenues) of the Big Six accounting practices, with a staff of 56,000 people operating from 647 offices in over 100 countries. Around the world, DTTI served over 600 companies with sales or assets greater than $1 billion, including six of the twenty-five largest banks, the two largest insurance companies, and the three largest trading companies. In addition to serving multinational corporations and large national enterprises, DTTI provided its services to public institutions as well as tens of thousands of fast-growing small to medium-sized businesses. To that end, it organized its services along three lines: audit, tax, and management consultancy. It divided its audit line further into audit and accounting, and tax into tax compliance and tax advisory. The range and type of management consultancy services offered by DTTI, however, varied depending on the size of local practices and the needs of their respective markets. In 1991 the company earned revenues of $4,800 million, distributed among accounting and auditing (70%), tax (15%), and management consultancy (15%).

Worldwide, DTT International was structured as a partnership of partnerships, composed of independent national practices with strong domestic multinational company (MNC) client portfolios. To provide strategic guidance for the entire family of DTTI practices, a Board of Directors (previously called the Directorate) made up primarily of Chief Executive Officers from national practices in Argentina, Australia, Canada, France, Germany, Japan, the Netherlands, the United Kingdom, and the United States, met twice a year. For the 1990s the Board of Directors had established five global objectives for DTTI:

1. Focus on MNCs with sales/assets in excess of $1 billion.

2. Provide, through each national practice or regional body, a range of core services that included audit, tax, and information technology consulting for all member practices, as well as financial systems consulting, operations consulting, strategy consulting, and corporate finance services for member practices in countries with a significant number of large MNCs.

3. Become as good as the strongest competition in all core service lines in terms of quality and service by hiring and developing the best people.

4. Become more balanced both functionally and geographically. Specifically, practices in countries with a significant number of MNCs were expected to achieve minimum target revenues of 40 percent audit, 15 percent tax, and 15 percent management consultancy. And, in comparison to the number three competitor among the Big Six on their respective markets, individual practices were expected to achieve at least 90 percent of total revenues, with large companies audited.

5. Share its skills and technology to improve the growth and profitability of all member practices.

To make recommendations to and monitor policies decided on by the Board of Directors, DTTI also had a nine-member Executive Committee (EXCO) that met up to six times per year; each member of the EXCO was also a member of the Board of Directors. As well, DTTI had an International Operations Group (IOG), which implemented decisions taken by the EXCO. Aside from the worldwide Board of Directors, the EXCO, and the International Operations Group, DTTI was organized into geographic regions, each with its own board. Typically, these regional boards also met up to six times per year and concentrated on developing practices in their region, as well as implementing the policies, plans, strategies, and programs of the Verein—the organization in which each national practice was a member. Similar to the Board of Directors and the International Operations Group, some of the regional boards had regional operating groups to respond to the needs of the marketplace and carry out decisions made by the regional boards (*Exhibit 1*).

Neither the Board of Directors nor the regional boards involved themselves in individual offices' daily operations; international management at DTTI reflected this structural arrangement. According to Jacques Manardo, Chairman, European Region, Deloitte Touche Tohmatsu International, DTTI's capital holdings were unique in that the various national practices held a share in the international organization and not the reverse. In describing the financing of national practices, Jerry Sullivan, Chief Financial Officer (CFO) for Deloitte & Touche Eastern Europe,

Exhibit 1 ● Relationship Among Member Practices, Boards, and Operating Groups

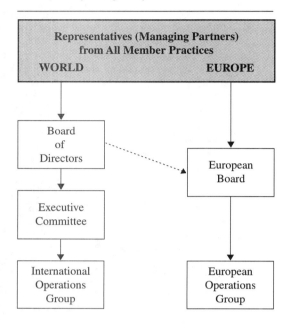

Source: Deloitte Touche Tohmatsu International.

explained that each practice was organized as a profit center and financing was determined within the geographic market of that practice. In short, Deloitte & Touche was a collection of nationally based partnerships whose partners drew their compensation from the revenue pool of their particular practice, rather than from a multicountry or worldwide revenue pool. Excluding the exceptions noted previously, Deloitte & Touche partners tended to work primarily within their own countries. There were also a few occasions when committees or groups of managing partners worked across national boundaries on task forces such as the one determining barriers to integration.

In Europe the regional board consisted of seven members: Jacques Manardo, Chairman, European Region, Deloitte Touche Tohmatsu International; John Roques, Senior Partner and Chief Executive, UK; Piet Hoogendoorn, Managing Partner, the Netherlands; Hoerst Thoennes, International Service Coor-

dinator and member of the management committee, Germany; Adolfo Mamoli, Chairman and CEO, Italy; Bent Hensen, member of the management board, Denmark; and Tom Presby. Like other regional boards, the European board of DTTI met several times a year to discuss governance and strategic issues pertaining to the 250 offices, 1,200 partners, and 17,000 employees that represented DTTI from Scandinavia to Turkey (**Exhibit 2**).

Because Presby reported to both the European Board and the East European Board, he provided a key link between DTTI's activities in Western and Eastern Europe. Together with John Christie and Archie Campbell, Deputy Regional Director, Projects and Deputy CEO Deloitte & Touche Eastern Europe, Presby believed that an arrangement like Deloitte & Touche Eastern Europe might be one way to help integrate Deloitte & Touche practices in Western Europe. Within DTTI Europe, however, there were substantial differences between the East and West European organizations. For example, the network of DTTI practices in Western Europe was far larger and had been established from nationally based practices with long histories. And, because some were started as joint ventures, some also retained their original names (**Exhibit 3**). By contrast, the firm's East European network was smaller, had been established within two years, and shared a common name. The shorter development period, and the fact that many of the expatriates had worked with Presby in the past or were recruited from places where Presby had been, gave the East European organization a team spirit that some believed would be difficult to repeat in Western Europe.

INDUSTRY BACKGROUND

In the 1980s audit and nonaudit accounting activities represented the majority of accounting and auditing services in the EC. In recent years, though, tax consulting, corporate finance, and management advisory services had grown in significance (**Exhibit 4**). In 1990 the National Economic Research Associates (NERA) was retained by the EC Commission to conduct a study into the audit and consultancy sectors of the EC economy.[3] Within these sectors, the European

3. Derek Ridyard and Jean de Bolle. *Competition in European Accounting.* Lafferty Publications, European Commission.

Exhibit 2 ● Deloitte Touche Tohmatsu Europe Operating Organization, from September 1, 1992

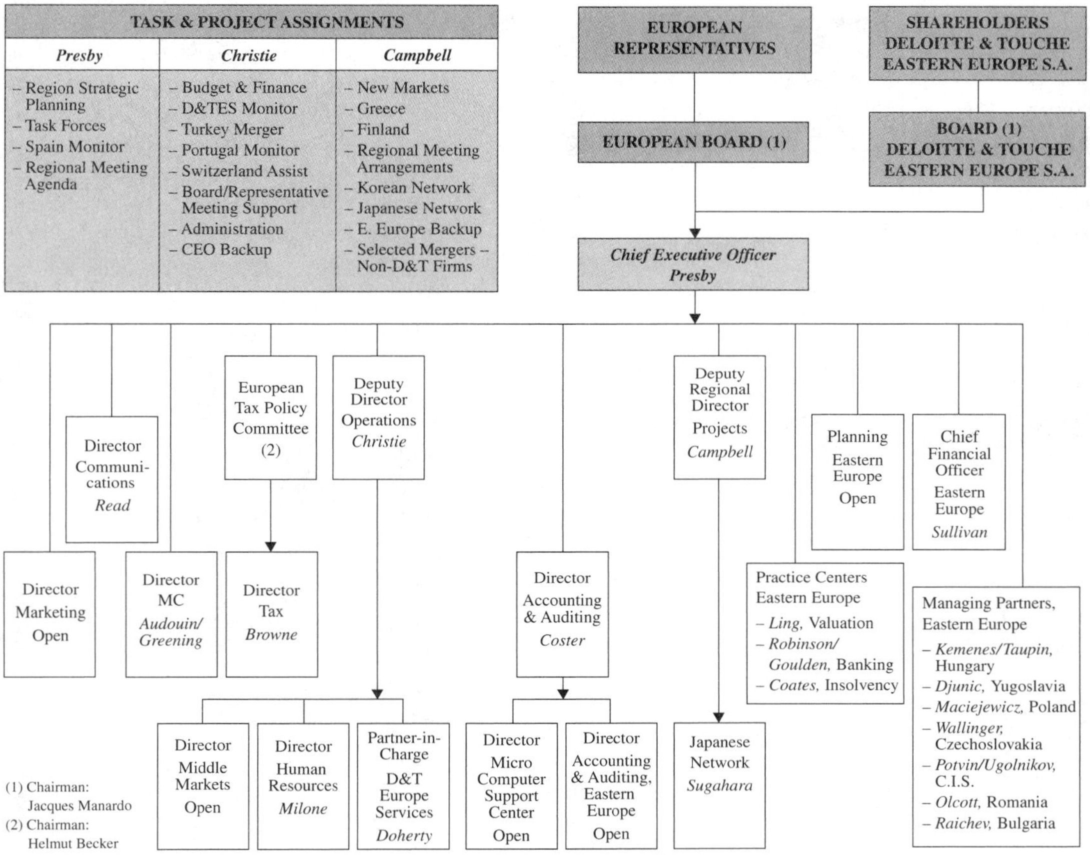

Source: Deloitte Touche Tohmatsu International

Commission was interested in how structural changes that occurred during the 1980s might affect the way firms competed in the 1990s. In the study, NERA identified three changes in particular that were most likely to influence the nature of competition in the industry over the coming decade: merger activity between accounting firms, changes in the composition of their business, and increased pressure for greater harmonization of techniques and mutual recognition of professional qualifications between EC member states.

Merger Activity

During the 1980s accounting firms embarked on a series of mergers to improve their network coverage, reduce costs, enhance or preserve status, increase client synergies, and defend their territories. Aside from

Exhibit 3 ● Deloitte Touche Tohmatsu International Offices in Europe (excludes Eastern Europe)

Market	Number of Offices	Total Staff	Name of Local Office(s)
Austria GmbH	2	50	Deloitte & Touche Danubia Treuhand
Belgium	2	200	Deloitte & Touche Consultants SA/NV Tinnemans, Pourbaix Vaes & Co SC/CV
Cyprus	3	70	Deloitte & Touche
Denmark	25	1,300	Schøebel & Marholt
Finland	11	126	Tilintarkastus Hietala, Paul & Tuominen
France	6	1,150	Deloitte & Touche BDA/BM3A/CPA Deloitte Touche Tohmatsu
Germany	14	1,050	Wollert-Elmendorff Deutsche Industrie-Treuhand GmbH
Greece	1	60	Deloitte & Touche
Ireland	3	550	Deloitte & Touche
Italy	15	300	Deloitte & Touche
Luxembourg	1	225	Fiduciaire Générale de, Luxembourg
Malta	2	60	Manduca, Mercieca & Co
Netherlands	45	3,100	Deloitte & Touche
Norway	8	440	Forum Touche Ross
Portugal	2	162	Deloitte & Touche
Spain	17	350	Deloitte & Touche
Sweden	56	750	TRG Revision
Switzerland	2	150	Deloitte & Touche
Turkey	2	130	DRT Denetim—Revizyon Tasdik Yeminli Mali Müsavirlik AS
United Kingdom	26	6,700	Touche Ross
Total	**243**	**16,923**	

Source: Deloitte Touche Tohmatsu International.

DTTI, a merger between Ernst & Whinney and Arthur Young in 1989/90 formed Ernst & Young, and the Peat Marwick Mitchell and Klynveld Main Goerdeler networks became KPMG Peat Marwick in 1987. By 1991 the Big Eight accounting firms of only a few years earlier had been consolidated into the Big Six, which also included Arthur Andersen, Coopers & Lybrand, and Price Waterhouse. As a result of the pre-vious decade's merger activity, a substantial realign-ment of market shares had occurred in all EC member states (*Exhibit 5*).

Changes in Business Composition

In addition to the intra-industry merger and acquisition activity of the 1980s, each of the Big Six expanded the

Exhibit 4 ● Deloitte Touche Tohmatsu International (A), Breakdown of Fees

Country	Audit Fee	Non-Audit Accounting	Tax Consulting	Corporate Finance	Management Consulting Services	Total Fees from Audit Clients
	%	%	%	%	%	%
Belgium	52	12	23	4	10	100
Denmark	59	14	11	5	11	100
France	82	5	5	5	5	100
Germany	65	5	21	5	5	100
Greece	63	4	13	15	4	100
Ireland	48	13	28	7	5	100
Italy	80	5	5	5	5	100
Luxembourg	69	9	9	0	12	100
Netherlands	57	10	23	5	5	100
Portugal	72	5	9	5	9	100
Spain	60	5	18	5	13	100
UK	51	12	27	5	5	100

Source: NERA accounting firm survey.

Exhibit 5 ● Deloitte Touche Tohmatsu International (A), 1989 Fees (In Ecu Million) and Market Share (%) of the Big Six Accounting Firms (Market share of six firms total 100 in each EC member state)

Country	KPMG	EY	CL	AA	PW	DTTI
Belgium	30.5 (23.2)	27.4 (20.8)	27.3 (20.7)	19.4 (14.7)	14.2 (10.8)	12.9 (9.8)
Denmark	49.7 (22.8)	24.9 (11.4)	47.8 (22.0)	13.1 (6.0)	9.8 (4.5)	72.6 (33.3)
France	335.4 (41.3)	119.1 (14.7)	67.06 (8.3)	155.2 (19.1)	74.0 (9.1)	61.5 (7.6)
Germany	208.7 (30.0)	132.9 (19.1)	180.9 (26.0)	79.7 (11.5)	33.3 (4.8)	60.4 (8.7)
Greece	1.2 (17.7)	1.72 (24.5)	1.5 (21.4)	1.7 (24.4)	0.9 (12.1)	NA
Ireland	31.5 (27.4)	19.3 (16.8)	18.0 (15.7)	13.1 (11.4)	24.7 (21.5)	8.2 (7.2)
Italy	52.5 (16.8)	38.7 (12.4)	49.5 (15.8)	114.2 (36.6)	32.0 (10.2)	25.5 (8.2)
Luxembourg	5.2 (19.9)	NA	2.4 (9.2)	3.1 (11.8)	4.3 (16.6)	11.1 (42.5)
Netherlands	227.0 (24.4)	259.4 (27.9)	253.1 (27.2)	27.9 (3.0)	23.7 (2.5)	140.0 (15.0)
Portugal	3.8 (15.1)	6.5 (25.8)	3.3 (13.0)	8.1 (32.0)	3.6 (14.1)	NA
Spain	28.9 (9.7)	26.1 (8.9)	18.4 (6.3)	149.5 (51.0)	51.4 (17.5)	19.2 (6.5)
UK	522.8 (22.1)	405.5 (17.1)	603.7 (25.5)	256.9 (10.9)	381.3 (16.1)	195.2 (8.3)

Note: KPMG = KPMG Peat Marwick   AA = Arthur Andersen
 EY = Ernst & Young   PW = Price Waterhouse
 CL = Coopers & Lybrand   DTTI = Deloitte Touche Tohmatsu International

Source: NERA accounting firm survey.

Exhibit 6 ● A Description of Strategy, Financial, and Operations Consulting Assignments

Study	Clients	Typical Requests	Typical Studies/Activities
Strategy	Chairman CEO President Business GMs	Mergers and Acquisitions Corporate Strategy Business Unit Strategy Organizational Planning Management Services	M&A Planning Takeover and Defenses Portfolio Analysis New Business Direction Mission Development Public Policy Cost Control Management Audits Strategic Capabilities	Customer Analysis Competitor Analysis Change Management Service Post Merger Integration Crisis Management Joint Venture and Alliances International Planning Simulation Modelling Control Systems Design
Finance and Accounting	Chairman CEO CFO Auditing Committee Financial Managers	Financial Strategy Planning Financial Management Management Control SEC Filings Investor Relations Risk Management	Raising Equity Raising Debt Asset Management Financial Reporting Annual Reports Shareholders Meetings Forecasting/Budgeting Reorganization Valuations	Int'l Currency Planning Shareholder Value Capital Structure Mergers and Acquisitions Capital Investments Cash Management Internal Auditing Assistance Operational Reviews
Operations	CEO COO VP Operations Plant Manager Senior Ops. Mgmt: (R&D or Engineering)	Production Planning Production Scheduling Production Management Regulatory Compliance	Plant Layout Strategic Facilities Design Operations Research Analysis Make or Buy Analysis Cost Reduction Statistical Process Control Inventory Control Systems Activity Subcontracting Anal.	Quality Control Programs Training Work Analysis Systems Modelling Sales/Production Forecasting Capacity Analysis and Util. Product Engineering Production Engineering

Information Technology			
CEO	Long-term Computing Strategy	Systems Analysis	Systems Design
President	Facilities Management	Programming	Network Design
Chief Info. Off.	Network Operation	Software Conversion	Installation
VP Information	Education and Training	Application Software Upgrades	Systems Security
Senior IS Managers	Systems Integration	Testing	Systems Maintenance
		Feasibility Analysis	Facilities Planning
		Requirement Specifications	New Business Direction
		Mission Development	Linking Strategy Analysis

Human Resources		
CEO	Executive Recruiting	Organizational Development
President	Temporary Help	Labour Relations
VH HR	Employee Leasing	Equal Employment Opportunity
Senior HR Mgmt	Outplacement	Risk Information Services
Junior HR Mgmt	Relocation	Employee Benefits
	Training	Job Design
	Career Guidance/Development	Remuneration Design

Source: The European Management Consulting Industry, by James Henderson and Ralf Boscheck, 1991 by IMD.

scope of their services by acquiring firms outside their traditional accounting and auditing areas—particularly in management consulting. Aside from the high growth rates that management consultancy offered over auditing in the 1980s, the addition and/or acquisition of consulting practices allowed the Big Six to cross-sell their services and provide a wide range of one-stop services to clients. Though some of the Big Six entered the management consulting area by specializing in Information Technology (IT), at the start of the 1990s, most of these firms offered a range of services (*Exhibit 6*). With management advisory services expected to grow at 16 percent per year through 1997, in contrast to the low-growth forecast for the audit and accounting portions of their businesses, competition in the management consulting field was expected to increase. One executive went so far as to say that, by the year 2000, 75 percent of the world's management consulting business might be handled by fewer than twenty firms, compared with forty firms in 1991.

Greater Harmonization and Mutual Recognition

Historically, accounting and audit services emerged during the industrial revolution when legislative and regulatory bodies required organizations to provide information about their commercial and financial affairs. Yet, because of different measurement principles among countries and their respective regulatory bodies, substantial differences existed on reporting financial information. In the EC, for example, each member state had distinct professional qualifications and regulations; several states had more than one professional body, offering different qualifications. Moreover, each member state also had different company laws specifying the type and/or size of company that had to have their accounts audited, and the financial reporting standards to be used. In the U.K., for example, all active companies—public and private—were required to publish an externally audited set of accounts, and roughly 1 million audits were performed each year. In Spain and Italy, on the other hand, the audit requirement was itself a relatively recent phenomenon, and was restricted to a comparatively small number of firms, usually only publicly listed companies.

As a result of these different cultural and legal backgrounds, national institutions tended to reinforce the differences in accountancy norms between firms

practicing in different member states. To overcome these differences, the EC passed the "Company Law Directive" to bring the different accounting standards and institutional arrangements of the EC together. Despite the legislation, the NERA found that substantial differences remained, which made it difficult for an accounting firm based in one member state to satisfy a client in another, because it would not have sufficient experience in the local requirements to carry out an audit in a cost-effective manner. Specifically, NERA cited three impediments to a client selecting a foreign firm to perform its audit: legal and institutional factors, professional rules and restrictions, and the organization and conduct of the major accounting firm networks. The report from NERA also mentioned that, for nonaudit services, most of the regulatory and legal restrictions to trade in audit services were absent but, because of strong links between audit and consultancy services, similar patterns were observed in nonaudit as well as in audit services (*Exhibit 7*).

THE EASTERN EUROPE INITIATIVE

According to Archie Campbell, DTTI's involvement in Eastern Europe began when Inaudit, the government auditing and accounting agency of the former Soviet Union, asked the United Kingdom office of Touche Ross to conduct a series of training courses.

Subsequent to that two-week program in Moscow in December 1988, we continued to follow up with Inaudit who was actively being courted by each of what were then the "Big Eight". Since they were the only licensed audit firm in the USSR, we saw them as key to our entering the market. In late 1989, after Ernst & Whinney merged with Arthur Young, they hired one of Inaudit's top managers to set up an independent office in Moscow. Inaudit realized that they had to pick one firm and, in 1990, agreed to a London-based joint venture with Touche Ross International with the understanding that a similar operation would eventually be opened in Moscow.

Despite Touche Ross's early involvement in the former Soviet Union, it was not until the spring of 1990, after Deloitte, Haskins, and Sells merged with Touche Ross, that the company accelerated its involvement in the region. In concert with that growing involvement,

Exhibit 7 ● Regulation in Different Sectors Throughout the EC

Country	Audit	Accounting	Public sector audit	Control of mergers	Insolvency	Legal representation	Investment advice	Tax advice	MAS
Belgium	R	R	R	R	F	X	F	F	F
Denmark	R	F	S	R	F	F	F	F	F
France	R	R	R	S	X	X	F	F	F
Germany	R/S	S	R	R	F	S	R	S	F
Greece	R/S	R	R	F	R	X	F	F	F
Ireland	R	F	F	F	F	F	F	F	F
Italy	S	S	S	S	S	S	F	S/F	F
Luxembourg	R	R	R	R	F	X	F	S	F
Netherlands	R	S	S	R	F	F	F	F	F
Portugal	R	F	X	R	S	S	F	F	F
Spain	R	F	R	R	—	S/F	F	S/F	F
United Kingdom	R	F	S	F	S	F	S	F	F

Keys: R = Regulated and reserved activity
      S = Regulated and shared activity
      F = Free activity
      X = Activity barred to accountants

Source: FEE Panorama de la Profession Comptable en Europe, 6 February 1990.

Deloitte & Touche Eastern Europe was created to start and operate practices in every important East European market. Presby emphasized, "The birth of this multilateral joint venture is the real secret to our success in Eastern Europe. Though five firms took the lead in forming Deloitte & Touche Eastern Europe, the 17 member practices most concerned with business in Eastern Europe put up the share capital" (***Exhibit 8***). Presby recalled,

The European leadership decided that Eastern Europe was going to be their responsibility. And they said this should be a multilateral joint venture, set up within the family of practices, where no practice would be dominant and the majority would be owned and controlled by Europeans. That's different from our competitors in that, for example, Price Waterhouse basically runs Eastern Europe out of their Lon-

don office; if you're not connected with their London firm, you can't participate too easily in Eastern Europe.

Among the members of the European Board, there was widespread agreement that only a profit center, not a cost center, would emphasize the viability of the East European offices—both at DTTI and among local staff. Within DTTI the fact that our West European firms were shareholders meant that Eastern Europe was a place our West European firms went to do work. For every dollar of volume booked in Eastern Europe in 1992, there was probably three-quarters of a dollar booked in Western Europe right next to it. And, with regard to local staff, we believed that, after years of state subsidies and government guarantees, an emphasis on profitability from day one was crucial in transforming the individual's mindset into taking more initiative.

Exhibit 8 ● Deloitte and Touche Tohmatsu Europe Practice

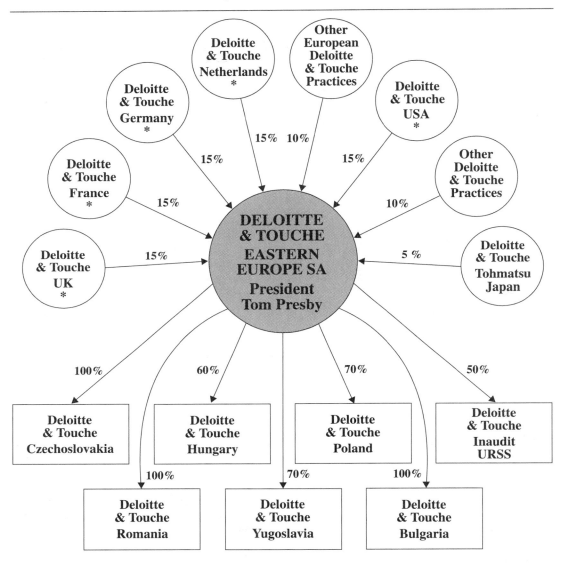

* = Founding members.

Source: Deloitte Touche Tohmatsu International.

Tom Presby added that as the company became more involved in Eastern Europe, he developed a list of policies and objectives (*Exhibit 9*). Beginning with the company's involvement in Russia—followed by Hungary, Czechoslovakia, Poland, Yugoslavia, Romania, and Bulgaria—these policies served as a compass for Deloitte & Touche activities throughout the region.

At the beginning of 1993, Tom Presby characterized Deloitte & Touche Eastern Europe's services as those provided by traditional public accounting or management consulting firms, yet adapted to Eastern Europe. He explained that in contrast to offices in Western Europe or North America, Deloitte & Touche Eastern Europe's offices had a more legal flavor when dealing with ministries and, in some Eastern (as well as Western) European markets, had fully fledged legal departments. Specifically, Deloitte & Touche's East European offering included accounting and auditing services such as bookkeeping, due diligence for acquisitions by Western firms, a limited review of local companies' systems and procedures in preparation for privatization, and financial statement transformation; management consulting, including financial planning and control, feasibility studies, market research, restructuring studies, privatization assistance, and treasury management; business advisory services such as asset valuation, business plan preparation, and joint venture structuring; fiscal services such as judicial advice, tax compliance, client representation in joint venture negotiations, tax consulting, and planning. The number and size of departments varied according to each market (*Exhibit 10*). Generally speaking, each practice derived its revenues from a mix of three sources: Western multinationals, local national enterprises (state-owned), and international lending agencies such as the World Bank, USAID, the European Bank for Reconstruction and Development (EBRD), and the EC PHARE program[4] (*Exhibit 11* and *Exhibit 12*).

4. Operation PHARE was the name given to the Poland and Hungary Assistance for Economic Restructuring program, a system for coordinating Organization for Economic Cooperation and Development (OECD) countries' aid to Hungary and Poland set up in 1989. In 1990, PHARE was extended to include Bulgaria, Czechoslovakia, East Germany, Romania, and Yugoslavia.

Though each of the practices in Eastern Europe was established as a profit center, their financing differed from Deloitte & Touche practices in Western Europe and elsewhere in two ways. First, each of Deloitte & Touche's East European practices was funded out of the Brussels-based holding company: Deloitte & Touche Eastern Europe SA. Money from the SA flowed to the respective East European practices in the form of investment capital or as loans and advances; in some cases, there was minority participation via joint ventures. Profits earned by the national East European practices were then allocated on the basis of Deloitte & Touche Eastern Europe SA ownership.

Sullivan added that Deloitte & Touche also used an override mechanism as an indirect means of financing activities in Eastern Europe. He explained that because of the national practices present in the region, West European practices were able to win proposals and do business in Eastern Europe for clients from their respective Western markets. However, when the founding practices used their own personnel to provide those services, they were obliged to pay 10 percent of the client fees to Deloitte & Touche Eastern Europe SA. In turn, half of this amount was returned to the local East European practice where the work was performed.

At the beginning of 1993, Presby commented that Deloitte & Touche's competitive standing in Eastern Europe varied depending on the market but that, overall, Deloitte & Touche was among the top firms in the region. In Hungary, for example, where the company was the last of the Big Six to enter the market, he believed it was in the bottom position. According to Presby,

In the summer of 1990, when Deloitte & Touche Hungary opened in Budapest with three people in a grocery store, Price Waterhouse and Ernst & Young already each had over 100 people. Given their lead, these same firms have been able to maintain a larger presence; in the fall of 1992, Deloitte & Touches Budapest office had roughly 50 people versus 180–200 at its competitors. Furthermore, as a result of their lead, Price Waterhouse secured several prestigious privatization issues, and assisted in the first Hungarian flotation on the Vienna stock exchange.

Exhibit 9 ● Deloitte & Touche Eastern Europe Objective and Policies

OBJECTIVE: To Be the Leaders in Our Profession in Central and Eastern Europe

POLICY	COMMENTS
1. Quality Client Service Is Our First Priority.	It Is a Core Value of the Deloitte Touche Tohmatsu International Group Everywhere. It Is the Best Way to Build a Successful Practice.
2. We Build Our Practice from "Top Down", Starting with Permanent Partner and Manager-Level Professionals First.	The Partners Know Best How to Build the Full Client Service Teams That We Need. The Nature of Our Work—Particularly in This Environment—Is Partner Intensive. Staff Alone Cannot Help Our Clients at This Time.
3. Our Practices Are Led by Teams of Partner-Level Professionals Both from Eastern Europe and from the West.	No One Professional Can Assimilate the Full Knowledge and Experience Needed to Both Serve National and Western Clients and Deal Effectively with the National Environments. The Blending Process Inherent in this Policy Will Produce Superior Results Than Would Otherwise Be Possible by Relying Solely on Either Expatriates or Nationals.
4. In General We Do Our Technical Training Locally and Our Professional and Language Training Abroad. English Is the Common Language of the Region.	Training Will be the Firm's Single Biggest Investment in This Region. The Technical Aspects Can Best Be Taught and Most Efficiently Delivered Locally. Technical Training Abroad Will Be Used Selectively. Professional Visits and Exchanges Abroad Are Needed to Give Our National Staff Direct Appreciation and Knowledge of the Rest of Our 56,000-Person Organization. English Is the Business Language Used Most Often by Our Clients and the National Infrastructures—Whether or Not they Are of English-Speaking Origin.
5. Our Scope of Services Matches the Needs of Our Clients in the Central and Eastern European Markets.	Because of Client Needs, We Are Not Bound by Our Traditional Western Scope of Services; However, Independent Objective Advice Will Remain Our Fundamental "Stock in Trade". We Will Not Become Investment Bankers or Financial Intermediaries. We Do Not Compete with Our Own Clients.

6. We Aim to Build a Significant National Client Base in Each Market along with Serving Our Western Clients.	Serving National, as Well as Western Clients, Assures That We Obtain the Necessary Experience to Give Good Advice within Each National Context. Ultimately, the National Clients Will Become the Dominant Participants on the National Scene. We Intend to Be Part of That Evolution.
7. We Build the Practices on Skills Practiced in Depth, i.e., "What We Do, We Do Well".	The Market Exerts Pressure on Emerging Practices to Be All Things to All Clients. Maintaining Quality Is the Challenge. Focus Helps Build Professional Expertise Relatively Quickly. Young and New People Who Are Specialized Will Be Able to Add Value to Our Clients Early in Their Careers. Skills Not Always Present in Each Marketplace Can Readily Be Brought in from Other Parts of the Organization.
8. We Manage on a Regional Basis and Encourage Cooperation and Resource-Sharing across the Region and with the Rest of the Firm.	Scarce Resources Can Be Readily Shared across National Boundaries to the Advantage of Our Clients. A Regional Approach Facilitates the Sharing of Experiences, Knowledge, and Facilities among the Markets. The Objective of Foreign Participation Will Be to Build Our National Practices in the Markets—Not Vice Versa.
9. Each Practice Must Be Financially Successful in the Intermediate and the Long Run.	Only Practices That Are Financially Successful Can Attract and Retain the Best People. Financial Success Provides the Funds Needed for Reinvestment in the Practices.
10. We Are Prepared—from the Very Beginning—to Turn the Practices over to the National Partners Who Build and Operate Them.	The Concept of National Ownership Is a Fundamental Part of the Deloitte Touche Tohmatsu Philosophy. Ultimately, Only National Entrepreneurs Can Build Practices of the Requisite Strength in the National Markets. Owners Work Better and Make Better Professionals Than Employees.

Source: Deloitte Touche Tohmatsu International

Exhibit 10 ● Deloitte & Touche Eastern Europe Organization Chart

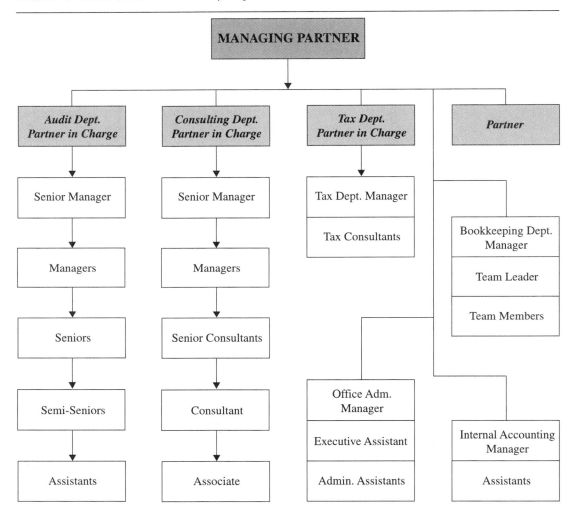

Source: Deloitte Touche Tohmatsu International.

With the exception of Hungary, the management of DTTI believed they held the first or second position, relative to the Big Six, in each of the remaining East European markets. In addition to the multilateral joint venture structure of Deloitte & Touche Eastern Europe, Presby believed that two important components of the company's success in Eastern Europe were the inclusion of foreign nationals in local practices and the center of expertise or practice center concept.

PRACTICE CENTERS

As Deloitte & Touche expanded into Eastern Europe, several partners felt that if they could develop a lead position in the financial services industry—one of DTT International's strengths—the company would be well poised to cross-sell the remainder of its services. Equally, if not more important, the financial services sector was the only real sector at the time that could pay hard currency, as the majority of manufacturing clients had not dealt with the West and lacked hard currency. Archie Campbell added,

Although we all agreed that that was the right thing to do, we also realized that we had no banking expertise in any of our East European offices. Rather than put in one banker for each office, which none of the local offices could afford, in February 1991 management concluded that the best way to serve the financial services industry was to establish a banking center, not unlike the Financial Services Center Tom had previously headed in New York.

Commenting on the Financial Services Center, one manager explained that in the United States in the 1980s a group of senior partners had set out to uncover new growth opportunities and had identified a tremendous market for financial services on Wall Street. In New York, after interviewing existing and potential clients, six services were defined and introduced: auditing, tax consulting, management consultancy, financial advisory services, reorganization advisory services, and regulatory consulting. Within only five years of its founding, the Financial Services Center had grown to include 350 people generating $30 million in revenues and was considered to be one of the most successful ventures in Touche Ross history.

Like the New York Financial Services Center, the services provided by the East European practice centers were determined by the needs of the market. Unlike the Financial Services Center, however, which marketed its services directly to clients, the practice centers in Eastern Europe provided their services directly to internal clients and indirectly to external clients. That is, practice centers provided services such as training and proposal writing to Deloitte & Touche practices throughout Eastern Europe. And, to meet the needs of the local practices' respective clients, practice centers worked through the local office. Also, in contrast to the Financial Services Center, it was expected that, as a market matured and knowledge was transferred from a practice center to local offices, both local offices and the practice centers would see the demand for and location of practice centers shifting from one market to another.

Banking

Presby recalled,

The banking center in Budapest came out of an identified need for banking talent and a strategy to build a banking business. We had a large proposal with the National Bank of Hungary. Although we had the pull, we did not have the talent, so Budapest seemed like the logical place to have the banking talent. To find that talent, Presby telephoned Jim Robinson, then Senior Banking Partner based in New York.

Robinson added his recollections:

It was not long after Presby's first phone call that I found myself Managing Director of Deloitte & Touche European Banking Services. My job in the region has been to assist in developing banking business through marketing, proposal writing, training local staff, managing and co-managing projects, and maintaining quality control. Regardless of the market we're in, we have three major objectives: provide the client with high-value service, bring the appropriate resources to a project, and develop our people. To that end, I assist each office to which I am invited. Generally speaking, I don't visit an office unless asked and, to preserve local office ownership of any project, I never call on a client without someone from that local office.

Exhibit 11 ● Deloitte & Touche Eastern Europe

WHERE WE ARE

National Offices

Bulgaria

Vasko Raichev/	Tel	+359 (2) 88 86 43
Renny Iordanova, Sofia	FAX	+359 (2) 88 87 69

Commonwealth of Independent States

Bill Potvin/	Tel	+7 (095) 281 66 46
Kirill Ugolnikov, Moscow	Fax	+7 (095) 971 64 19
	Telex	612134 SMAIL SU

For services in Kiev, Naborezhny Chelney, Odessa and
St. Petersburg, contact Moscow office.

Czech Republic

Trevor Wallinger/	Tel	+42 (2) 232 11 34
Karel Hampl, Prague	Fax	+42 (2) 232 57 00

Hungary

Emo Kemenes/	Tel	+36 (1) 131 2514
Didier Taupin, Budapest	Fax	+36 (1) 131 2330

Poland

Jan Maciejewicz/	Tel	+48 (2) 661 53 00
George Szyman, Warsaw	Fax	+48 (2) 661 53 50

Romania

Rick Olcott/	Tel	+40 (1) 312 40 40
Constantin Sandu, Bucharest	Fax	+40 (1) 312 40 40

Slovak Republic

Mel Mraz, Bratislava	Tel	+42 (7) 211 603
	Fax	+42 (7) 673 00

Yugoslavia

Danko Kjunic, Belgrade	Tel	+38 (11) 688 255
	Fax	+39 (11) 687 627

Practice Centres

Banking

James R. Robinson/	Tel	+36 (1) 131 2514
Andrew Goulden, Budapest	Fax	+36 (1) 131 2330

Valuation

Robert Ling, Prague	Tel	+42 (2) 232 1134
	Fax	+42 (2) 232 57 00

Insolvency

Richard Coates, Budapest	Tel	+36 (1) 131 2514
	Fax	+36 (1) 131 2330

Regional Management

J. Thomas Presby (Paris)	Tel	+33 (1) 40 88 29 20
Chief Executive Officer	Fax	+33 (1) 40 88 29 29
Archie Campbell (London)	Tel	+44 (71) 936 3000
Deputy Chief Executive Officer	Fax	+44 (71) 583 8517
Jerry Sullivan (Frankfurt)	Tel	+49 (69) 75695 313
Chief Financial Officer	Fax	+49 (64) 75695 333

WHAT WE DO

Accounting and Auditing Services
- Bookkeeping
- Financial Statement Transformation
- International Auditing
- Management Accounting
- Statutory Auditing

Management Consulting Services
- Environmental Consulting
- Financial Planning and Control
- Large-Scale Infrastructure and Privatization Systems
- Privatization Assistance
- Productivity Improvement
- Restructuring
- Strategic Planning Systems Design and Implementation
- Treasury Management

Business Advisory Services
- Asset Valuations
- Business Plans
- Business Valuations
- Insolvency
- Joint Venture Structuring and Set-Up
- Ministerial Consulting

Fiscal Services
- Judicial Advice
- Tax Compliance
- Tax Consulting and Planning

Industries Served
- Banking and Financial Services
- Chemicals
- Energy and Petroleum
- Government
- Hotel and Tourism
- Insurance
- Manufacturing
- Real Estate and Construction
- Retail
- Telecommunications
- Transportation

CLIENTS WE SERVE

National Enterprises

Bulgaria
- Bulgarian Committee
- Post and Telecommunications Company

CIS
- AMC
- Desta
- ELOX
- Frasmo
- GUM
- Huntsmen Aromar
- Imperial Bank
- Kamaz Motor Works
- Mosbusiness Bank
- Rosvomchur
- Solub
- Sovamit

Hungary
- AEB-Bank
- Alkaloidal
- Biogal
- Hungarian Electrical
- Energy Trust
- Hungarian Gas & Oil Trust
- IPAR Bank
- National Bank of Hungary

Donor Agencies
- British Know-How Fund
- European Bank for Reconstruction and Development

Western Companies
- Accor
- Aer Rianta
- Bank Austria
- BASF
- Begheyn Sey
- Cariplo
- Coats Viyella
- Computerland
- Conagra
- Deutsche Babcock
- Dow Chemical
- General Motors
- Group 4
- Honeywell
- Hypo Bank

Czechoslovakia
- Chemlon Humenne
- CKD
- Desta Decin
- Ferona Praha
- Istrochem Bratislava
- Kablo Decin
- Metrostav
- Prerovska Strojiny
- SR Praha
- Tesla
- Velke Fopovice

Poland
- Bank lnicjatyw Spoleczno-Ekonomicznych
- Bydgoski Bank Komunalny
- Cooperation Fund
- Gazeta Wyborcza
- Marie Curie Fund

Romania
- Petrobrazi
- Rocim

Yugoslavia
- Beogradska Banka
- IMT
- Jugobanka Bank System
- Jugometal
- Jugoslav Airlines
- Trgovacka Banka

- European Economic Community
- PHARE Program
- USAID
- World Bank

- IKEA
- Isoflex
- Machines Bull
- Maersk
- Marsh & McLennan
- Microsoft
- Mitsubishi Corporation
- Mitsui
- Norsk Hydro
- Penta Hotels
- Procter & Gamble
- Rhone Poulenc
- RJ Reynolds
- Société Générale (France)
- 3M

January 1993

Source: Deloitte Touche Tohmatsu International.

Exhibit 12 ● Information on Deloitte & Touche Eastern Europe Practices

	1992 Revenues ($US Million)	Revenue Mix by: Service ($US Million)	Market Sector ($US Million)	Total Number of Personnel End 1992	Mix of Personnel by: Service	Management Level	Expat vs. Local
BULGARIA	0.035	T&L .002 MC .022 A&A .012	ILA .024 MNC .002 LNE .009	18	T&L 3 MC 3 A&A 8 Other 2	MGT 11 Staff 7	Expat 0 Local 18
C.I.S.	4.2	T&L 0.29 MC 2.31 A&A 1.6	ILA 2.1 MNC 0.97 LNE 1.13	147	T&L 5 MC 28 A&A 45 Other 30	MGT 26 Staff 92	Expat 15 Local 132
CSFR	4.4	T&L 0.2 MC 1.7 A&A 2.5	ILA 1.8 MNC 1.5 LNE 1.1	54	T&L 3 MC 17 A&A 34 Other 0	MGT 19 Staff 35	Expat 11 Local 43
HUNGARY	4.39	T&L 0.22 MC 1.27 A&A 2.7	ILA 0.4 MNC 0.66 LNE 3.34	55	T&L 4 MC 15 A&A 34 Other 2	MGT 17 Staff 38	Expat 11 Local 44
POLAND	2.7	T&L 0.6 MC 1.1 A&A 1.0	ILA 1.2 MNC 0.5 LNE 1.0	52	T&L 9 MC 17 A&A 22 Other 4	MGT 12 Staff 40	Expat 14 Local 38
ROMANIA	0.23	T&L 0.02 MC 0.18 A&A 0.03	ILA 0.03 MNC 0.11 LNE 0.09	6	T&L 1 MC 3 A&A 2 Other 0	MGT 3 Staff 3	Expat 2 Local 4
YUGOSLAVIA	Not available						

NOTES: *Numbers may vary due to rounding*
    T&L = Tax & Legal
    MC = Management Consultancy
    A&A = Audit & Accounting
    ILA = International Lending Agency
    MNC = Multinational Corporation
    LNE = Local National Enterprise
    MGT = Management

Source: Deloitte Touche Tohmatsu International.

As an example of the shifting demand pattern for practice center services, Jim Robinson explained that when he arrived in Budapest in 1991, the majority of his chargeable hours were in Hungary, working on local projects. By the end of 1992, however, Robinson estimated that he spent roughly 30 percent of his time in Budapest, 34 percent in Moscow and Kiev, 25 percent in Prague, 7 percent in Sophia, 2 percent in Warsaw, and 1 percent in both Belgrade and Bucharest.

In late 1992, Andrew Goulden, also Managing Director of Deloitte & Touche European Banking Services, joined Jim Robinson in the Banking Center. Though both initially provided the full range of banking consulting services to Deloitte & Touche clients, in recent months the two had begun to divide work as a function of market demand, knowledge of individual markets, and experience in certain areas of banking. Generally speaking, Jim Robinson tended to work more often than Andrew Goulden in Poland, Romania, Bulgaria, and Russia, and on projects pertaining to central banks and payment systems. Andrew Goulden, on the other hand, tended to work more often in the Czech Republic, Slovakia, and Hungary, and on projects pertaining to savings and commercial banks.

Valuation

Presby continued, "Valuation was different from banking. Although it was created at about the same time as the banking center, it turned out that our principal professional product in Eastern Europe was valuations because it was the first thing that Western companies asked us to do." Robert van Ling, Managing Director of the Deloitte & Touche Valuation Center, commented, "Valuations were the biggest fee earners in Eastern Europe at the time and, not surprisingly, each valuation reflected the national bias of the individuals who carried them out. That is, if you came from Canada, you did it the Canadian way, if you came from Germany, you did it the German way; everybody did it their own way." Presby added, "I was vaguely aware of this and I read one of the valuation reports and it scared me. But I couldn't blame anybody because the knowledge really wasn't present anywhere; we didn't know where to go and wherever you did go, somebody did it differently." To attain greater consistency in valuations throughout the re-

gion, and minimize any liability, both legally and professionally, management decided to set up a valuation center with Robert van Ling in charge.

After a tour of the region, Ling picked Prague for the valuation center because of its central location as well as for personal reasons. He commented,

The valuation practice has a different scope than the banking practice. I believe their mission is more to define the market and then develop it. By contrast, the first thing we did was to establish a set of policies and procedures concerning valuation. I spent a year writing a valuation manual, which was issued in July 1991. The manual is not intended to train people how to do valuations; rather, how to manage an engagement within Deloitte & Touche. So, it covers issues such as client acceptance, how to write a proposal that includes key points such as the date of value, the definition of value encompassed by the appraisal, which assets are being valued, work plans, generally accepted valuation procedures, and professional service revenues.

In late 1992 I was joined by Alan Trotter, Director of Real Estate Valuation. His work differs from mine in that I specialize in business valuation and value companies as going concerns. Typically, that entails looking at intangible assets such as copyrights and goodwill, as well as tangible assets such as machinery and equipment and real estate. Though we tend to bring in expats to value machinery and equipment, Trotter is specialized in real estate valuation and thus handles those aspects of valuations dealing with land, improvements, and buildings.

Insolvency

"Insolvency differs from the banking and valuation center in that, first of all, it's a totally new service in these countries," said Richard Coates, Managing Director of the Deloitte & Touche Insolvency Center. "Until the bankruptcy law was introduced in Hungary in January 1992, they never had any bankruptcies in Hungary. In that sense, the demand for insolvency is a function of legislation and Hungary had the most developed set of laws." He added that, beyond the legislative requirements, the idea for a practice center based on insolvency came about as a result of the restructuring being initiated by locals in Eastern Europe and the tremendous amount of money flowing into Eastern Europe from Western companies and from international lending agencies. Coates explained,

Within Deloitte & Touche, management recognized that before many of the state-owned enterprises in Eastern Europe were transformed into privately owned companies, some would fail—either in part or in their entirety. Those that did fail would have to go through a number of further proceedings of which insolvency is really the most extreme form of restructuring. Combined, the inflow of funds and the reorganization of industry in Eastern Europe created a market opportunity for someone with a background in insolvency, which is basically breaking up and selling businesses. I therefore came to Budapest in September 1992 from the mainstream insolvency department in the U.K. to identify and appraise opportunities for work in the region. No sooner had I arrived than two jobs appeared which have occupied all my time in 1992. Though that has allowed us to earn some fees, I haven't had a chance to do any market research in the region.

Practice Center Economics

Because no revenues flowed directly to the practice centers, but to the national practices they served, the central office (Deloitte & Touche Eastern Europe SA) allocated the costs of running the practice centers using two formulas, collectively referred to as "push-downs." In the first case, the national practices were billed on the basis of usage. That is, for activities such as training and proposal writing, each national practice in Eastern Europe was billed at an hourly rate. Similarly, when individuals from the practice centers were involved in direct client engagements, the time spent on that engagement was also billed to the national practices based on an hourly rate. Although the total of salary and nonsalary expenses was roughly $150 per hour, local offices were free to charge their own rates to their clients. "However," Jerry Sullivan added, "the usage mechanism does not always cover all of the practice center costs, and it is therefore necessary to use a second billing technique based on a percentage of the individual offices' net service revenues." To clarify, he said that if one office's revenues represented 10 percent of the combined revenues for

Deloitte & Touche Eastern Europe, that same office would pay 10 percent of the costs not covered by the usage method.

Local Practice Reaction to Practice Centers

Generally speaking, the managing partners in each of the East European offices thought that practice centers were a cost-effective means to transfer expertise into individual markets and that, over time, the role of the centers would diminish as their own national practices absorbed the centers' expertise. The managing partners also believed that in those cases where a practice center shared the same building as a national practice, national practice tended to build up its expertise the fastest. In other words, because of their common domicile, the Budapest and Prague offices of Deloitte & Touche had a certain learning advantage in banking and valuation, respectively. "And," one manager added, "even though the practice centers consist of one or two persons each, market and legal differences among the East European countries have helped to avoid placing simultaneous demands on the centers." On the few occasions where such demands did arise, the managers reported that they had no problem in avoiding conflicts by rescheduling.

In Moscow, Bill Potvin, Managing Partner of Deloitte & Touche in the Commonwealth of Independent States (CIS), commented that his office had made extensive use of the banking center but did not foresee an immediate need for services from the other practice centers.

A valuation is an exercise to estimate what the market will pay for an asset. And, there is no market yet in Russia because of the lack of privatization. Also, bankruptcy applies when a firm is unable to meet its long-term debts. Most organizations here are debt-free. In other words, bankruptcy and valuation are Western market concepts. In a place like Hungary, those concepts are more mature than in Russia, which never had any real experience with such concepts until recently. However, the demand for valuation and insolvency will certainly grow as the market evolves.

In Budapest, Didier Taupin, Managing Partner of Deloitte & Touche Hungary, described the practice centers as a cost-effective solution for a region with limited resources and virtually infinite demand. Of the three centers, Taupin mentioned that he had used the banking and insolvency services the most, but that, in the valuation area, he was fortunate to have hired an individual with five years of valuation experience in Hungary. "Because that person was hired before the creation of the Valuation Center," Taupin explained, "our valuation needs were already being met." Commenting on the evolution of practice centers, Taupin felt that the market in Hungary had already changed and that he now needed people to manage projects and in areas other than those originally established. Rather than the fundamentals of banking, for example, he felt that the market was now ready for more specific banking activities such as organizing a dealing room or a back office.

Like the national managing partners, Jim Robinson believed that the practice centers had been well received. "On the other hand," he commented, "in a region where the national practices are so short of talent, it's only natural that our services would be in demand. What I think is more important in Eastern Europe is the fact that everyone knows and trusts each other and we all work as a team."

By contrast, Robert Ling felt that the valuation center had not gone as well as he would have preferred, and he believed that it was because the center had not been granted any authority. Specifically, Ling believed that he should have had the final say on all valuations performed by Deloitte & Touche national practices in Eastern Europe. He added that a memorandum to this effect had, in fact, been issued to each of the respective managing partners. Yet, despite the memo, he felt that some practices had all but ignored it, while others had followed it completely.

Despite the success of the practice centers, there were two issues that the managing partners of the national offices felt were not being adequately addressed: namely, the formulas used to allocate practice center costs; and training. Though formulas existed for distributing the costs of the practice centers' activities to the national practices, few if any of the managing partners in the national practices understood exactly how the cost allocations were made. For example, one manager saw that the national practices were charged on the basis of usage, but felt that he could not accurately measure or influence the costs of such usage un-

less the practice center representatives were physically present in the managing partner's market.

In addition to costs, all the East European managing partners stressed that there was an urgent need for training. Jan Maciejewicz, Managing Partner of Deloitte & Touche Poland, commented,

Our biggest challenge is not being able to train people fast enough to keep pace with the market's rapid growth. From the time I started in August 1990 to the end of 1992, the office has grown from two to eighty people. To make matters worse, some of the employees that have been trained by Deloitte & Touche were poached by local and international clients. In a market like Poland, where the demand for qualified help far exceeds the supply, some companies are doubling the salaries of our employees to lure them away.

Trevor Wallinger, Managing Partner of Deloitte & Touche in the Czech Republic, added,

We are gradually getting squeezed between increasing demands from a growing client base and the need to serve those clients with highly qualified people. Like my colleagues in neighboring practices, if I had to choose between allocating staff to an immediate client need versus training and development activities, I invariably would opt for the client.

TASK FORCE REPORT ON BARRIERS TO INTEGRATION IN WESTERN EUROPE

In one of its strategic planning meetings, the European Board concluded that if Europe developed into a truly single market, Deloitte & Touche could choose to lead or follow the competition in providing pan-European services. To that end, the European Board appointed Soren Bjerre-Nielsen, one of three joint managing partners in Denmark, to chair a task force on the barriers to integration facing Deloitte & Touche in Europe. The task force had recently completed its report and presented its findings to the European Board. In his presentation, Soren Bjerre-Nielsen pointed out that, as clients had become more international, the size and status of DTTI's practices in national markets had become an important element in presenting a global and regional image. To a large extent, he emphasized, the need to present a consistent image across practices stemmed from referral work, as in the case of an audit for a multinational client. Though the amount of work referred among the European practices of Deloitte & Touche was relatively limited, there was far more work referred in from outside Europe, especially from North America.

As the internal market within the EC countries evolved, however, the task force believed that the amount of referred work would increase and the need to present a consistent image would become as important to European practices as it was to North American and Japanese practices that already perceived Europe as a single market. On the other hand, the task force pointed out that as long as the nature of audit work demanded a physical presence at a client's premises, and as long as national languages and cultural differences still existed, the majority of work in the European practices would be nationally oriented.

In the report, it was clear that the interest in integrating Deloitte & Touche's European practices differed little from the motivation that led to the development of national practices themselves. In both cases, practices reacted to the changes taking place in their marketplace and the need to perform professional work at locations where offices did not already exist, the creation of larger markets for existing products and skills, the maintenance of cost competitiveness through economies of scale, and the improvement of DTTI's overall standing in the marketplace. As in individual markets, where practices effected mergers or invested in new offices or products, and gradually adopted national partnership structures with democratically elected management and profit sharing among partners, the creation of a single market raised questions on issues such as culture, governance, management, and profit sharing. Based on information exchanged between members of the task force and the many European practices, Soren Bjerre-Nielsen and his colleagues prepared a list of the different barriers to integration in Europe and their perceived level of difficulty (*Exhibit 13*).

The report went on to say that, even though a lot of integrated activities were already taking place among the European practices, the following advantages were seen as becoming more integrated: better implementation of duly made decisions; stronger willingness to invest in new markets, services and products; differentiation from competitors by ensuring that the best people available were assigned to the most important jobs; competitive advantage through cost effectiveness in areas such as management information systems, transfer of know-how, application of methodologies, quality assurance, marketing and product development; and securing the network through contractual agreements, software and methodology application, and mutual investments.

On the other hand, there were a number of concerns raised regarding the move to a more integrated practice. Among the disadvantages cited were risk of centralism and loss of autonomy; risk of ignoring local market conditions and characteristics; individual partners feeling dissociated from the decision-making process, with the risk of loss of entrepreneurship; litigation problems spreading to countries where litigation was never a great concern in the past; risk of possible loss of beneficial aspects of the practice culture; and risk of losing member practices that disagreed with the concept.

Given the information provided by Deloitte & Touche's many practices, the task force prepared what it saw as five components to a fully integrated pan-European partnership (*Exhibit 13*). Lastly, the task force proposed taking four steps to achieve more integration among European member practices. In the first of these steps, the task force proposed that each member practice make a formal commitment, as set forth in a European Document, toward adopting a pan-European strategy. For those who did not implement previously agreed policies, it was further proposed that they be subject to an annual tax, to be reimbursed only after implementation occurred. Also, to present a pan-European image, the task force recommended that its strategy include adopting one name—Deloitte & Touche—across Europe in as timely a manner as possible.

In a second step towards greater integration among member practices, it was suggested that Deloitte & Touche exchange financial results among its European practices for incorporation into a European Annual Report, for distribution to partners. Though intended for internal use only, the task force believed that such an annual report could be used to monitor compliance with policy objectives set forth in step number one.

Thirdly, the task force proposed that, instead of each national practice acting independently, they

Exhibit 13 ● Barriers

Barrier	Perceived Level of Difficulty
Cultural difference (firm-wise and national)	Very difficult
Governance	Very difficult
Fear of centralism	Very difficult
Litigation climate	Very difficult
Legal aspects	Difficult, but can be overcome
Taxation	Difficult, but can be overcome
Profit level and distribution	Difficult, but can be overcome
Lack of consensus (between firms and partners)	Difficult, but can be overcome
Organization	Difficult, but can be overcome
Partner definition (admission)	Difficult, but can be overcome
Size of firms	Difficult, but can be overcome
Professional aspects (name)	Easy
Costs (financial and other)	Easy
Clients	Easy

Five Components to a Fully-Integrated Pan-European Partnership

1. A partnership consisting of individual partners owning equity in a limited liability company.

2. A Representative Committee elected by the partners on a regional basis to take into account the proper balance in representation from practices and countries respectively.

3. A Supervisory Board elected by the Representatives' Committee. The Board would appoint and supervise the Executive Committee, approve admission of partners, review and approve the plan of the European practice, plan major financial commitments and mergers.

4. An Executive Committee responsible for the overall management of the firm subject to the plan approved by the Supervisory Board, with the right to nominate senior management in the European practice subject to local partner approval when, for example, the appointment was that of a national managing partner.

5. A National Management to be responsible for developing and implementing the plans approved by the Executive Committee and the Supervisory Board.

Source: Deloitte Touche Tohmatsu International.

cede some of their autonomy in marketing to the European organization. At the same time, the task force also recommended that Deloitte & Touche implement a system of sharing and advising member practices of new products, that the network of practices improve information about European activities, including information and control of joint ventures, and that

Deloitte & Touche encourage more joint ventures among practices.

Lastly, the task force proposed that Deloitte & Touche initiate a number of human resource activities. Among these activities, it was suggested that the company hold educational and development programs that encouraged younger partners to think and act as European partners. It was also envisioned that any follow-up programs be orchestrated in such a way as to keep the original members of a group together. Similar programs were also proposed for managing and senior partners. Additional human resource activities included taking a more international approach to recruiting graduates and expanding participation in national partners' meetings to share information about Europe.

MODELS FOR PAN-EUROPEAN INTEGRATION

With clients' businesses increasingly defined on a regional if not a global basis, the management of DTTI Europe was eager to draw upon those parts of the organization with experience in serving customers from a multicountry perspective. Aside from the practice centers within Deloitte & Touche Eastern Europe, Deloitte & Touche Europe Services and D & T Corporate Finance Europe were the other European entities within the organization accustomed to providing cross-border services on a regular basis. When one considered those parts of the organization that had built their business on a particular expertise, there was also the Financial Services Center in New York. As well, Deloitte & Touche practices in the United States had engaged in one other type of multipractice activity—special interest groups (SIGs).

Deloitte & Touche Europe Services

Richard Doherty, Partner-in-Charge of the Deloitte & Touche Europe Services practice, explained that Deloitte & Touche had established the Brussels-based entity in 1988 for two reasons. First, it was intended to serve EC institutions such as the European Commission and the European Parliament located in Brussels and second, to advise clients on EC-led changes and policies that had become increasingly important with the planned completion of the single market under the 1992 program. "More recently," Doherty explained, "Deloitte & Touche Europe Services has added a third service: preparing a comprehensive information service on Eastern Europe. Given the pan-European nature of our services and our regular contact with EC institutions, it made sense to coordinate the East European information effort from Brussels, where money for Eastern Europe projects is often approved." Doherty commented further,

We are not a European office replicating the three classic disciplines that you get at the national level—audit, tax, and management consultancy. We are an EC specialist office; you come to us if you have an EC-related problem. Generally speaking, we do work such as EC regulatory and legal projects, explaining recent developments at the EC level to clients, which is easier for a Brussels-based EC group to do than for someone in a member state. Over the past four years, the office has learned how to sell better to the EC and what type of relationship we should have with our national practices. Regarding the latter, we tend to do EC-related work on the request of our national practices, when they have a client whose business is being influenced in some way by EC policies. Where rivalry with national firms has emerged, we have pulled back. In short, we have minimized that rivalry by specializing in an area which the national practices would find too costly to duplicate.

Doherty went on to say that revenues for Deloitte & Touche Europe Services came from two sources: EC institutions and Deloitte & Touche national practices. In the latter case, Deloitte & Touche Europe Services acted as a marketing agent to win work for national practices and received a percentage of the revenues. Alternatively, national practices sometimes referred clients directly to Deloitte & Touche Europe Services which, in turn, billed the client directly for advisory and consulting services. Doherty explained,

Our role in trying to get West European practices to work together occurs more when we do the work for the EC itself or when the work is funded by the EC in Eastern Europe. An unwritten part of our mission is, I think, to promote cross-border cooperation among our national practices. It is unwritten but it is natural, because these guys are our shareholders and we're interested in keeping our shareholders happy. A lot of them look at us in terms of how much work we've created for them. So, if we have an opportunity and we know there are capabilities in one or two countries, it's in our interest to try and get these people to work together. We are able to do that because we have a certain amount of moral authority as we are the EC experts and, if a job comes from the EC, we can say to our practices: "Guys, the angles on this in Europe are different, it will make us look more professional and give us a better chance of winning this assignment if we can show that we're in touch with the issue in different parts of the community."

D & T Corporate Finance

Andrew Curwen, Partner at D & T Corporate Finance in London, explained that Deloitte & Touche had established its corporate finance business in 1991 for two reasons: First, it was set up to respond to the needs of clients already looking at Europe as a single market. "To be successful," Curwen emphasized, "the single market concept required a single market approach to providing the full range of local, technical, and industry expertise." To this end, D & T Corporate Finance Europe assisted clients exclusively on cross-border transactions and followed a transaction through from conception to completion and post acquisition integration. "Secondly," Curwen added, "corporate finance provided an excellent opportunity to develop new business relationships with non-DTTI clients and, hopefully, cross-sell the remainder of our services. In this respect, corporate finance was perhaps an easier way to ultimately get a client to switch auditing firms."

Like Deloitte & Touche Europe Services, D & T Corporate Finance secured its revenues from two sources: nonclients and Deloitte & Touche national practices. In the latter case, D & T Corporate Finance either billed the referring Deloitte & Touche national practice or, in some cases, billed the local client directly. Curwen explained,

We help clients with strategic acquisitions in Europe, looking at Europe as one market. Together with Daniel Quirici, Partner, we have a specialized team of eight people and work only on cross-border merger and acquisition jobs. Because of our expertise, we are often called upon by other Deloitte & Touche national practices in Europe. If we do our job properly, however, within ten years we will have transferred our knowledge to each Deloitte & Touche local practice and we won't be needed. Ultimately, each local practice will work on both domestic and cross-border corporate finance deals.

Special Interest Groups (SIGs)

In the United States, partners in the management consultancy part of Deloitte & Touche sometimes met with colleagues from other practices to discuss ongoing events in a particular industry. These special interest groups (SIGs) thus provided a vehicle for linking consultants nationwide who shared a common interest. According to one executive, Deloitte & Touche relied on SIGs in many areas—such as technology, finance, operations, and health care to promote communication—to focus resources on critical issues in the marketplace and build national networks. The executive added that the networking that occurred within each SIG enabled consultants to get to know colleagues from offices around the country both personally and professionally and that, in turn, helped them know whom to call when a need arose for special skills, background, or advice.

Because SIGs tended to be national in nature, they eventually led to the creation of national partners. In addition to acting as practice leaders on a countrywide basis, national partners coordinated programs in their industry, and promoted their industry expertise to offices across the country. Unlike partners who worked primarily from one office, however, and who drew their earnings from the profits of that one office, those promoted to national partner were taken out of individual profit centers and were compensated according to how much they sold.

Practice Centers for Western Europe

Within DTTI Europe, almost everyone agreed that their services would become more pan-European in the future. Nonetheless, there were some concerns about using existing models as a way to create a pan-European service offering. Richard Doherty commented,

In Eastern Europe, for example, the practice centers and their respective expertise is not owned by any one of the national practices; they belong to everyone. There is a feeling that the practice centers belong to everyone so there's no sense of "We're calling in the Hungarians" or "We're calling in the Czechs." In Western Europe, on the other hand, the expertise is owned by national practices and the feeling is "We're calling in the Brits, or the Dutch, etc."

Another manager added,

In Western Europe, the national practices have different agendas than in Eastern Europe. I believe that in

Western Europe there is a fear that, if we establish practice centers, the U.K. office will be the expert in everything because they am the single biggest practice in Europe. There is already a perception that personnel from the U.K. practice invade other markets of the world, and it aggravates our colleagues in those practices where they feel they're losing revenues to the U.K. In short, no other country in Western Europe has access to manpower like the U.K.

Bill Potvin contrasted the idea of applying practice centers to Western Europe with an experience in one of his prior jobs.

In one of my positions in the United States, I was a "National Partner" and not attached to any one office. In that role, I sought to get offices from different parts of the country to work together within the Financial Services industry by staffing jobs jointly. When completed, the billings for each job were based on time inputs per office. The billings required that one work diligently to make sure that everyone got their fair share, and that required a certain amount of negotiating and trust. Once people began to trust that the system wouldn't give them a disadvantage, then they put more into it.

But Western Europe is not the United States. In the latter, the fact that it is one country may have imparted some common or national goal, but the offices were still individual profit centers. Europe will be a lot harder because you really don't have any economic ties across the offices and countries. Also, to do things on a pan-European basis, you need product managers that take products across Europe. But, those "products" need to be more closely defined than "banking" or "valuation." There are certainly market issues, but there are technology issues as well.

Didier Taupin held a similar view:

In Western Europe, I don't think one or two people in a center are enough, you need teams of specialists in a certain area because, when a practice calls up for specialists, these specialists may not be well matched for the speciality sought. For example, the term "banking" is so comprehensive that it is difficult for one practice to cover the entirety of expertise in the

banking sector. And that's true of other sectors as well; no one practice has a specialist that knows everything about the full spectrum of activities in his respective field of expertise. Moreover, once their expertise has been sold, you need to define new areas of expertise. In Hungary, for example, we have saturated pockets of demand for some services. Having sold a service with practice center experts, we can now do some things on our own, but we'll need to keep repeating the process of identifying and selling new services if centers are to be adopted more widely.

SUMMARY

Turning to Tom Presby, John Christie shared his views on extending the practice center concept to Western Europe:

The need to spread around expertise in Western Europe as Ling, Robinson, or Coates is doing in Eastern Europe does exist but it's not in valuation, or banking, or insolvency. It's in other areas. For example, in Western Europe, the opportunities are in things like environmental auditing to help corporations with their approach toward environmental management. Other possibilities can be found in markets that have not traditionally been at the heart of management consulting as seen by the practices. For example, in hotel and leisure, it so happens that the U.K. firm acquired a hotel and leisure specialist company— Greene, Belfield-Smith—which had a very good market presence. And so people are saying, "They have a good reputation, let's get one of the specialists in and help our client in this local market." And that's happening. In other words, the same reasons for having the centers in Eastern Europe also exist in Western Europe. But, it is much more difficult to get it going in Western Europe, because the organizational structure is very different. In Western Europe we do have a lot of local practices—just as we have in Eastern Europe, yet we don't have a single holding company with a reporting line going to a CEO in charge of the region. In the absence of a multilateral construct as we have in Eastern Europe, I'm still uncertain about what is the best way to manage the barriers to integration that we face in Western Europe.

Case 16

The SWATCH Project

"This watch is the product which will reintroduce Switzerland to the low and middle price market. It is the first step of our campaign to regain dominance of the world watch industry," said Dr. Ernst Thomke, president of ETA SA, a subsidiary of Asuag and Switzerland's largest watch company. Ernst Thomke had made this confident declaration about SWATCH to Franz Sprecher, project marketing consultant, in late spring 1981. Sprecher had accepted a consulting assignment to help ETA launch the watch, which was at that time still in the handmade prototype phase and as yet unnamed. This new watch would come in a variety of colored plastic cases and bracelets with an analog face. ETA had designed an entire production process exclusively for SWATCH. This new process was completely automated and built the quartz movement directly into the watch case. Sprecher's key concern was how to determine a viable proposal for moving this remarkable new product from the factory in Grenchen, Switzerland, into the hands of consumers all over the world.

COMPANY BACKGROUND: ETA, EBAUCHES, AND ASUAG

SWATCH was only one brand within a large consortium of holding companies and manufacturing units controlled by Allgemeine Schweizer Uhrenindustrie (Asuag, or General Company of Swiss Watchmak-

ing). SWATCH was to be produced by ETA, a movement manufacturer, which was part of Ebauches SA, the subsidiary company overseeing watch movement production within the Asuag organization.

Asuag was founded in 1931 when the Swiss government orchestrated the consolidation of a wide variety of small watchmakers. The major purpose of this consolidation was to begin rationalization of a highly fragmented, but vital, industry suffering the effects of one world war and a global depression. By 1981, Asuag had become the largest Swiss producer of watches and watch components. Asuag was the third-largest watchmaker in the world, behind two Japanese firms, Seiko and Citizen. Asuag had a total of 14,499 employees, 83 percent of whom worked within Switzerland. Asuag accounted for about one-third of all Swiss watch exports, which were estimated at SFr. 3.1 billion in 1980.[1] Major activities were movement manufacture and watch assembly. Bracelets, cases, dials, and crystals were sourced from independent suppliers.

Ebauches SA, a wholly owned subsidiary of Asuag, controlled the various movement manufacturers. The Swiss government played an important role in encouraging and funding Ebauches' formation in 1932. An "Ebauche" was the base upon which the movement was built, and Ebauches companies produced almost all of the movements used in watches produced by Asuag group companies. Sixty-five percent of Ebauches production was used by Asuag group companies, and the rest was sold to other Swiss watch manufacturers. Ebauches SA recorded sales of SFr. 675.0 million in 1980, a 3.1 percent increase over the previous year. Ebauches companies employed a total of 6,860 people, 90 percent of them in Switzerland.

ETA SA, the manufacturer of SWATCH, produced a full range of watch movements and was known as the creator of the ultrathin movements used in expensive watches. The quality of ETA movements

This case was prepared by Susan W. Nye and Barbara Priovolos under the direction of Visiting Professor Jean-Pierre Jeannet as a basis for class discussion rather than to illustrate either effective or ineffective handling of an administrative situation. Copyright © 1985 by IMD, Lausanne, Switzerland. The International Institute for Management Development (IMD), resulting from the merger between IMEDE, Lausanne, and IMI, Geneva, acquires and retains all rights. Not to be used or reproduced without written permission from IMD, Lausanne, Switzerland.

1. U.S. $1 = SFr. 2.00; SFr. 1 = U.S. $0.50.

was so renowned that some watches were marked with "ETA Swiss Quartz" as well as the name brand. ETA movements were distributed on a virtual quota basis to a select group of watch manufacturers. The demand for its movements had always equaled or exceeded its production capacity. In 1980, ETA employed over 2,000 people and produced more than 14 million watch movements for revenues of approximately SFr. 362 million and profits of about SFr. 20 million.

Dr. Ernst Thomke had joined ETA as president in 1978. Early in his career, he had worked as an apprentice in production at ETA. He left the watch industry to pursue university degrees in chemistry and cancer research, earning both a Ph.D. and a medical degree. He then moved on to a career in research at British-owned Beecham Pharmaceutical. Thomke did not stay in the lab for long. He moved into the marketing department, where he boosted Beecham sales with ski trips and concerts for physicians and their families. His unorthodox selling techniques led to skyrocketing sales. He looked for a new challenge when faced with a transfer to another country. His colleagues at Asuag and throughout the watch industry described Thomke as a tough negotiator and as iron willed. After joining ETA he agreed to provide advertising and support allowances to movement customers. However, these agreements stated that ETA only provided aid if it had a role in product planning and strategy formulation.

THE GLOBAL WATCH INDUSTRY

To understand the global watch industry, three key variables were considered: watch technology, watch price, and the watch's country of origin.

Watch Movement Technology

Watch design underwent a revolutionary change in the early 1970s when traditional mechanical movement technology was replaced with electronics. A mechanical watch's energy source came from a tightened mainspring which was wound by the user. As the spring unwound, it drove a series of gears to which the watch hands were attached; the hands moved around the analog (or numerical) face of the watch to indicate the time. Highly skilled workers were required to produce and assemble the movements in accurate mechanical watches, and the Swiss were world renowned in this area.

The first electronic watch was built by a Swiss engineer, Max Hetzel, in 1954, but it was U.S. and Japanese companies that first commercialized electronic technology. Bulova, a U.S. company, was the first to bring an electronic watch to market in the early 1960s, based upon tuning-fork technology. A vibrating tuning fork stimulated the gears' movements and moved the hands on a traditional analog face. At the end of the decade, quartz crystal technology began to appear in the marketplace. An electric current was passed through a quartz crystal to stimulate high frequency vibration. This oscillation could be converted to precise time increments with a step motor. Quartz technology was used to drive the hands on traditional analog watches and led to an innovation: digital displays. Digital watches had no moving parts, and the conventional face and hands were replaced with digital readouts. Electronic watches revolutionized the industry because, for the first time, consumers could purchase an inexpensive watch with accuracy within one second per day or less.

Ebauches-owned companies had been involved in electronic watch technology since its pioneering stages. In 1962, Ebauches was among a number of Swiss component manufacturers and watch assembly firms which established the "Centre Electronique Horlogère" (CEH). The center's immediate goal was to develop a movement which could compete with Bulova's tuning-fork movement. CEH was never able to successfully produce a tuning-fork movement which did not violate Bulova's patents. In 1968, Ebauches entered into a licensing agreement with Bulova to manufacture and sell watches using Bulova's tuning-fork technology. In 1969, CEH introduced its first quartz crystal models, and Ebauches subsequently took over manufacture and marketing for the new movement, introducing its first quartz line in 1972.

Ebauches also worked with the U.S. electronic firm, Texas Instruments, and FASEC[2] in the early

2. FASEC was a laboratory for joint research in semiconductors, integrated circuits, and lasers. It was formed in 1966 by the Swiss Watch Federation (FHS), Brown Boveri, Landis & Gyr, and Philips of the Netherlands.

1970s to pursue integrated circuit and display technology. By 1973, Ebauches was producing movements or watches for three generations of electronic technology: tuning-fork, quartz analog, and digital. Ebauches did not stay in the assembled watch market for long and returned to its first mission of producing and supplying watch movements to Asuag companies. Between 1974 and 1980 the Swiss watch industry as a whole spent SFr.1 billion toward investment in new technology, and Asuag accounted for half the expenditure. Ebauches Electronique on Lake Neuchâtel was a major use of investment funds and was created to produce electronic components.

Price

Price was the traditional means of segmenting the watch market into three categories. "AA" and "A" watches were sold at prices above SFr. 1,200 and accounted for 42 percent of the total value of watches sold and 2 percent of total volume. "B" watches priced at SFr. 120–1,200 made up 25 percent of the market in value and 12 percent in units. "C" watches were priced under SFr. 120 and accounted for 33 percent of the market in value and 86 percent of total units.

Players in the Global Watch Industry

Japan, Hong Kong, and Switzerland together accounted for almost 75 percent of total world watch production. In 1980, watch producers worldwide were faced with inventory buildups at factory warehouses and retail stores. A worldwide recession had slowed demand for watches, and overproduction compounded the problem. Projections for 1980 were not being met, and factory-based price-cutting, particularly by large producers, was becoming common as a substitute for production cuts.

The Swiss Watch Industry   The Swiss watchmakers' position was viewed by many industry observers as being more precarious than others. Since 1970, when the Swiss accounted for 80 percent, their share of the world watch market in units had declined to 25 percent of the world's watch exports. The Swiss ranked third in unit production but remained first in the value of watches sold. Twenty-five percent of all Swiss

watch factories were permanently shut down during the 1970s, and 30,000 workers lost their jobs.

Despite extensive factory and company shutdowns within the Swiss industry, in 1981 the Swiss still owned the rights to 10,000 registered brand names, although less than 3,000 were actively marketed. Most Swiss watches were priced in the mid- to expensive price ranges, above SFr.100 ex-factory and SFr. 400 retail. In 1981, industry analysts were congratulating the Swiss for their adherence to the upper price segments, because the low-price segments were beginning to turn weak. Industry observers also noted that the Swiss seemed to be emerging from a decade of uncertainty and confusion and were focusing on higher quality segments of the watch market. Swiss component manufacturers had been supplying their inexpensive components to Far East assemblers, and analysts believed that this practice would continue.

Swiss watch manufacturers generally fell into one of three categories. First, there were the well-established, privately owned companies which produced expensive, handmade watches. These firms included Rolex, Patek-Philippe, Vacheron Constantin, Audemars-Piguet, and Piaget. For the most part, these firms were in good health financially. Stressing high quality as the key selling point, these manufacturers maintained tight control through vertical integration of the entire production and marketing processes from movement and component production through assembly and out into the market. The recession had cost them some customers, but these had been replaced by new Middle Eastern clients.

Second, there were a number of relatively small, privately owned companies that concentrated on watch components—bracelets, crystals, faces, hands, or movements. This group included an ETA competitor, Ronda SA. The financial health of these companies was mixed.

The third sector of the industry was the largest participants, Asuag and Société Suisse de l'Industrie Horlogère (SSIH). SSIH was an organization similar to but smaller than Asuag, producing 10 percent of all Swiss watch and movements output. Its most famous brand, Omega, had for years been synonymous with high quality. Omega had recently run into trouble and had been surpassed by the Asuag brand Rado as Switzerland's best-selling watch. In June 1981, SSIH announced a loss of SFr. 142 million for the fiscal year ending March 31, 1981. This loss gave SSIH a negative net worth of SFr. 27.4 million. A consortium of Swiss banks and the Zurich trading group Siber Hegner & Co., AG were brought together to save the company.

In the late 1970s, Asuag and SSIH began working in a cooperative effort to cut costs through the use of common components. However, this effort did not affect individual brand identities or brand names. Industry analysts did not rule out the eventual possibility of a full merger. Asuag was noted for its strength in production and quality but was reported to have a weakness in the marketing function. SSIH was noted for strong marketing skills but had recently been faced with a slippage in product quality. It was believed that both companies would stand to gain from closer ties in research and production.

The watch industry played a significant role in Switzerland's economy. The banks and the government took a serious interest in its operations and the performance of individual companies. Between 1934 and 1971 the Swiss government made it illegal to open, enlarge, transform, or transfer any watch manufacturing plant without government permission. This action was justified as a defensive move to combat potential unemployment due to foreign competition. It was also illegal to export watch components and watchmaking technology without a government issued permit. The government essentially froze the industry by dictating both prices and the supplier-manufacturer relationship. These constraints were gradually removed beginning in 1971 and by 1981 were no longer in effect.

The Japanese Watch Industry   Japan was the world's second largest watch producer in 1980 with approximately 67.5 million pieces, up from 12.2 million pieces in 1970. The growth of the watch industry in Japan was attributed to the Japanese watchmakers' ability to commercialize the electronic watch. K. Hattori, which marketed the Seiko, Alba, and Pulsar brands, was Japan's largest watchmaker and responsible for approximately 42 million units. Selling under three different brand names allowed Hattori to compete across a broad price range. Seiko watches fell into the "B" category. Alba and Pulsar competed in the "C" range.

Casio entered the watch market in 1975, selling low cost digital watches. Philip Thwaites, the U.K. marketing manager, described Casio as follows: "Casio's strategy is simple; we aim to win market share by cutting prices to the bone." Casio's product line was exclusively digital. The company was noted for adding "gadgetry" to its watches, such as timers, stopwatches, and calculators. In Casio's view, the watch was no longer just a timepiece but a "wrist instrument."

In contrast to Switzerland, Japan's "big three" watch producers, the Hattori group, Casio, and Citizen, had a combined product line of fewer than twelve brands. All three firms were fully integrated, producing movements and most components and assembling and distributing worldwide through wholly owned distribution subsidiaries. These watchmakers made extensive use of automated equipment and assembly line production techniques.

The Hong Kong Watch Industry   Hong Kong manufacturers had only entered the market in 1976, but by 1980 unit output had reached 126 million units. Ten major producers accounted for an estimated 70 percent of total volume. Watch design costs were minimized by copying Swiss and Japanese products. As many as 800 "loft workshops" were in operation in the late 1970s. These facilities could be started at low cost and ran with minimum overheads. The expanded capacity led to the rapid fall of Hong Kong watch prices: prices of simple watches in the SFr. 15–20 range in 1978 dropped to SFr. 10 the next year, with margins of less than SFr. 1. Hong Kong watches were sold under private label in minimum lot sizes of 1,000–2,000 units, with average ex-factory costs of SFr. 20 for mechanical watches and SFr. 50 for quartz analog and SFr. 10 for electronic digitals. Most watchmaking activity in Hong Kong was concentrated on assembly. The colony had become Switzerland's client for watch components and movements. Swiss movement exports to Hong Kong had grown from 13.3 million pieces in 1977 to 38.5 million in 1980.

THE POPULARIUS PROJECT

The SWATCH project began under the code name "Popularius." Thomke's goal was to discover what the market wanted and then to supply it. He told his engineers that he wanted a plastic, analog watch that could be produced at less than SFr. 10 and sold ex-factory at SFr. 15. He also wanted to use the technology which ETA had developed for its high-priced, ultrathin "Delirium" movements to enter the low-priced watch segment. Thomke was convinced that ETA's long term viability and profitability depended on increasing the company's volume and integrating downstream into fully assembled watch production and marketing. Thomke had seen the demand for ETA movements dwindle when exports of finished Swiss watches declined from 48 million pieces in 1970 to 28.5 million in 1980. The mass market "C" watch had all but disappeared from Swiss production, replaced by inexpensive Japanese and Hong Kong models. The Swiss manufacturers pushed their products up-market, and sales value of exports moved from SFr. 2,383.7 million in 1970 to SFr. 3,106.7 million in 1980.

With electronic technology, movements were no longer a major cost factor in the end price of a watch. The average price of an ETA movement was SFr. 18 and applied whether the watch sold ex-factory at SFr. 80 or SFr. 500. Thomke wanted to increase ETA volume output and knew that Asuag transfer pricing policies made this difficult. Asuag was a loose consortium of companies, each operating as an independent profit center. Transfer pricing reflected this fact. At each point of production and sales—movements, components, assembly and through the distribution channels—a profit was taken by the individual unit. Thomke believed that this system weakened the Swiss brands' competitive position for the volume business which his movement business needed to be profitable. Thomke believed that if he wanted to introduce a successful new product, he would need to sell it to 1 percent of the world's population, which amounted to about 10 percent of the "C" market segment. He knew that the Japanese companies were fully integrated and that the Hong Kong assemblers, which already operated with low overheads, were moving increasingly toward full integration.

Thomke knew he could turn over the Popularius project to another Asuag unit, but he did not have a great deal of confidence in the production and marketing capabilities of Asuag branded watch assemblers. ETA was the only company within the Asuag group

which had extensive experience in automated manufacturing. If the Popularius was to succeed as the latest entry in the low-price market, it would have to be produced in an automated environment. Furthermore, Thomke had watched many of the finished watch companies steadily lose market share to Japanese and Hong Kong competitors over the last decade, and he had little confidence in their marketing capabilities. ETA currently sold 65 percent of its output to Asuag companies, and Thomke wanted to reduce this dependence. He planned to use the Popularius as ETA's own entry into the finished watch market (*Exhibit 1*).

ETA engineers and technicians, responding to Thomke's specifications, developed the Popularius. To meet the low unit ex-factory price was no small accomplishment. A cost analysis at that time showed that the required components without assembly would have cost SFr. 20. Quartz technology provided accuracy within one second per day, and the watch was waterproof, shock resistant, and powered by a readily available and inexpensive three-year battery. The watch weighed 20 grams and was 8 mm thick with an analog face. The face and strap were made of durable mat finished plastic, and the strap was attached with a special hinge flush with the face. It was considered stylish and attractive. Further aesthetic enhancements could be made with the careful selection of color and face design. Ultrasonic welding produced a finished product which would not be reopened after it left the assembly line. In the event of failure, designers believed, the watch was essentially unrepairable and would be replaced rather than repaired. Batteries were replaceable by the owner and inserted in the back of the watch (*Exhibit 2*).

The product line was, at that time, limited to one size, a large "man's" watch, which could be produced in a number of solid colors with several designs or patterns on the face. Although a 25 percent smaller version for women and children was being considered, no definite introduction plans had as yet been developed. Management believed that the young were a potentially strong secondary market for the new product. A number of ideas were in development for "novelty" watches with special functions, a button watch, and special colors and motifs. A day/date calendar with a quick reset feature was available. The production system was designed for strict quality

Exhibit 1 ● Comparison of Ebauches SA Sales to World Market

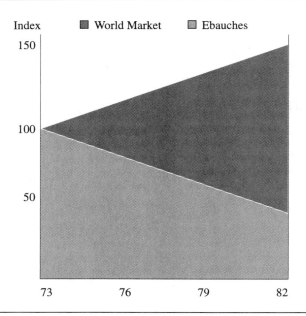

---

control conditions to produce highly reliable watches. The movement was designed with a theoretical life of thirty years, and Popularius would be sold with a one-year guarantee.

Manufacturing Systems for Popularius

The ability to produce and sell a watch with the Popularius features, for a low price, was largely dependent upon unique production technology developed at ETA. ETA's product development staff was respected throughout the watch industry for its technical abilities in mass production. Its production technology was considered by industry observers to be equal to that of the best Japanese companies. In the early stages of electronic movement production, even with high-priced luxury movements, automated assembly was not only possible but a practical means of production. The production equipment planned for Popularius was entirely Swiss made and would in its final form consist of a fully automated production line that consumed raw materials at one end and delivered complete watches at the other.

ETA technology built the movement right into the base of the watch and required only 51 parts versus the 90 to 150 parts found in most electronic and mechanical watches. ETA had already used this technology to create the "Delirium," the world's thinnest movement, measuring .98 mm at its thickest point. These movements were used in high-precision luxury watches measuring 2.4 mm at their thickest point and selling at retail SFr. 40,000.

The Popularius production process and the equipment that made the technology possible were protected by seven patents. The ETA technical staff felt that it would be impossible for a competitor to duplicate Popularius, especially at low ex-factory price, because the watch was closely linked to its unique production process. ETA engineers had already invested nearly two years on this project, including the efforts of 200 employees and more than SFr. 10 million in research and development funds.

Production was still limited to hand production of prototype watches and watches for test marketing purposes. ETA expected the line to have semi- but not full automation with forecasted production levels of

Exhibit 2 ● Photograph of the Product

SWATCH.
THE REVOLUTIONARY NEW TECHNOLOGY.

swatch ✚
SWATCH. THE NEW WAVE IN SWISS WATCHES.

600,000 men's watches and 150,000 smaller versions for women or children in the first year. Fully automated lines which would produce 2 million units per year were targeted for the second year. Production goals of 3 million units had been set for the third year. Production quotas for later years had not yet been finalized. Management expressed the desire to reach production and sales levels of 5 million units after three years (*Exhibit 3*).

Initially it was expected that full unit cost could go as high as SFr. 16. As volume increased the per unit cost would drop, and the full unit cost was expected to be less than SFr. 10 at production levels of 5 million watches per annum. The project was not considered technically feasible at annual production levels below 5 million, and higher volume was expected to drive the unit price just below SFr. 7. Asuag pricing and costing policy suggested that individual projects should reach contribution margins of 60 percent for marketing, sales and administrative expenses, fixed

costs, and profits. Each size model would require a separate production line. Within each line, economic order runs were 10,000 units for each color and 2,000 units for each face style. Maximum annual production per line was 2 million units, and the initial cost of installing a line was SFr. 5 million, including engineering costs of SFr. 2 million. Additional assembly lines could be installed at an estimated cost of SFr. 3 million. Production costs included depreciation of this equipment over four years. The equipment occupied space which was already available, and no additional real estate investments were expected.

ETA had applied for special financing packages with local authorities. No response had as yet been received. However, obtaining the necessary financing was not viewed as a problem.

Initial plans suggested a marketing budget of SFr. 5 per unit. The brand was expected to break even in the third year and begin earning profits for ETA in the fourth year. Per unit marketing costs were expected to decline as volume increased. Decisions as to how the budgeted marketing funds would be distributed had not been finalized. It was expected that they would be divided between ETA and its distributors, but on what basis and how the "campaigns" would be coordinated could not be decided until distribution agreements had been finalized. Thomke was a firm believer in joint ventures and wanted to develop 50/50 relationships with distributors.

Still to be decided were questions of packaging, advertising, production line composition, and distribution. Packaging alternatives centered around who should do it. ETA needed to decide if the product would leave the factory prepackaged and ready to hang or display, or be shipped in bulk and packaged by the distributor or retailer, or even be sold "as is." Advertising budgets and campaigns had not been finalized. The size of the budgets and the question of whether or not advertising costs would be shared between ETA and the distributors were still open. The advertising agencies had not yet been chosen, and no media decisions had been finalized.

DISTRIBUTING POPULARIUS

Sprecher felt that distribution was the most important and problematic of the issues still outstanding. Discussions at ETA on developing an introduction strategy

Exhibit 3 ● Projected Marketing Costs and Profits for SWATCH

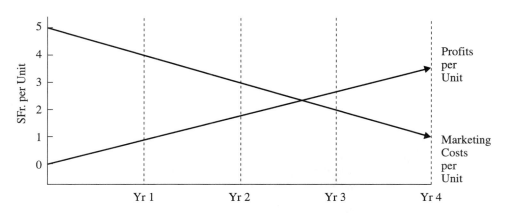

Per Unit:
Full Cost to Produce = SFr. 10 (with Long Range Target of Less than SFr. 7,
                                 Including Depreciation for Production Machinery)
Ex-Factory Price = SFr. 15
Contribution Margin for Marketing Costs and Profit = SFr. 5

were confined to five industrial markets. Although it was not as yet definitive, the emerging consensus seemed to be that distribution would begin in Switzerland, the United States, the United Kingdom, France, and West Germany. Distribution in Japan, other industrialized countries, and certain developing countries was also being discussed for a later date.

Market and Country Selection

A major motivation in choosing the target entry markets would be the probability of gaining high volume sales. Thomke had in mind a goal of reaching an annual potential volume of 1 percent of the country's population in each targeted market. The United States would be an important market for Popularius success. It was the world's single largest watch market, and success with a product in the United States often signaled global success. Thomke planned to keep the watch priced below $30 in the United States. Germany and the United Kingdom were significantly large in terms of population but could be difficult markets to enter, because they were known to be particularly price sensitive. Germany was also noted as

being particularly slow in accepting new innovations in consumer goods. Switzerland was chosen because it was the home market. ETA management assumed that their next move would be into Canada and the rest of Europe. If ETA decided to enter Japan and the less developed countries (LDCs), management would have some special considerations. Japan would be a particularly difficult market to crack, because almost all "B" and "C" class watches sold in Japan were produced domestically. Furthermore, Sprecher had heard that Seiko was considering plans for introducing a new quartz analog watch which would be priced under SFr. 50. The LDCs of Africa and Latin America provided ETA with opportunities for volume sales. Sprecher expected that consumers in these markets would use price as the only criteria for choosing a watch. Selling the Popularius to LDCs would put ETA in competition with the Hong Kong producers' inexpensive digital watches.

Selecting Distributing Organizations

Within each market there was a range of distribution alternatives. But a fundamental need was a central marketing, sales, and distribution unit within ETA with sole responsibility for Popularius. However, at that time, there was no marketing or sales department within the ETA organization. ETA's products, watch movements, had always been distributed to a select and consistent group of users. Distribution at ETA had essentially been a question of arranging "best way" shipping, letters of credit, and insurance. The annual costs of establishing a central marketing division within ETA was estimated at SFr. 1–1.5 million. This figure would cover management and administrative salaries for a marketing manager, regional managers, product managers, service, sales planning, and advertising and promotion planning. Sprecher believed that eight to ten people would be required for adequate staffing of the department. Furthermore, he estimated that wholly owned subsidiaries in any of the major target markets could be staffed and run at a similar cost.

Contracting individual, independent marketing organizations in each country and then coordinating the marketing, sales, and distribution from the Grenchen office would, Sprecher believed, allow ETA to retain a much greater degree of control over the product. He felt that this type of organization would allow ETA to enter the market slowly and to learn about it gradually without having to relinquish control.

Following Thomke's suggestion, throughout the summer of 1981 Sprecher took a number of trips to the United States to determine possible solutions to this and other marketing problems. Sprecher's agenda included visits to a number of distributors, advertising agencies, and retail stores. Sprecher completed his investigation with visits to some of the multinational advertising agencies' Zurich offices. Sprecher made his rounds with a maquette which he described as an "ugly, little black strap." The Popularius prototype still had a number of bugs to iron out, and Sprecher could only make promises of the variety of colors and patterns which were planned.

The United States would be essential to Popularius success because it was the world's largest watch market. Thomke and Sprecher also believed that the U.S. market would be more open to this new idea and felt they would gain the best advice from U.S. distributors and advertising agencies (*Exhibit 4*).

Retailer and Wholesaler Reactions

Sprecher began his first U.S. trip with a visit to Zales Corporation. The Zales organization included both a large jewelry and watch wholesale business and a chain of jewelry stores. Sprecher met with a high level marketing manager, who responded positively to the product but said that Zales could not seriously consider it at this early stage. He invited Sprecher to return when the project was further along. Zales management did advise Sprecher that if ETA decided to go ahead with the project and start production and sales, then "do it right." Doing it "right" meant heavy spending on advertising, point-of-purchase displays and merchandising, and aggressive pricing.

Sprecher also paid a visit to Gluck and Company. Gluck was a jewelry, watch, and accessory wholesaler operating in the low price end of the market. An aggressive trader, Gluck operated mainly on price, and much of its business involved single lots or short-term arrangements to catalog and discount houses. Gluck executives told Sprecher that they did not believe in advertising but relied on low prices to push goods through the distribution chain and into the hands of the customer. If Gluck agreed to take on Popularius, it would have to be sold with a retail price of under SFr. 40. Sprecher attempted to discuss the possibility of a long term relationship between ETA and Gluck, but the wholesaler did not appear particularly interested.

Sprecher's reception at Bulova's New York offices was very different from Gluck. The first reaction of Andrew Tisch, president of the company, was that the Popularius should be packaged as a fashion watch. Tisch, who had substantial experience in consumer goods marketing and believed that Popularius should be heavily advertised and promoted, suggested a budget of SFr. 20 million. He was sufficiently impressed with the project and voiced some interest in establishing a separate company with ETA to market the watch.

Considering OEM Arrangements

Sprecher was concerned that he might be taking a "hit-or-miss" approach to his investigation and decided to pay a visit to Arthur Young and Company. Arthur Young was among the largest accounting firms

Exhibit 4A ● Retail Watch Purchases in the United States: Summary of Market Research

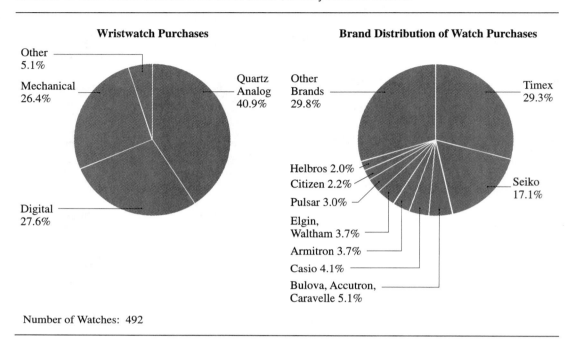

Wristwatch Purchases

Other 5.1%

Mechanical 26.4%

Quartz Analog 40.9%

Digital 27.6%

Brand Distribution of Watch Purchases

Other Brands 29.8%

Timex 29.3%

Helbros 2.0%
Citizen 2.2%
Pulsar 3.0%
Elgin, Waltham 3.7%
Armitron 3.7%
Casio 4.1%
Bulova, Accutron, Caravelle 5.1%

Seiko 17.1%

Number of Watches: 492

Exhibit 4B ● Retail Watch Purchases in the United States: Watch Purchases by Retail Price (sample size = 465)

	% Quartz analog	% Digital	% Mechanical
Number of watches	200	135	130
Price categories			
$1,000 or more	.5%	.7%	1.5%
$300 to $999	4.0	.7	1.5
$100 to $299	38.0	8.9	14.6
$50 to $99	33.5	31.9	35.4
$30 to $49	24.0	57.8	47.0

Note: 46.6 percent of all watches are purchased on sale or discount.

Exhibit 4C ● Retail Watch Purchases in the United States: Watch Purchases by Outlet Type (sample size = 485)

	% Watches (all)	% Quartz analog	% Digital
Number of items	485	198	134
Jewelry Store	27.6%	34.3%	12.0%
Department Store	26.2	26.3	27.6
Discount Store	16.7	14.7	23.1
Catalog Showroom	10.3	14.7	10.4
Mail Order	5.4		11.2
Wholesaler	2.1		1.5
Drugstore	5.1		6.0
Flea Market	0.4		
Other Outlets	6.2		7.5

Exhibit 4D ● Retail Watch Purchases in the United States: Distribution of Watch and Jewelry Purchase Prices by Age of Purchaser

	18–24 yrs.	25–34 yrs.	35–54 yrs.	55 and over
NUMBER OF CUSTOMERS	150	419	821	431
$25 to $99	39.4%	39.6%	35.7%	32.3%
$100 to $299	20.7	24.8	25.3	28.5
$300 to $999	27.3	25.3	26.7	27.6
$1,000 or more	11.3	8.8	9.0	10.4

in the world, one of the "Big Eight," and was noted for its industry analysis and consulting. Sprecher visited Arthur Young to see if its consultants might have some suggestions on potential partners for ETA. The accounting firm put together a proposal on how to attack the problem of finding a distribution partner. Sprecher was well aware that his investigation was still incomplete, and he returned to Switzerland with the Arthur Young proposal to work out a new agenda of visits.

Included in the Arthur Young proposal was the possibility of turning all marketing responsibilities of Popularius over to an independent company. Sprecher investigated this possibility and entered into negotiations with two well-known multinational consumer goods companies: Timex and Duracell. Both of these companies had their own extensive and established distribution channels. ETA executives believed that an agreement with either of these two firms might, provide Popularius with a virtual guarantee of high-volume sales due to the extensive and intensive marketing resources at both.

The Duracell Proposal   Duracell produced and distributed high quality batteries worldwide and was interested in becoming the exclusive distributor of Popularius. Contact was initiated with the U.S. battery company's general manager in Zurich and followed up by a visit at Duracell's U.S. headquarters. The company had a distribution system in place which covered the entire globe. Duracell batteries were sold through drugstores, supermarkets, and hardware stores. Duracell made batteries for watches as well and therefore had some contacts in the retail

watch trade. The company employed an experienced and well-trained sales force and had a wealth of marketing knowledge. Duracell had unused distribution capacity, and its management was looking for extensions to the product line and felt that an electronic watch could be complementary to and a logical extension of Duracell batteries.

Sprecher felt that an agreement with Duracell could be interesting but was concerned that ETA was being relegated to the role of product supplier, with little or no impact on marketing decisions. Duracell wanted to establish itself in an original equipment manufacture relationship with ETA. Duracell would buy the watch from ETA and then control the product's marketing strategy. ETA would be supplying the product, the product's name, and some marketing funds but would be left out of most mass marketing decisions. Furthermore, while Duracell continued to express interest, it was proceeding at what ETA executives considered to be a snail's pace. In late summer, Duracell management informed ETA that they were continuing their evaluation of Popularius as a product and that their investigation of its potential market was still incomplete.

The Timex Organization   Timex was known for producing durable, inexpensive watches. The U.S.-based company had become famous in the late 1950s and 1960s for circumventing traditional watch outlets and jewelry stores and distributing through mass outlets such as drug, department, and hardware stores and even cigar stands. At its peak, Timex had sold watches through an estimated 2.5 million retail outlets. In 1982,

Timex had an estimated 100,000 to 150,000 retail accounts worldwide. Timex and ETA were considering the possibility of ETA production of a limited range of watches under the Timex name. The Timex Popularius would be produced in black with a different, but ETA approved, design. The hinge which attached the plastic strap to the watch case would be different, and "Swiss Made" would not be stamped on the face. Timex was willing to guarantee a minimum annual order of 600,000 units, at SFr. 10 ex-factory price.

Sprecher knew that ETA executives considered private label production as a viable option which could be implemented in either the introductory phase of distribution or later when the brand was well established. However, they felt that the Timex arrangement had some drawbacks. First, they perceived the Timex organization as somewhat stodgy and bureaucratic, and ETA executives were unsure as to how close a working relationship they could establish with Timex management. Second, Timex seemed to want Popularius for "nothing." Sprecher did not think that they could keep Popularius to a SFr. 50 retail price and gain a profit in the Timex agreement. Sprecher considered the Timex distribution system very costly. Sprecher estimated that Timex watches were distributed with a retail price of 4 to 4.5 times the ex-factory watch price. ETA wanted to maintain a 3 to 3.5 ex-factory ratio. Sprecher believed that the Timex system was costly because it used a direct sales force as well as two middlemen (distributor and broker) to get watches into the retail store. Finally, ETA management was also concerned with Timex's most recent performance. The company had been steadily losing market share.

Positioning Options

Toward the end of his second trip to the states, Sprecher hit upon the "perfect" name for the new product—SWATCH. He had arranged to spend two weeks with the advertising agency Lintas SSC&B to work on developing a possible product and advertising strategy. This arrangement initiated a quasi-partnership between the two firms; Lintas invested its time and talent in the Popularius project and would receive payment later if they were to get the advertising account.

Lintas had been influenced by their work with another client, Monet, a producer of costume jewelry. Monet supported its products with heavy point-of-sale promotion activities. Lintas believed that this kind of promotion would be beneficial to Popularius.

Lintas saw a number of positioning options for the Popularius: a (new) Swiss watch, a second watch, an activity watch, a fashion watch, or a combination of images. The agency had suggested approaching the Popularius positioning with a combination of a fashion and sports image while emphasizing the watch's Swiss origin. The copy staff was excited about stressing the Swiss watch concept and the contraction S'watches was repeated throughout their notes. Sprecher looked at the abbreviation and was struck by the idea of taking it one step further to SWATCH, and the Popularius finally had a name.

Considering Direct Mail

Back in Switzerland, Sprecher continued interviewing advertising agencies. He visited the Zurich office of McCann-Erickson, a large multinational advertising agency, to discuss advertising strategy and to look into the mail-order market. McCann-Erickson made an investigation of the mail-order market for the SWATCH in West Germany. The purpose of this study was to demonstrate what a mail-order approach might accomplish for SWATCH.

McCann-Erickson's proposal suggested using mail order as an initial entry strategy for SWATCH. This arrangement would later be expanded into a mail-order business through specialized companies with a full range of watches and jewelry. Target group would be young men and women between 20 and 29 years, as well as people who "stay young." The target group would be motivated and interested in fashion, pop culture, and modern style.

To achieve sufficient penetration of the target market, which the agency estimated at 12.5 million, advertising support of about SFr. 1 million would have to be spent. Orders were estimated anywhere from 50,000 units to 190,000. This estimate included volume of 4,500 to 18,000 for a test market with total advertising costs of about SFr. 150,000. The effort would be organized in two waves, one in the spring and a second in the fall.

Additional costs to be considered were mailing at SFr. 2.50 per unit as well as an unknown amount for coupon handling. Furthermore, experience indicated that about 10 percent of all orders would not be paid.

Considering an Exclusive Distributorship

Zales had suggested that Sprecher contact Ben Hammond, a former Seiko distributor for the southwestern region of the United States. Sprecher was unable to make this contact, but Thomke followed up on this lead on a separate visit to the United States in late summer. Ben Hammond, president of Bhamco, was interested in the exclusive distribution rights for North America for SWATCH and a second Asuag brand, Certina. Bhamco was a gemstone firm, and Hammond had been in the jewelry and watch business in the southwest for several years. Up until the recent past, he had been the southwest distributor for Seiko. Hammond reported that he and Seiko had had a falling out when the Japanese manufacturer opened a parallel distribution system, selling its watches through new distributors to mass merchandise and discounters in direct competition to its traditional outlets and "exclusive" distributors. He proposed to start a new company, Swiss Watch Distribution Center (SWDC), and wanted an agreement for three years. Hammond was very enthusiastic about the SWATCH and told Thomke that he could "sell it by the ton." Hammond projected first year sales of 500,000 units, growing to 1.2 million and 1.8–2 million in years two and three and then leveling off at 2.5 million.

Hammond felt that the watch should be positioned as a fashion item and sold through jewelry and fine department stores. He believed that a heavy advertising and point-of-sale budget would be important to gaining large volume sales and felt that SFr. 5 per watch was a reasonable figure. Furthermore, after his experience at Seiko, he promised a careful monitoring of consumer takeoff and a close relationship with retail buyers to avoid discounting and to give service support. Based in Texas, Hammond had substantial financial backing from a group of wealthy investors. He planned to begin initial efforts in the Southwest and then promised to spread rapidly to all major U.S. cities and Canada.

Next Week's Meeting

Thomke had just returned from the United States and briefed Sprecher on his meeting with Ben Hammond. Thomke was anxious to get moving on the project and planned to make a proposal to Pierre Renggli, the president of Asuag, in mid-September, less than three weeks away. At the end of the briefing, they had scheduled a strategy planning session for the next week. Sprecher now had less than one week to evaluate his information and to prepare his proposals for Thomke in preparation for their final presentation to Renggli. Sprecher knew that Thomke expected to receive approval for ETA production and marketing of SWATCH at that presentation. Sprecher knew that his proposals to Thomke needed to be operationally feasible, and with a target launch date of January 1, 1982, available implementation time was short. Sprecher knew that they could pursue negotiations with some of the companies which he had visited or "go it alone" with a direct sales force. Sprecher needed to balance the economic restraints which required minimum annual sales volume of 5 million with Thomke's desire to keep strategic control of the product within ETA. Sprecher needed to consider ETA's lack of marketing experience and what that would mean in the international marketplace.

DATE DUE

HIGHSMITH 45230

DISCARDED